MARVEL

ANT-MAN

PRELUDE

MARVEL

ANT-MAN

PRELUDE

WRITER: **WILL CORONA PILGRIM**
PENCILER: **MIGUEL SEPULVEDA**
INKER: **BIT**
COLORISTS: **JAY DAVID RAMOS** with **DAVID CURIEL**
LETTERER: **VC'S CLAYTON COWLES**
CONSULTING EDITOR: **EMILY SHAW**
EDITORS: **BILL ROSEMANN & MARK BASSO**

EDITOR IN CHIEF: **AXEL ALONSO**
CHIEF CREATIVE OFFICER: **JOE QUESADA**
PUBLISHER: **DAN BUCKLEY**

SPECIAL THANKS **TO MARK PANICCIA**

MARVEL STUDIOS
VP PRODUCTION & DEVELOPMENT: **BRAD WINDERBAUM**
PRESIDENT: **KEVIN FEIGE**

ANT-MAN CREATED BY **STAN LEE, LARRY LIEBER AND JACK KIRBY**

MARVEL'S ANT-MAN PRELUDE. Contains material originally published in magazine form as MARVEL'S ANT-MAN PRELUDE #1-2, MARVEL'S ANT-MAN - SCOTT LANG: SMALL TIME MCU INFINITE COMIC #1, MARVEL PREMIERE #47-48, ANT-MAN #1 and AGE OF ULTRON #10AI. First printing 2015. ISBN# 978-0-7851-9798-0. Published by MARVEL WORLDWIDE, INC., a subsidiary of MARVEL ENTERTAINMENT, LLC. OFFICE OF PUBLICATION: 135 West 50th Street, New York, NY 10020. Copyright © 2015 MARVEL No similarity between any of the names, characters, persons, and/or institutions in this magazine with those of any living or dead person or institution is intended, and any such similarity which may exist is purely coincidental. **Printed in the U.S.A.** ALAN FINE, President, Marvel Entertainment; DAN BUCKLEY, President, TV, Publishing and Brand Management; JOE QUESADA, Chief Creative Officer; TOM BREVOORT, SVP of Publishing; DAVID BOGART, SVP of Operations & Procurement, Publishing; C.B. CEBULSKI, VP of International Development & Brand Management; DAVID GABRIEL, SVP Print, Sales & Marketing; JIM O'KEEFE, VP of Operations & Logistics; DAN CARR, Executive Director of Publishing Technology; SUSAN CRESPI, Editorial Operations Manager; ALEX MORALES, Publishing Operations Manager; STAN LEE, Chairman Emeritus. For information regarding advertising in Marvel Comics or on Marvel.com, please contact Jonathan Rheingold, VP of Custom Solutions & Ad Sales, at jrheingold@marvel.com. For Marvel subscription inquiries, please call 800-217-9158. **Manufactured between 4/3/2015 and 5/11/2015 by R.R. DONNELLEY, INC., SALEM, VA, USA.**

10 9 8 7 6 5 4 3 2 1

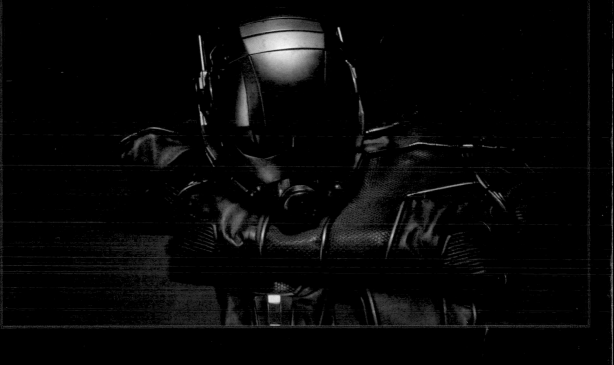

MARVEL'S ANT-MAN PRELUDE #1

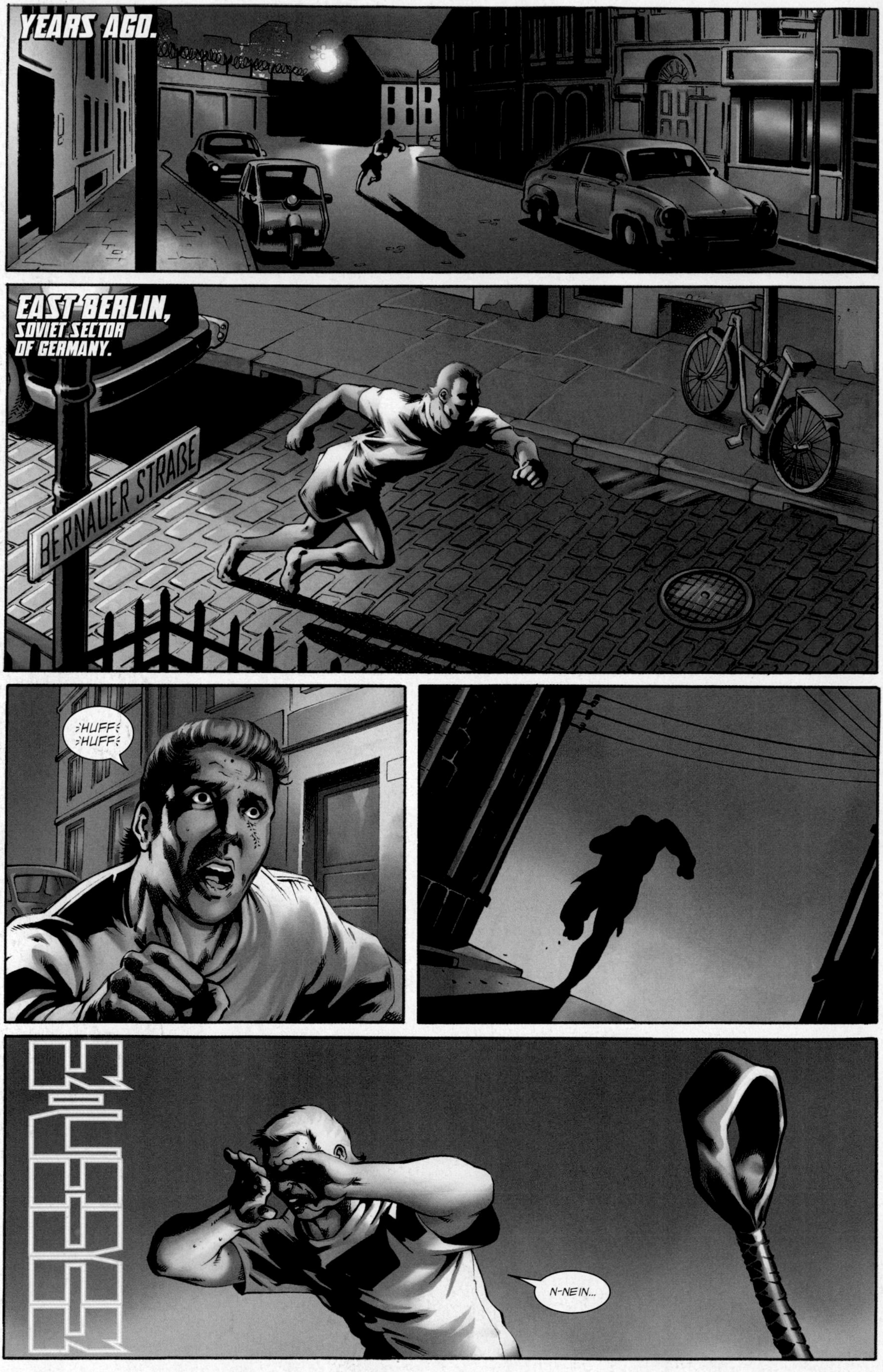
YEARS AGO.
EAST BERLIN,
SOVIET SECTOR OF GERMANY.
BERNAUER STRAßE
HUFF HUFF
N-NEIN...

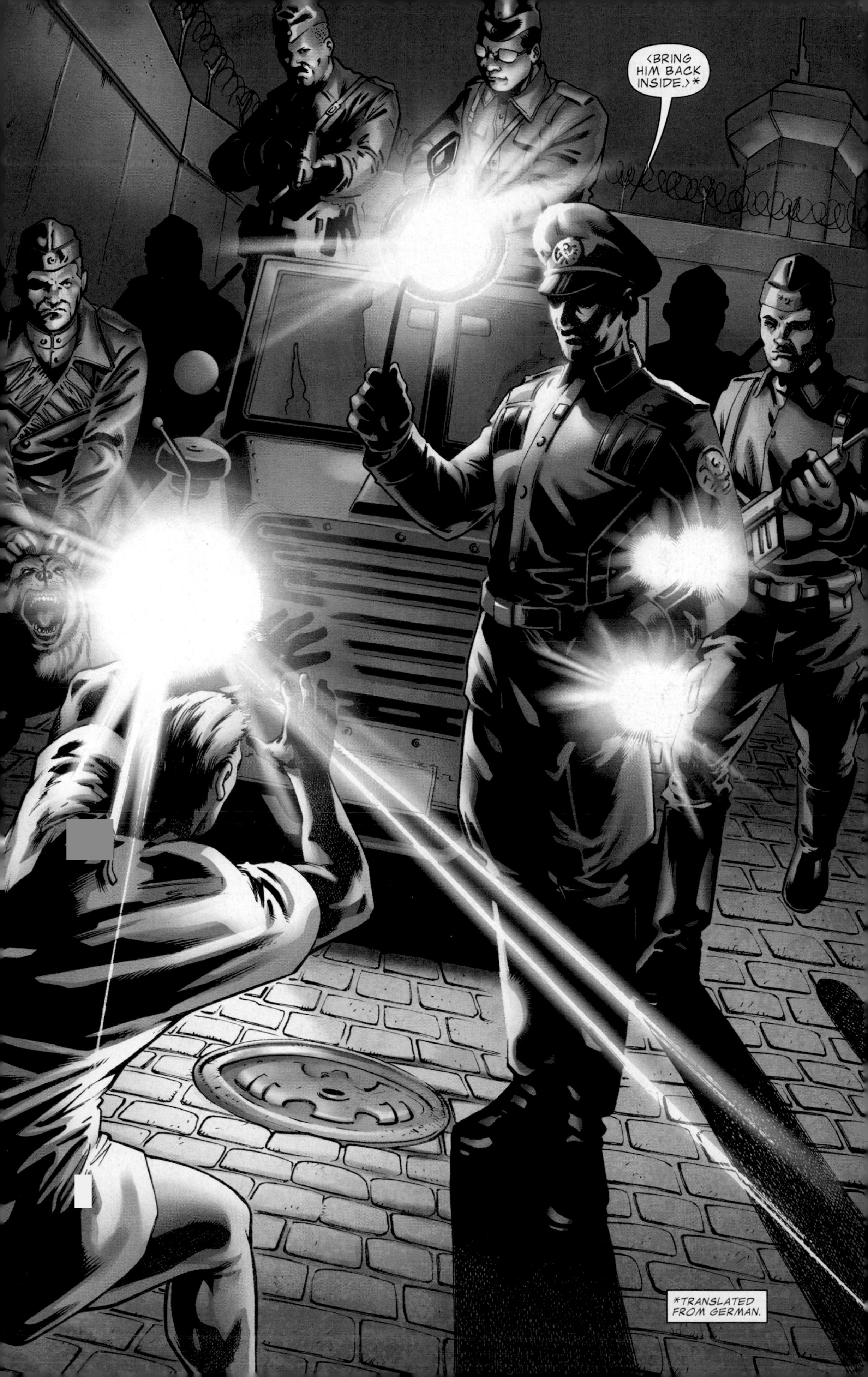
<BRING HIM BACK INSIDE.>*
*TRANSLATED FROM GERMAN.

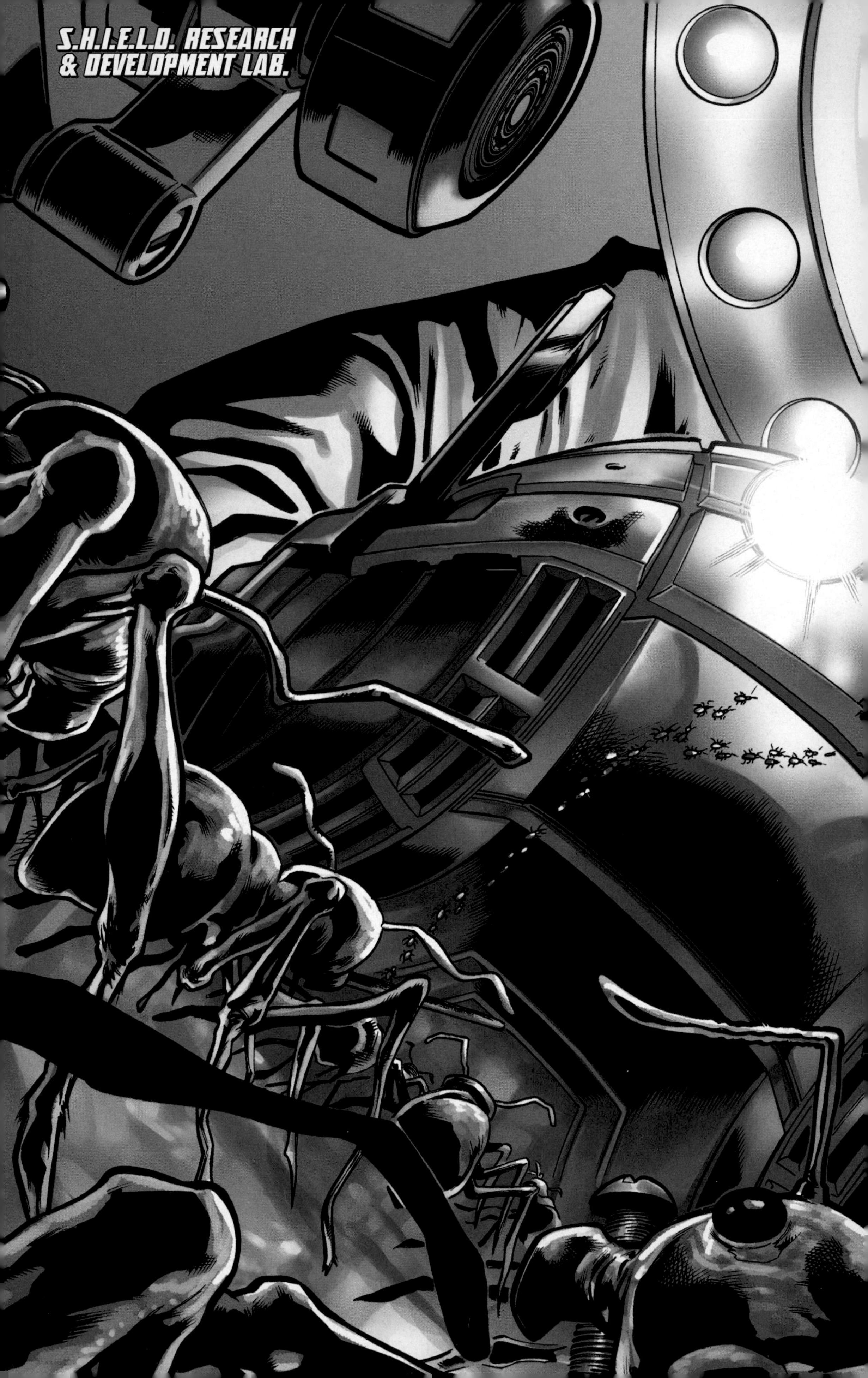
S.H.I.E.L.D. RESEARCH & DEVELOPMENT LAB.

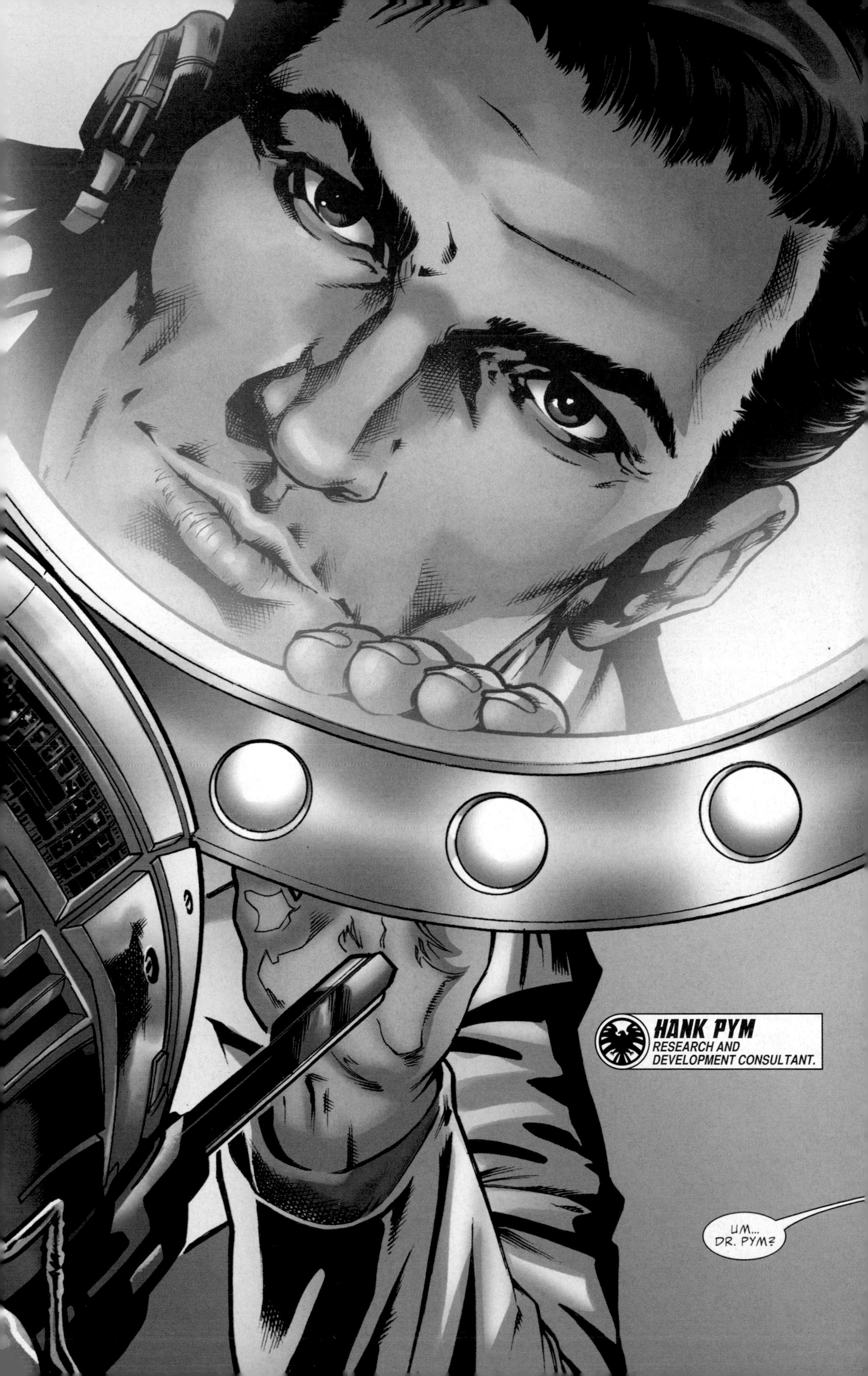
HANK PYM
RESEARCH AND
DEVELOPMENT CONSULTANT.
UM... DR. PYM?

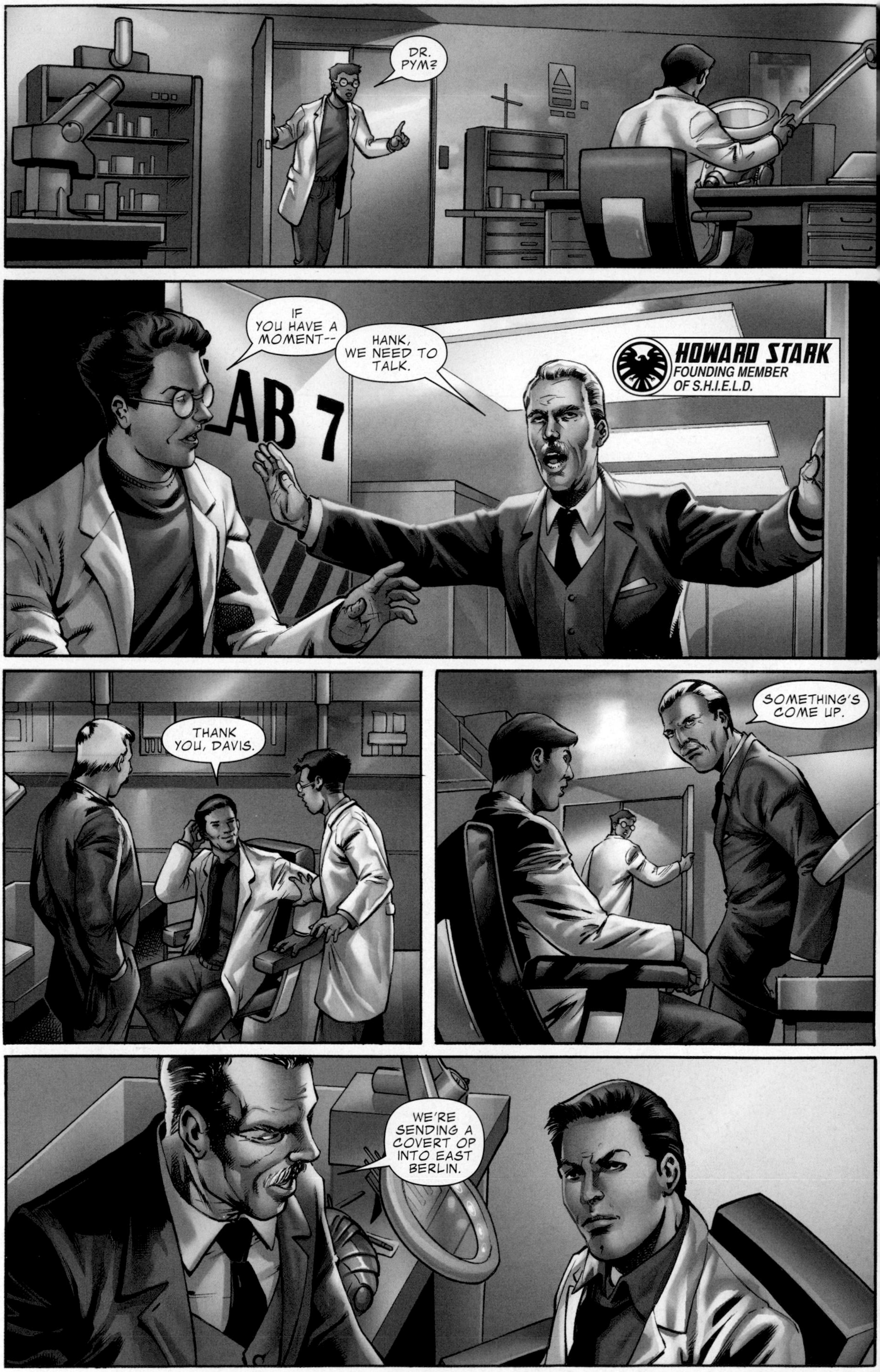
DR. PYM?
IF YOU HAVE A MOMENT--
HANK, WE NEED TO TALK.
HOWARD STARK FOUNDING MEMBER OF S.H.I.E.L.D.
LAB 7
THANK YOU, DAVIS.
SOMETHING'S COME UP.
WE'RE SENDING A COVERT OP INTO EAST BERLIN.

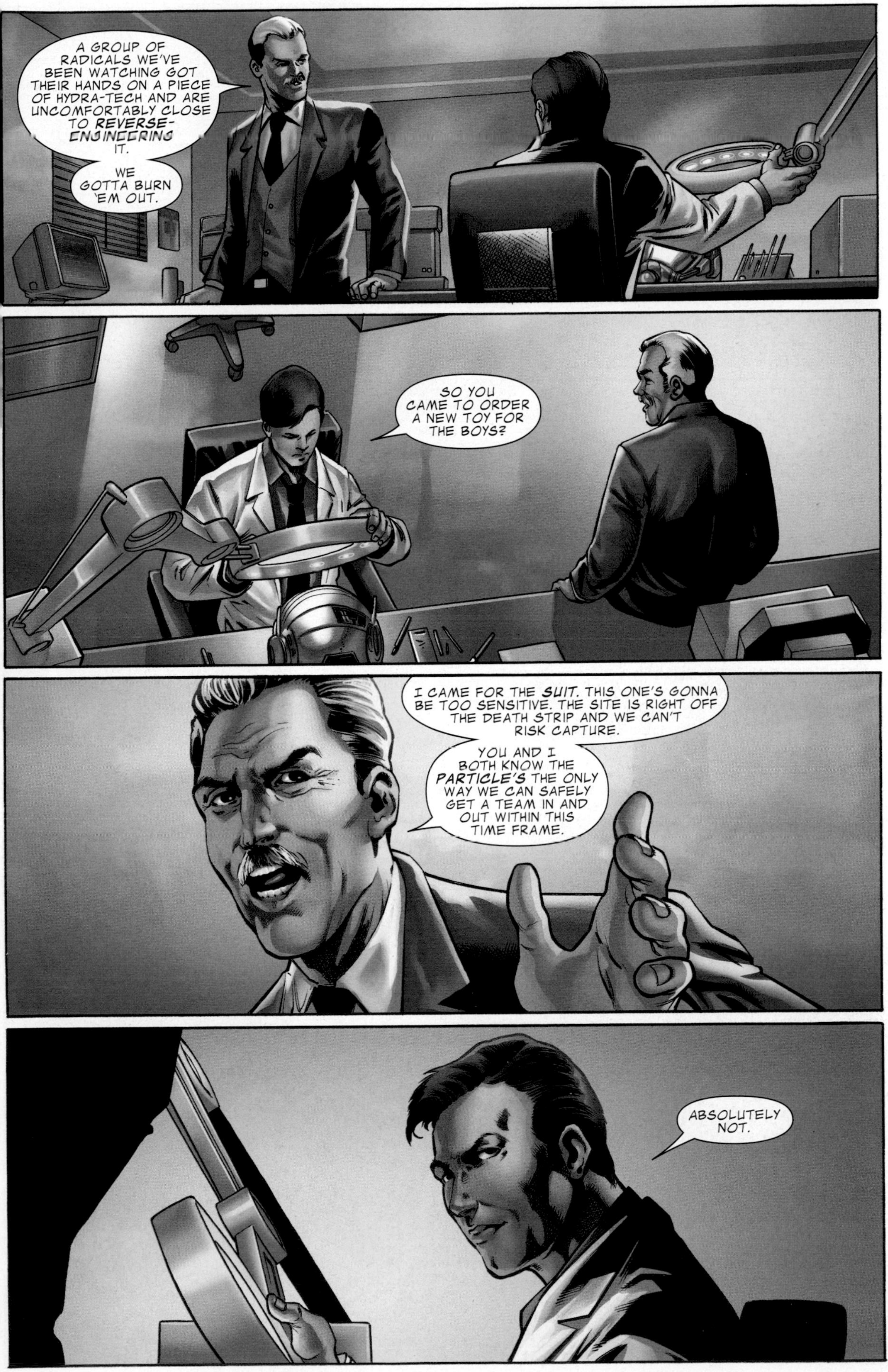
A GROUP OF RADICALS WE'VE BEEN WATCHING GOT THEIR HANDS ON A PIECE OF HYDRA-TECH AND ARE UNCOMFORTABLY CLOSE TO REVERSE-ENGINEERING IT.
WE GOTTA BURN 'EM OUT.
SO YOU CAME TO ORDER A NEW TOY FOR THE BOYS?
I CAME FOR THE SUIT. THIS ONE'S GONNA BE TOO SENSITIVE. THE SITE IS RIGHT OFF THE DEATH STRIP AND WE CAN'T RISK CAPTURE.
YOU AND I BOTH KNOW THE PARTICLE'S THE ONLY WAY WE CAN SAFELY GET A TEAM IN AND OUT WITHIN THIS TIME FRAME.
ABSOLUTELY NOT.

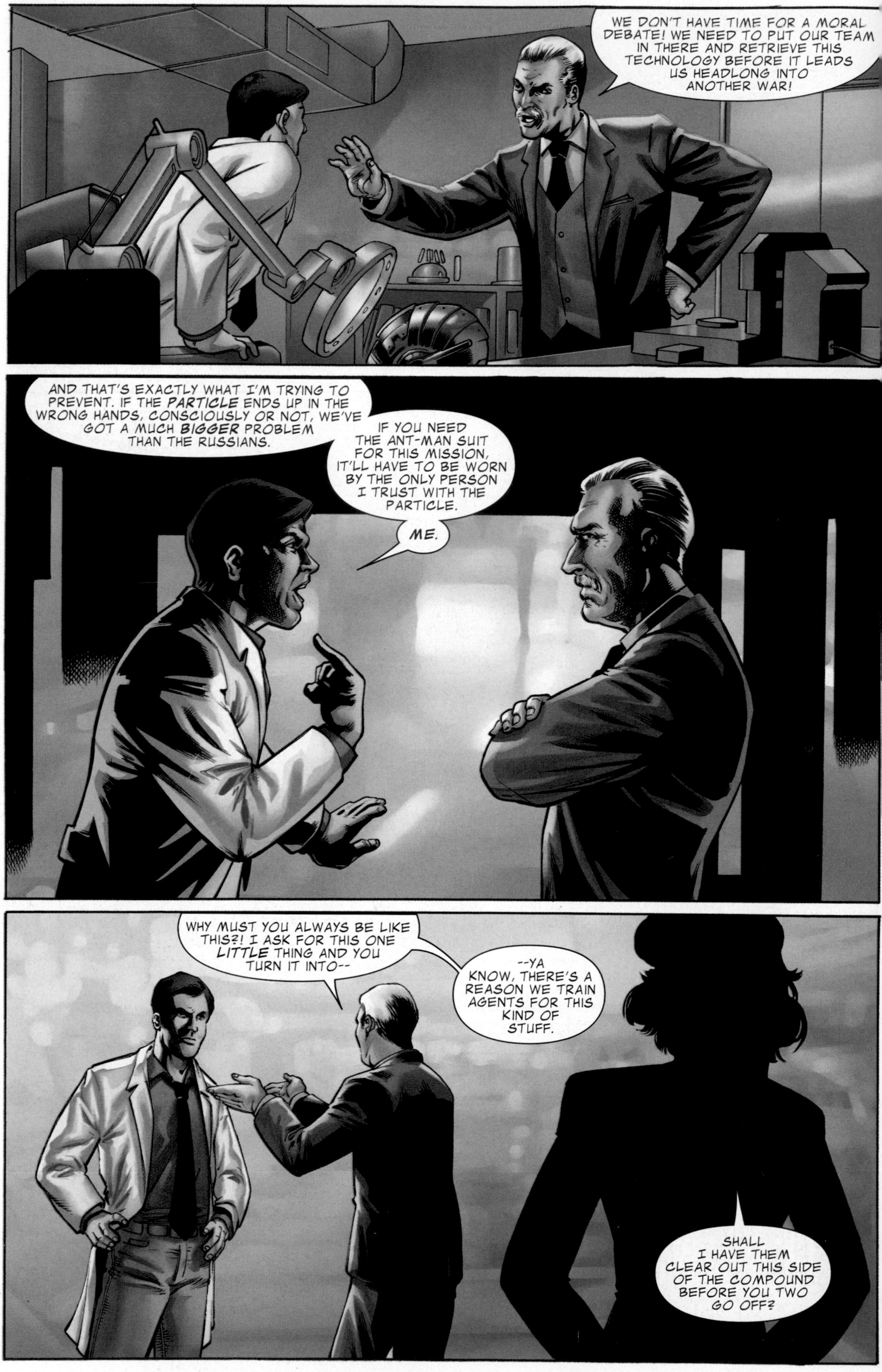
WE DON'T HAVE TIME FOR A MORAL DEBATE! WE NEED TO PUT OUR TEAM IN THERE AND RETRIEVE THIS TECHNOLOGY BEFORE IT LEADS US HEADLONG INTO ANOTHER WAR!
AND THAT'S EXACTLY WHAT I'M TRYING TO PREVENT. IF THE PARTICLE ENDS UP IN THE WRONG HANDS, CONSCIOUSLY OR NOT, WE'VE GOT A MUCH BIGGER PROBLEM THAN THE RUSSIANS.
IF YOU NEED THE ANT-MAN SUIT FOR THIS MISSION, IT'LL HAVE TO BE WORN BY THE ONLY PERSON I TRUST WITH THE PARTICLE.
ME.
WHY MUST YOU ALWAYS BE LIKE THIS?! I ASK FOR THIS ONE LITTLE THING AND YOU TURN IT INTO--
--YA KNOW, THERE'S A REASON WE TRAIN AGENTS FOR THIS KIND OF STUFF.
SHALL I HAVE THEM CLEAR OUT THIS SIDE OF THE COMPOUND BEFORE YOU TWO GO OFF?

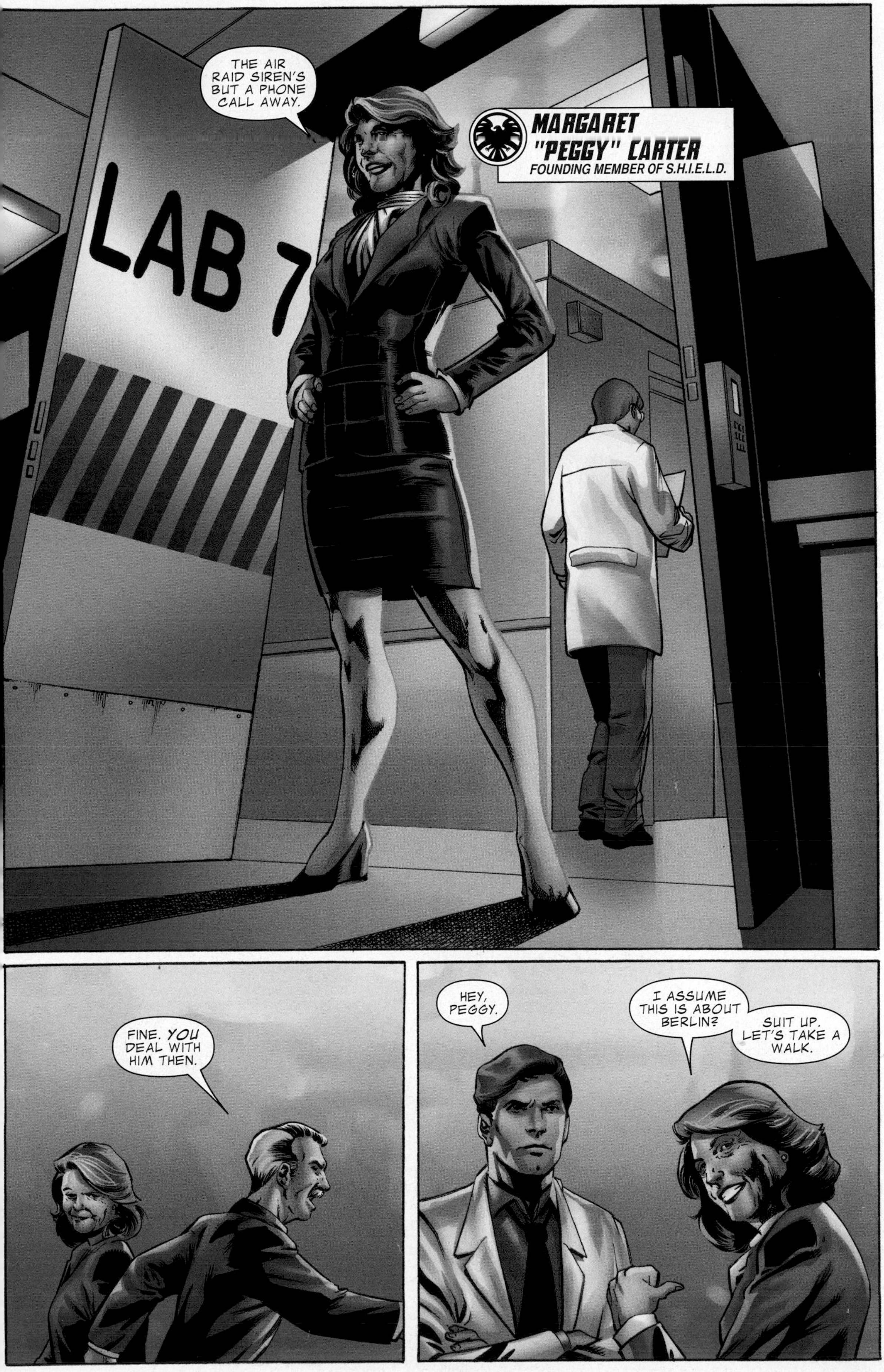
THE AIR RAID SIREN'S BUT A PHONE CALL AWAY.
LAB 7
MARGARET "PEGGY" CARTER
FOUNDING MEMBER OF S.H.I.E.L.D.
FINE. YOU DEAL WITH HIM THEN.
HEY, PEGGY.
I ASSUME THIS IS ABOUT BERLIN?
SUIT UP. LET'S TAKE A WALK.

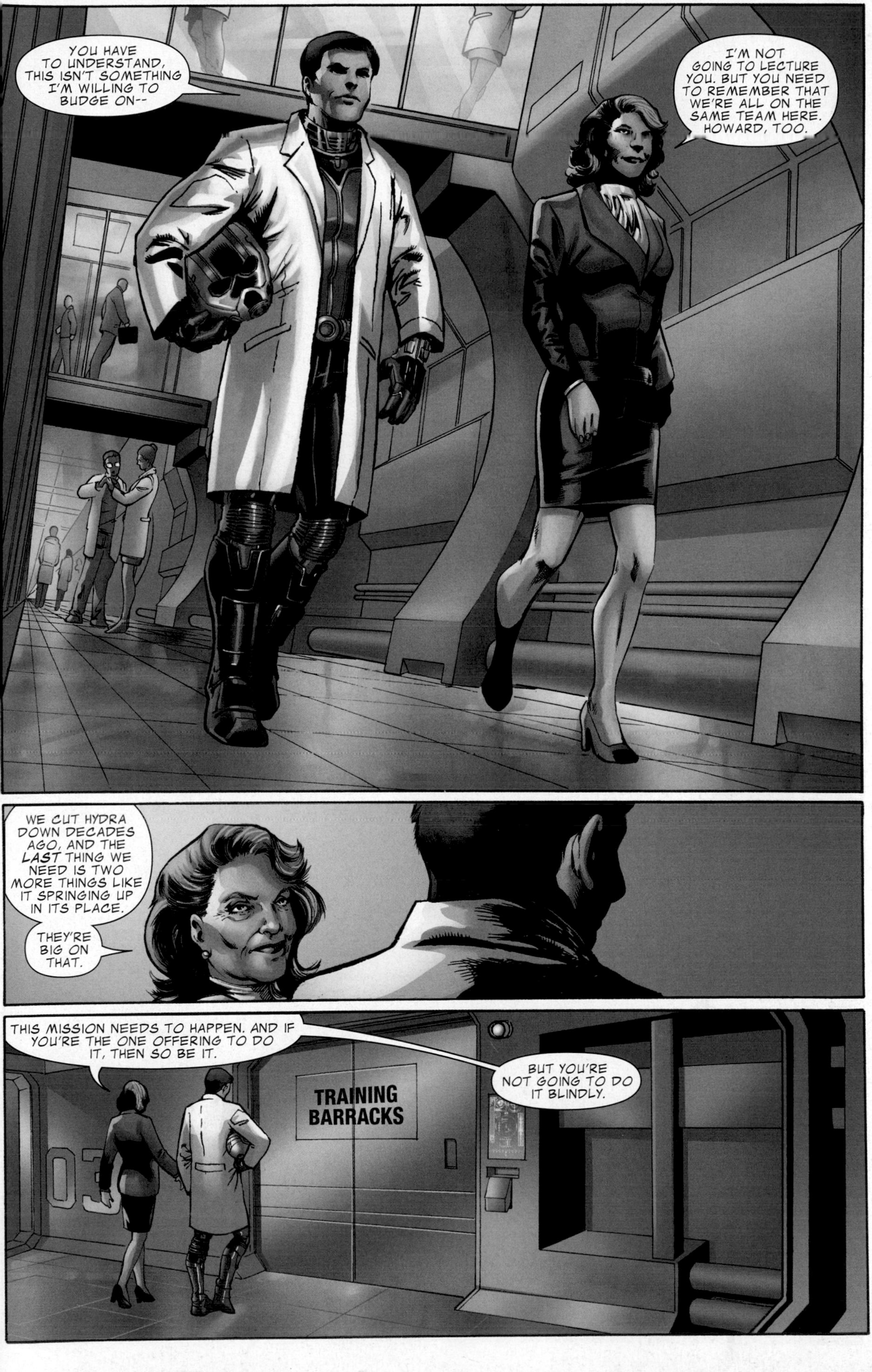
YOU HAVE TO UNDERSTAND, THIS ISN'T SOMETHING I'M WILLING TO BUDGE ON--
I'M NOT GOING TO LECTURE YOU. BUT YOU NEED TO REMEMBER THAT WE'RE ALL ON THE SAME TEAM HERE. HOWARD, TOO.
WE CUT HYDRA DOWN DECADES AGO, AND THE LAST THING WE NEED IS TWO MORE THINGS LIKE IT SPRINGING UP IN ITS PLACE.
THEY'RE BIG ON THAT.
THIS MISSION NEEDS TO HAPPEN, AND IF YOU'RE THE ONE OFFERING TO DO IT, THEN SO BE IT.
TRAINING BARRACKS
03
BUT YOU'RE NOT GOING TO DO IT BLINDLY.

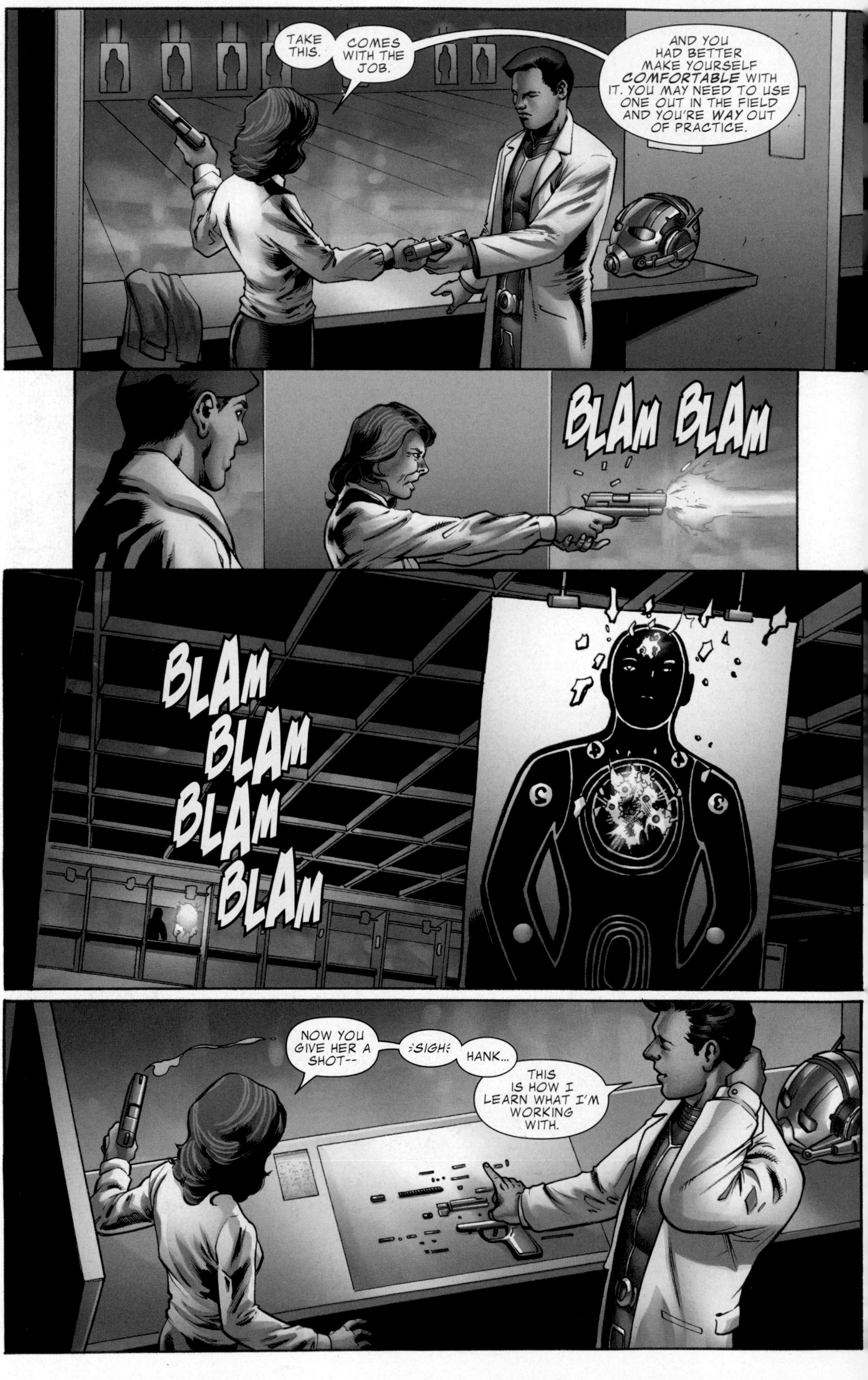
TAKE THIS.
COMES WITH THE JOB.
AND YOU HAD BETTER MAKE YOURSELF COMFORTABLE WITH IT. YOU MAY NEED TO USE ONE OUT IN THE FIELD AND YOU'RE WAY OUT OF PRACTICE.
BLAM BLAM
BLAM BLAM BLAM BLAM
NOW YOU GIVE HER A SHOT--
SIGH
HANK...
THIS IS HOW I LEARN WHAT I'M WORKING WITH.

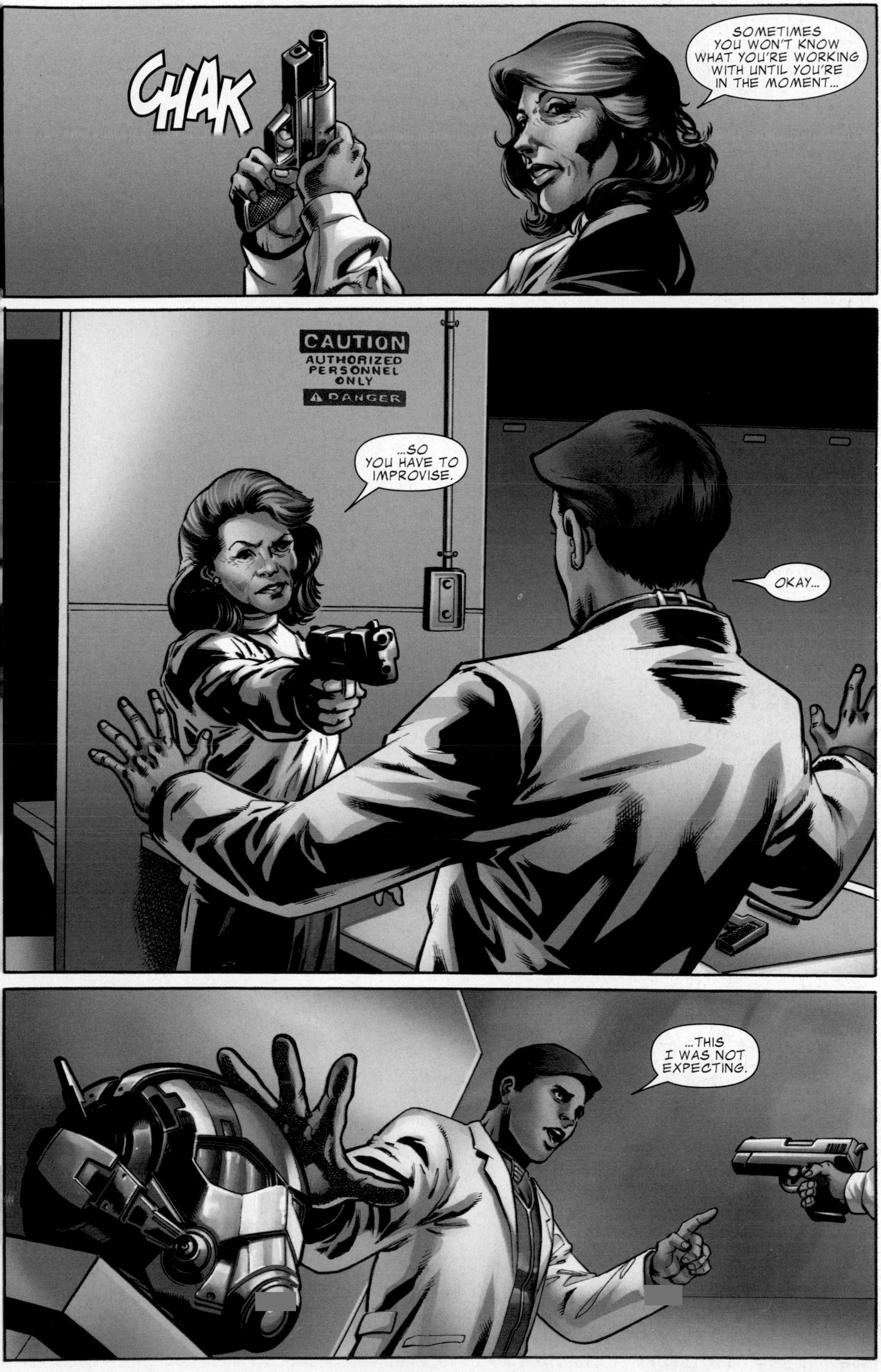
CHAK
SOMETIMES YOU WON'T KNOW WHAT YOU'RE WORKING WITH UNTIL YOU'RE IN THE MOMENT...
CAUTION
AUTHORIZED PERSONNEL ONLY
DANGER
...SO YOU HAVE TO IMPROVISE.
OKAY...
...THIS I WAS NOT EXPECTING.

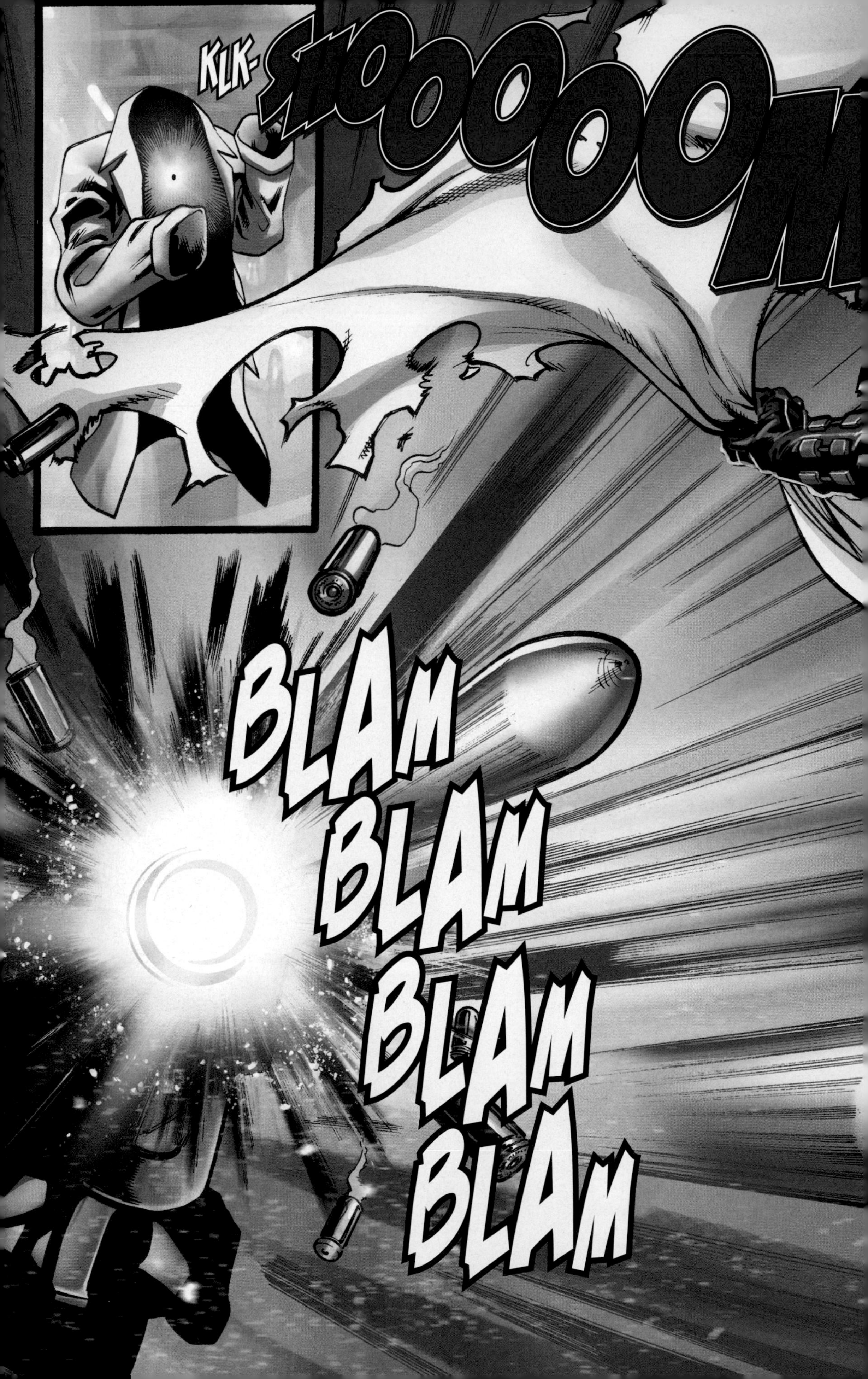
KLK-
SHOOOOOM
BLAM
BLAM
BLAM
BLAM

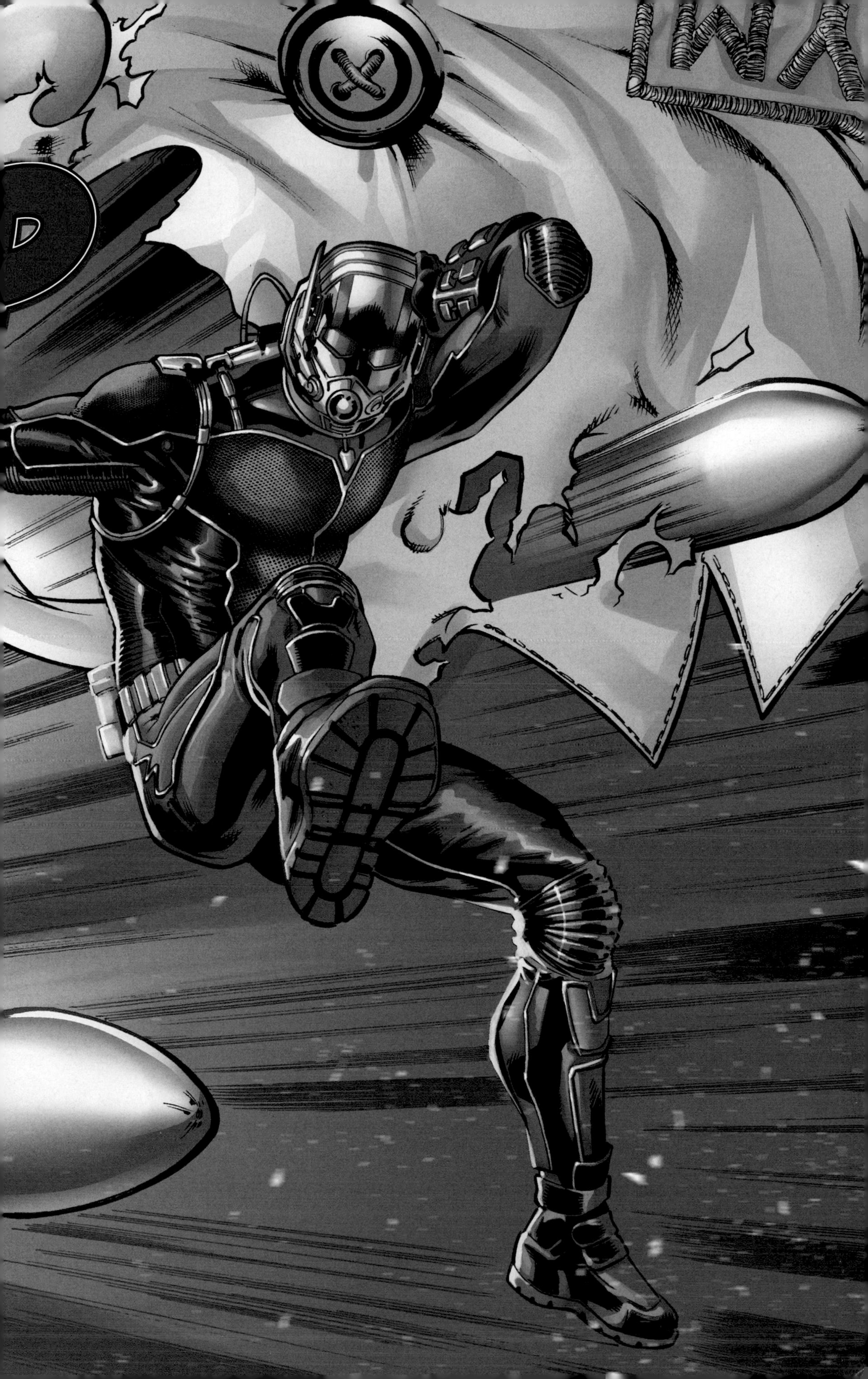

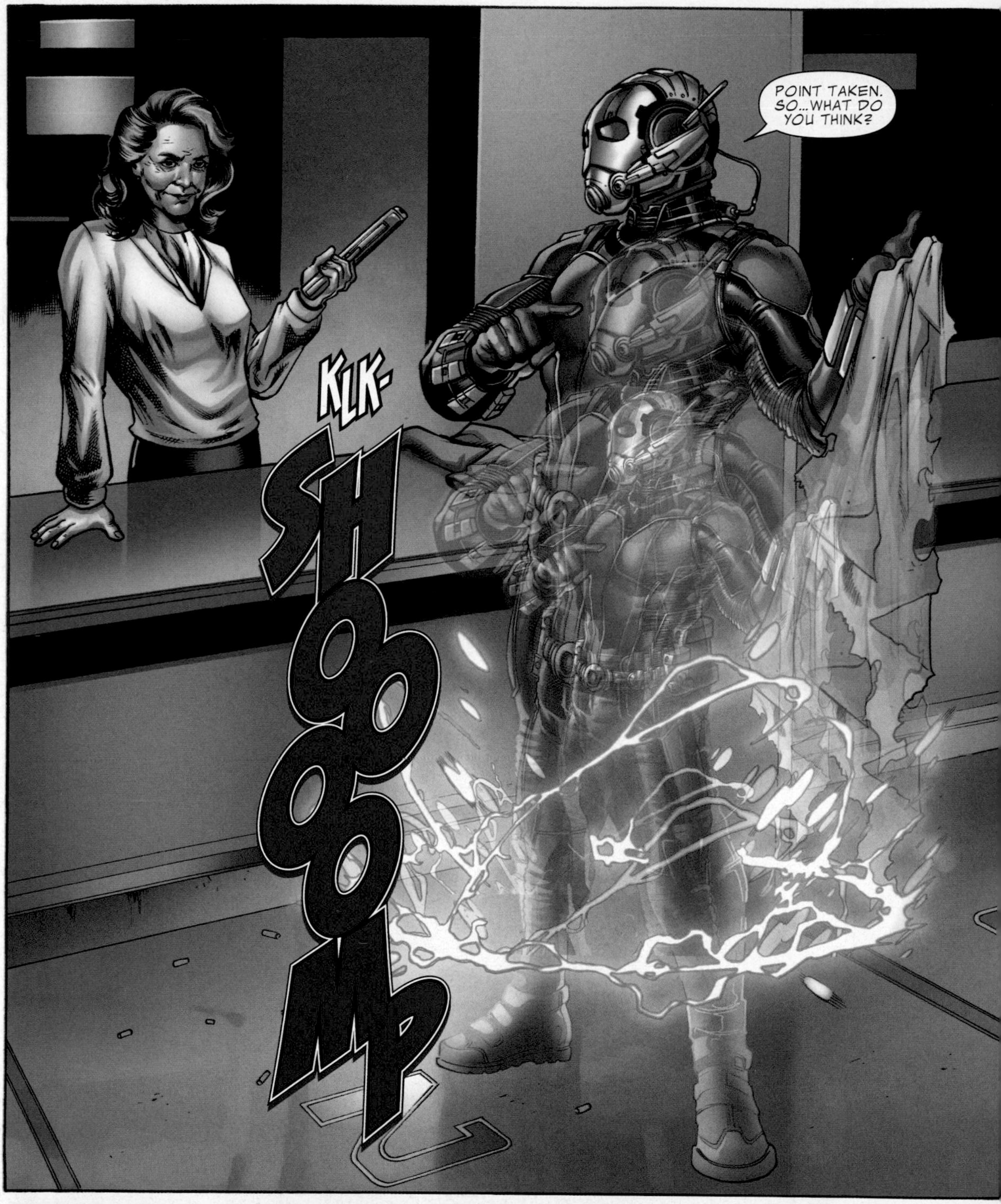
POINT TAKEN. SO...WHAT DO YOU THINK?
KLK-
SHOOOMP

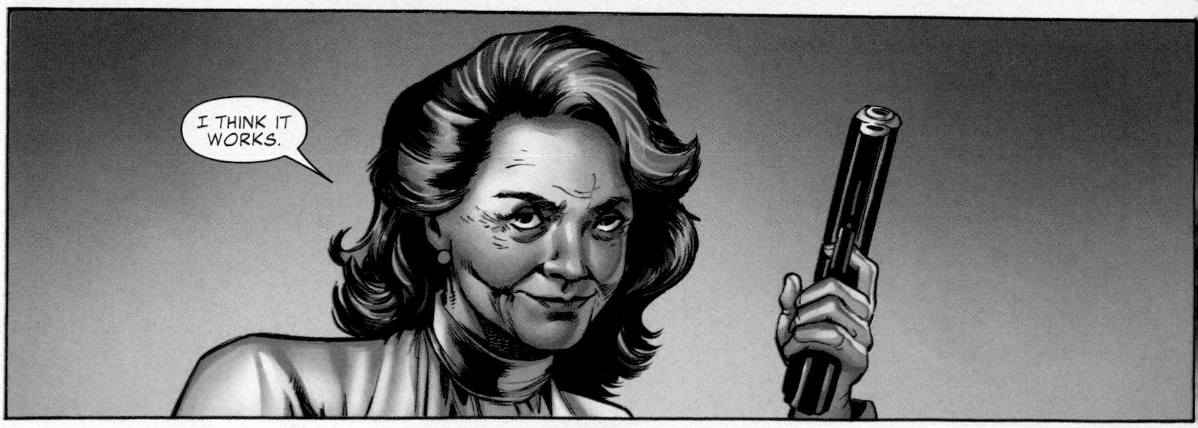
I THINK IT WORKS.

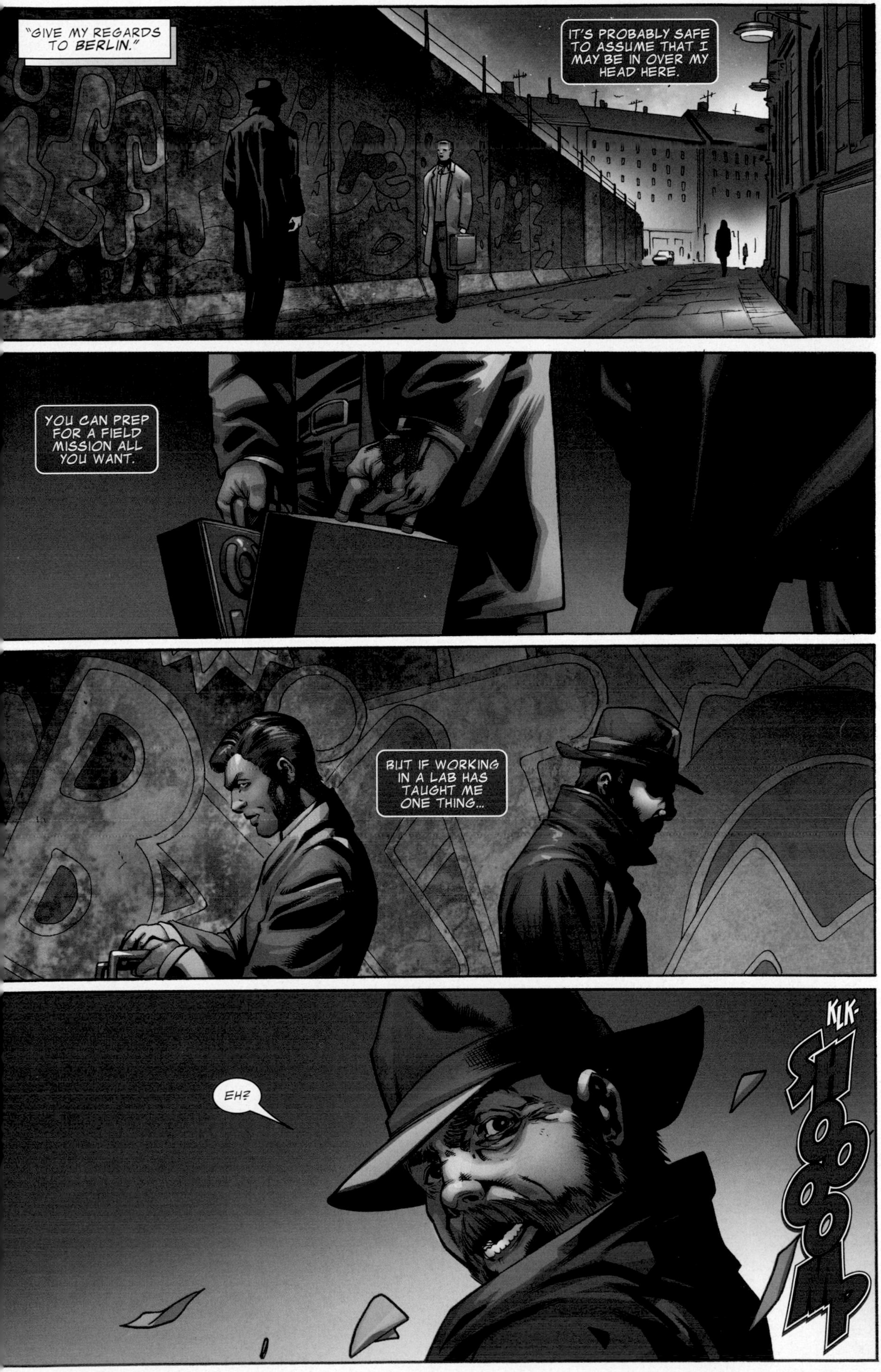
"GIVE MY REGARDS TO BERLIN."
IT'S PROBABLY SAFE TO ASSUME THAT I MAY BE IN OVER MY HEAD HERE.
YOU CAN PREP FOR A FIELD MISSION ALL YOU WANT.
BUT IF WORKING IN A LAB HAS TAUGHT ME ONE THING...
EH?
KLK-SHOOOMP

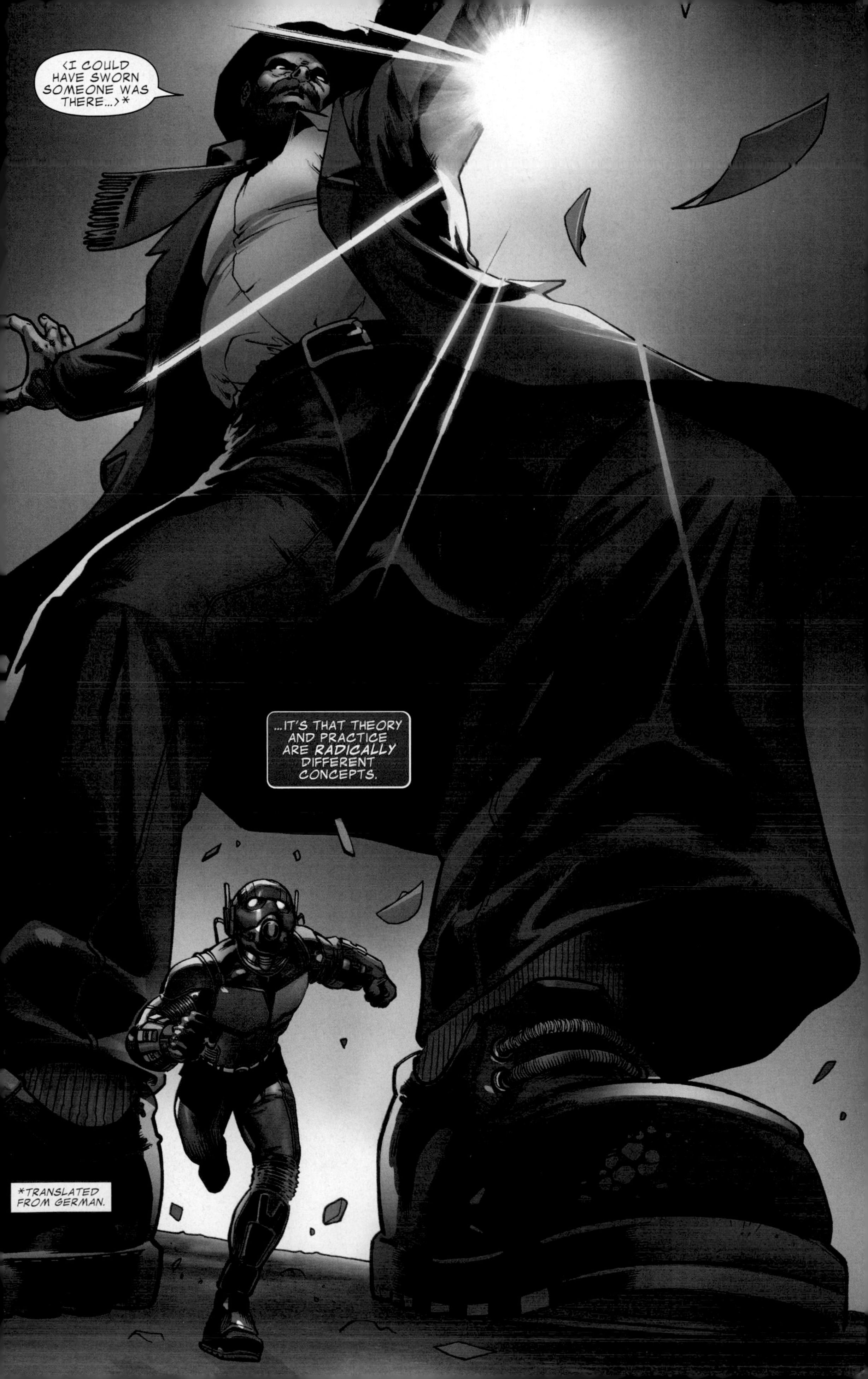
<I COULD HAVE SWORN SOMEONE WAS THERE...>*
...IT'S THAT THEORY AND PRACTICE ARE RADICALLY DIFFERENT CONCEPTS.
*TRANSLATED FROM GERMAN.

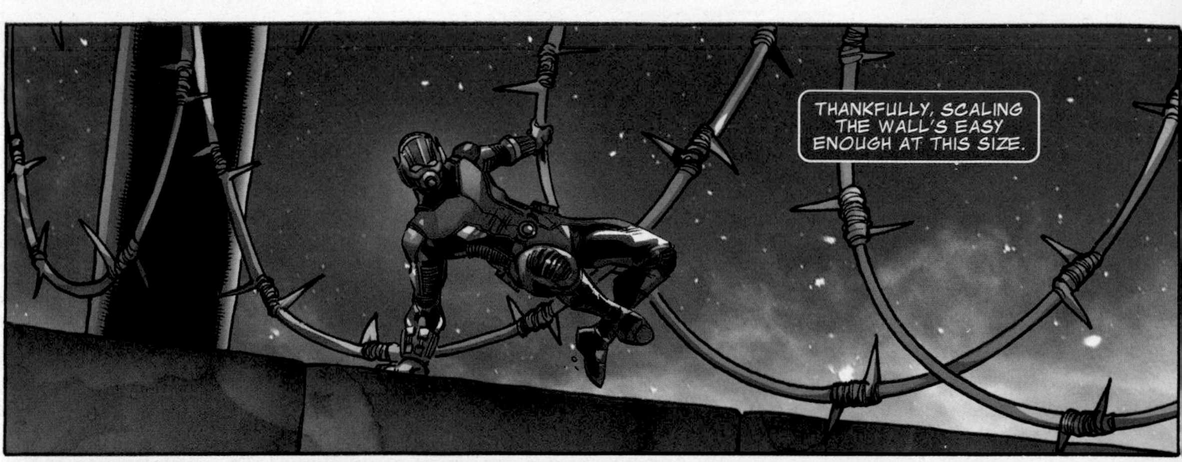
THANKFULLY, SCALING THE WALL'S EASY ENOUGH AT THIS SIZE.

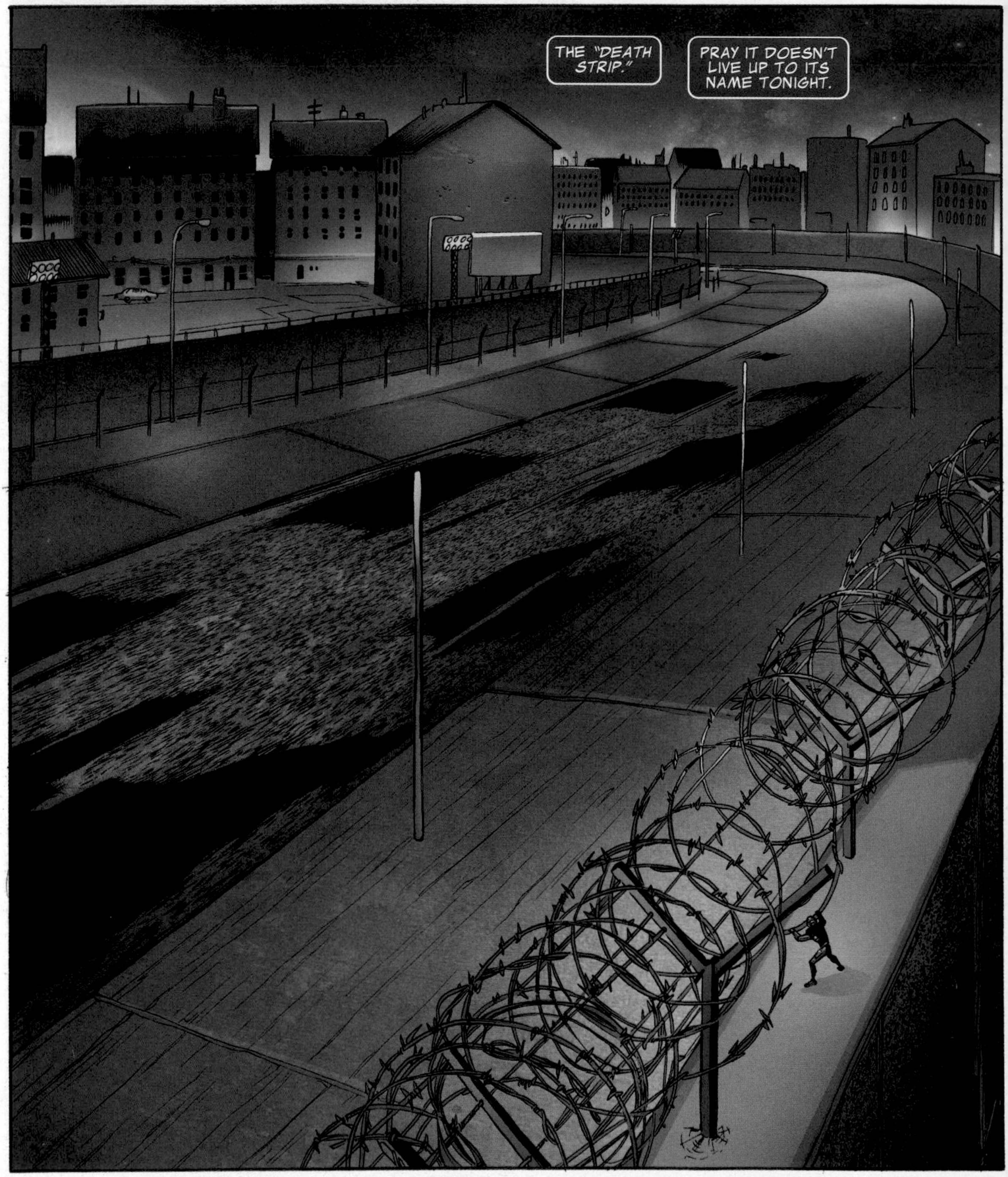
THE "DEATH STRIP."
PRAY IT DOESN'T LIVE UP TO ITS NAME TONIGHT.

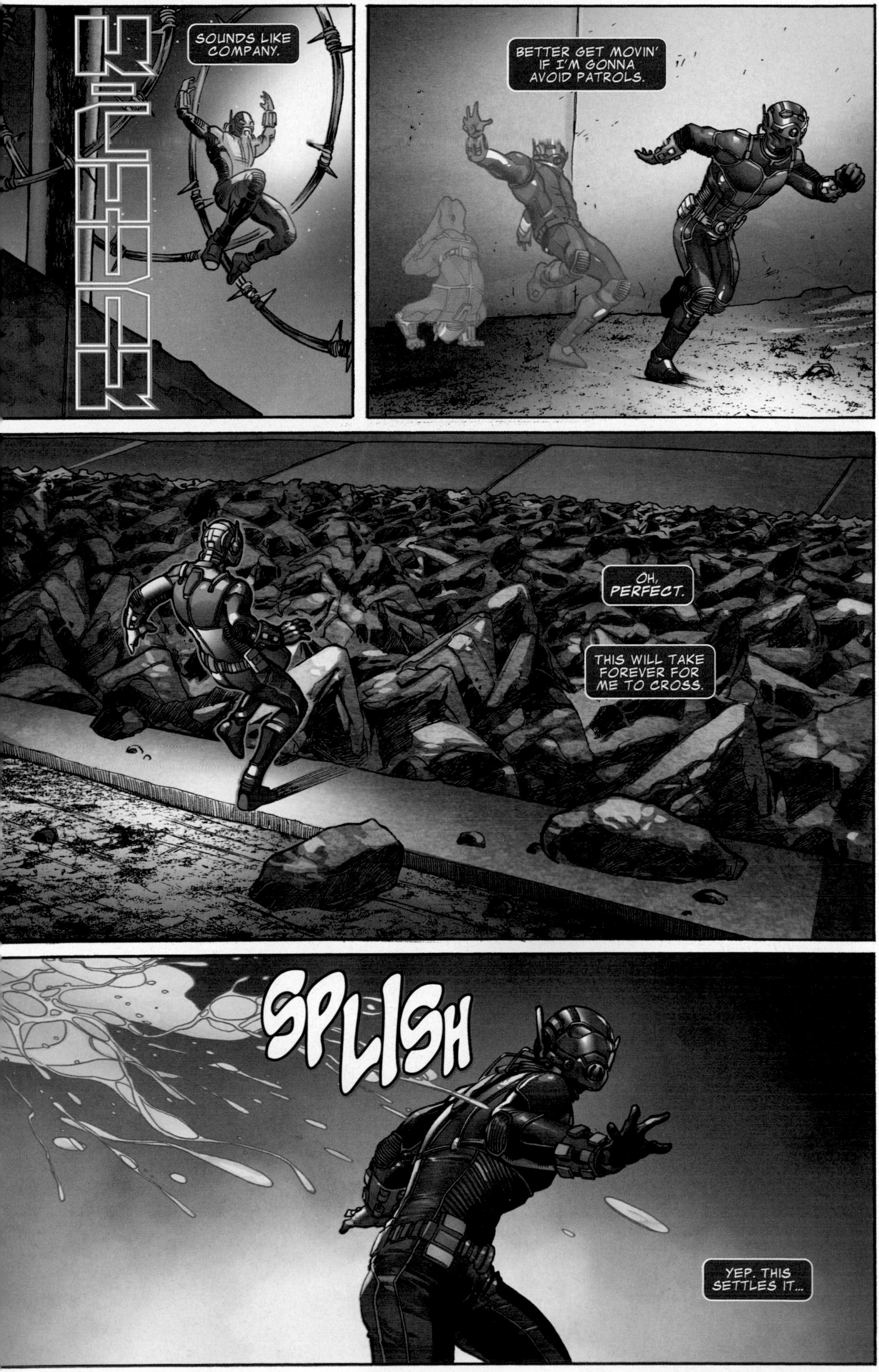
SOUNDS LIKE COMPANY.
BETTER GET MOVIN' IF I'M GONNA AVOID PATROLS.
OH, PERFECT.
THIS WILL TAKE FOREVER FOR ME TO CROSS.
SPLISH
YEP. THIS SETTLES IT...

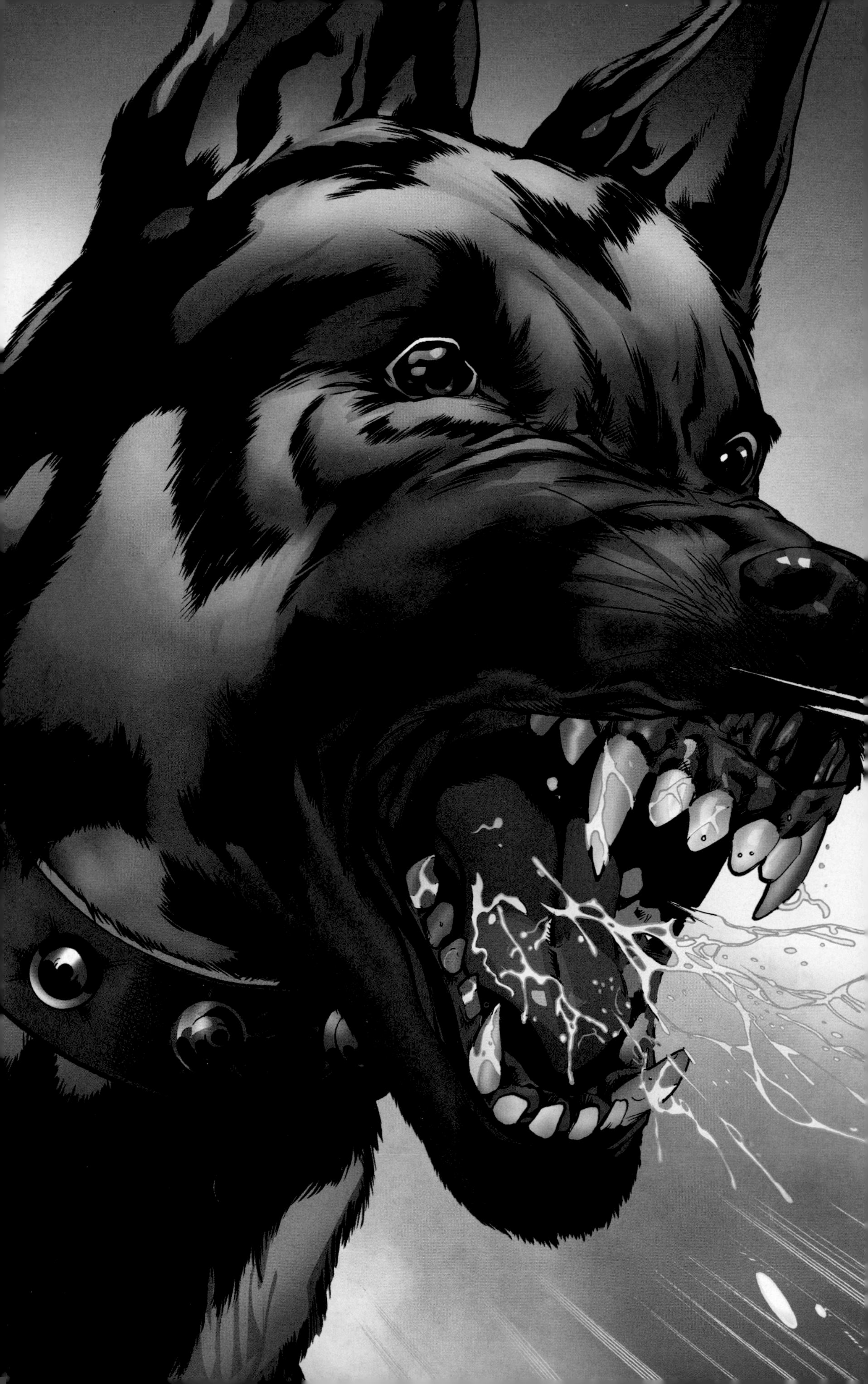

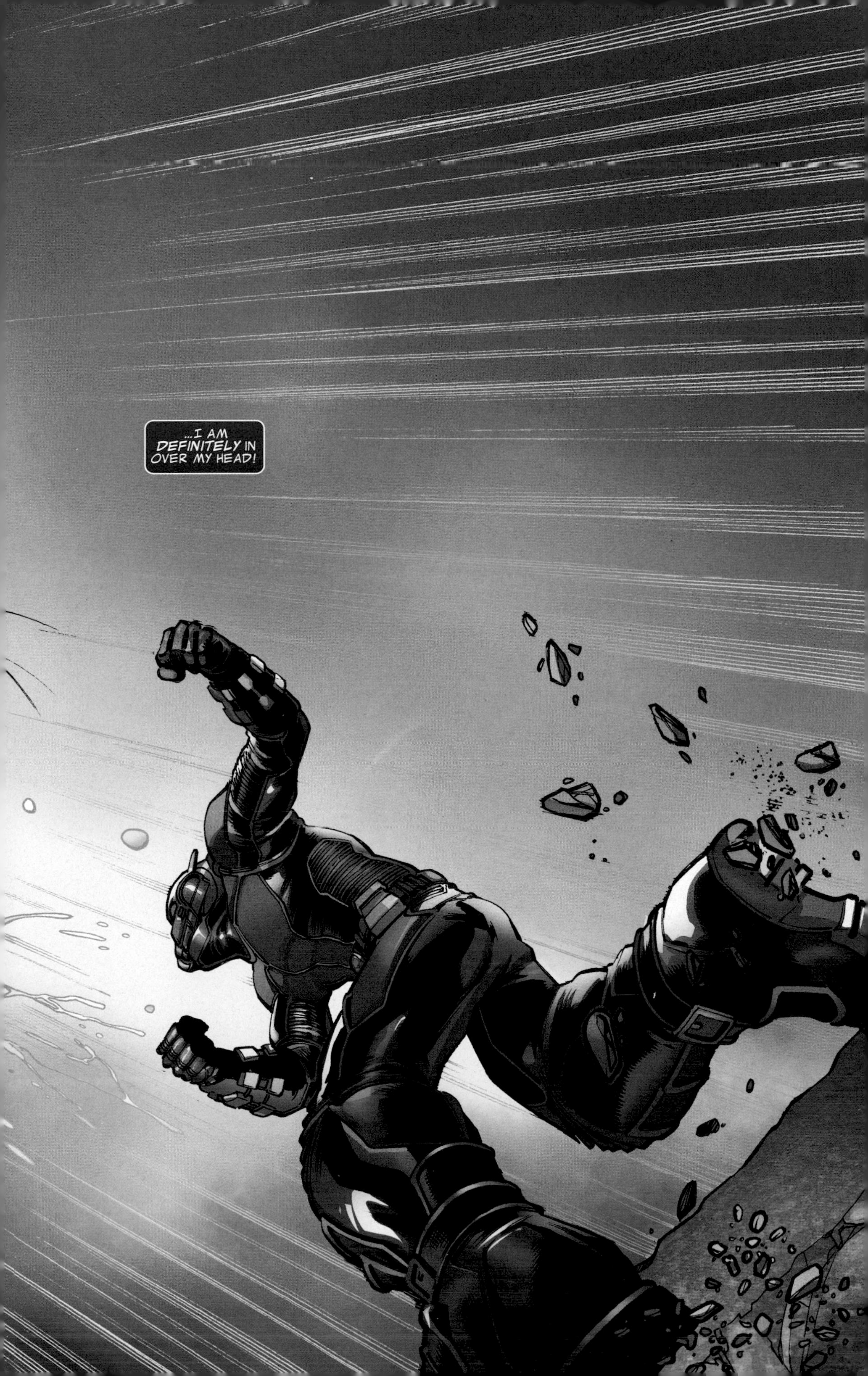
...I AM DEFINITELY IN OVER MY HEAD!

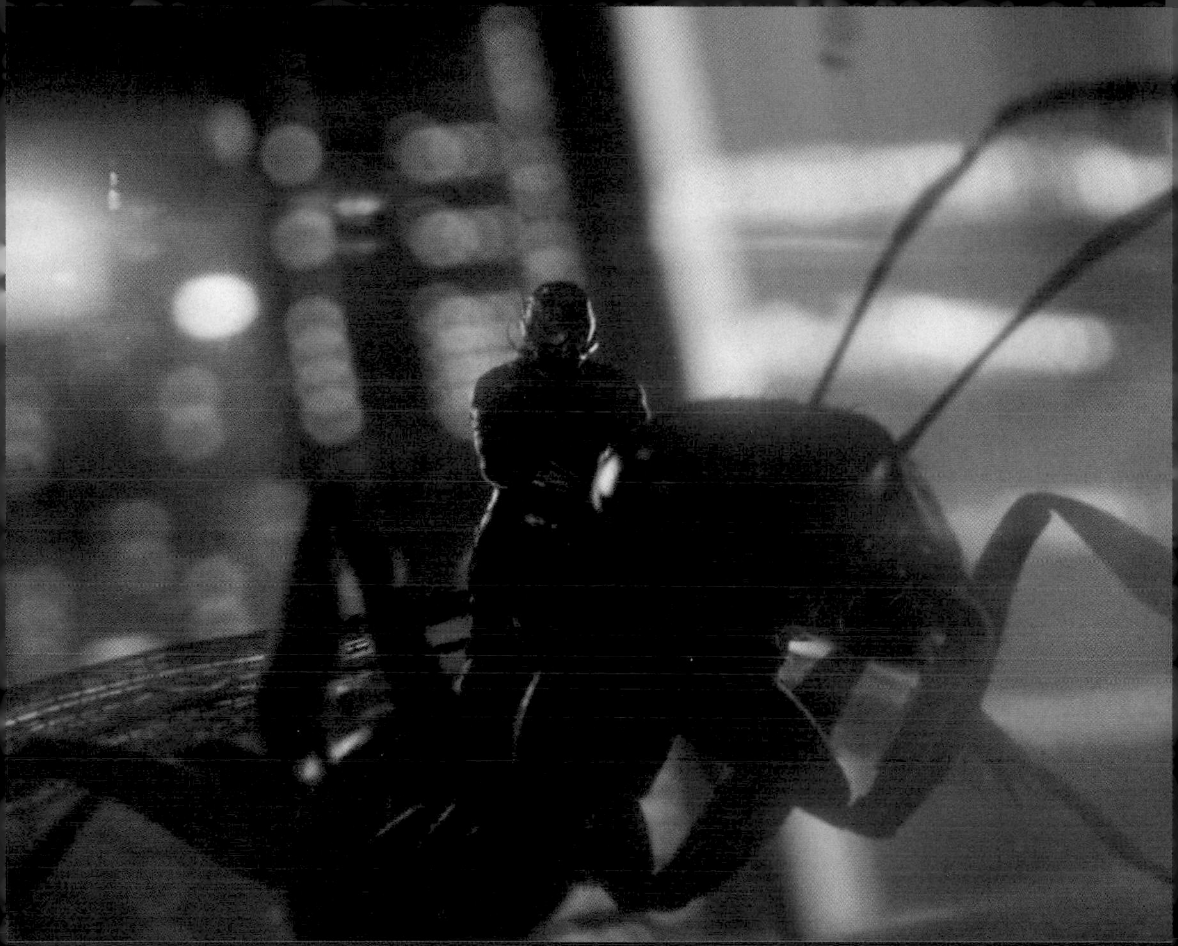

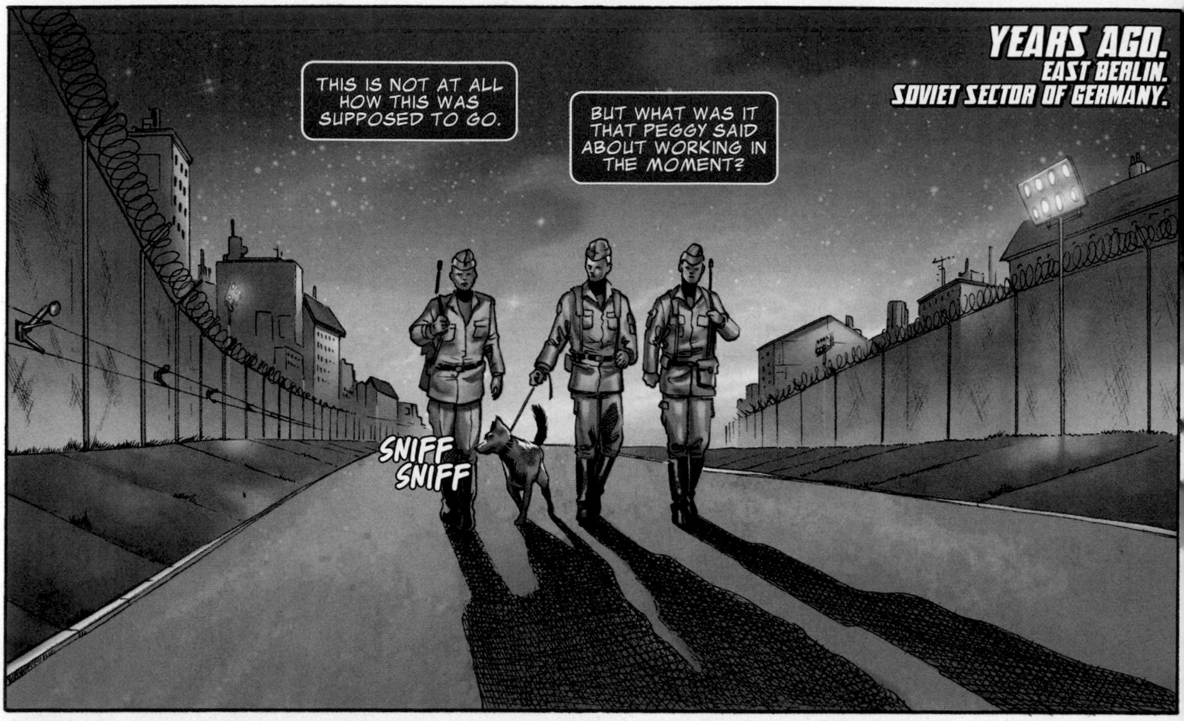
YEARS AGO.
EAST BERLIN.
SOVIET SECTOR OF GERMANY.
THIS IS NOT AT ALL HOW THIS WAS SUPPOSED TO GO.
BUT WHAT WAS IT THAT PEGGY SAID ABOUT WORKING IN THE MOMENT?
SNIFF SNIFF

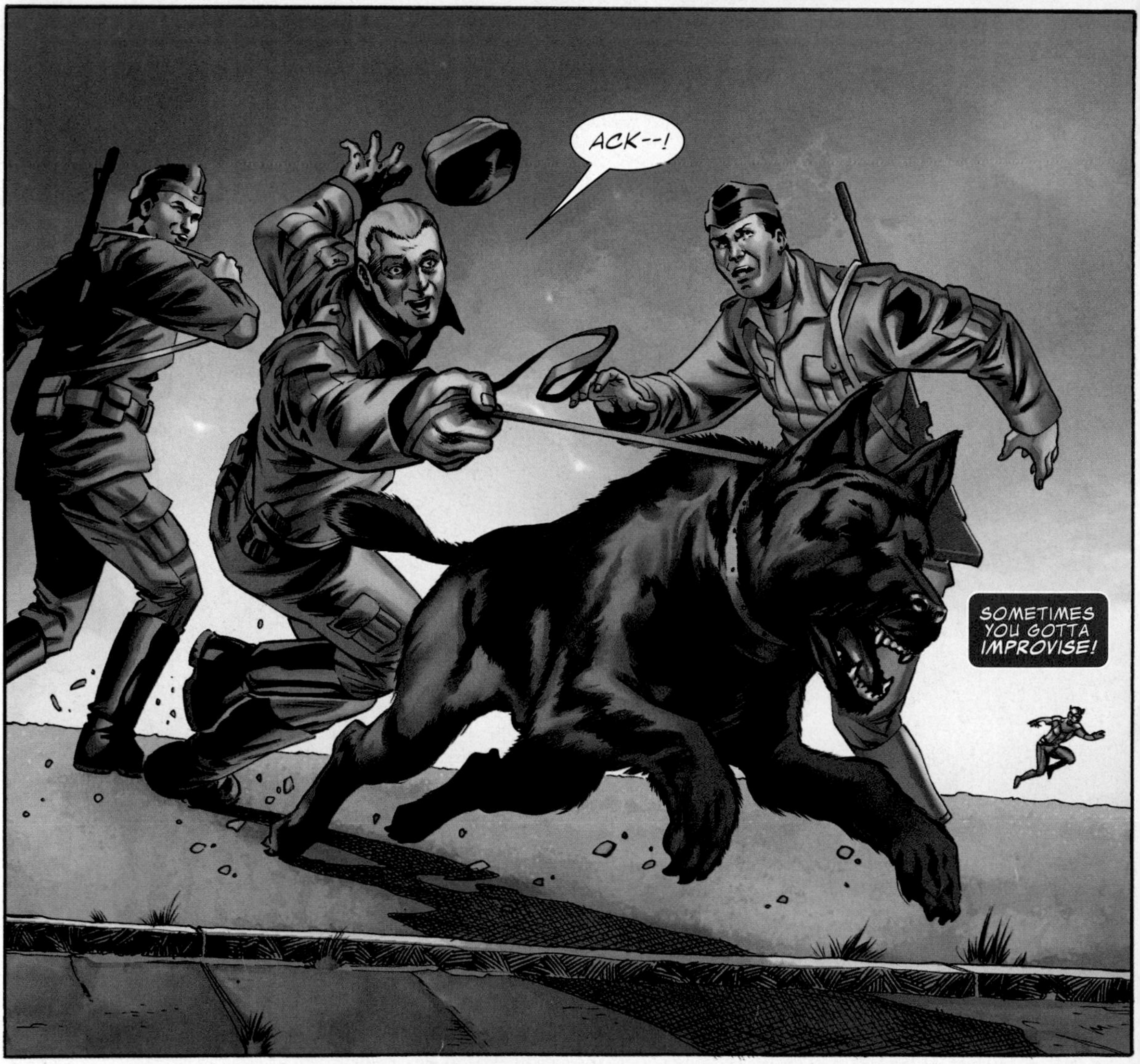
ACK--!
SOMETIMES YOU GOTTA IMPROVISE!

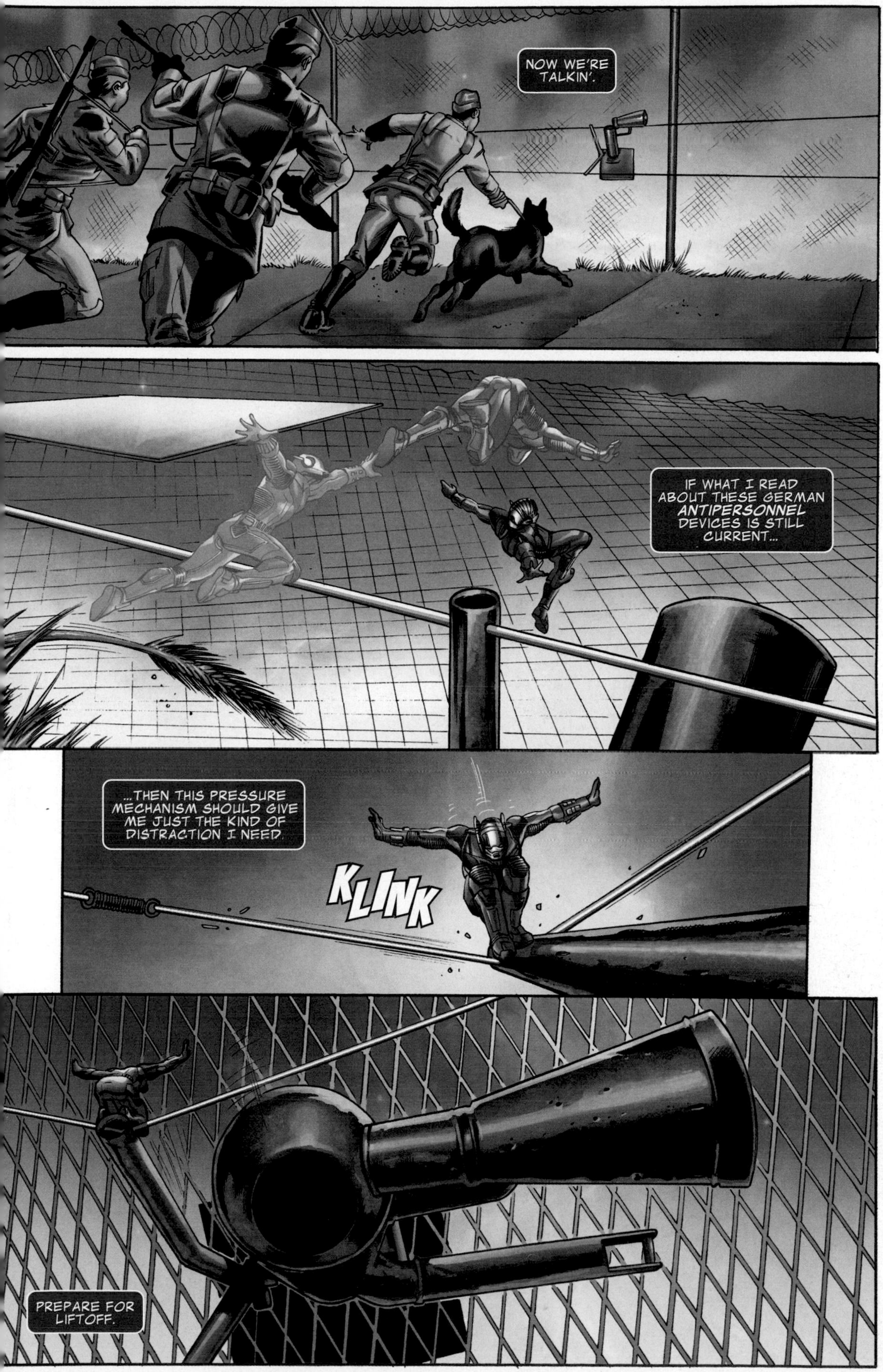
NOW WE'RE TALKIN'.
IF WHAT I READ ABOUT THESE GERMAN ANTIPERSONNEL DEVICES IS STILL CURRENT...
...THEN THIS PRESSURE MECHANISM SHOULD GIVE ME JUST THE KIND OF DISTRACTION I NEED.
KLINK
PREPARE FOR LIFTOFF.

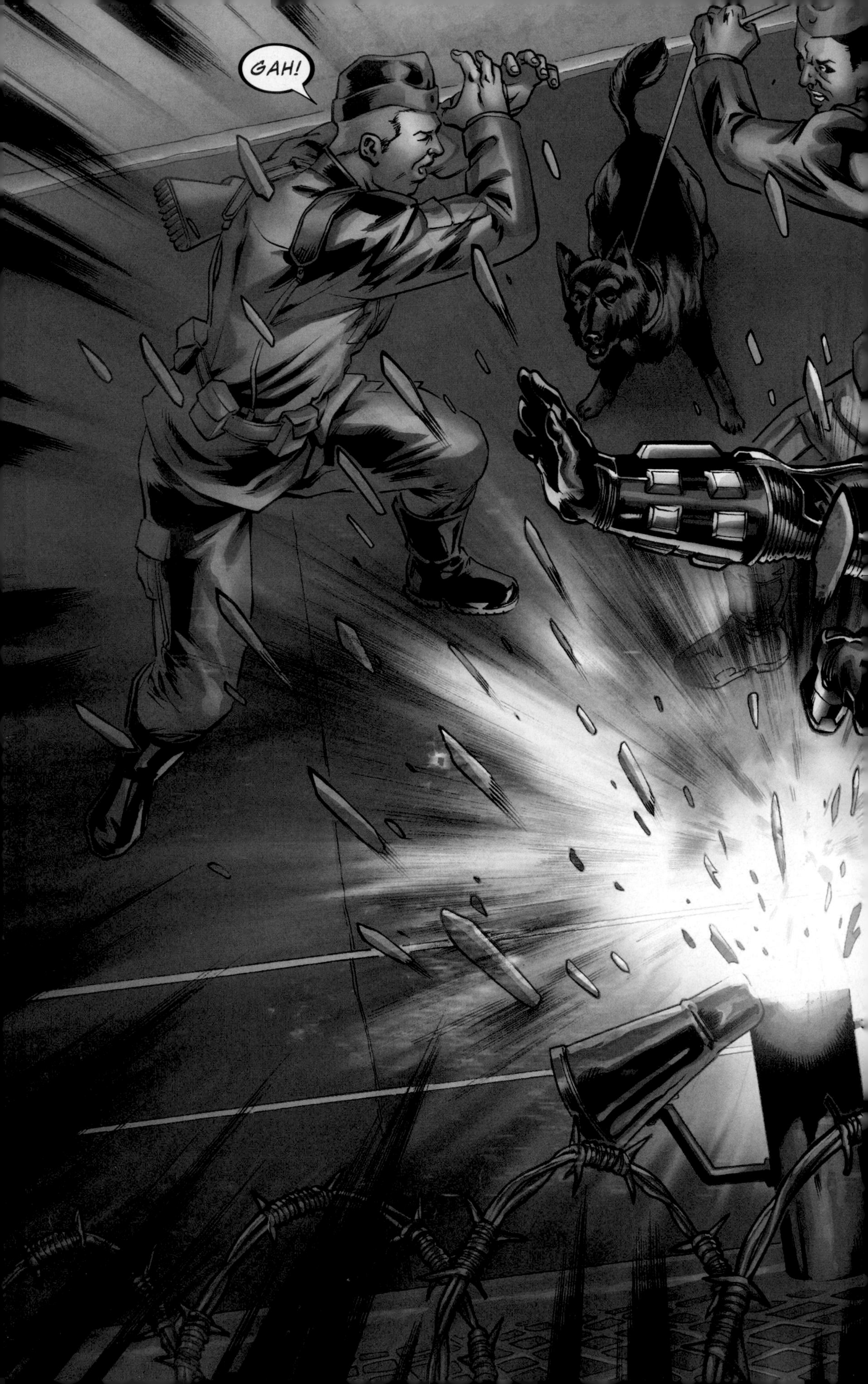
GAH!

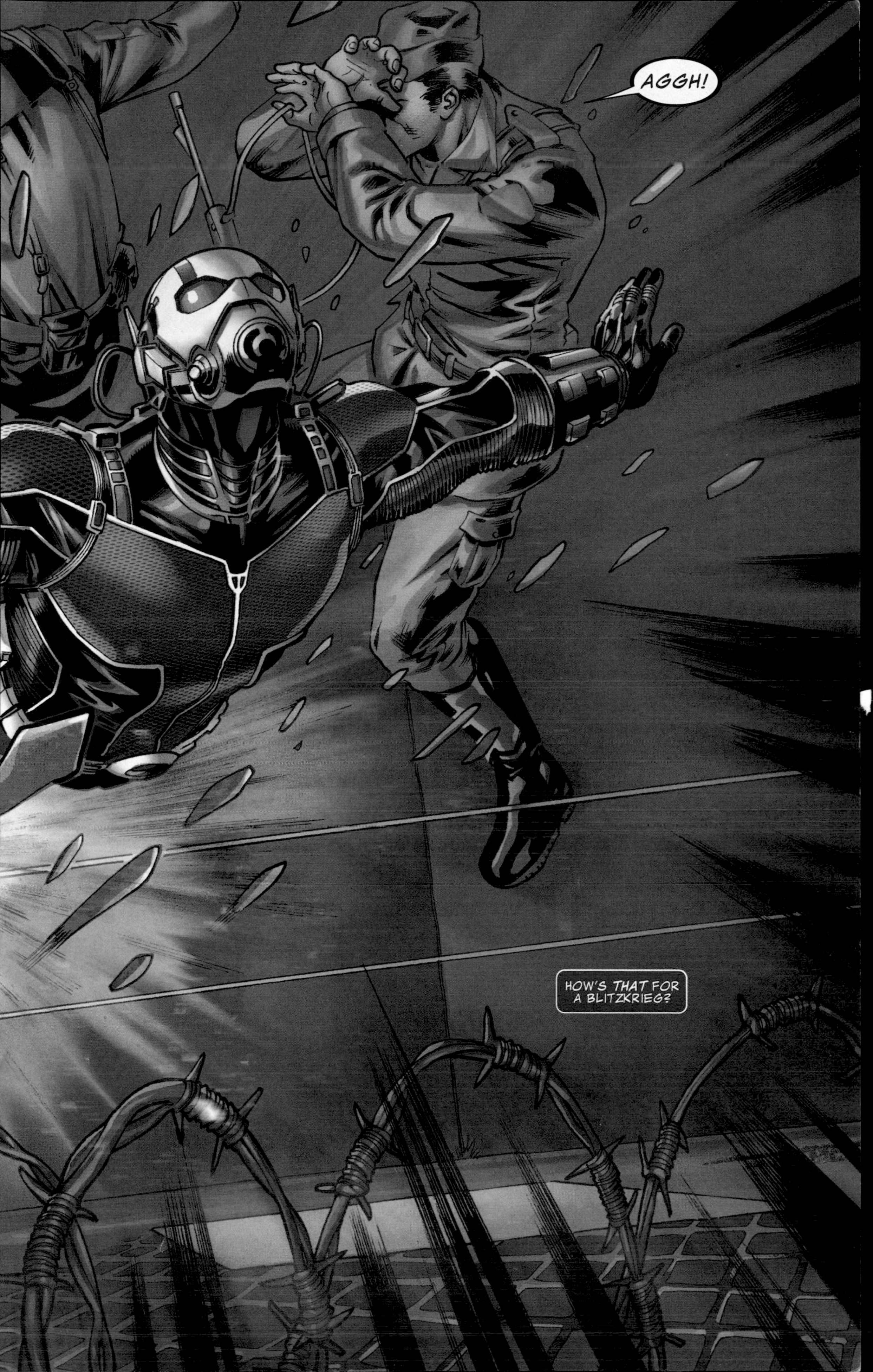
AGGH!
HOW'S THAT FOR A BLITZKRIEG?

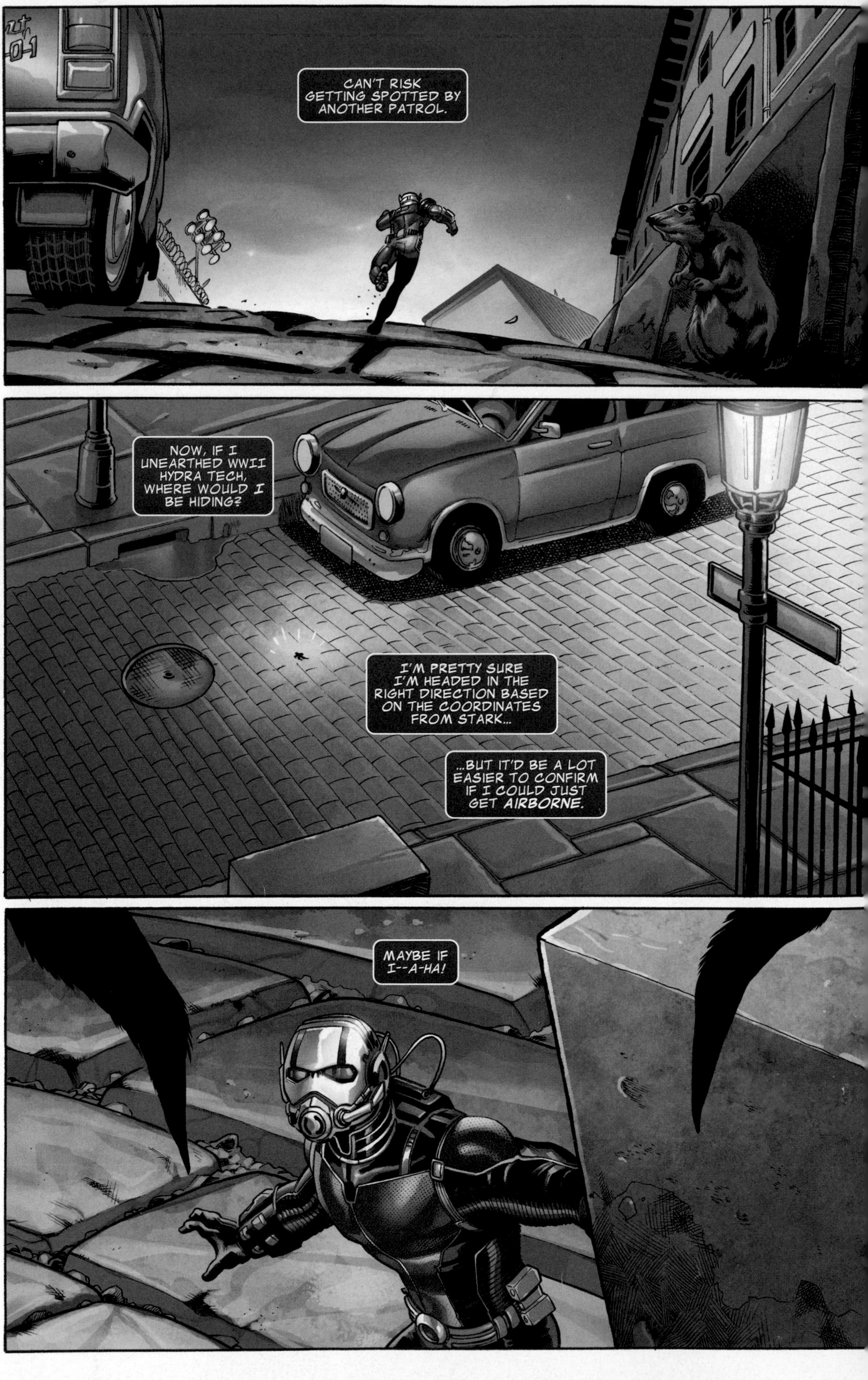
CAN'T RISK GETTING SPOTTED BY ANOTHER PATROL.
NOW, IF I UNEARTHED WWII HYDRA TECH, WHERE WOULD I BE HIDING?
I'M PRETTY SURE I'M HEADED IN THE RIGHT DIRECTION BASED ON THE COORDINATES FROM STARK...
...BUT IT'D BE A LOT EASIER TO CONFIRM IF I COULD JUST GET AIRBORNE.
MAYBE IF I--A-HA!

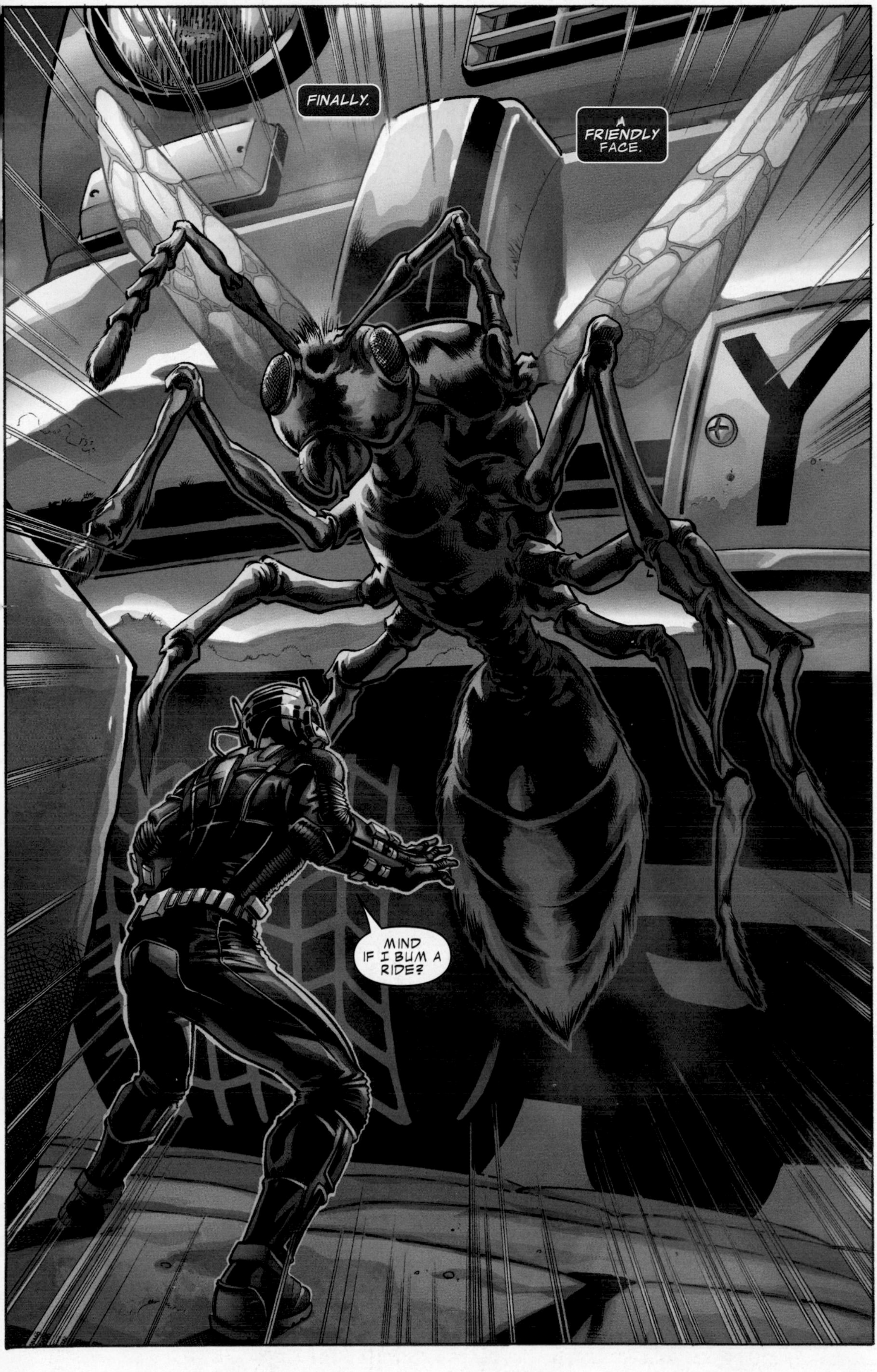
FINALLY.
A FRIENDLY FACE.
MIND IF I BUM A RIDE?

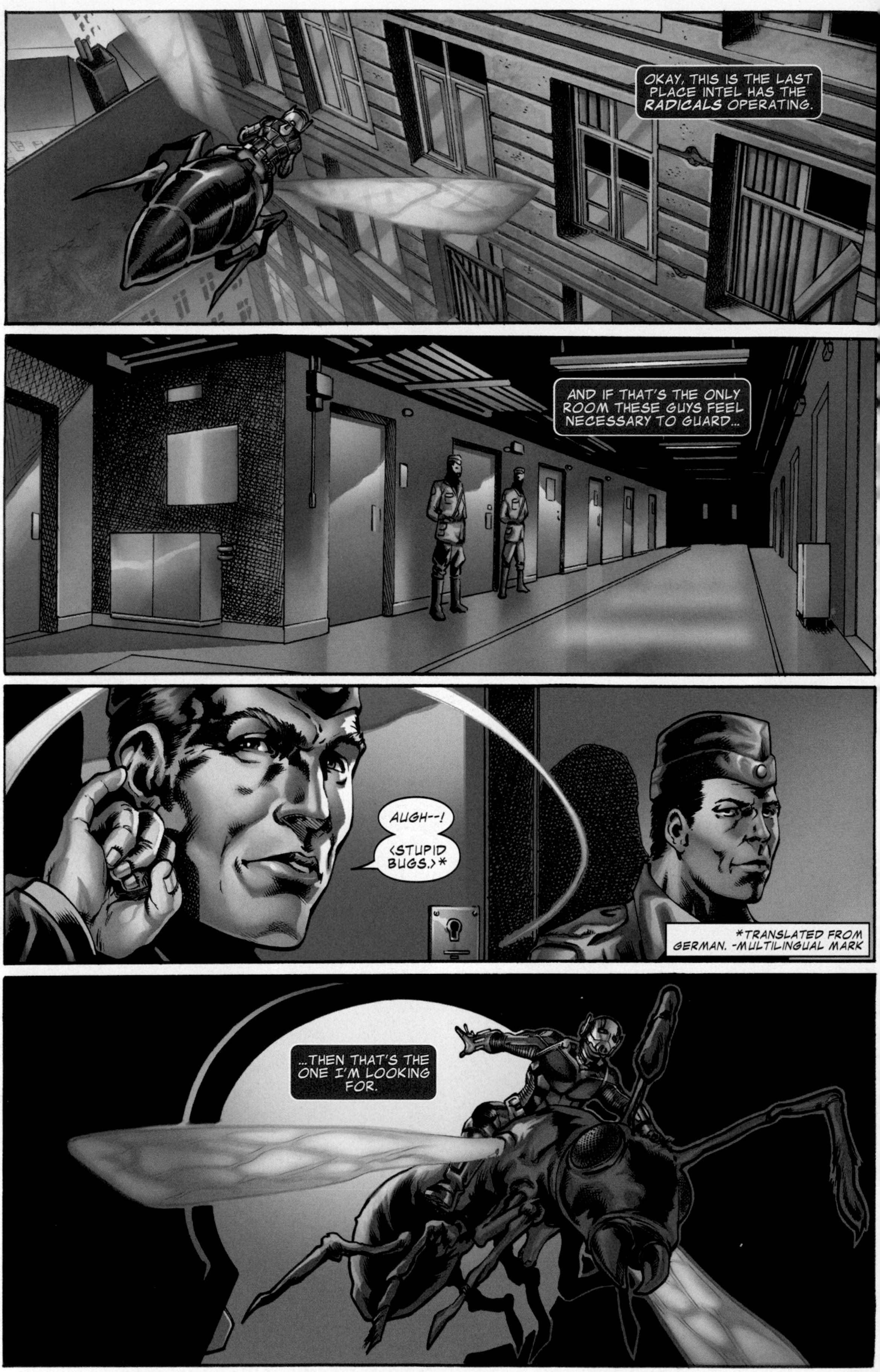
OKAY, THIS IS THE LAST PLACE INTEL HAS THE RADICALS OPERATING.
AND IF THAT'S THE ONLY ROOM THESE GUYS FEEL NECESSARY TO GUARD...
AUGH--!
<STUPID BUGS.>*
*TRANSLATED FROM GERMAN. -MULTILINGUAL MARK
...THEN THAT'S THE ONE I'M LOOKING FOR.

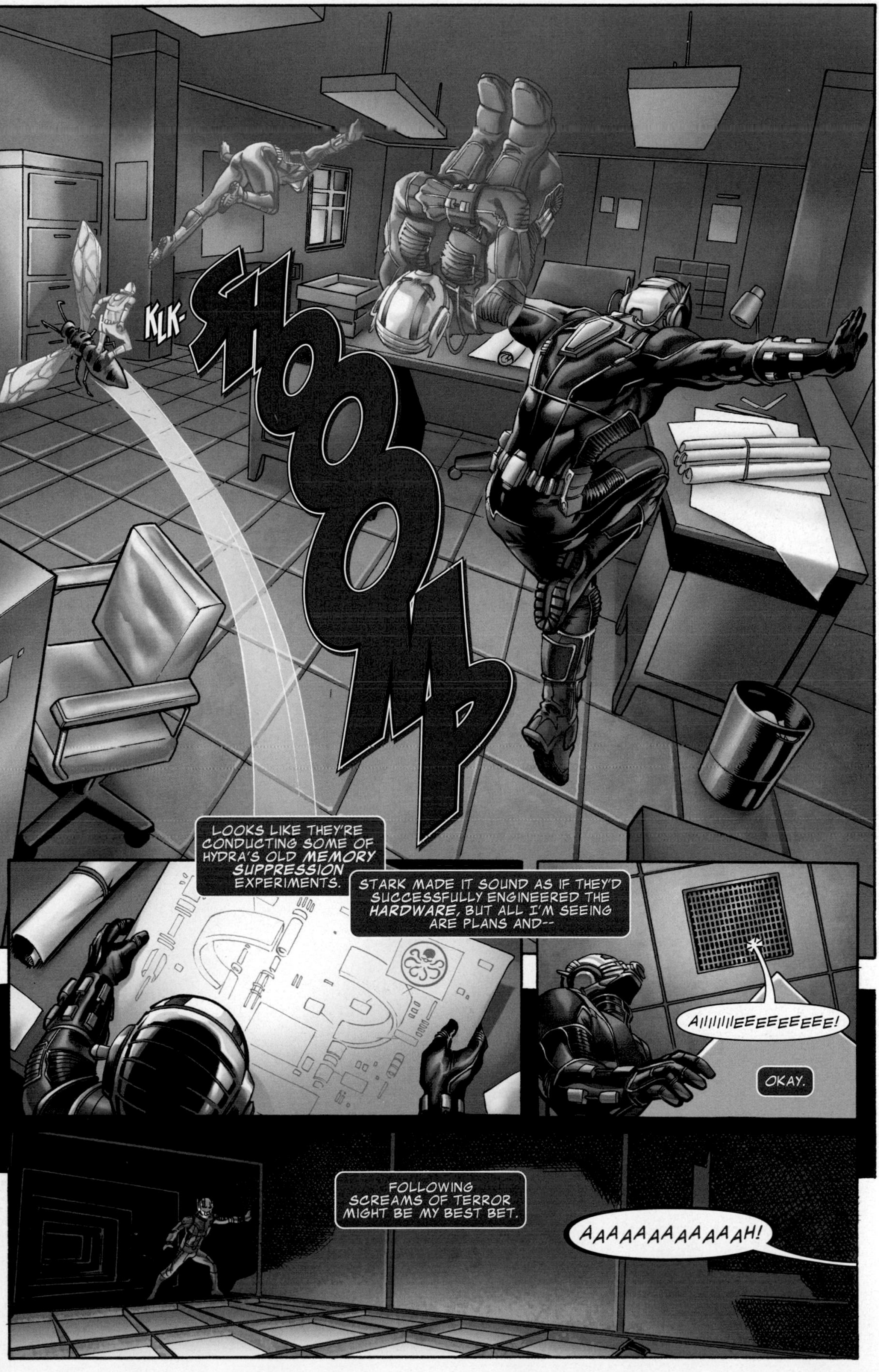
KLK-
SHOOMP
LOOKS LIKE THEY'RE CONDUCTING SOME OF HYDRA'S OLD MEMORY SUPPRESSION EXPERIMENTS.
STARK MADE IT SOUND AS IF THEY'D SUCCESSFULLY ENGINEERED THE HARDWARE, BUT ALL I'M SEEING ARE PLANS AND--
AIIIIIIIEEEEEEEEE!
OKAY.
FOLLOWING SCREAMS OF TERROR MIGHT BE MY BEST BET.
AAAAAAAAAAAAH!

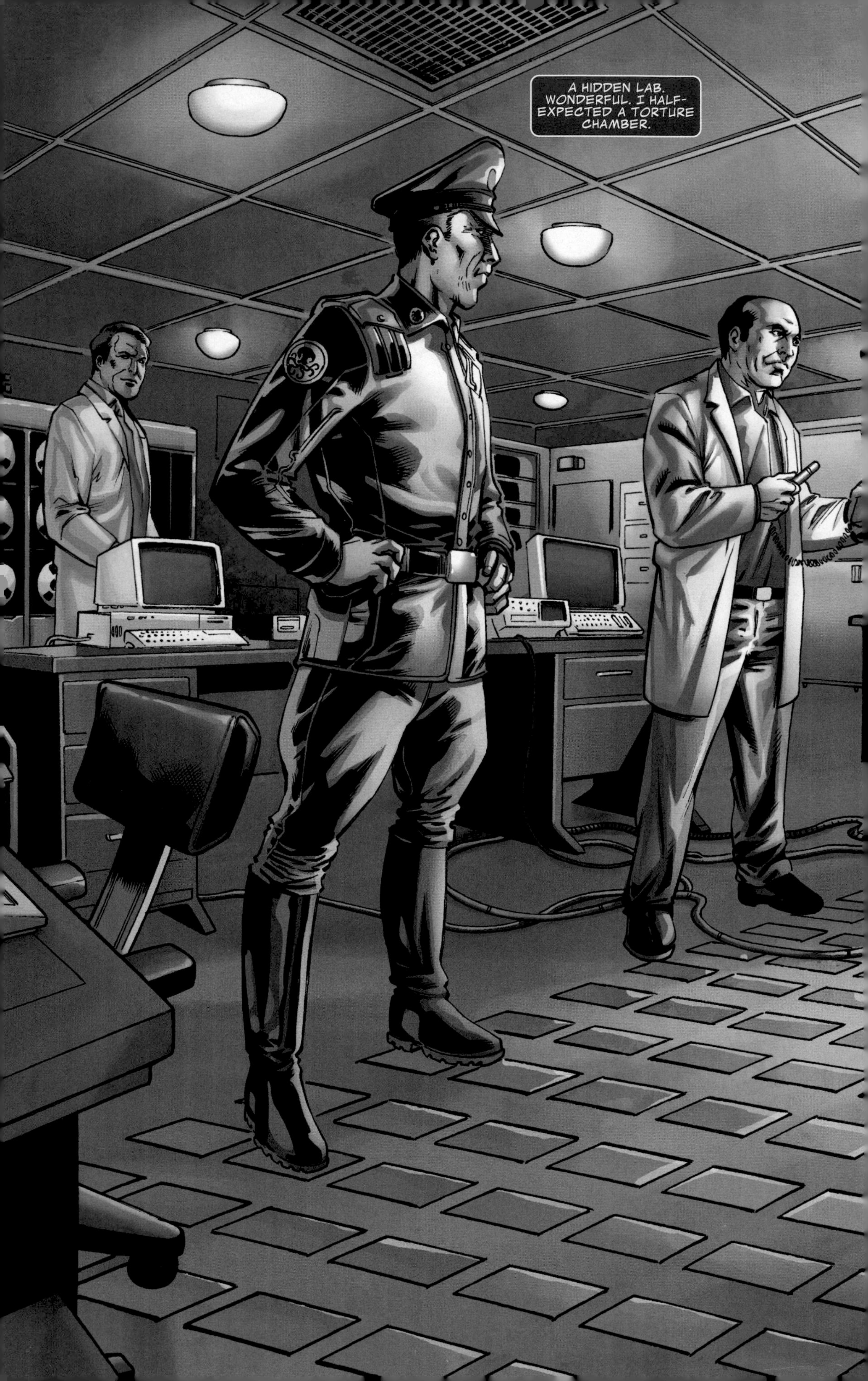
A HIDDEN LAB. WONDERFUL. I HALF-EXPECTED A TORTURE CHAMBER.

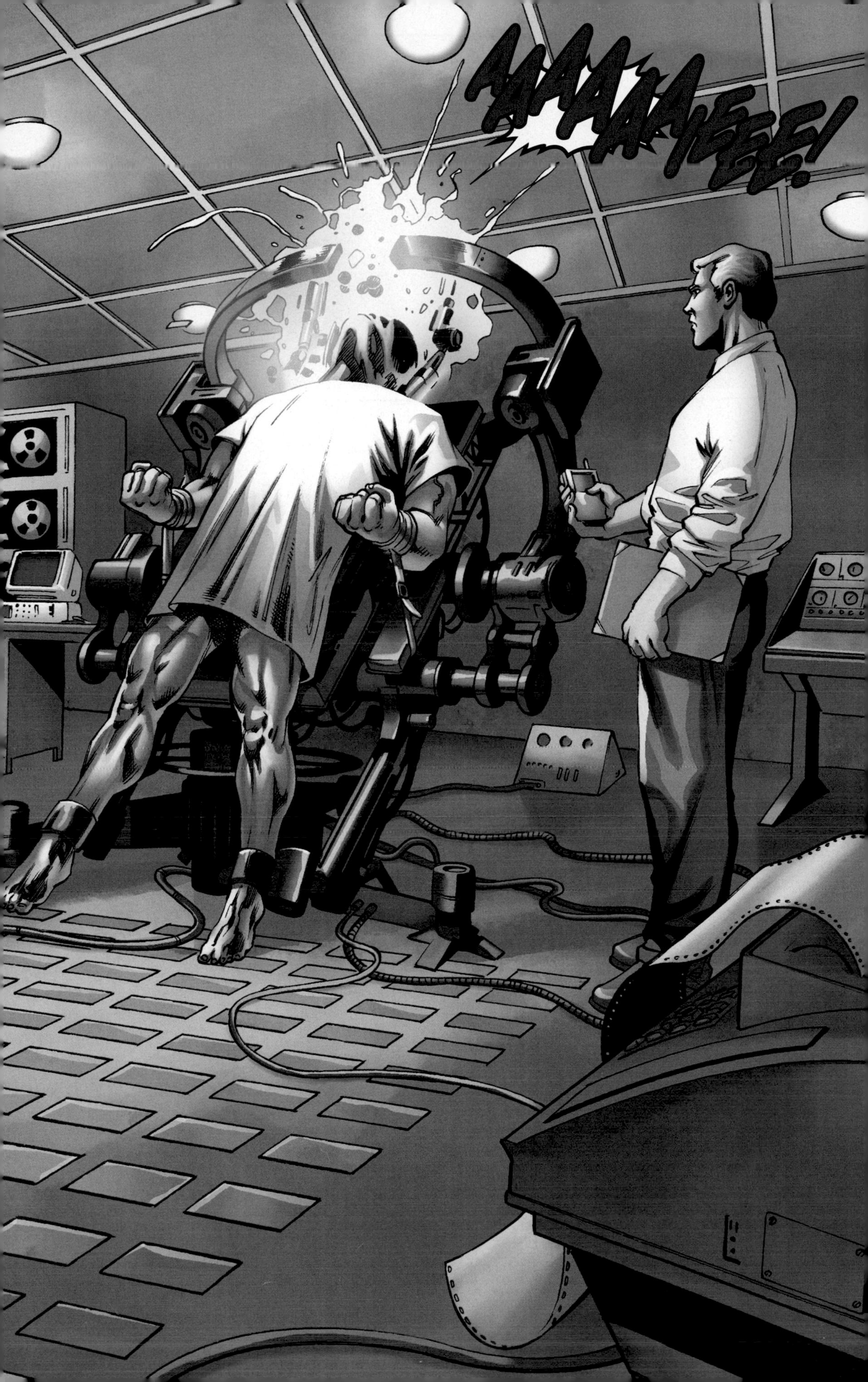
AAAAAIEEEE!

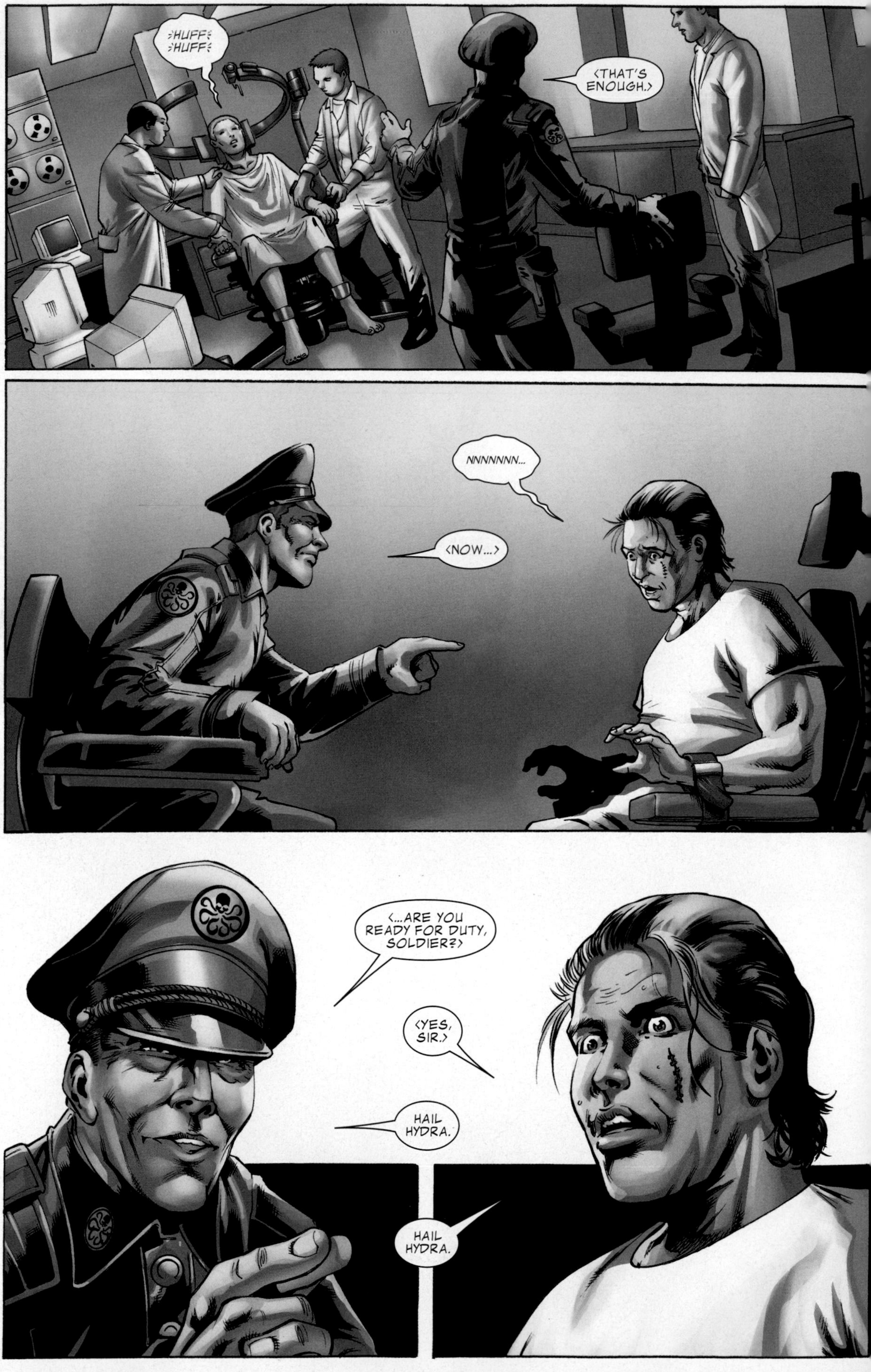

HUFF HUFF
<THAT'S ENOUGH.>
NNNNNNN...
<NOW...>
<...ARE YOU READY FOR DUTY, SOLDIER?>
<YES, SIR.>
HAIL HYDRA.
HAIL HYDRA.

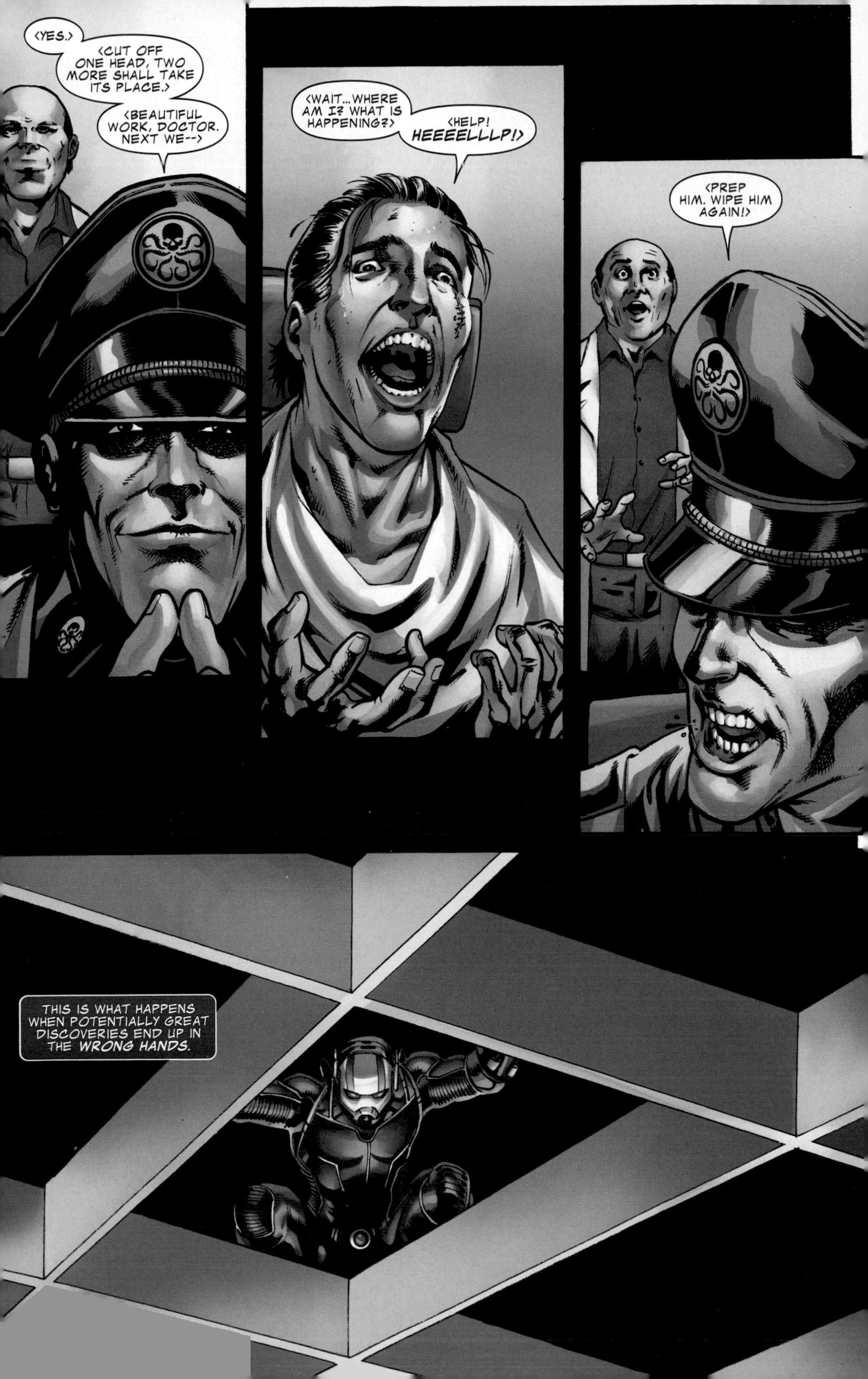

<YES.>
<CUT OFF ONE HEAD, TWO MORE SHALL TAKE ITS PLACE.>
<BEAUTIFUL WORK, DOCTOR. NEXT WE-->
<WAIT... WHERE AM I? WHAT IS HAPPENING?>
<HELP! HEEEELLLP!>
<PREP HIM. WIPE HIM AGAIN!>
THIS IS WHAT HAPPENS WHEN POTENTIALLY GREAT DISCOVERIES END UP IN THE WRONG HANDS.

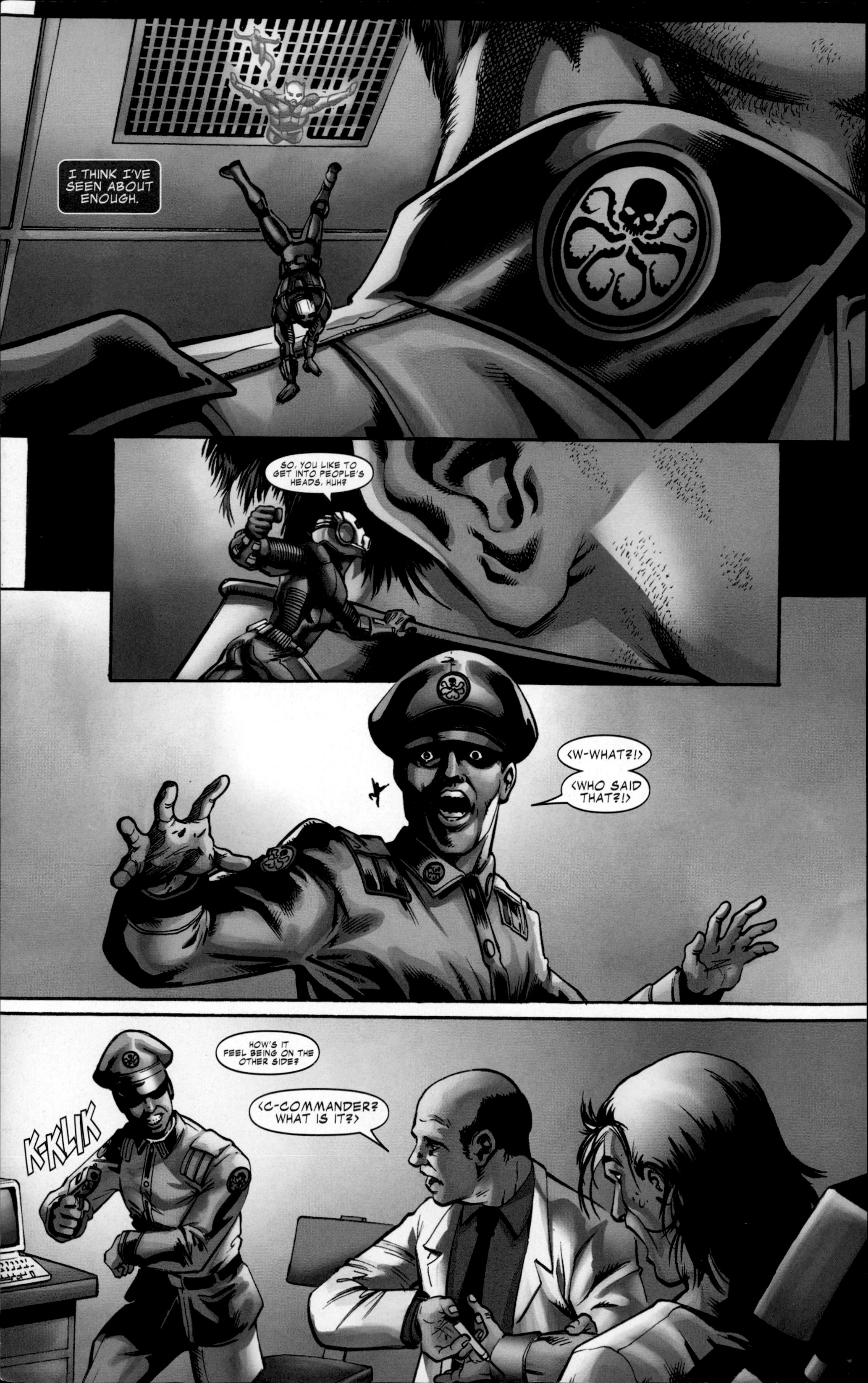
I THINK I'VE SEEN ABOUT ENOUGH.
SO, YOU LIKE TO GET INTO PEOPLE'S HEADS, HUH?
‹W-WHAT?!›
‹WHO SAID THAT?!›
HOW'S IT FEEL BEING ON THE OTHER SIDE?
‹C-COMMANDER? WHAT IS IT?›
K-KLIK

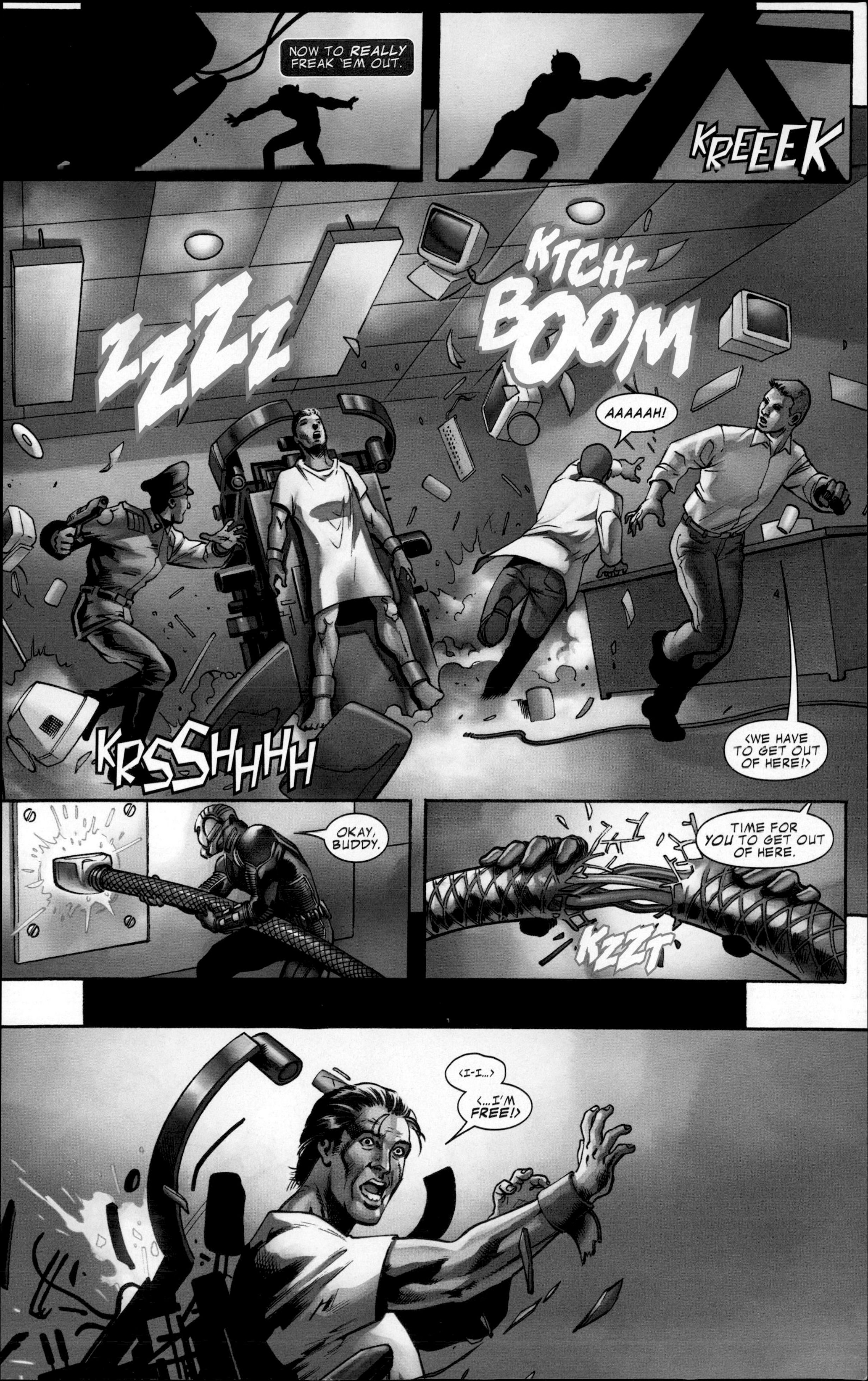
NOW TO REALLY FREAK 'EM OUT.
KREEEK
ZZZZZ
KTCH-BOOM
AAAAAH!
<WE HAVE TO GET OUT OF HERE!>
KRSSHHHH
OKAY, BUDDY.
TIME FOR YOU TO GET OUT OF HERE.
KZZZT
<I-I...>
<...I'M FREE!>

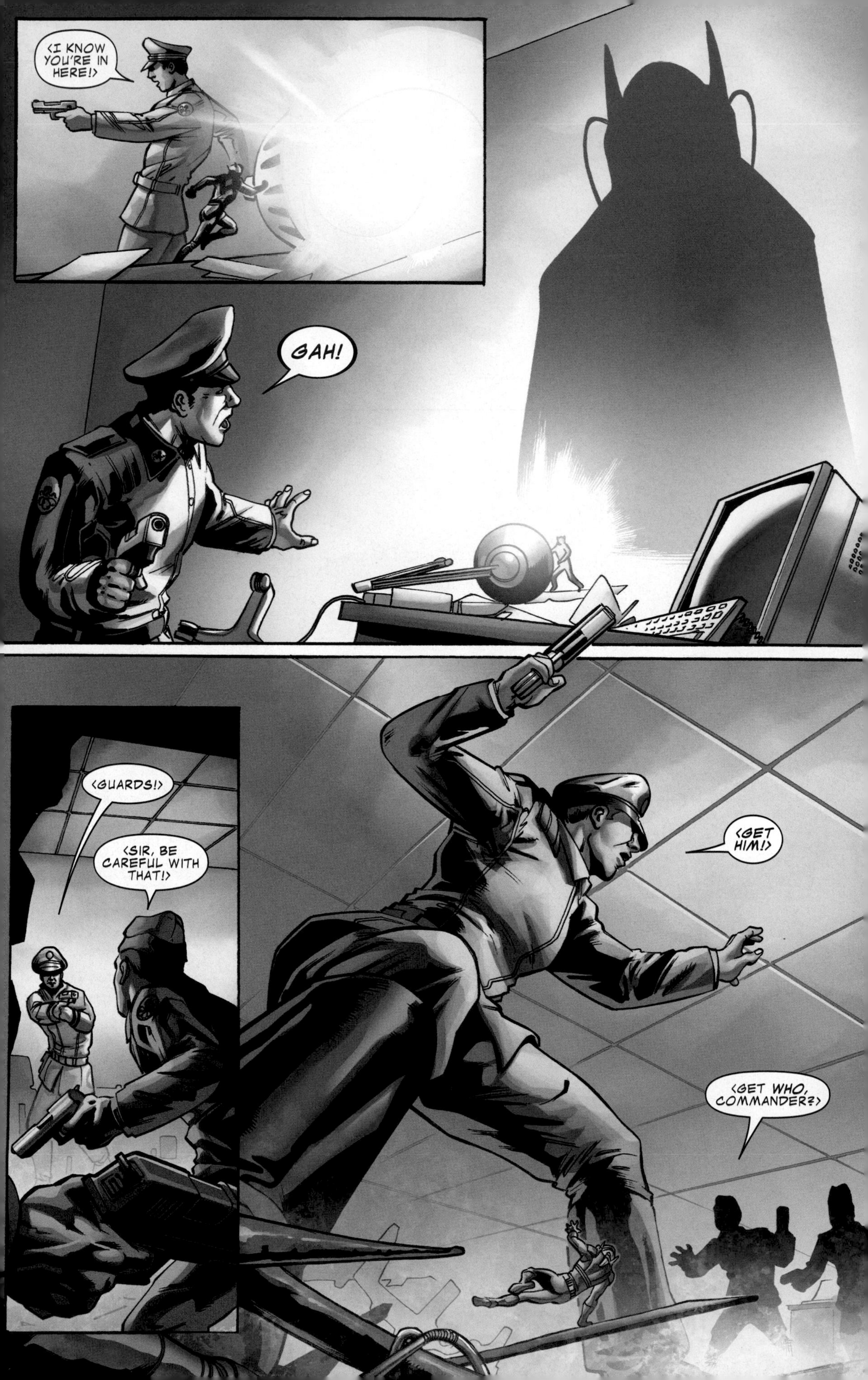

<I KNOW YOU'RE IN HERE!>
GAH!
<GUARDS!>
<SIR, BE CAREFUL WITH THAT!>
<GET HIM!>
<GET WHO, COMMANDER?>

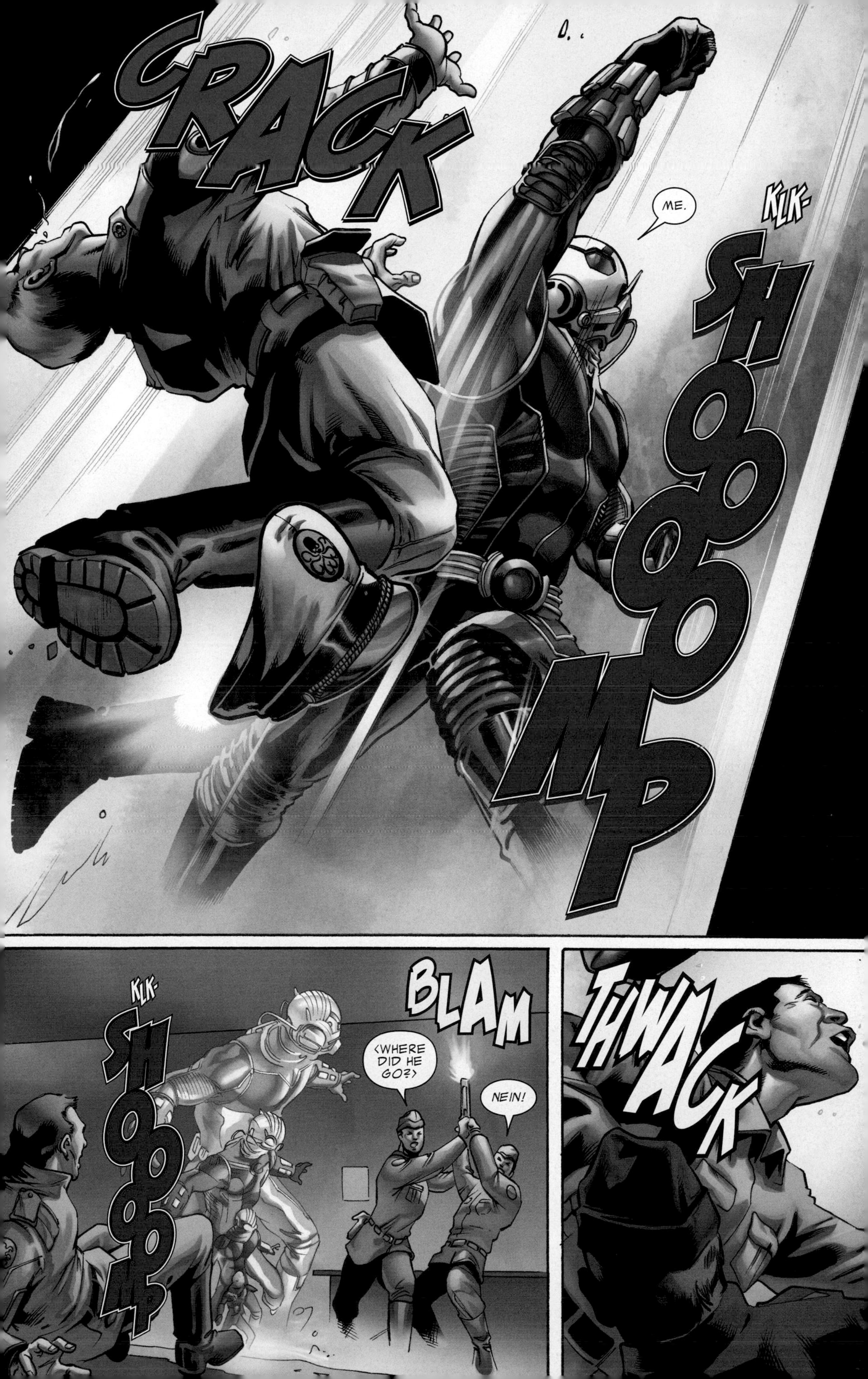
CRACK
ME.
KLK-
SHOOOOMP
KLK-
SHOOOOMP
BLAM
‹WHERE DID HE GO?›
NEIN!
THWACK

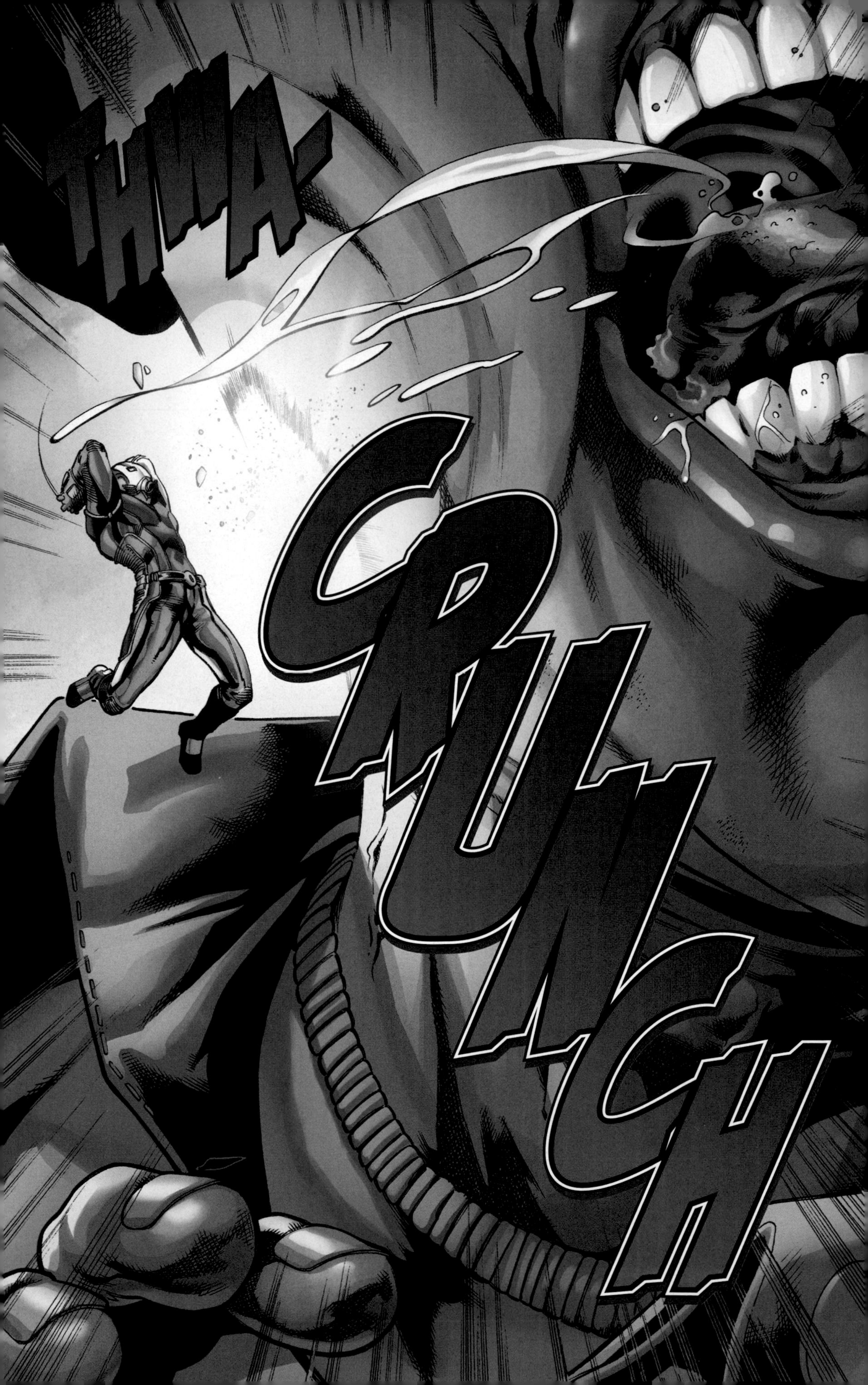
THWA-
CRUNCH

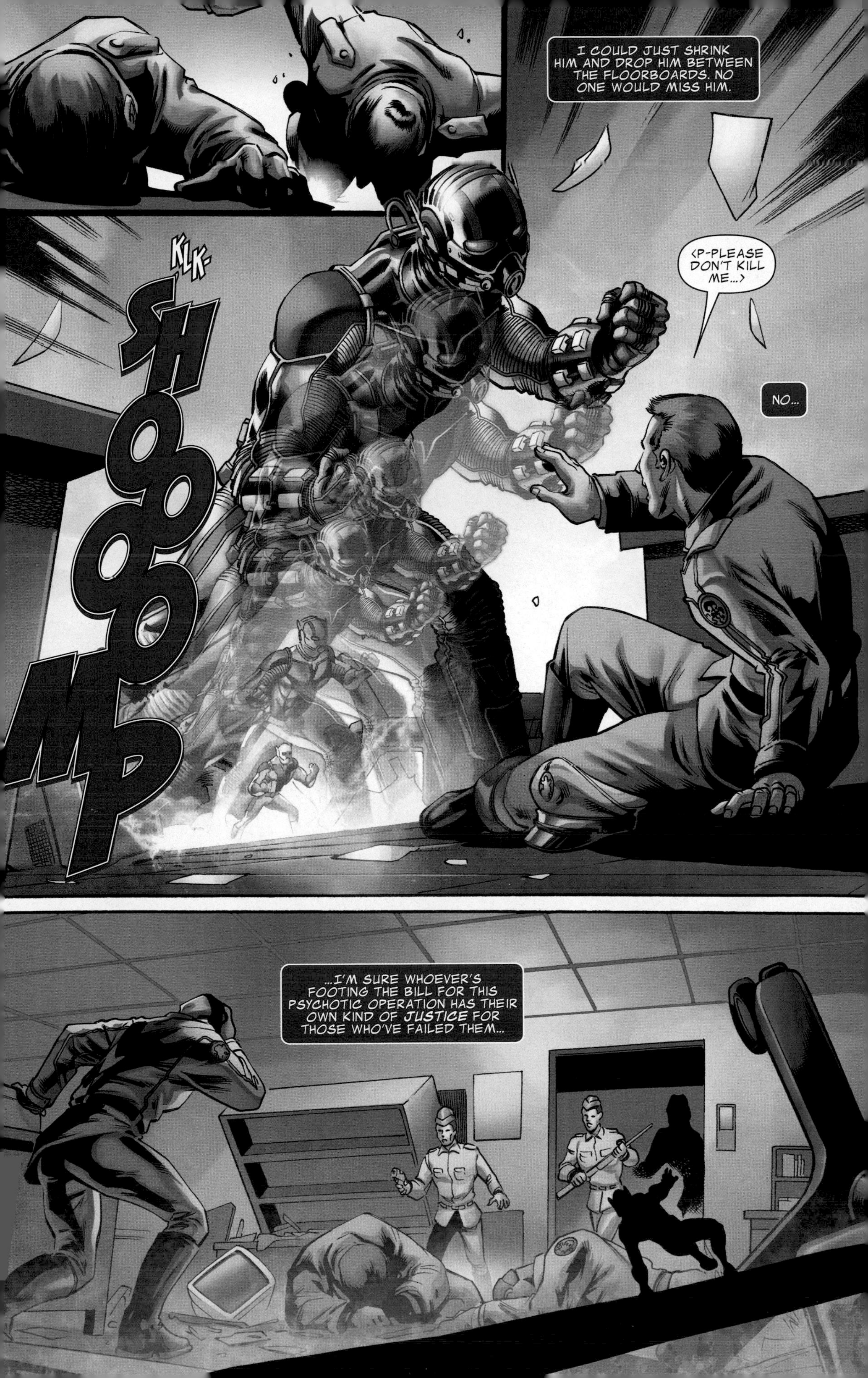
I COULD JUST SHRINK HIM AND DROP HIM BETWEEN THE FLOORBOARDS. NO ONE WOULD MISS HIM.
<P-PLEASE DON'T KILL ME...>
NO...
KLK-
SHOOOOMP
...I'M SURE WHOEVER'S FOOTING THE BILL FOR THIS PSYCHOTIC OPERATION HAS THEIR OWN KIND OF JUSTICE FOR THOSE WHO'VE FAILED THEM...

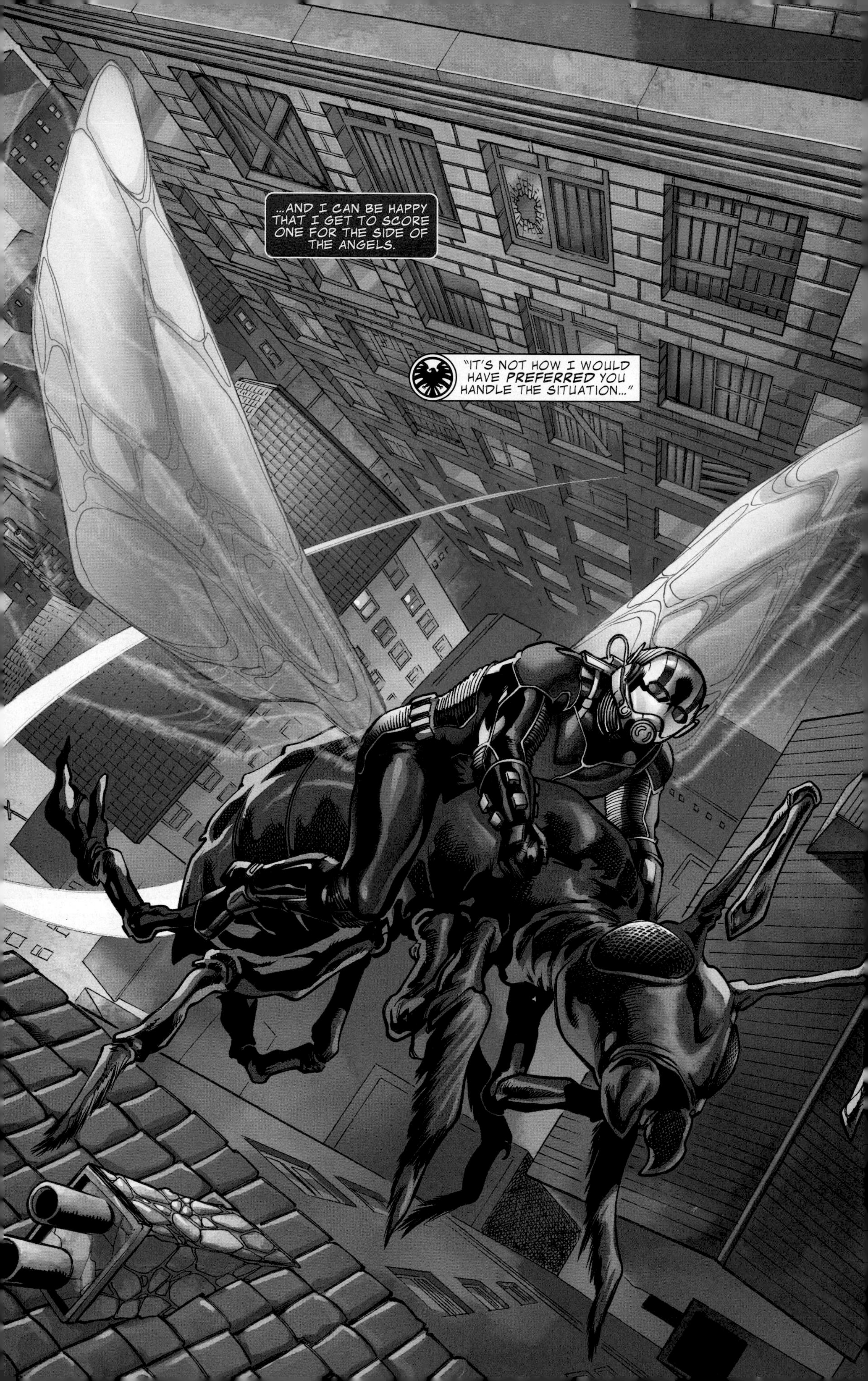
...AND I CAN BE HAPPY THAT I GET TO SCORE ONE FOR THE SIDE OF THE ANGELS.
"IT'S NOT HOW I WOULD HAVE PREFERRED YOU HANDLE THE SITUATION..."

HOWARD STARK.

PEGGY CARTER.

...BUT I CAN'T DENY THE RESULTS. WHAT DID YOU END UP DOING WITH THE PLANS FOR THE TECH?

I DESTROYED THEM. CLEARLY TECHNOLOGY LIKE THAT WILL NEVER BE USED FOR *GOOD*.

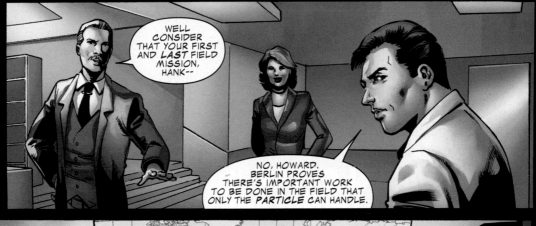

WELL CONSIDER THAT YOUR FIRST AND *LAST* FIELD MISSION, HANK--

NO, HOWARD. BERLIN PROVES THERE'S IMPORTANT WORK TO BE DONE IN THE FIELD THAT ONLY THE *PARTICLE* CAN HANDLE.

AND I TOLD YOU BEFORE, THE ONLY WAY S.H.I.E.L.D. GETS THE PYM PARTICLE IS WITH A *PYM* OPERATING IT.

SO... WHERE TO NEXT?

TO BE CONTINUED IN MARVEL'S ANT-MAN! COMING SOON TO THEATERS!

MARVEL

ANT-MAN

SCOTT LANG: SMALL TIME

WILL CORONA PILGRIM - WRITER
DANIEL GOVAR - STORYBOARD ARTIST
WELLINTON ALVES - PENCILER
MANNY CLARK - INKER
ANDRES MOSSA - COLORIST
VC'S CLAYTON COWLES - LETTERER

ARLIN ORTIZ - PRODUCTION
TIM SMITH 3 - PRODUCTION MANAGER
EMILY SHAW - CONSULTING EDITOR
BILL ROSEMANN & **MARK BASSO** - EDITORS
AXEL ALONSO - EDITOR IN CHIEF
JOE QUESADA - CHIEF CREATIVE OFFICER
DAN BUCKLEY - PUBLISHER

MARVEL STUDIOS:
BRAD WINDERBAUM - SVP PRODUCTION & DEVELOPMENT
KEVIN FEIGE - PRESIDENT

ANT-MAN CREATED BY **STAN LEE**, **LARRY LIEBER**, AND **JACK KIRBY**

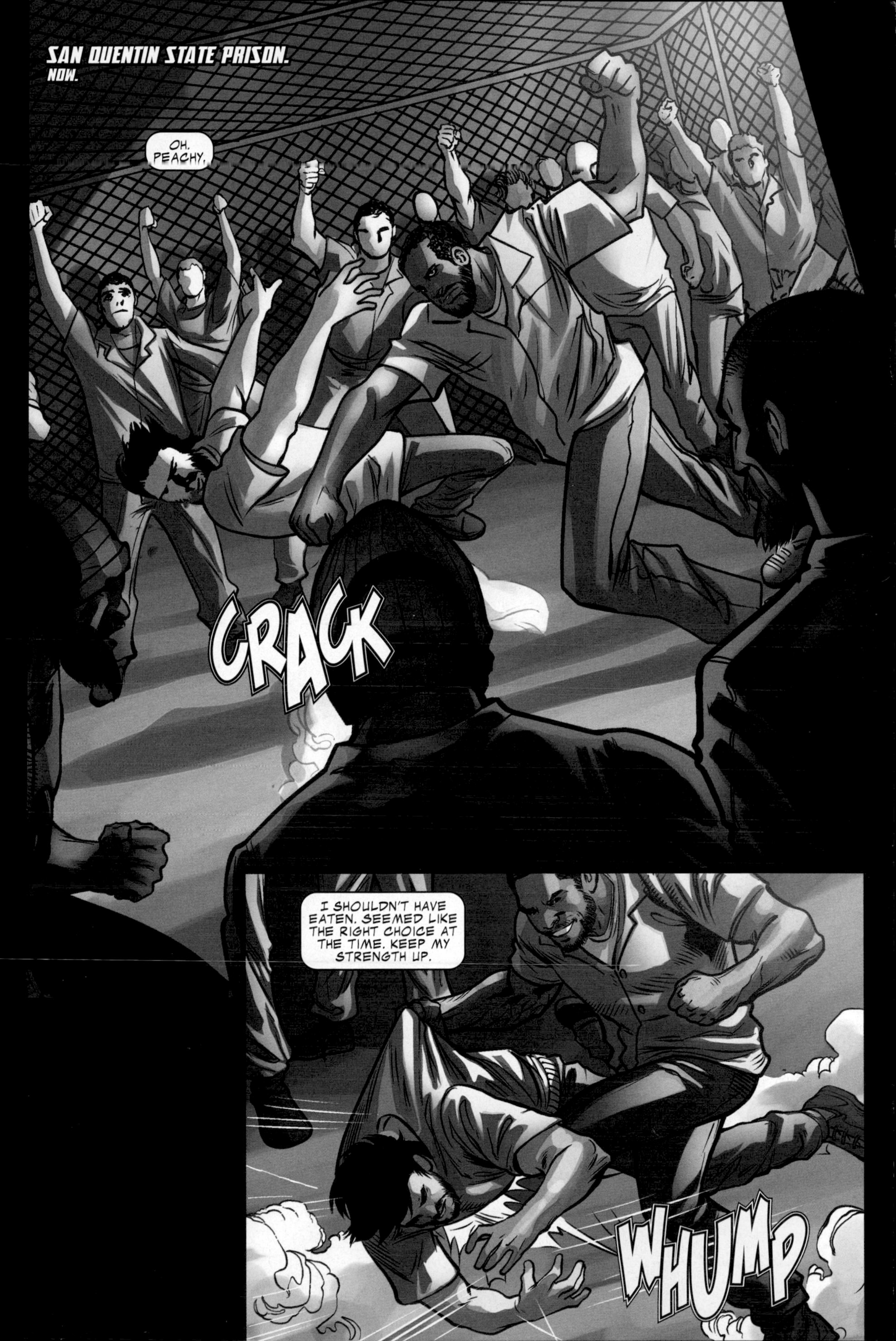
SAN QUENTIN STATE PRISON.
NOW.
OH. PEACHY.
CRACK
I SHOULDN'T HAVE EATEN. SEEMED LIKE THE RIGHT CHOICE AT THE TIME. KEEP MY STRENGTH UP.
WHUMP

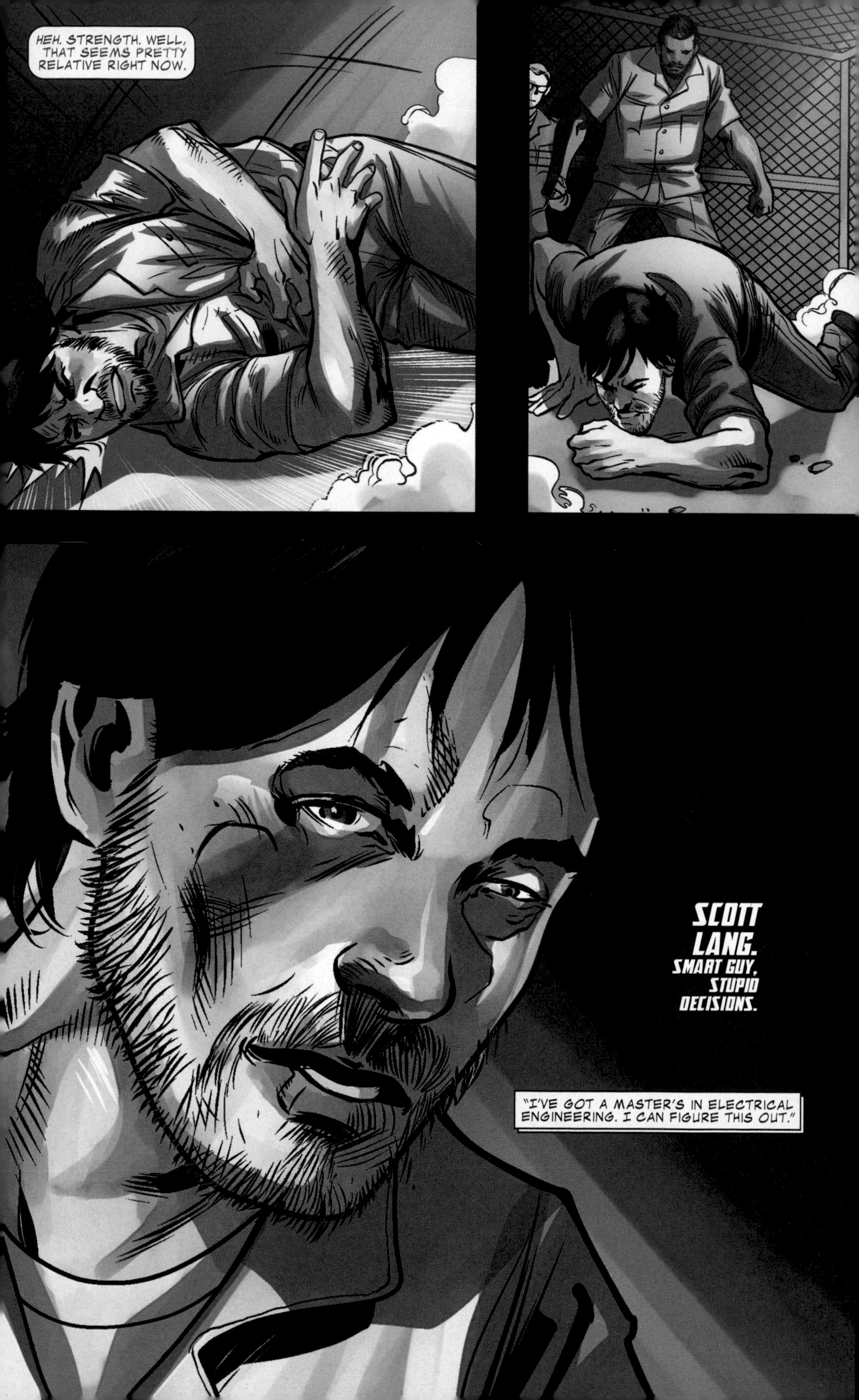
HEH. STRENGTH. WELL, THAT SEEMS PRETTY RELATIVE RIGHT NOW.
SCOTT LANG. SMART GUY, STUPID DECISIONS.
"I'VE GOT A MASTER'S IN ELECTRICAL ENGINEERING. I CAN FIGURE THIS OUT."

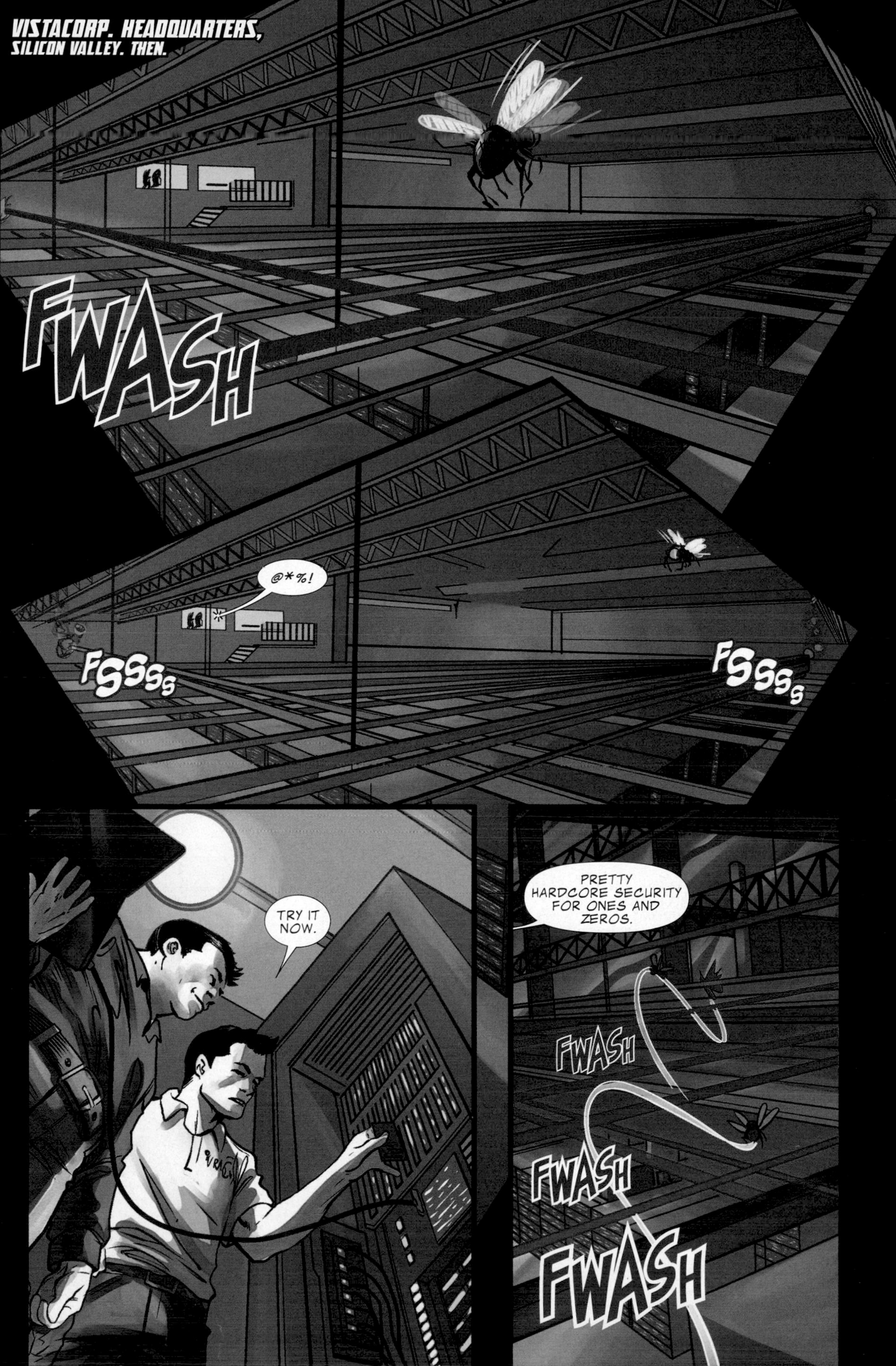
VISTACORP. HEADQUARTERS, SILICON VALLEY. THEN.
FWASH
@*%!
FSSSS
FSSSS
TRY IT NOW.
PRETTY HARDCORE SECURITY FOR ONES AND ZEROS.
FWASH
FWASH
FWASH

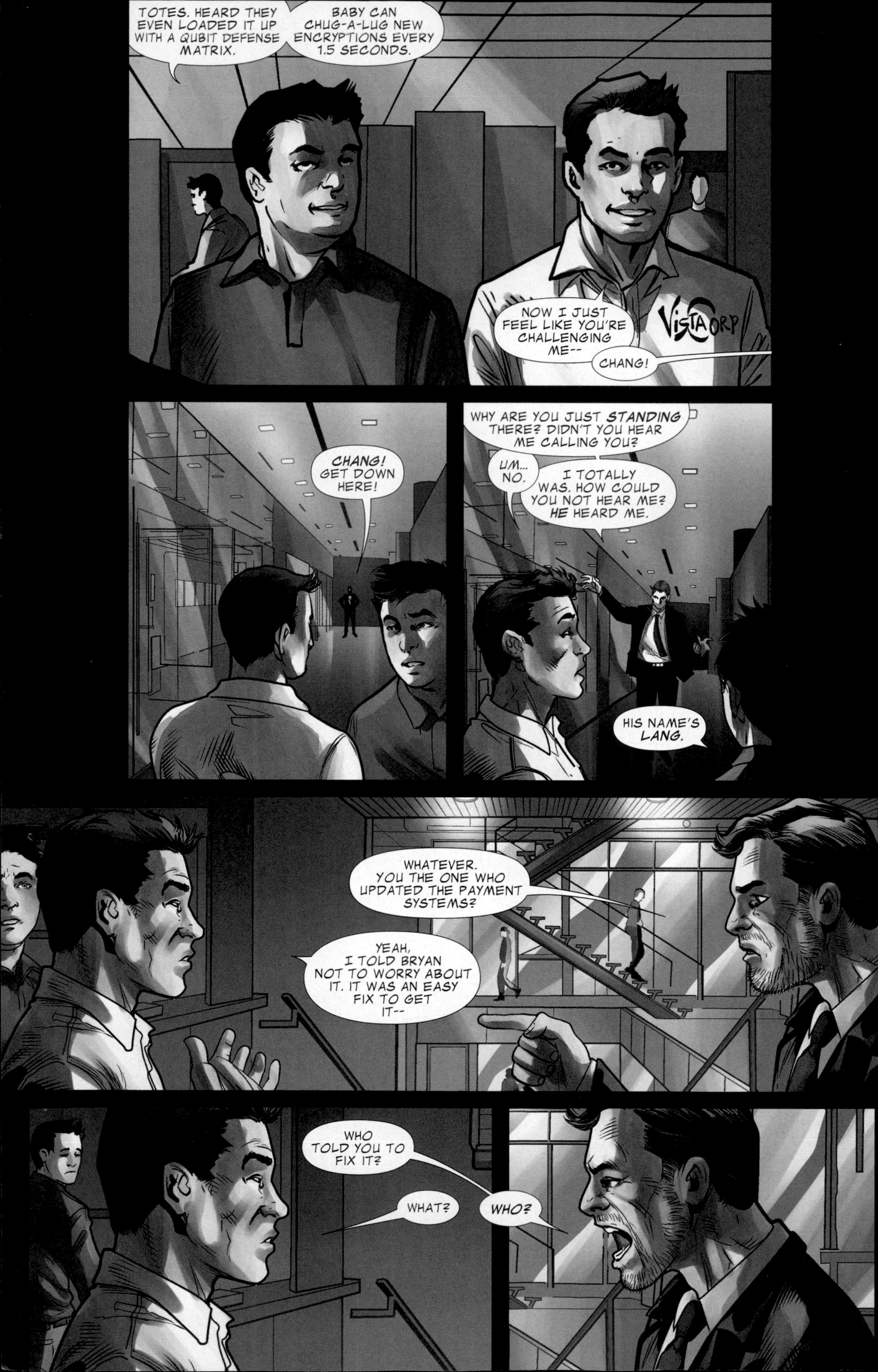
TOTES. HEARD THEY EVEN LOADED IT UP WITH A QUBIT DEFENSE MATRIX.
BABY CAN CHUG-A-LUG NEW ENCRYPTIONS EVERY 1.5 SECONDS.
VISTACORP
NOW I JUST FEEL LIKE YOU'RE CHALLENGING ME--
CHANG!
CHANG! GET DOWN HERE!
WHY ARE YOU JUST STANDING THERE? DIDN'T YOU HEAR ME CALLING YOU?
UM... NO.
I TOTALLY WAS. HOW COULD YOU NOT HEAR ME? HE HEARD ME.
HIS NAME'S LANG.
WHATEVER. YOU THE ONE WHO UPDATED THE PAYMENT SYSTEMS?
YEAH, I TOLD BRYAN NOT TO WORRY ABOUT IT. IT WAS AN EASY FIX TO GET IT--
WHO TOLD YOU TO FIX IT?
WHAT?
WHO?

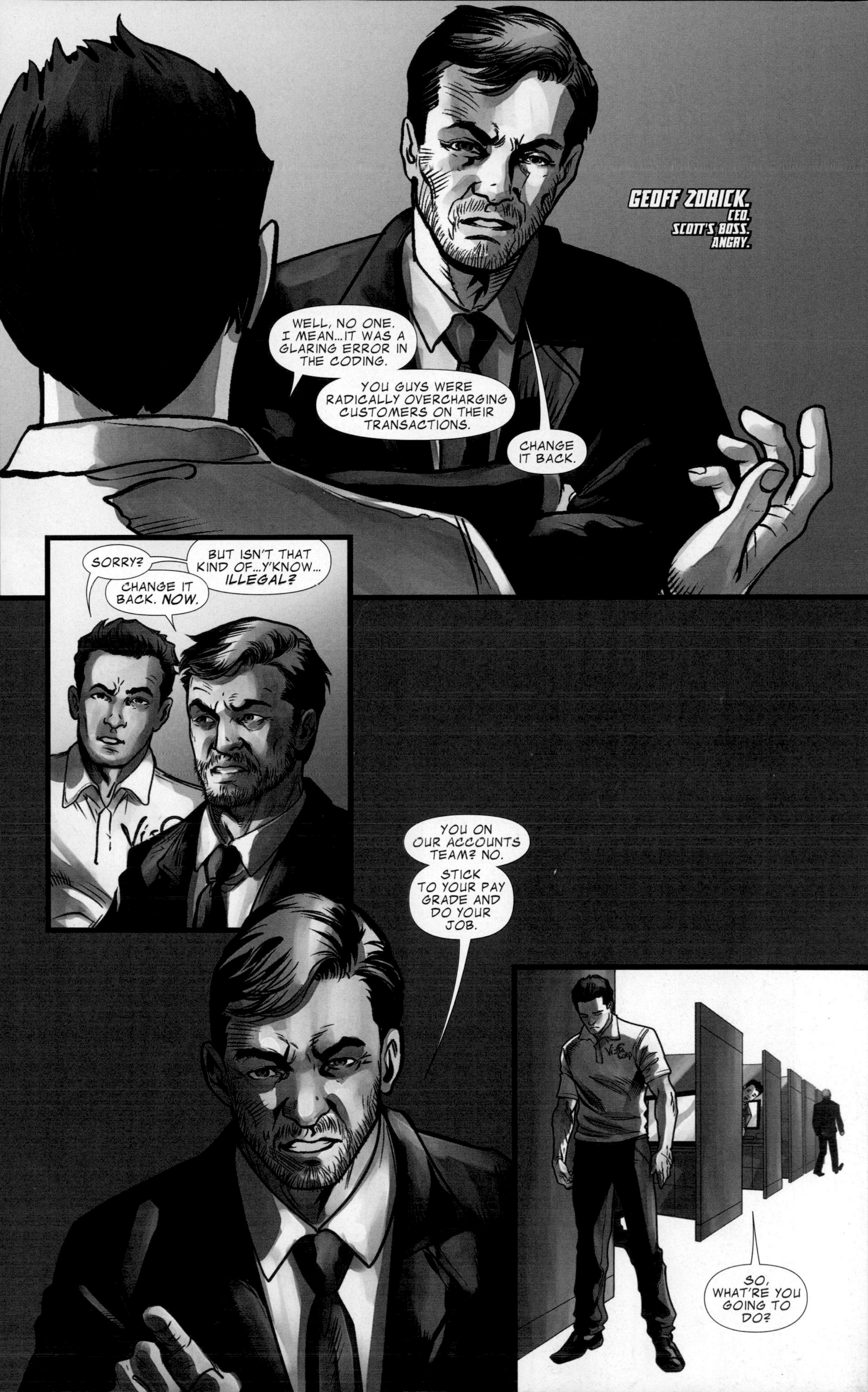
GEOFF ZORICK.
CEO.
SCOTT'S BOSS.
ANGRY.
WELL, NO ONE. I MEAN...IT WAS A GLARING ERROR IN THE CODING.
YOU GUYS WERE RADICALLY OVERCHARGING CUSTOMERS ON THEIR TRANSACTIONS.
CHANGE IT BACK.
SORRY?
CHANGE IT BACK. NOW.
BUT ISN'T THAT KIND OF...Y'KNOW... ILLEGAL?
YOU ON OUR ACCOUNTS TEAM? NO.
STICK TO YOUR PAY GRADE AND DO YOUR JOB.
SO, WHAT'RE YOU GOING TO DO?

HUMAN RESOURCES.

WHAT CAN I HELP YOU WITH, SCOTT?

WHISTLE BLOWER KNOW YOUR RIGHTS

VISTACORP

DISGRUNTLED FORMER EMPLOYEE TRIES TO EXTORT HARDWORKING CORPORATION

VISTACORP

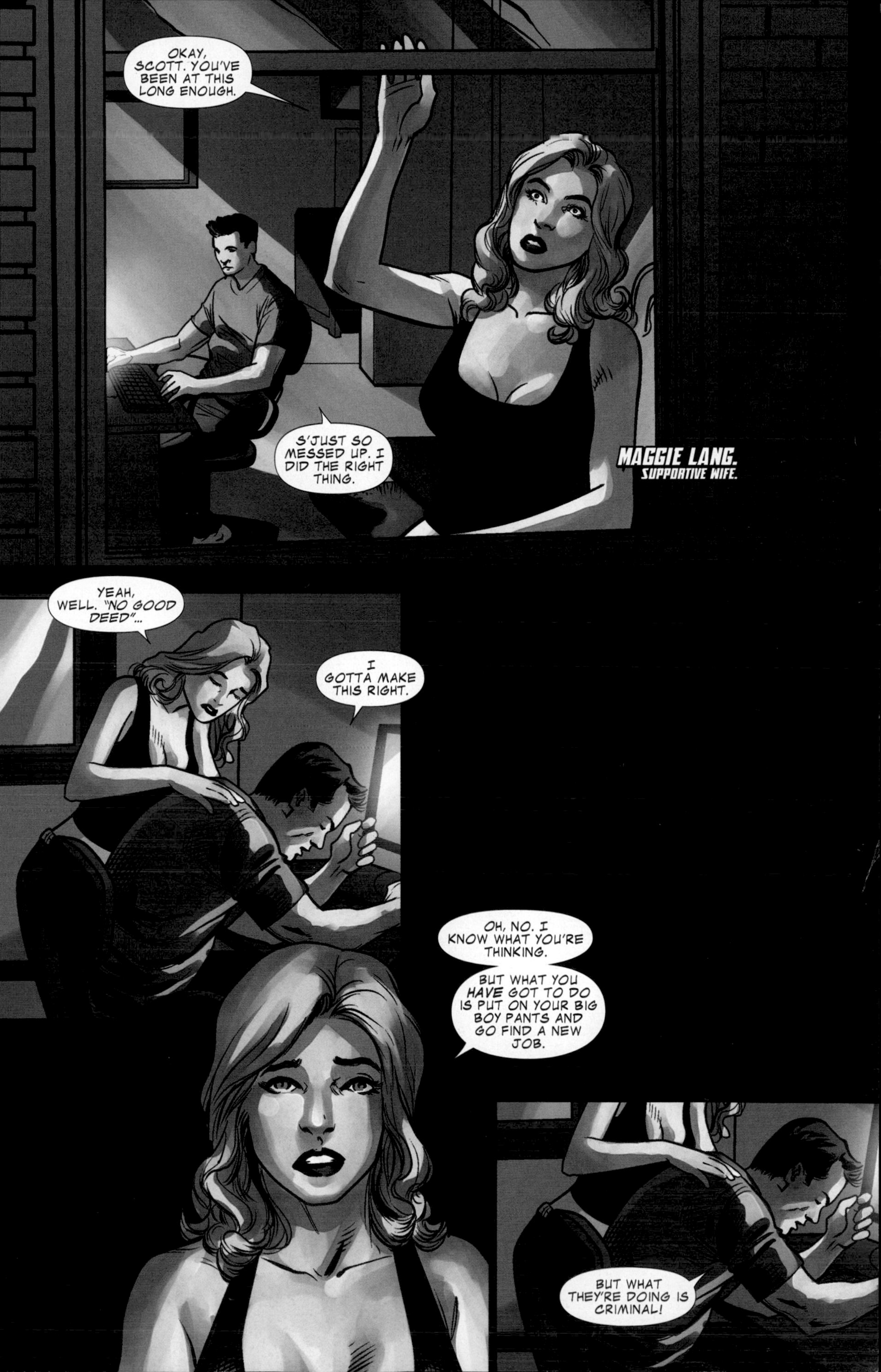
OKAY, SCOTT. YOU'VE BEEN AT THIS LONG ENOUGH.
S'JUST SO MESSED UP. I DID THE RIGHT THING.
MAGGIE LANG. SUPPORTIVE WIFE.
YEAH, WELL. "NO GOOD DEED"...
I GOTTA MAKE THIS RIGHT.
OH, NO. I KNOW WHAT YOU'RE THINKING.
BUT WHAT YOU HAVE GOT TO DO IS PUT ON YOUR BIG BOY PANTS AND GO FIND A NEW JOB.
BUT WHAT THEY'RE DOING IS CRIMINAL!

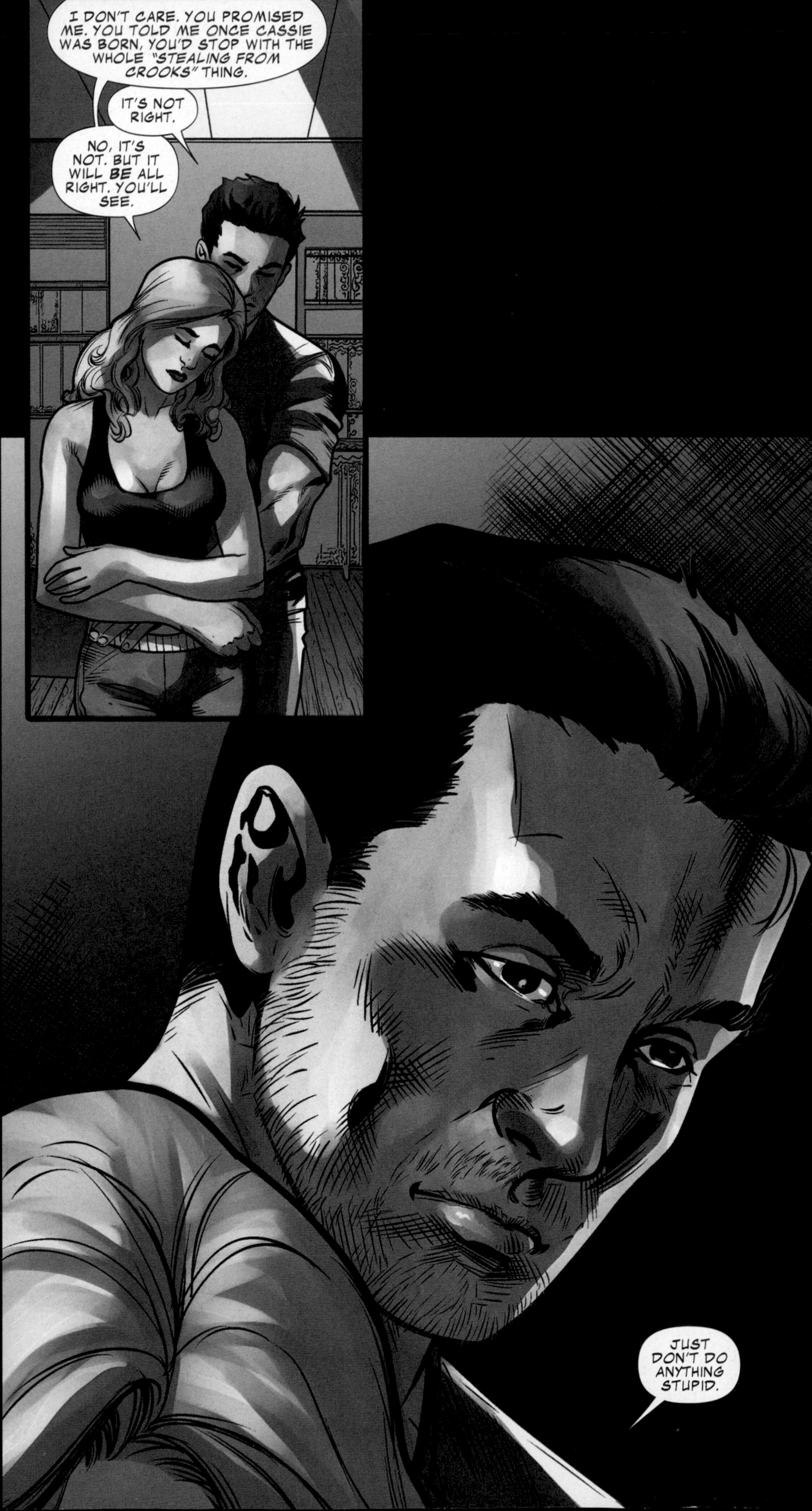
I DON'T CARE. YOU PROMISED ME. YOU TOLD ME ONCE CASSIE WAS BORN, YOU'D STOP WITH THE WHOLE "STEALING FROM CROOKS" THING.
IT'S NOT RIGHT.
NO, IT'S NOT. BUT IT WILL BE ALL RIGHT. YOU'LL SEE.
JUST DON'T DO ANYTHING STUPID.

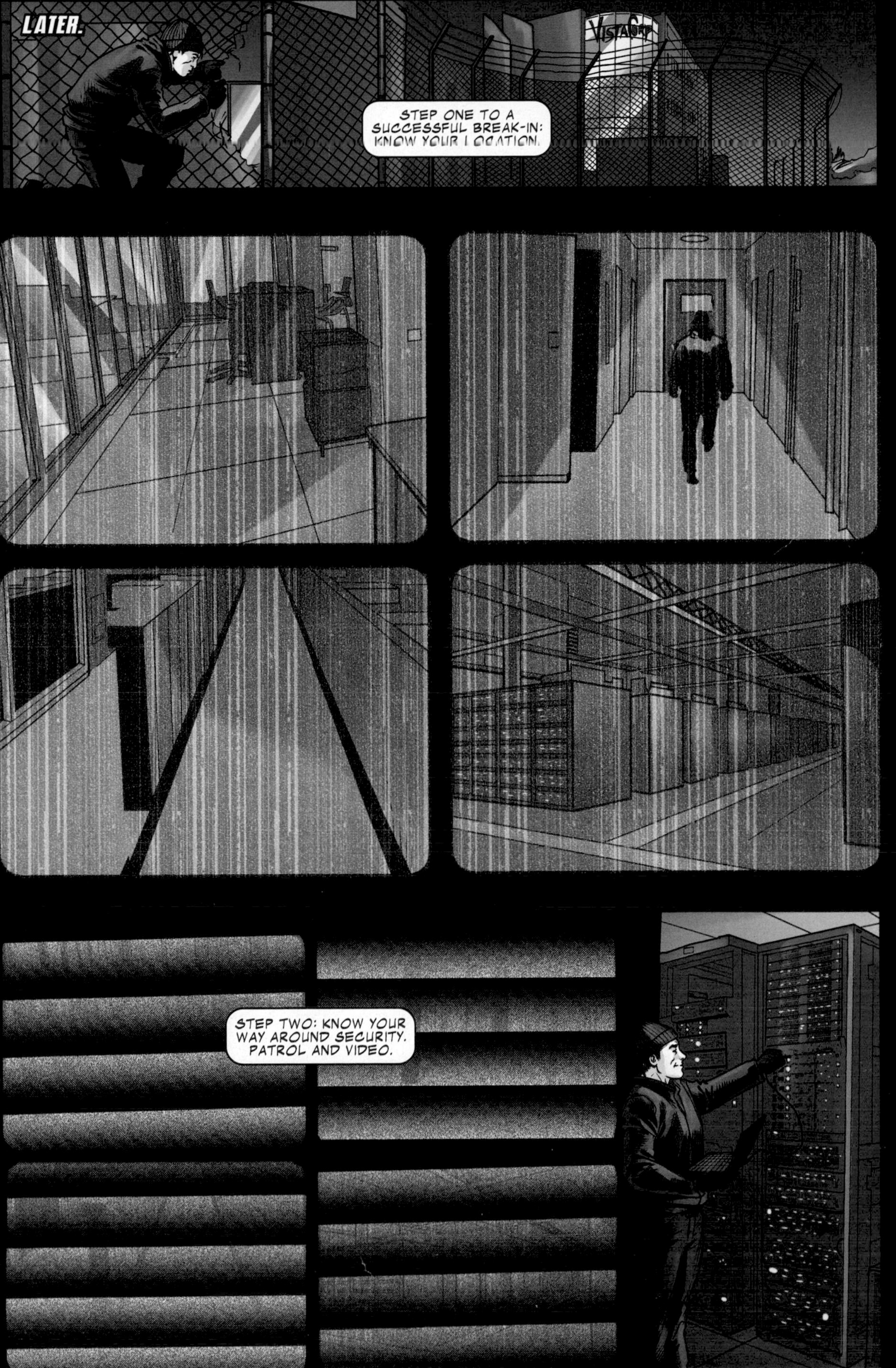
LATER.
VistaCorp
STEP ONE TO A SUCCESSFUL BREAK-IN: KNOW YOUR LOCATION.
STEP TWO: KNOW YOUR WAY AROUND SECURITY. PATROL AND VIDEO.

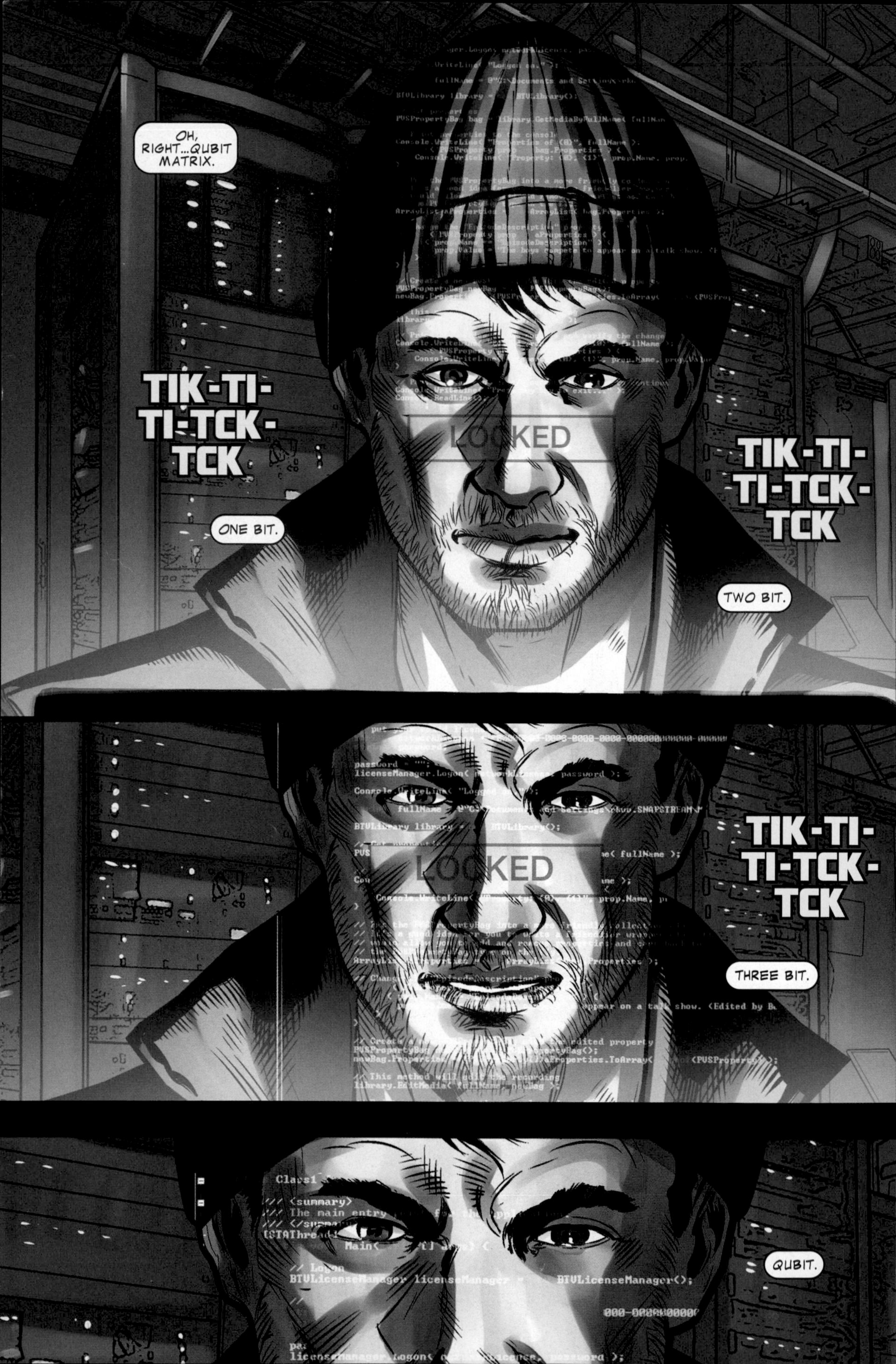
OH, RIGHT...QUBIT MATRIX.
TIK-TI-TI-TCK-TCK
LOCKED
ONE BIT.
TIK-TI-TI-TCK-TCK
TWO BIT.
LOCKED
TIK-TI-TI-TCK-TCK
THREE BIT.
QUBIT.

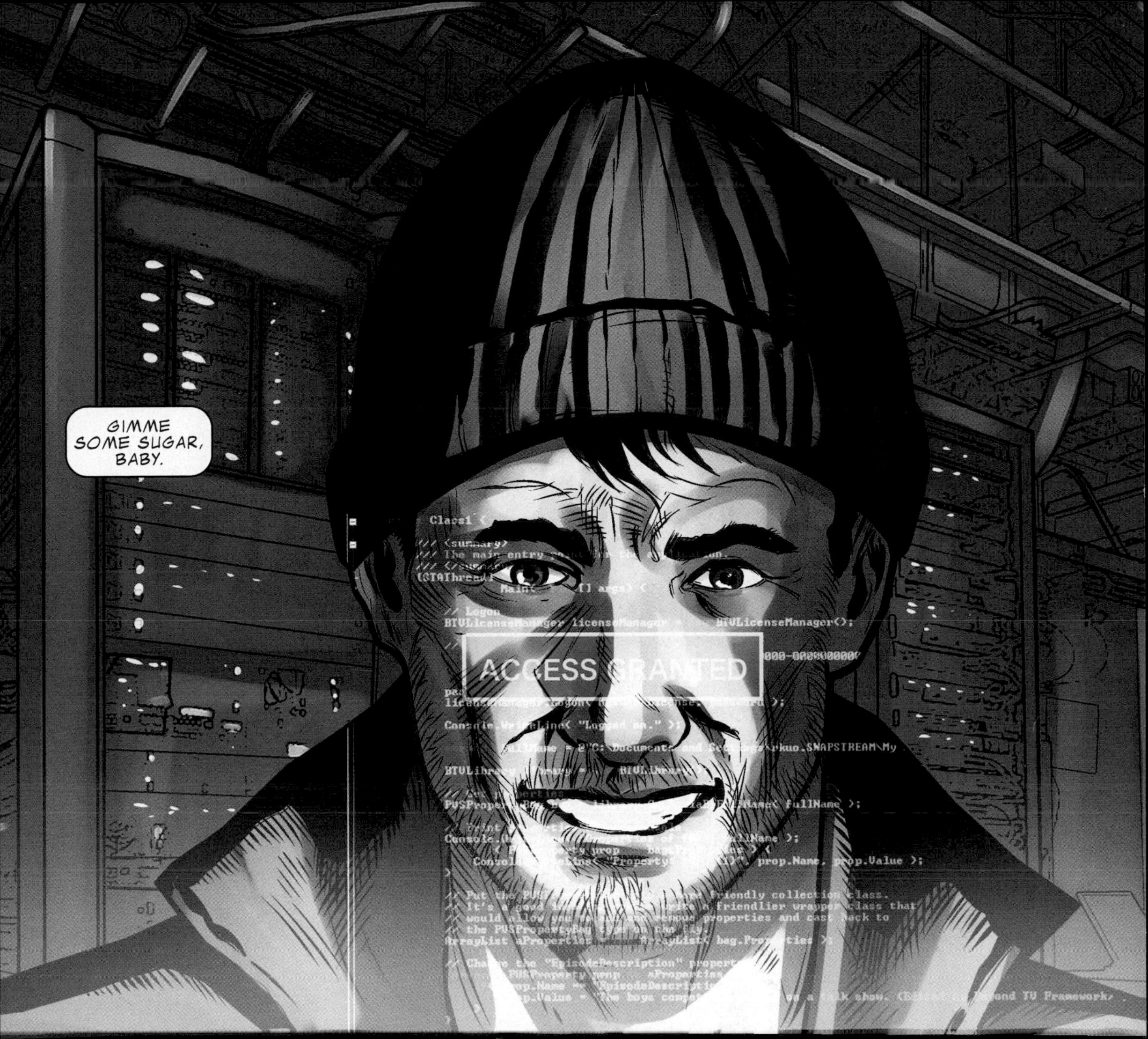
GIMME SOME SUGAR, BABY.
ACCESS GRANTED

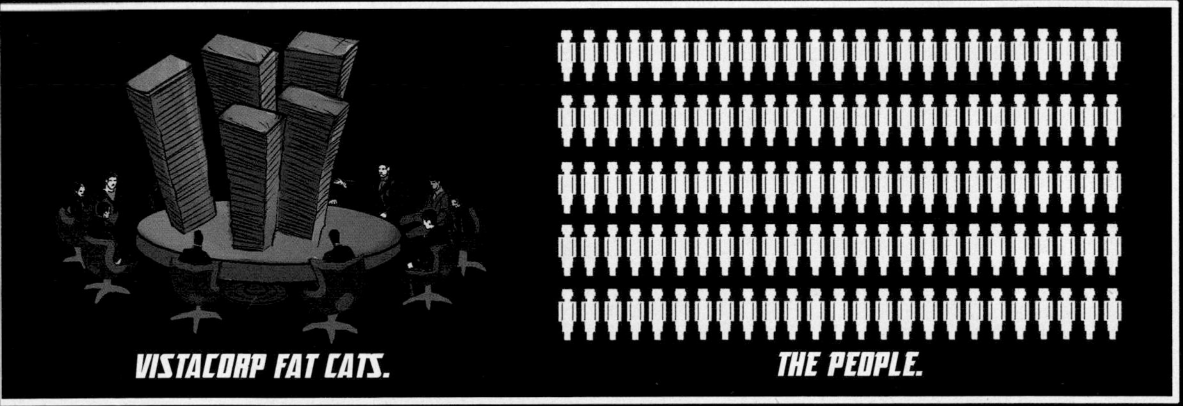
VISTACORP FAT CATS.
THE PEOPLE.

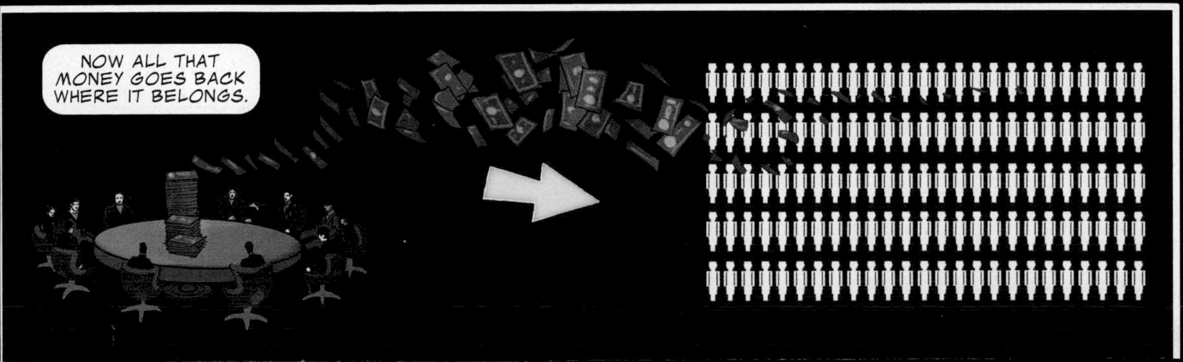
NOW ALL THAT MONEY GOES BACK WHERE IT BELONGS.

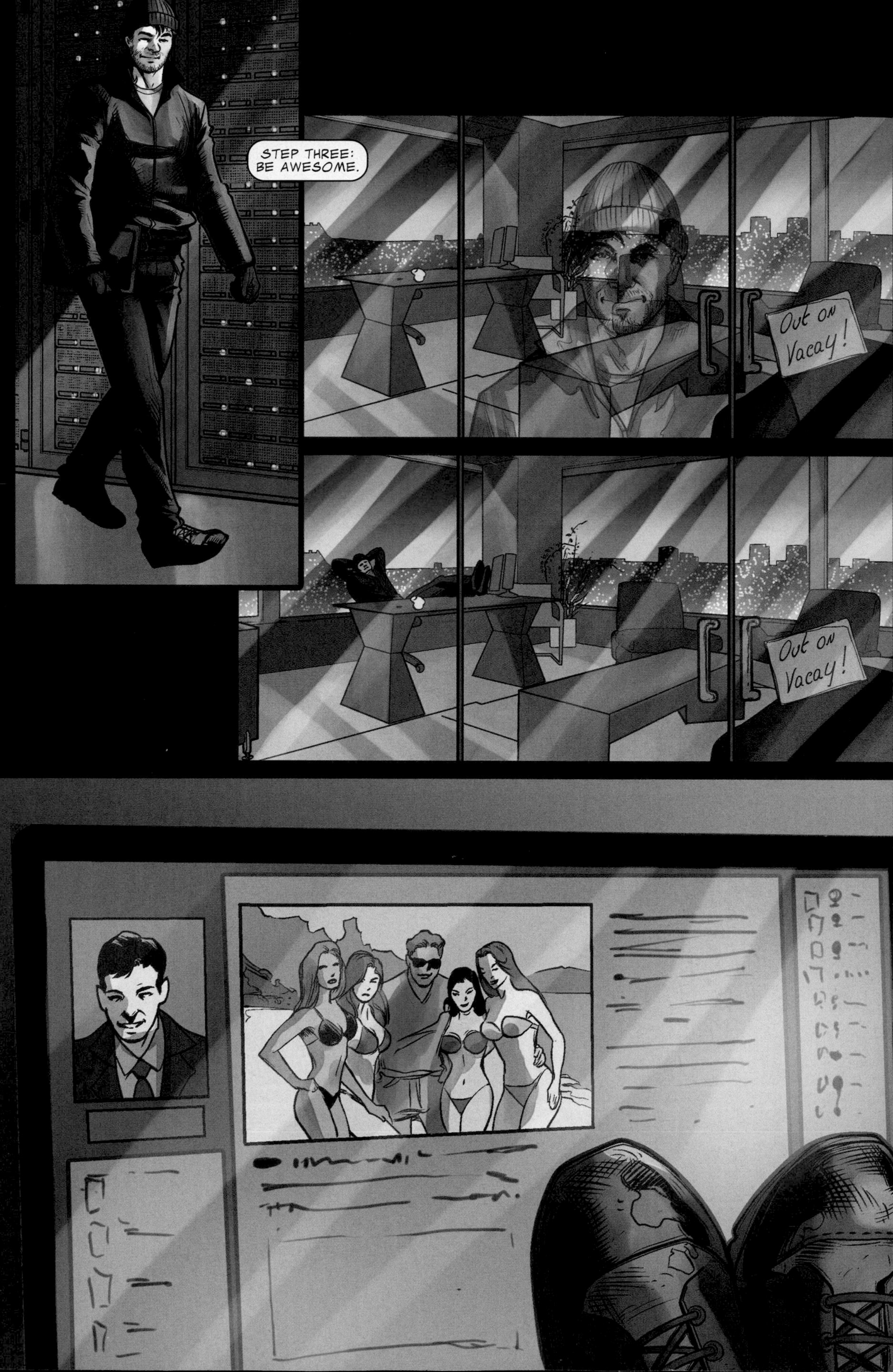
STEP THREE: BE AWESOME.
Out on Vacay!
Out on Vacay!

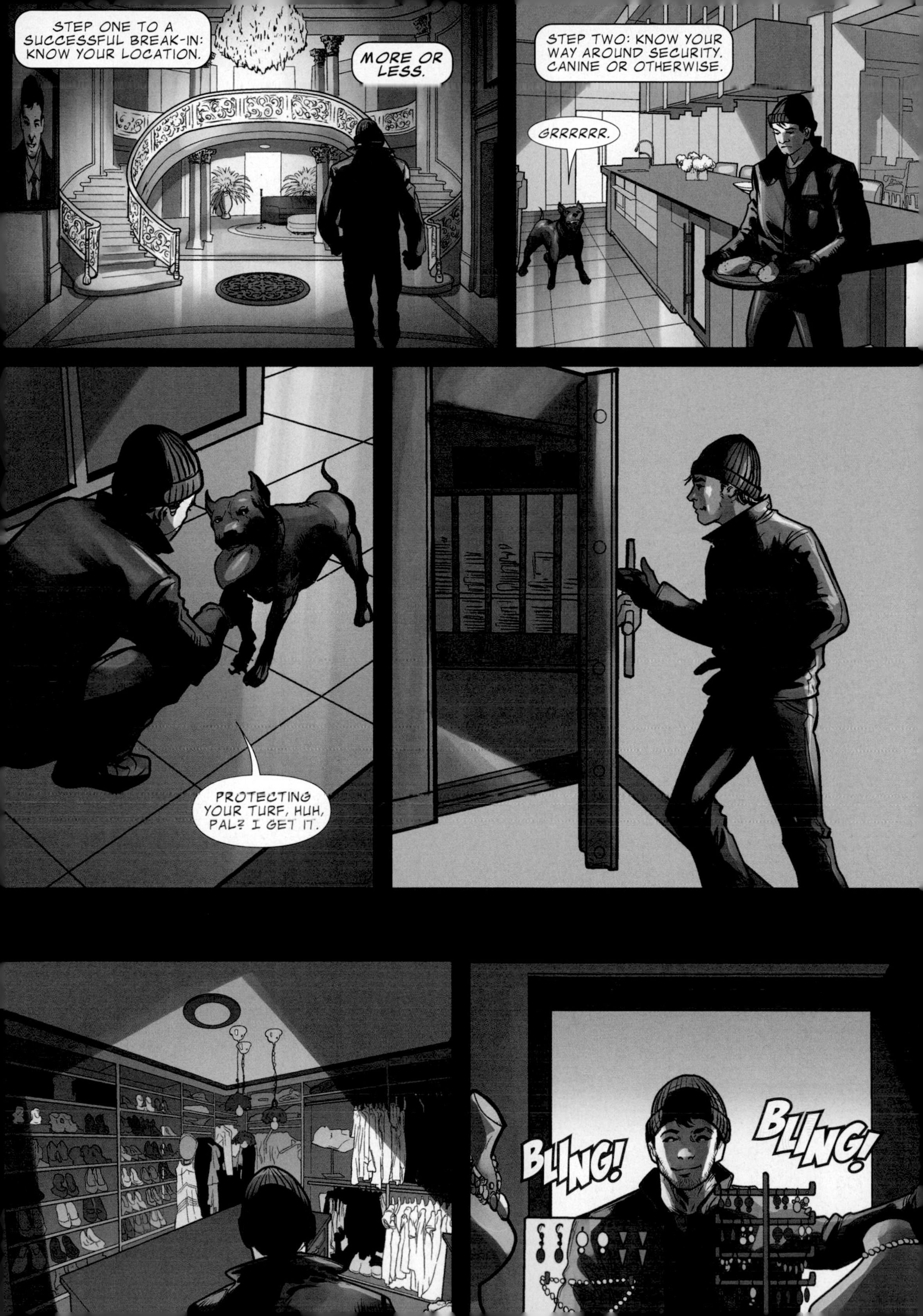

STEP ONE TO A SUCCESSFUL BREAK-IN: KNOW YOUR LOCATION.
MORE OR LESS.
STEP TWO: KNOW YOUR WAY AROUND SECURITY. CANINE OR OTHERWISE.
GRRRRRR.
PROTECTING YOUR TURF, HUH, PAL? I GET IT.
BLING!
BLING!

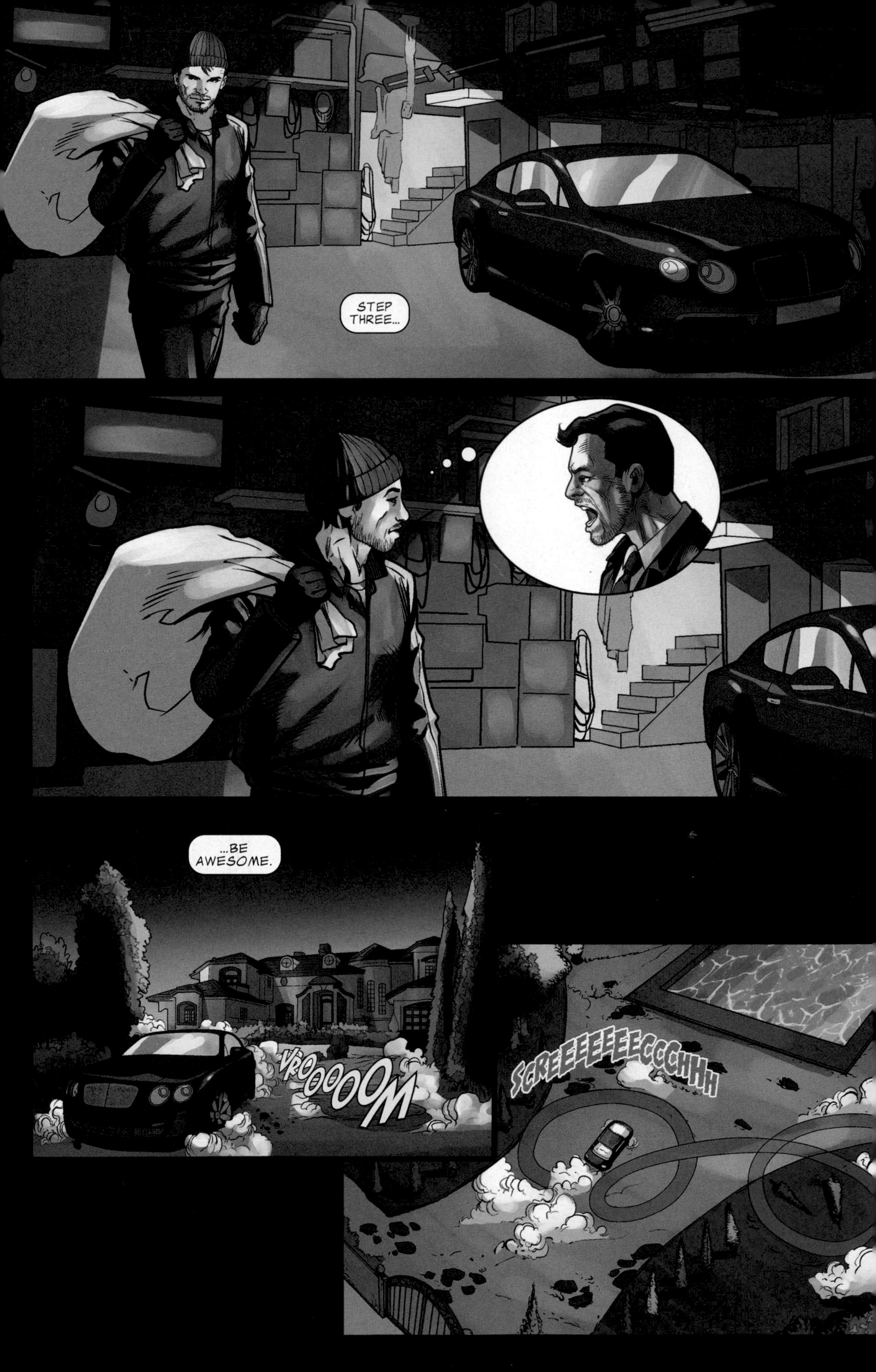
STEP THREE...
...BE AWESOME.
VROOOOOM
SCREEEEEEECCCHHH

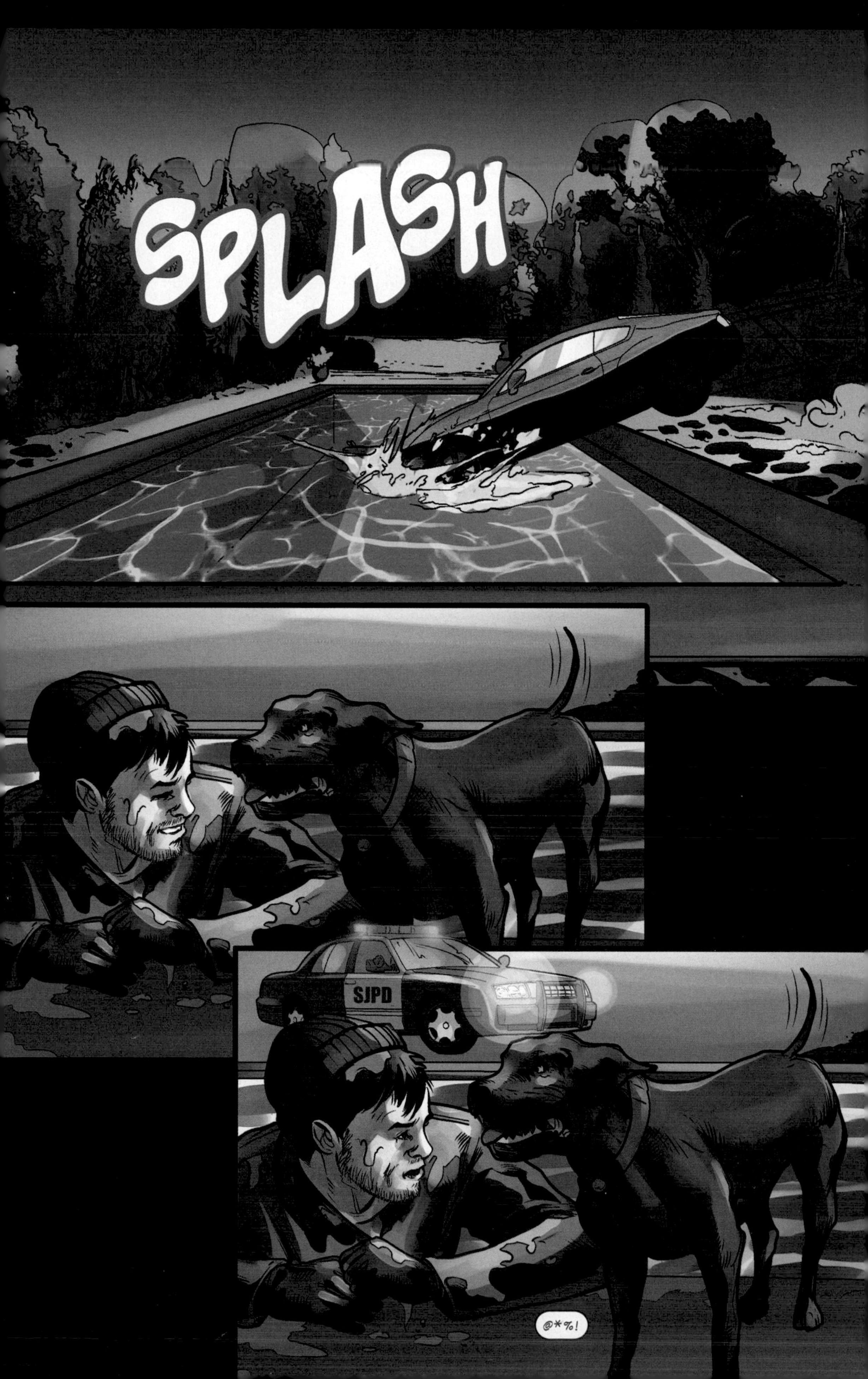
SPLASH
SJPD
@*%!

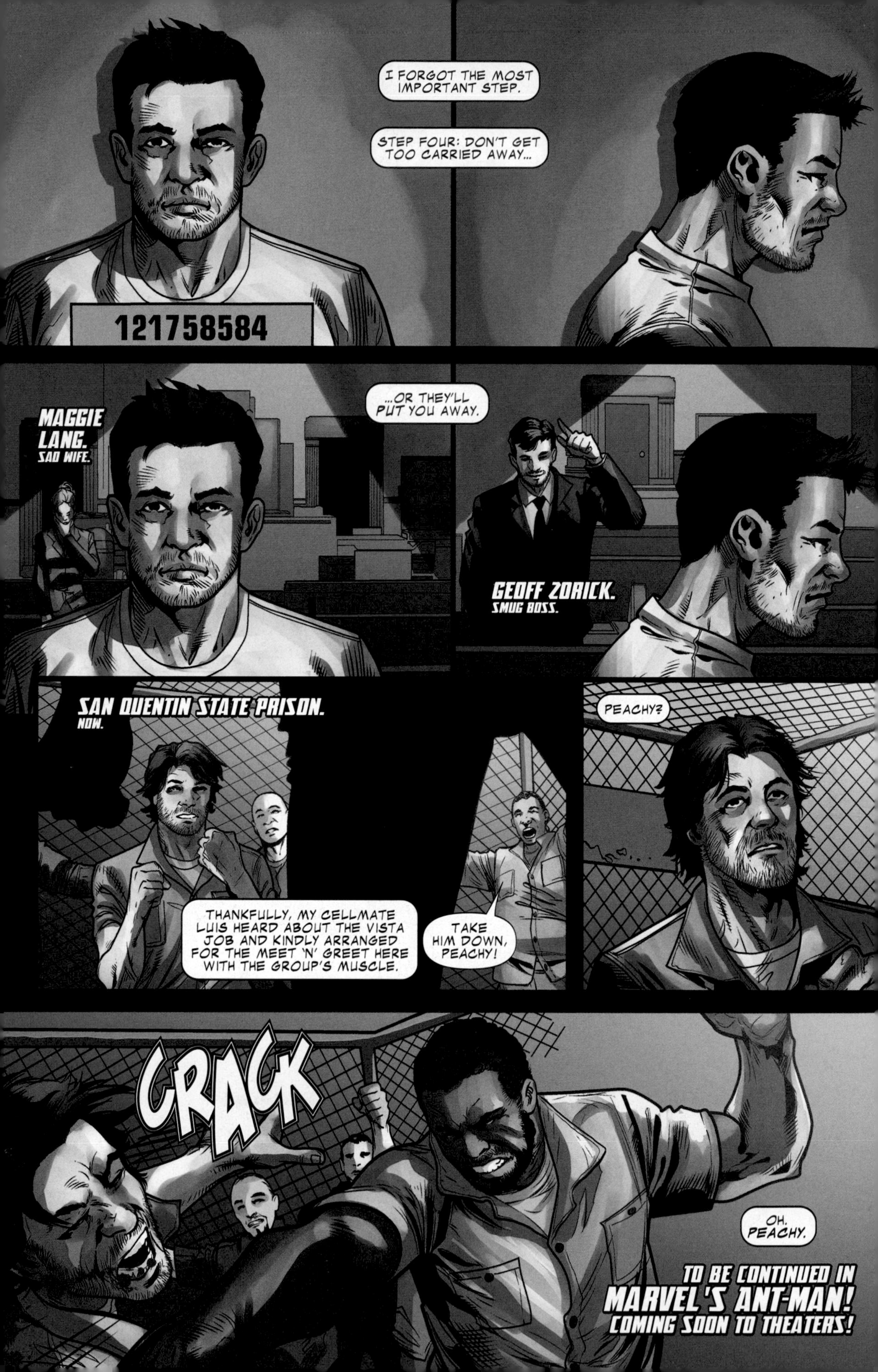
121758584
I FORGOT THE MOST IMPORTANT STEP.
STEP FOUR: DON'T GET TOO CARRIED AWAY...
MAGGIE LANG.
SAD WIFE.
...OR THEY'LL PUT YOU AWAY.
GEOFF ZORICK.
SMUG BOSS.
SAN QUENTIN STATE PRISON.
NOW.
THANKFULLY, MY CELLMATE LUIS HEARD ABOUT THE VISTA JOB AND KINDLY ARRANGED FOR THE MEET 'N' GREET HERE WITH THE GROUP'S MUSCLE.
TAKE HIM DOWN, PEACHY!
PEACHY?
CRACK
OH. PEACHY.
TO BE CONTINUED IN
MARVEL'S ANT-MAN!
COMING SOON TO THEATERS!

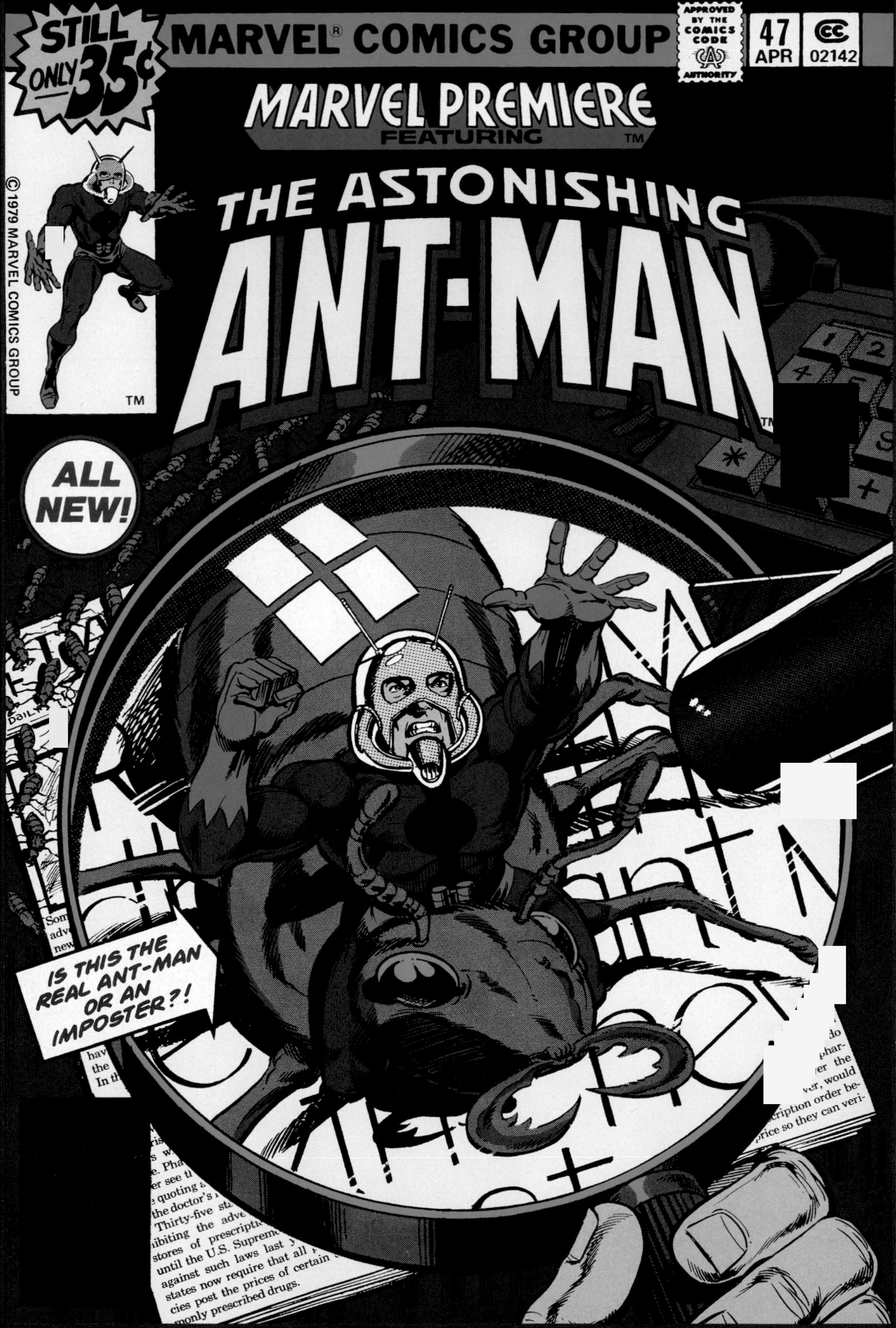

STILL ONLY 35¢
MARVEL® COMICS GROUP
APPROVED BY THE COMICS CODE AUTHORITY
47 APR
CC 02142
MARVEL PREMIERE
FEATURING
THE ASTONISHING ANT-MAN™
© 1979 MARVEL COMICS GROUP
ALL NEW!
IS THIS THE REAL ANT-MAN OR AN IMPOSTER?!

Stan Lee Presents: **THE ALL-NEW ANT-MAN** ™

DAVID MICHELINIE, *writer* •• JOHN BYRNE & BOB LAYTON, *artists*

TOM ORZECHOWSKI, *letterer* • BOB SHAREN, *colorist* • ROGER STERN, *editor* • JIM SHOOTER, *editor-in-chief*

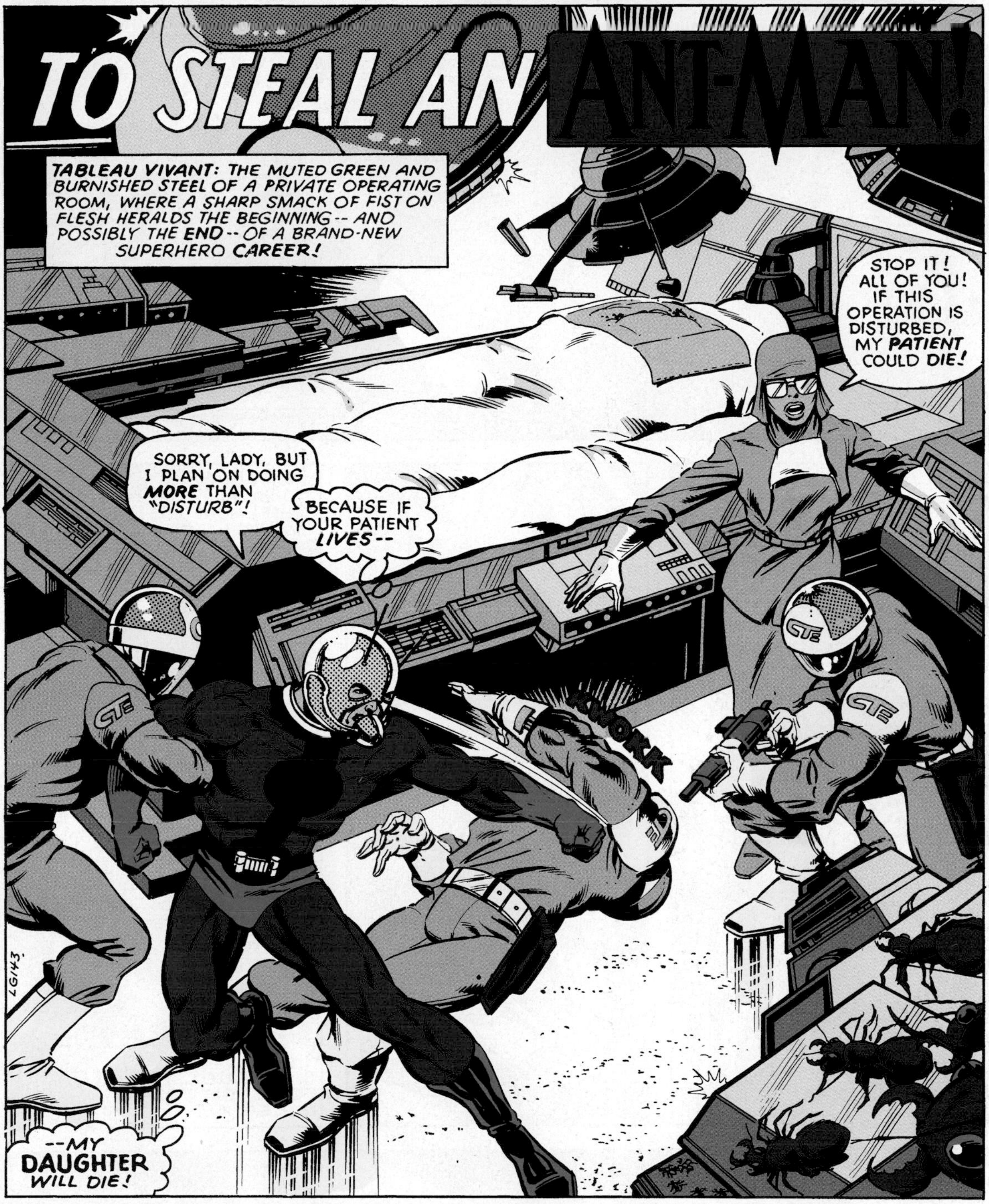

TO STEAL AN ANT-MAN!
TABLEAU VIVANT: THE MUTED GREEN AND BURNISHED STEEL OF A PRIVATE OPERATING ROOM, WHERE A SHARP SMACK OF FIST ON FLESH HERALDS THE BEGINNING -- AND POSSIBLY THE END -- OF A BRAND-NEW SUPERHERO CAREER!
STOP IT! ALL OF YOU! IF THIS OPERATION IS DISTURBED, MY PATIENT COULD DIE!
SORRY, LADY, BUT I PLAN ON DOING MORE THAN "DISTURB"!
BECAUSE IF YOUR PATIENT LIVES --
KWOKK
--MY DAUGHTER WILL DIE!
LG/143

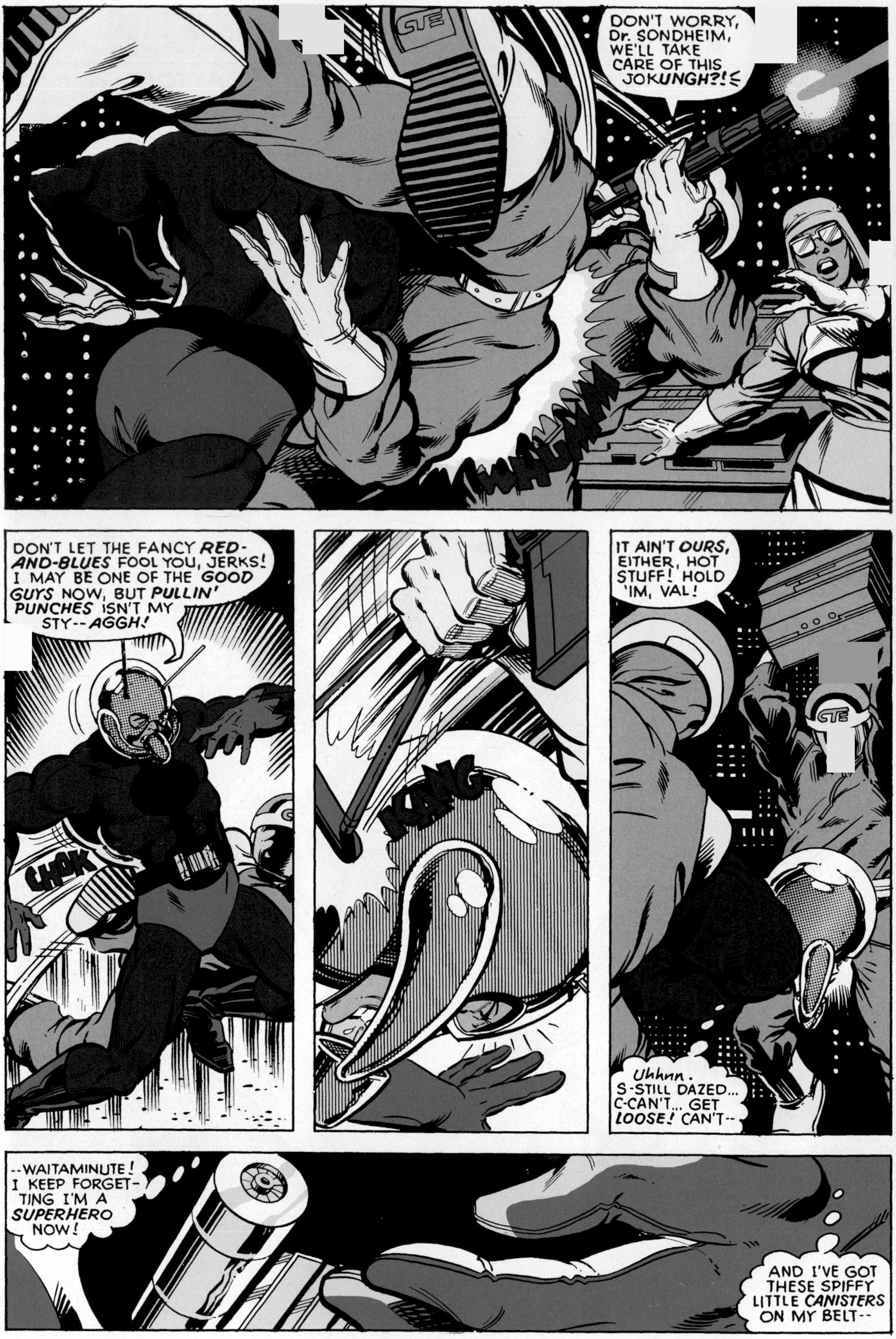
DON'T WORRY, Dr. SONDHEIM, WE'LL TAKE CARE OF THIS JOKUNGH?!
DON'T LET THE FANCY RED-AND-BLUES FOOL YOU, JERKS! I MAY BE ONE OF THE GOOD GUYS NOW, BUT PULLIN' PUNCHES ISN'T MY STY--AGGH!
CHOK
KANG
IT AIN'T OURS, EITHER, HOT STUFF! HOLD 'IM, VAL!
Uhhnn. S-STILL DAZED... C-CAN'T... GET LOOSE! CAN'T--
--WAITAMINUTE! I KEEP FORGET-TING I'M A SUPERHERO NOW!
AND I'VE GOT THESE SPIFFY LITTLE CANISTERS ON MY BELT--

"--TO **PROVE** IT!"

HEY! W-WHAT HAPPENED? WHERE'D HE GO?

WHUDD

WITH APOLOGIES TO *STEVE MARTIN*, PAL, I "*GOT SMALL*"--

--THANKS TO THE HANDY *SHRINK GAS* IN THESE CANISTERS!

NOW ALL ME AND MY *ANT* BUDDIES HAVE TO DO IS MANEUVER AROUND *BEHIND* THESE BOZOS AND WE'RE *HOME FREE*, RIGHT GUYS?

Uh·uh...

HEY, RICH, LOOK! THERE'S *ANTS* ALL OVER THE PLACE!

ANTS? I *THOUGHT* I RECOGNIZED THAT *COSTUME!* THAT TURKEY'S THE *ANT-MAN!*

AND NOW WE KNOW WHAT WE'RE *UP* AGAINST, WE CAN GET *RID* OF THE LITTLE SQUIRT--

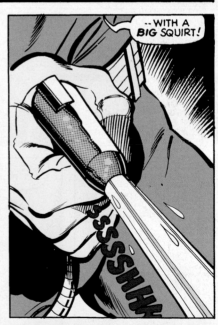

--WITH A *BIG SQUIRT!*

SSSSHHH

≥Ung≤ W-WATER--! L-LIKE A *TIDAL WAVE!*

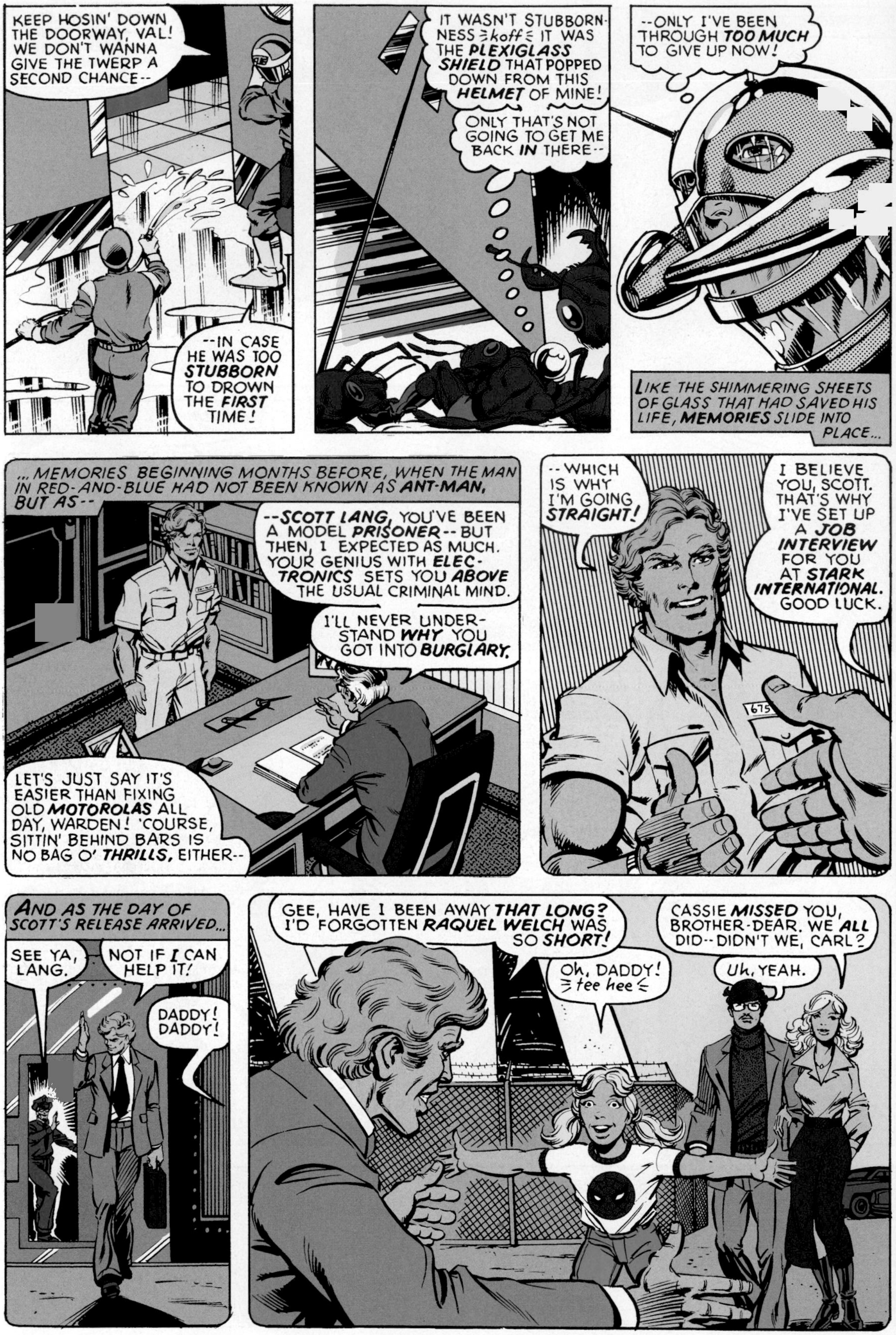
KEEP HOSIN' DOWN THE DOORWAY, VAL! WE DON'T WANNA GIVE THE TWERP A SECOND CHANCE--
--IN CASE HE WAS TOO STUBBORN TO DROWN THE FIRST TIME!
IT WASN'T STUBBORNNESS ≷koff≶ IT WAS THE PLEXIGLASS SHIELD THAT POPPED DOWN FROM THIS HELMET OF MINE!
ONLY THAT'S NOT GOING TO GET ME BACK IN THERE--
--ONLY I'VE BEEN THROUGH TOO MUCH TO GIVE UP NOW!
LIKE THE SHIMMERING SHEETS OF GLASS THAT HAD SAVED HIS LIFE, MEMORIES SLIDE INTO PLACE...
...MEMORIES BEGINNING MONTHS BEFORE, WHEN THE MAN IN RED-AND-BLUE HAD NOT BEEN KNOWN AS ANT-MAN, BUT AS--
--SCOTT LANG, YOU'VE BEEN A MODEL PRISONER--BUT THEN, I EXPECTED AS MUCH. YOUR GENIUS WITH ELECTRONICS SETS YOU ABOVE THE USUAL CRIMINAL MIND.
I'LL NEVER UNDERSTAND WHY YOU GOT INTO BURGLARY.
LET'S JUST SAY IT'S EASIER THAN FIXING OLD MOTOROLAS ALL DAY, WARDEN! 'COURSE, SITTIN' BEHIND BARS IS NO BAG O' THRILLS, EITHER--
--WHICH IS WHY I'M GOING STRAIGHT!
I BELIEVE YOU, SCOTT. THAT'S WHY I'VE SET UP A JOB INTERVIEW FOR YOU AT STARK INTERNATIONAL. GOOD LUCK.
AND AS THE DAY OF SCOTT'S RELEASE ARRIVED...
SEE YA, LANG.
NOT IF I CAN HELP IT!
DADDY! DADDY!
GEE, HAVE I BEEN AWAY THAT LONG? I'D FORGOTTEN RAQUEL WELCH WAS SO SHORT!
Oh, DADDY! ≷tee hee≶
CASSIE MISSED YOU, BROTHER-DEAR. WE ALL DID--DIDN'T WE, CARL?
Uh, YEAH.

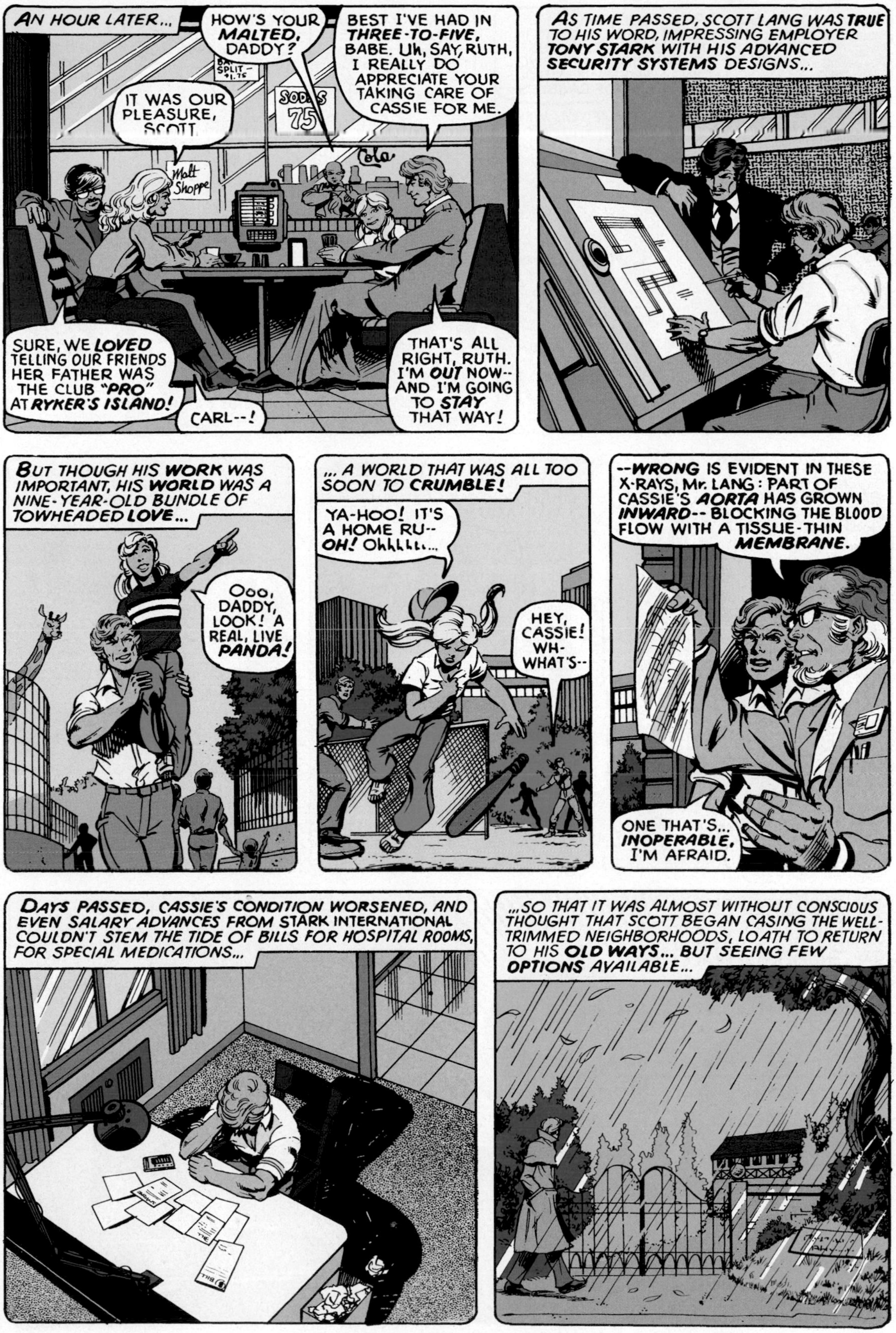
AN HOUR LATER...
HOW'S YOUR MALTED, DADDY?
BEST I'VE HAD IN THREE-TO-FIVE, BABE. Uh, SAY, RUTH, I REALLY DO APPRECIATE YOUR TAKING CARE OF CASSIE FOR ME.
IT WAS OUR PLEASURE, SCOTT.
SODAS 75
Cola
Malt Shoppe
SURE, WE LOVED TELLING OUR FRIENDS HER FATHER WAS THE CLUB "PRO" AT RYKER'S ISLAND!
CARL--!
THAT'S ALL RIGHT, RUTH. I'M OUT NOW-- AND I'M GOING TO STAY THAT WAY!
AS TIME PASSED, SCOTT LANG WAS TRUE TO HIS WORD, IMPRESSING EMPLOYER TONY STARK WITH HIS ADVANCED SECURITY SYSTEMS DESIGNS...
BUT THOUGH HIS WORK WAS IMPORTANT, HIS WORLD WAS A NINE-YEAR-OLD BUNDLE OF TOWHEADED LOVE...
Ooo, DADDY, LOOK! A REAL, LIVE PANDA!
... A WORLD THAT WAS ALL TOO SOON TO CRUMBLE!
YA-HOO! IT'S A HOME RU-- OH! Ohhhhh...
HEY, CASSIE! WH-WHAT'S--
--WRONG IS EVIDENT IN THESE X-RAYS, Mr. LANG: PART OF CASSIE'S AORTA HAS GROWN INWARD-- BLOCKING THE BLOOD FLOW WITH A TISSUE-THIN MEMBRANE.
ONE THAT'S... INOPERABLE, I'M AFRAID.
DAYS PASSED, CASSIE'S CONDITION WORSENED, AND EVEN SALARY ADVANCES FROM STARK INTERNATIONAL COULDN'T STEM THE TIDE OF BILLS FOR HOSPITAL ROOMS, FOR SPECIAL MEDICATIONS...
BILL
...SO THAT IT WAS ALMOST WITHOUT CONSCIOUS THOUGHT THAT SCOTT BEGAN CASING THE WELL-TRIMMED NEIGHBORHOODS, LOATH TO RETURN TO HIS OLD WAYS... BUT SEEING FEW OPTIONS AVAILABLE...

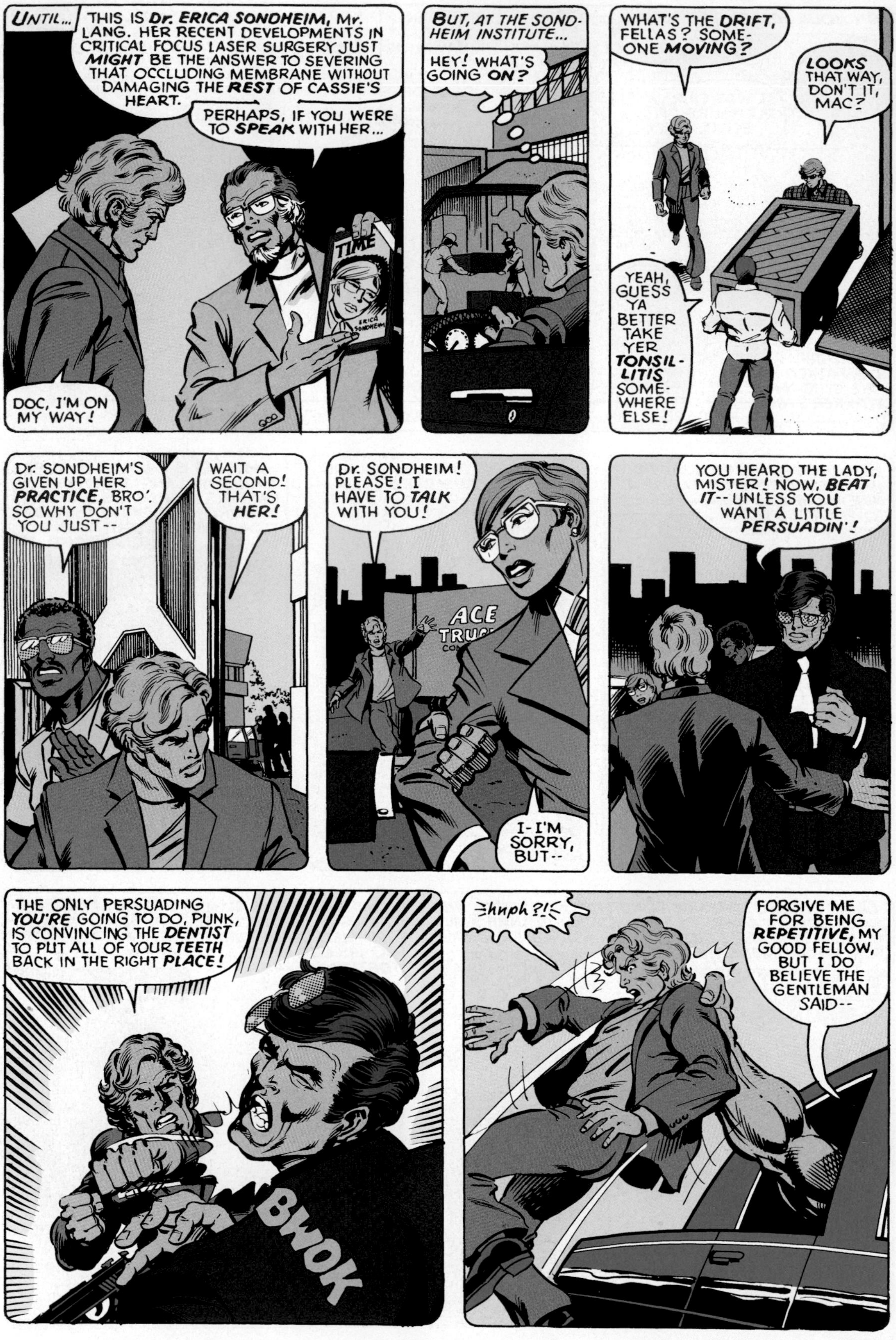
UNTIL...
THIS IS Dr. ERICA SONDHEIM, Mr. LANG. HER RECENT DEVELOPMENTS IN CRITICAL FOCUS LASER SURGERY JUST MIGHT BE THE ANSWER TO SEVERING THAT OCCLUDING MEMBRANE WITHOUT DAMAGING THE REST OF CASSIE'S HEART.
PERHAPS, IF YOU WERE TO SPEAK WITH HER...
TIME
ERICA SONDHEIM
DOC, I'M ON MY WAY!
BUT, AT THE SONDHEIM INSTITUTE...
HEY! WHAT'S GOING ON?
WHAT'S THE DRIFT, FELLAS? SOMEONE MOVING?
LOOKS THAT WAY, DON'T IT, MAC?
YEAH, GUESS YA BETTER TAKE YER TONSILLITIS SOMEWHERE ELSE!
Dr. SONDHEIM'S GIVEN UP HER PRACTICE, BRO'. SO WHY DON'T YOU JUST--
WAIT A SECOND! THAT'S HER!
Dr. SONDHEIM! PLEASE! I HAVE TO TALK WITH YOU!
ACE
I-I'M SORRY, BUT--
YOU HEARD THE LADY, MISTER! NOW, BEAT IT-- UNLESS YOU WANT A LITTLE PERSUADIN'!
THE ONLY PERSUADING YOU'RE GOING TO DO, PUNK, IS CONVINCING THE DENTIST TO PUT ALL OF YOUR TEETH BACK IN THE RIGHT PLACE!
BWOK
hnph?!
FORGIVE ME FOR BEING REPETITIVE, MY GOOD FELLOW, BUT I DO BELIEVE THE GENTLEMAN SAID--

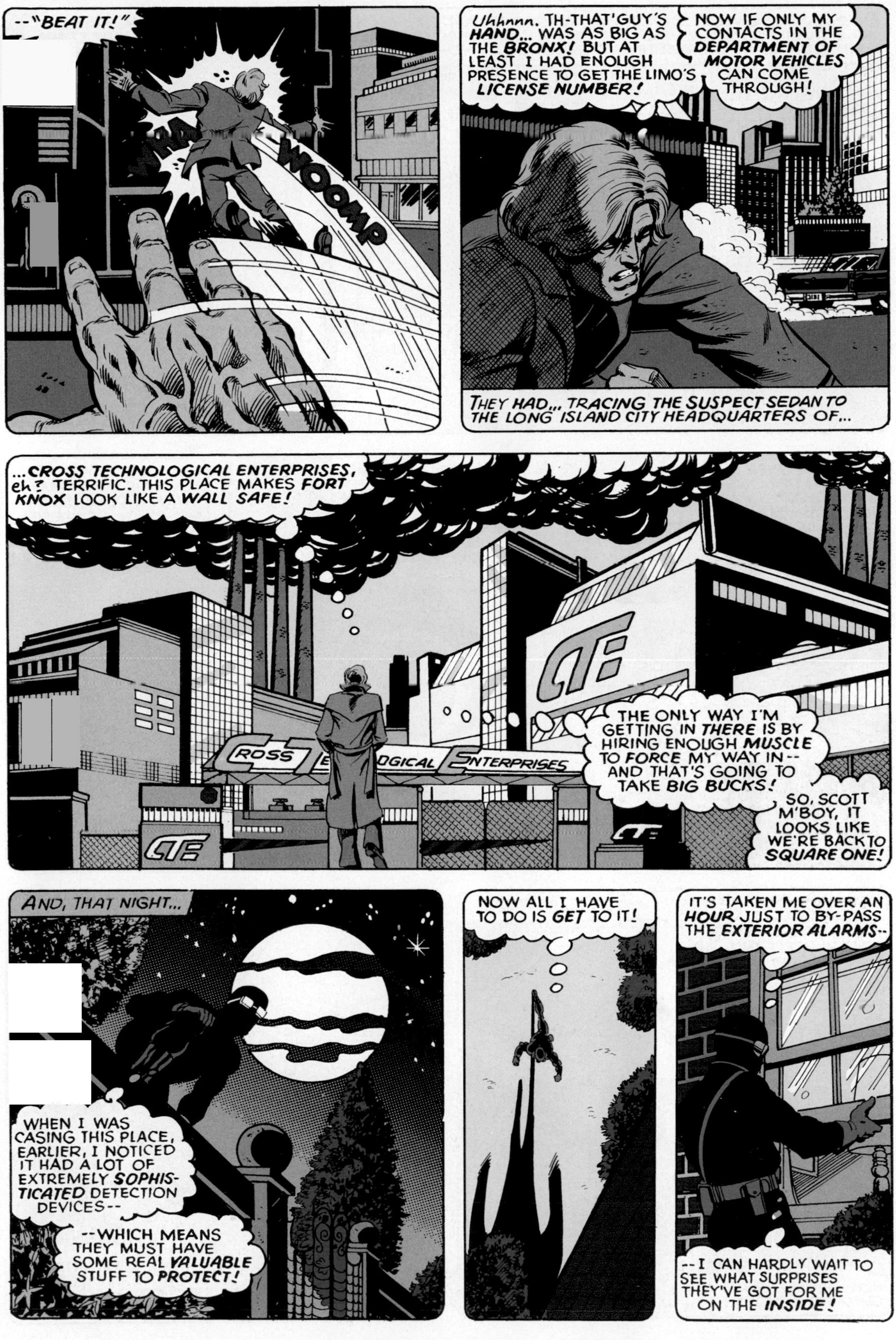
--"BEAT IT!"
WOOMP
Uhhnnn. TH-THAT GUY'S HAND... WAS AS BIG AS THE BRONX! BUT AT LEAST I HAD ENOUGH PRESENCE TO GET THE LIMO'S LICENSE NUMBER!
NOW IF ONLY MY CONTACTS IN THE DEPARTMENT OF MOTOR VEHICLES CAN COME THROUGH!
THEY HAD... TRACING THE SUSPECT SEDAN TO THE LONG ISLAND CITY HEADQUARTERS OF...
...CROSS TECHNOLOGICAL ENTERPRISES, eh? TERRIFIC. THIS PLACE MAKES FORT KNOX LOOK LIKE A WALL SAFE!
THE ONLY WAY I'M GETTING IN THERE IS BY HIRING ENOUGH MUSCLE TO FORCE MY WAY IN -- AND THAT'S GOING TO TAKE BIG BUCKS!
SO, SCOTT M'BOY, IT LOOKS LIKE WE'RE BACK TO SQUARE ONE!
AND, THAT NIGHT...
WHEN I WAS CASING THIS PLACE, EARLIER, I NOTICED IT HAD A LOT OF EXTREMELY SOPHISTICATED DETECTION DEVICES--
--WHICH MEANS THEY MUST HAVE SOME REAL VALUABLE STUFF TO PROTECT!
NOW ALL I HAVE TO DO IS GET TO IT!
IT'S TAKEN ME OVER AN HOUR JUST TO BY-PASS THE EXTERIOR ALARMS--
--I CAN HARDLY WAIT TO SEE WHAT SURPRISES THEY'VE GOT FOR ME ON THE INSIDE!

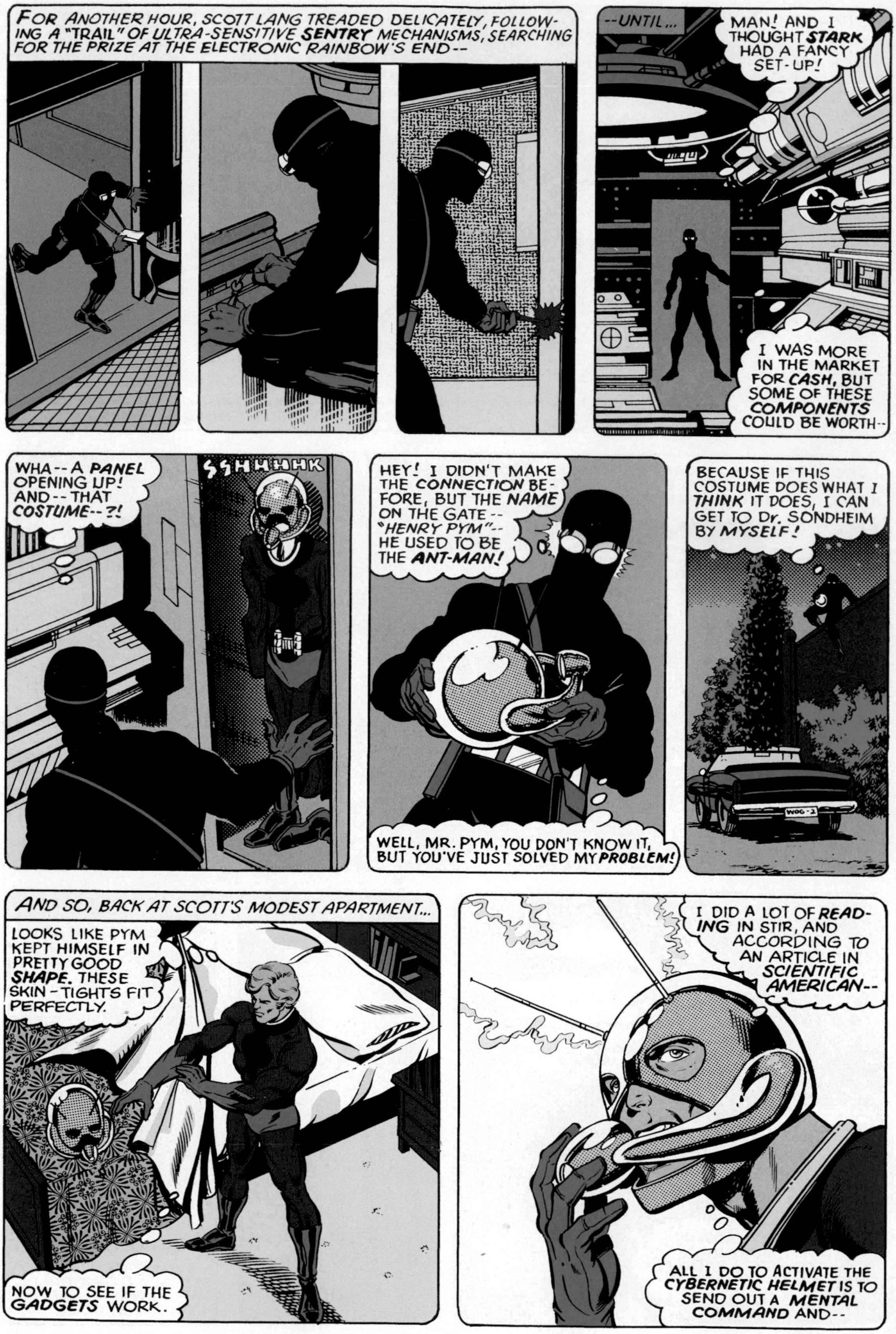

FOR ANOTHER HOUR, SCOTT LANG TREADED DELICATELY, FOLLOWING A "TRAIL" OF ULTRA-SENSITIVE SENTRY MECHANISMS, SEARCHING FOR THE PRIZE AT THE ELECTRONIC RAINBOW'S END--
--UNTIL...
MAN! AND I THOUGHT STARK HAD A FANCY SET-UP!
I WAS MORE IN THE MARKET FOR CASH, BUT SOME OF THESE COMPONENTS COULD BE WORTH--
WHA-- A PANEL OPENING UP! AND-- THAT COSTUME--?!
SSHHHHHK
HEY! I DIDN'T MAKE THE CONNECTION BEFORE, BUT THE NAME ON THE GATE -- "HENRY PYM"-- HE USED TO BE THE ANT-MAN!
WELL, MR. PYM, YOU DON'T KNOW IT, BUT YOU'VE JUST SOLVED MY PROBLEM!
BECAUSE IF THIS COSTUME DOES WHAT I THINK IT DOES, I CAN GET TO Dr. SONDHEIM BY MYSELF!
WOG-2
AND SO, BACK AT SCOTT'S MODEST APARTMENT...
LOOKS LIKE PYM KEPT HIMSELF IN PRETTY GOOD SHAPE. THESE SKIN-TIGHTS FIT PERFECTLY.
NOW TO SEE IF THE GADGETS WORK.
I DID A LOT OF READING IN STIR, AND ACCORDING TO AN ARTICLE IN SCIENTIFIC AMERICAN--
ALL I DO TO ACTIVATE THE CYBERNETIC HELMET IS TO SEND OUT A MENTAL COMMAND AND--

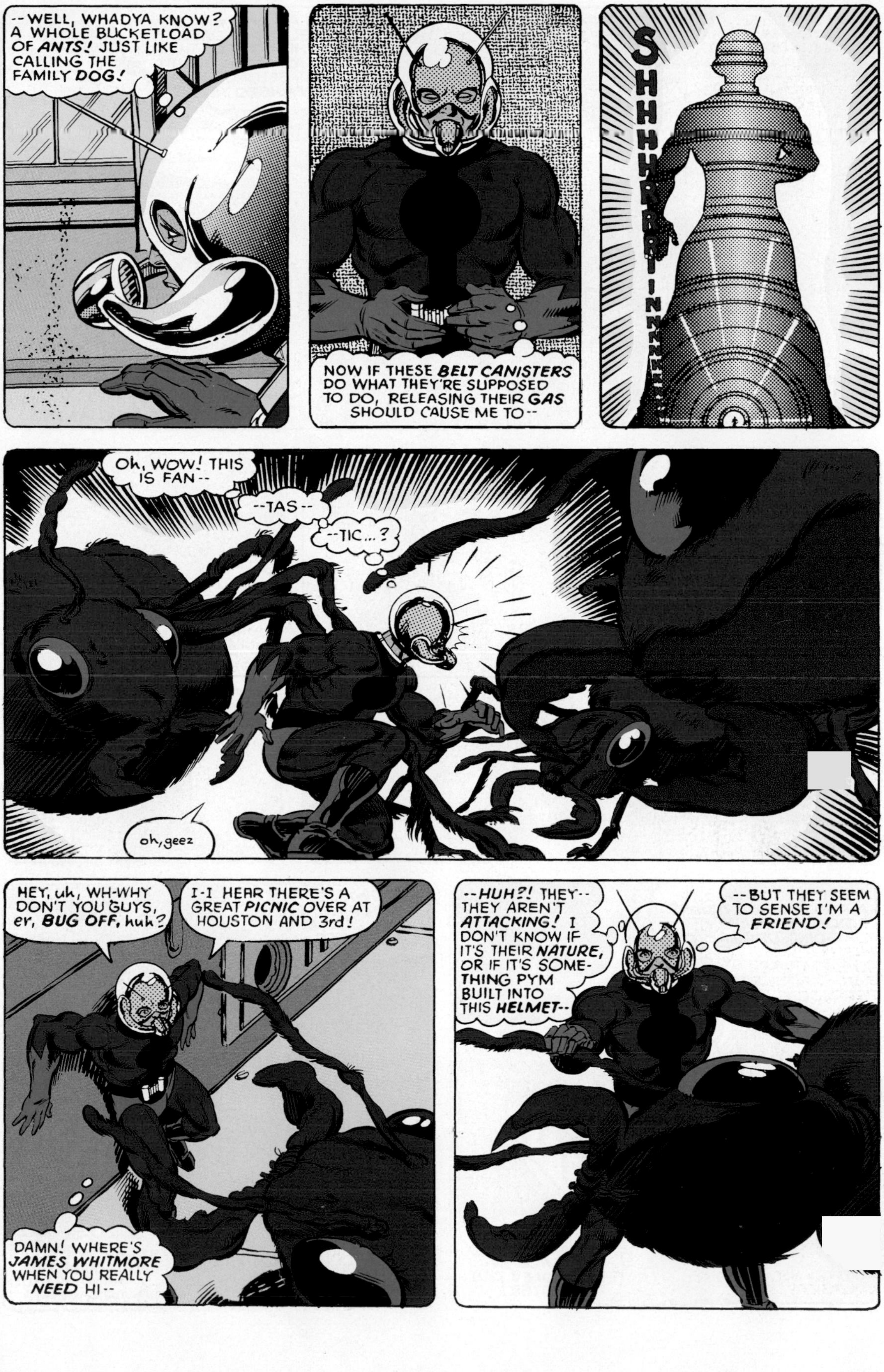
--WELL, WHADYA KNOW? A WHOLE BUCKETLOAD OF ANTS! JUST LIKE CALLING THE FAMILY DOG!
NOW IF THESE BELT CANISTERS DO WHAT THEY'RE SUPPOSED TO DO, RELEASING THEIR GAS SHOULD CAUSE ME TO--
SHHHHRRRIINNN
Oh, WOW! THIS IS FAN--
--TAS--
--TIC...?
oh, geez
HEY, uh, WH-WHY DON'T YOU GUYS, er, BUG OFF, huh?
I-I HEAR THERE'S A GREAT PICNIC OVER AT HOUSTON AND 3rd!
DAMN! WHERE'S JAMES WHITMORE WHEN YOU REALLY NEED HI--
--HUH?! THEY-- THEY AREN'T ATTACKING! I DON'T KNOW IF IT'S THEIR NATURE, OR IF IT'S SOME-THING PYM BUILT INTO THIS HELMET--
--BUT THEY SEEM TO SENSE I'M A FRIEND!

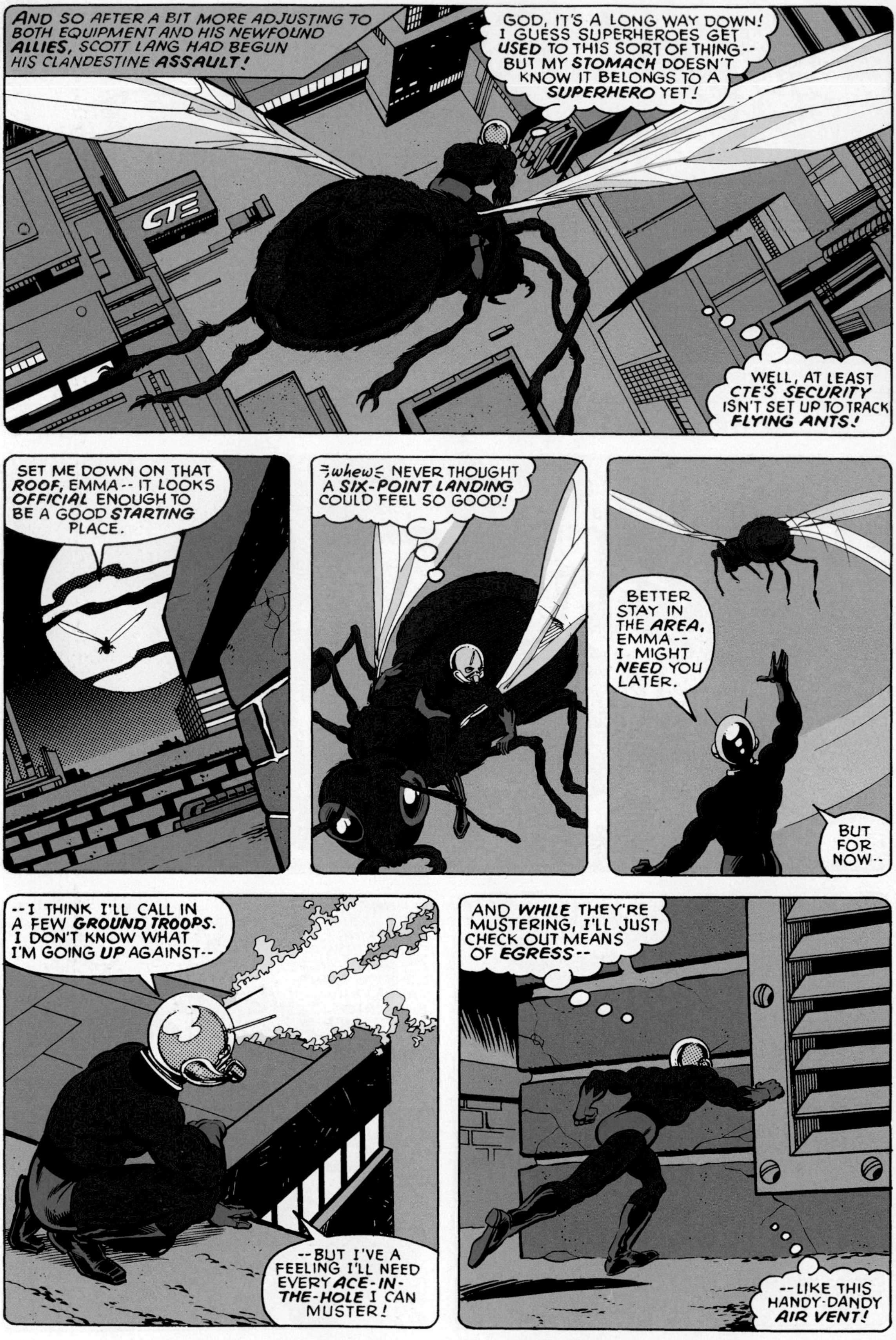
AND SO AFTER A BIT MORE ADJUSTING TO BOTH EQUIPMENT AND HIS NEWFOUND ALLIES, SCOTT LANG HAD BEGUN HIS CLANDESTINE ASSAULT!
GOD, IT'S A LONG WAY DOWN! I GUESS SUPERHEROES GET USED TO THIS SORT OF THING-- BUT MY STOMACH DOESN'T KNOW IT BELONGS TO A SUPERHERO YET!
CTE
WELL, AT LEAST CTE'S SECURITY ISN'T SET UP TO TRACK FLYING ANTS!
SET ME DOWN ON THAT ROOF, EMMA-- IT LOOKS OFFICIAL ENOUGH TO BE A GOOD STARTING PLACE.
=whew= NEVER THOUGHT A SIX-POINT LANDING COULD FEEL SO GOOD!
BETTER STAY IN THE AREA, EMMA-- I MIGHT NEED YOU LATER.
BUT FOR NOW--
--I THINK I'LL CALL IN A FEW GROUND TROOPS. I DON'T KNOW WHAT I'M GOING UP AGAINST--
--BUT I'VE A FEELING I'LL NEED EVERY ACE-IN-THE-HOLE I CAN MUSTER!
AND WHILE THEY'RE MUSTERING, I'LL JUST CHECK OUT MEANS OF EGRESS--
--LIKE THIS HANDY-DANDY AIR VENT!

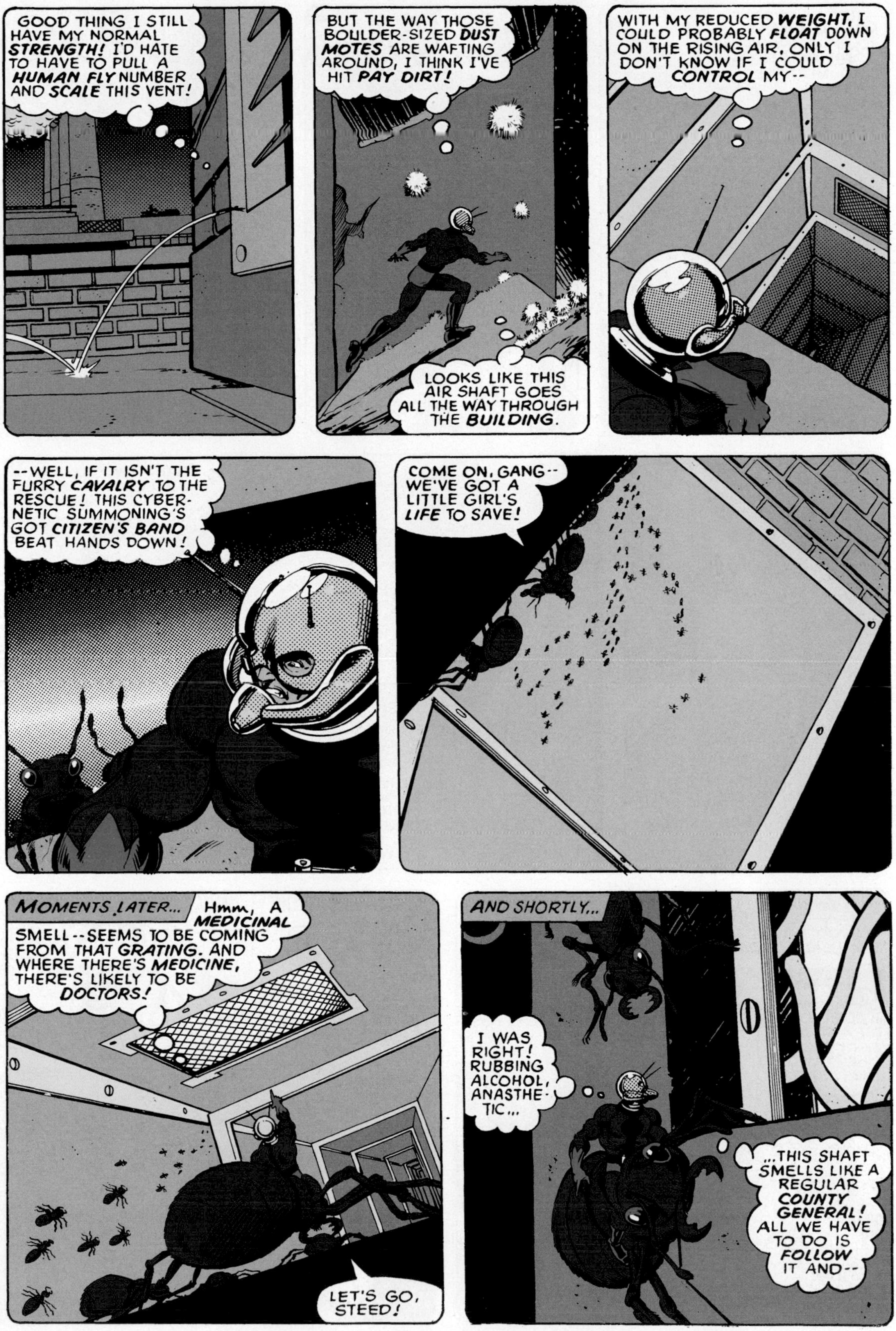

GOOD THING I STILL HAVE MY NORMAL STRENGTH! I'D HATE TO HAVE TO PULL A HUMAN FLY NUMBER AND SCALE THIS VENT!
BUT THE WAY THOSE BOULDER-SIZED DUST MOTES ARE WAFTING AROUND, I THINK I'VE HIT PAY DIRT!
LOOKS LIKE THIS AIR SHAFT GOES ALL THE WAY THROUGH THE BUILDING.
WITH MY REDUCED WEIGHT, I COULD PROBABLY FLOAT DOWN ON THE RISING AIR, ONLY I DON'T KNOW IF I COULD CONTROL MY--
--WELL, IF IT ISN'T THE FURRY CAVALRY TO THE RESCUE! THIS CYBERNETIC SUMMONING'S GOT CITIZEN'S BAND BEAT HANDS DOWN!
COME ON, GANG-- WE'VE GOT A LITTLE GIRL'S LIFE TO SAVE!
MOMENTS LATER...
Hmm, A MEDICINAL SMELL--SEEMS TO BE COMING FROM THAT GRATING. AND WHERE THERE'S MEDICINE, THERE'S LIKELY TO BE DOCTORS!
LET'S GO, STEED!
AND SHORTLY...
I WAS RIGHT! RUBBING ALCOHOL, ANASTHETIC...
...THIS SHAFT SMELLS LIKE A REGULAR COUNTY GENERAL! ALL WE HAVE TO DO IS FOLLOW IT AND--

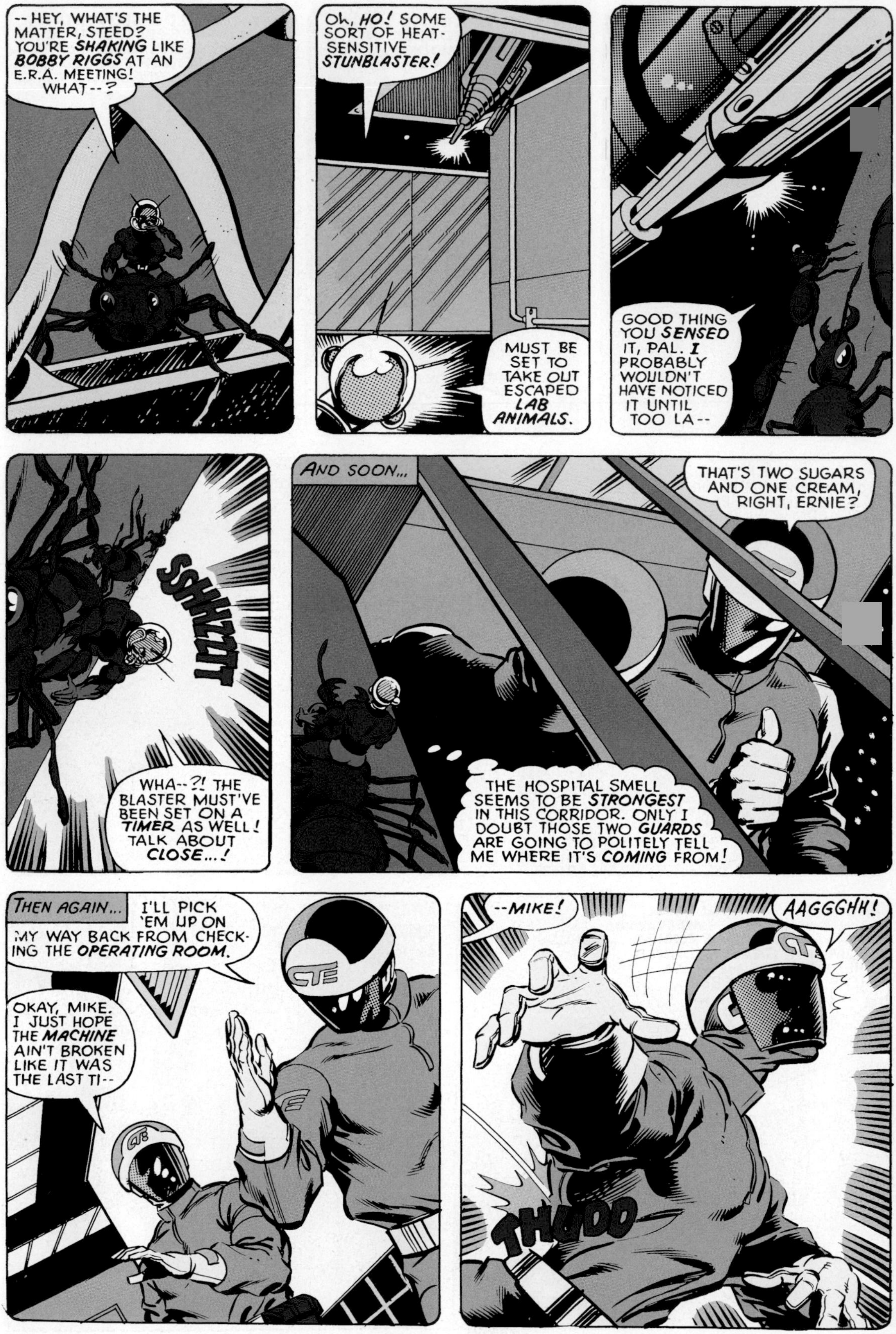
-- HEY, WHAT'S THE MATTER, STEED? YOU'RE SHAKING LIKE BOBBY RIGGS AT AN E.R.A. MEETING! WHAT--?
Oh, HO! SOME SORT OF HEAT-SENSITIVE STUNBLASTER!
MUST BE SET TO TAKE OUT ESCAPED LAB ANIMALS.
GOOD THING YOU SENSED IT, PAL. I PROBABLY WOULDN'T HAVE NOTICED IT UNTIL TOO LA--
SSHHZZTT
WHA--?! THE BLASTER MUST'VE BEEN SET ON A TIMER AS WELL! TALK ABOUT CLOSE...!
AND SOON...
THAT'S TWO SUGARS AND ONE CREAM, RIGHT, ERNIE?
THE HOSPITAL SMELL SEEMS TO BE STRONGEST IN THIS CORRIDOR. ONLY I DOUBT THOSE TWO GUARDS ARE GOING TO POLITELY TELL ME WHERE IT'S COMING FROM!
THEN AGAIN...
I'LL PICK 'EM UP ON MY WAY BACK FROM CHECKING THE OPERATING ROOM.
OKAY, MIKE. I JUST HOPE THE MACHINE AIN'T BROKEN LIKE IT WAS THE LAST TI--
--MIKE!
AAGGGHH!
THUDD

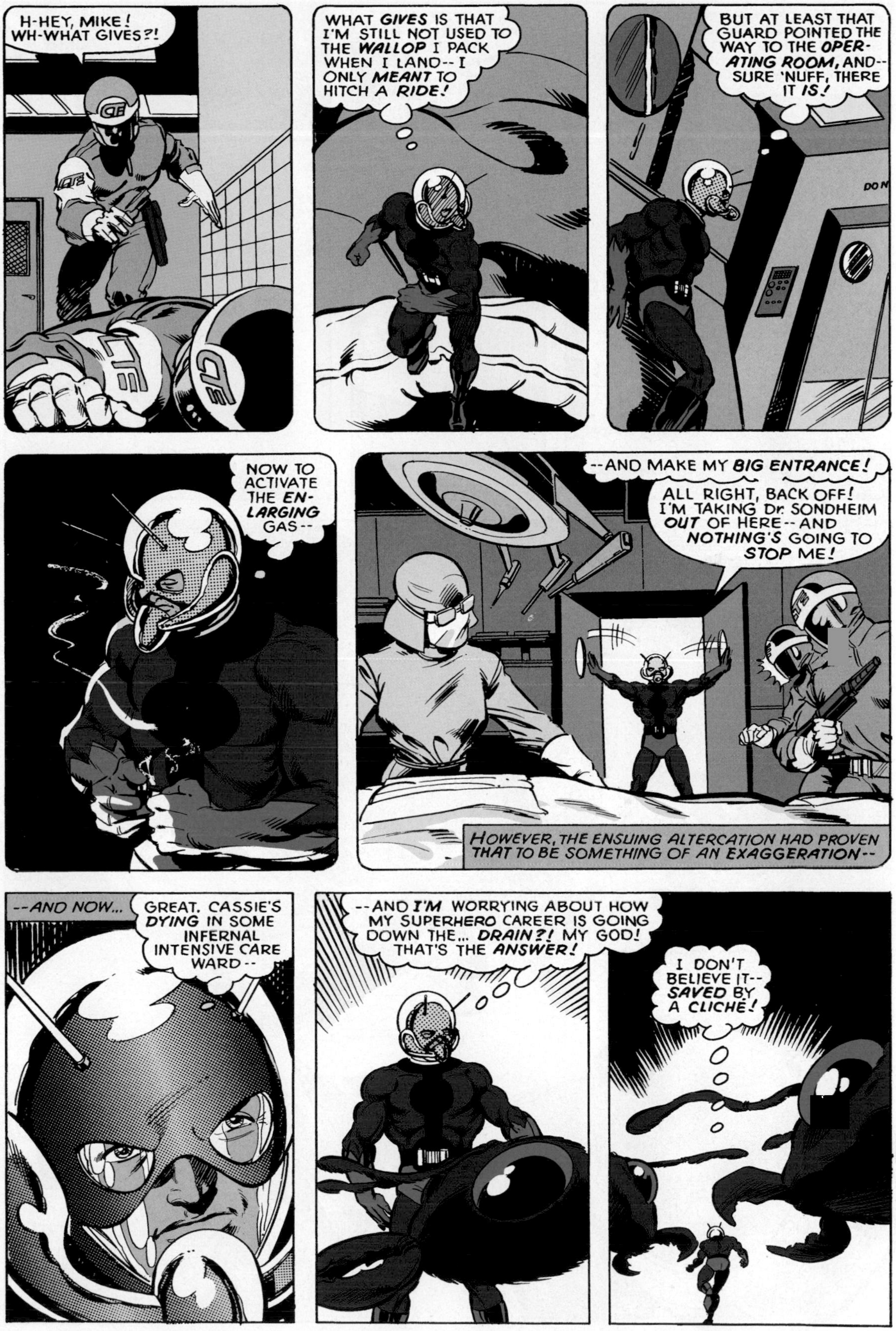
H-HEY, MIKE! WH-WHAT GIVES?!
WHAT GIVES IS THAT I'M STILL NOT USED TO THE WALLOP I PACK WHEN I LAND-- I ONLY MEANT TO HITCH A RIDE!
BUT AT LEAST THAT GUARD POINTED THE WAY TO THE OPER-ATING ROOM, AND-- SURE 'NUFF, THERE IT IS!
NOW TO ACTIVATE THE EN-LARGING GAS--
--AND MAKE MY BIG ENTRANCE!
ALL RIGHT, BACK OFF! I'M TAKING Dr. SONDHEIM OUT OF HERE--AND NOTHING'S GOING TO STOP ME!
HOWEVER, THE ENSUING ALTERCATION HAD PROVEN THAT TO BE SOMETHING OF AN EXAGGERATION--
--AND NOW...
GREAT. CASSIE'S DYING IN SOME INFERNAL INTENSIVE CARE WARD--
--AND I'M WORRYING ABOUT HOW MY SUPERHERO CAREER IS GOING DOWN THE... DRAIN?! MY GOD! THAT'S THE ANSWER!
I DON'T BELIEVE IT-- SAVED BY A CLICHÉ!

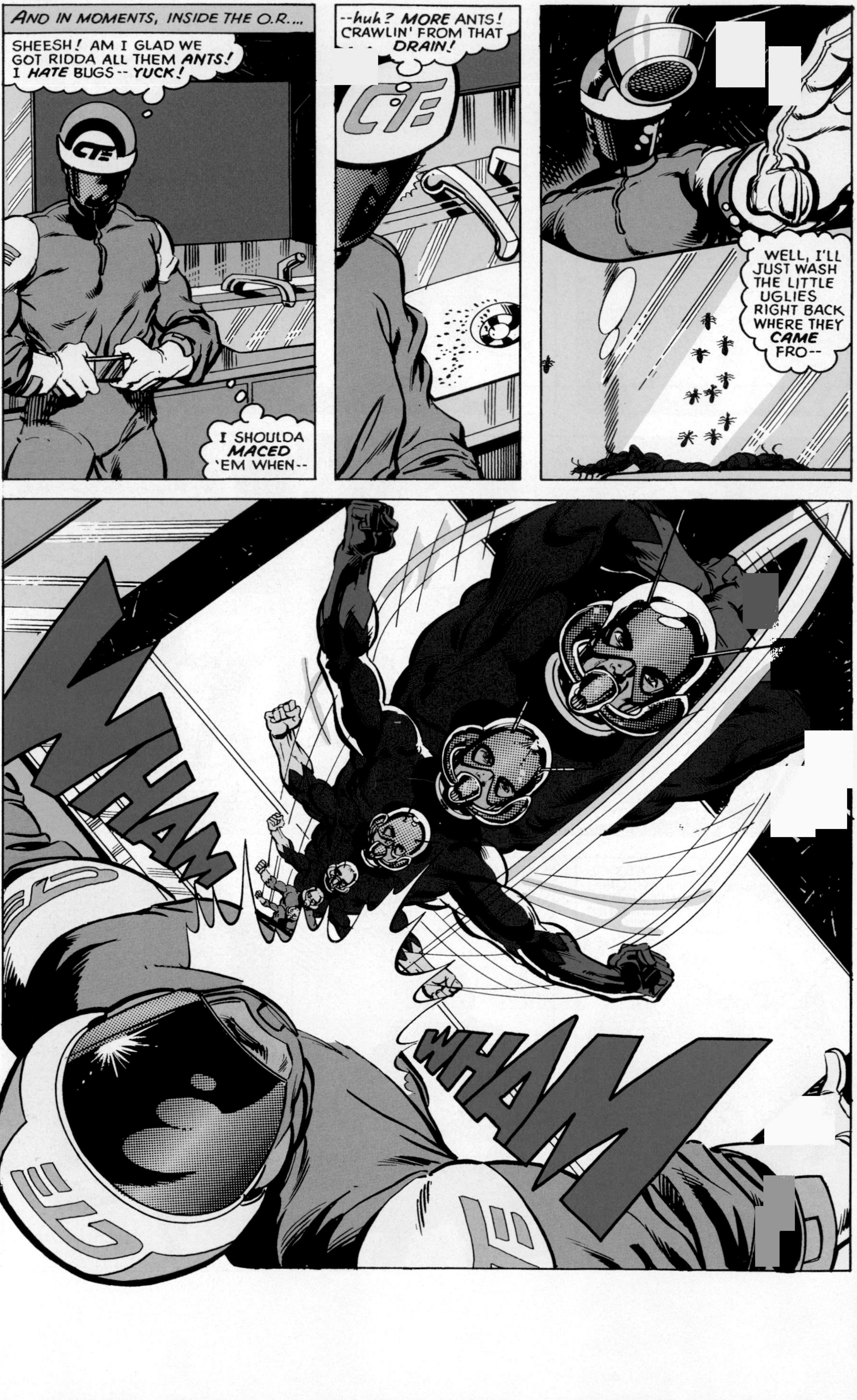
AND IN MOMENTS, INSIDE THE O.R....
SHEESH! AM I GLAD WE GOT RIDDA ALL THEM ANTS! I HATE BUGS -- YUCK!
I SHOULDA MACED 'EM WHEN --
--huh? MORE ANTS! CRAWLIN' FROM THAT DRAIN!
WELL, I'LL JUST WASH THE LITTLE UGLIES RIGHT BACK WHERE THEY CAME FRO--
WHAM
WHAM

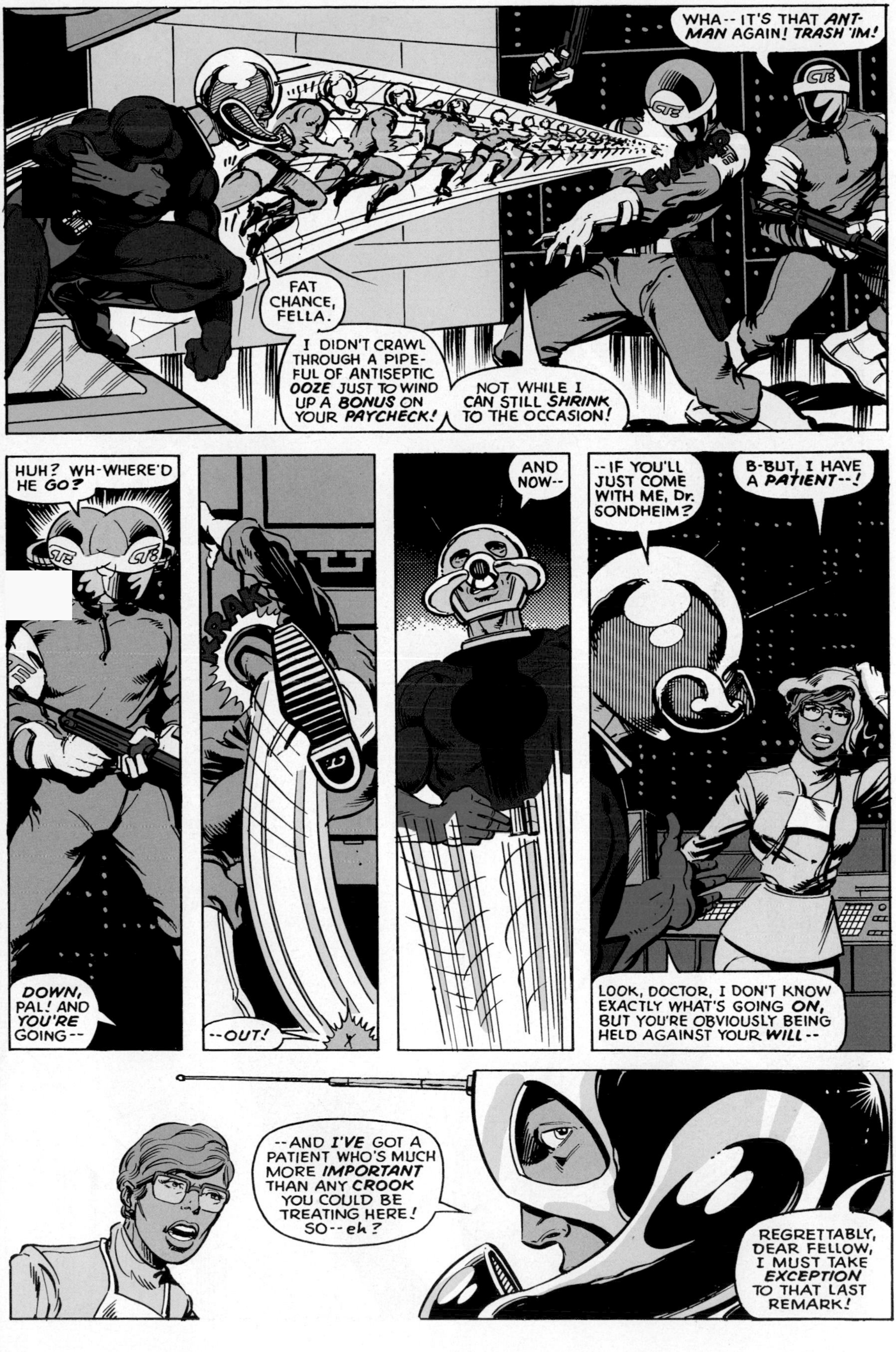

WHA-- IT'S THAT ANT-MAN AGAIN! TRASH 'IM!
FAT CHANCE, FELLA.
I DIDN'T CRAWL THROUGH A PIPE-FUL OF ANTISEPTIC OOZE JUST TO WIND UP A BONUS ON YOUR PAYCHECK!
NOT WHILE I CAN STILL SHRINK TO THE OCCASION!
HUH? WH-WHERE'D HE GO?
DOWN, PAL! AND YOU'RE GOING--
--OUT!
AND NOW--
--IF YOU'LL JUST COME WITH ME, Dr. SONDHEIM?
B-BUT, I HAVE A PATIENT--!
LOOK, DOCTOR, I DON'T KNOW EXACTLY WHAT'S GOING ON, BUT YOU'RE OBVIOUSLY BEING HELD AGAINST YOUR WILL--
--AND I'VE GOT A PATIENT WHO'S MUCH MORE IMPORTANT THAN ANY CROOK YOU COULD BE TREATING HERE! SO--eh?
REGRETTABLY, DEAR FELLOW, I MUST TAKE EXCEPTION TO THAT LAST REMARK!

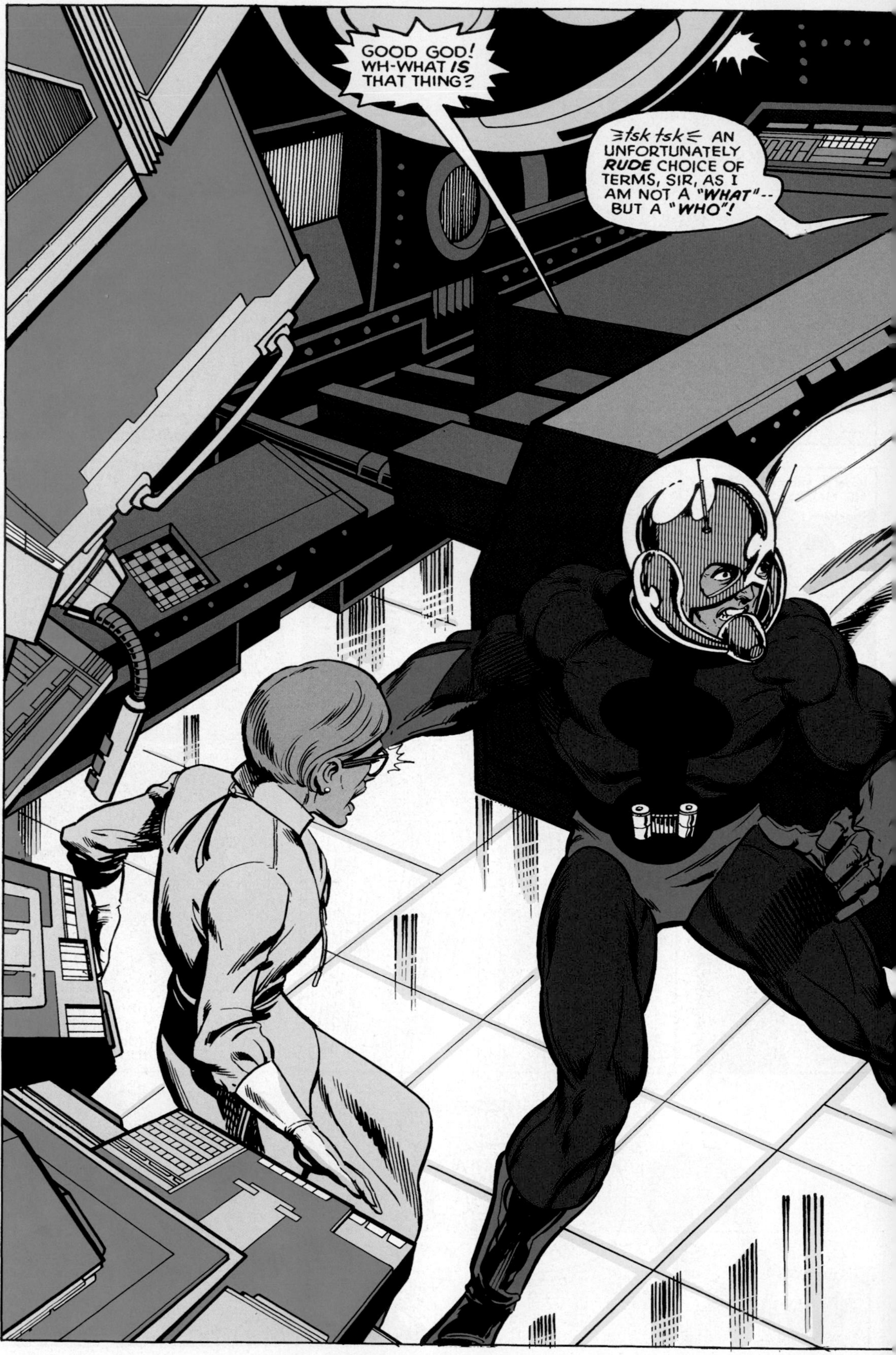
GOOD GOD! WH-WHAT IS THAT THING?
≡tsk tsk≡ AN UNFORTUNATELY RUDE CHOICE OF TERMS, SIR, AS I AM NOT A "WHAT"-- BUT A "WHO"!

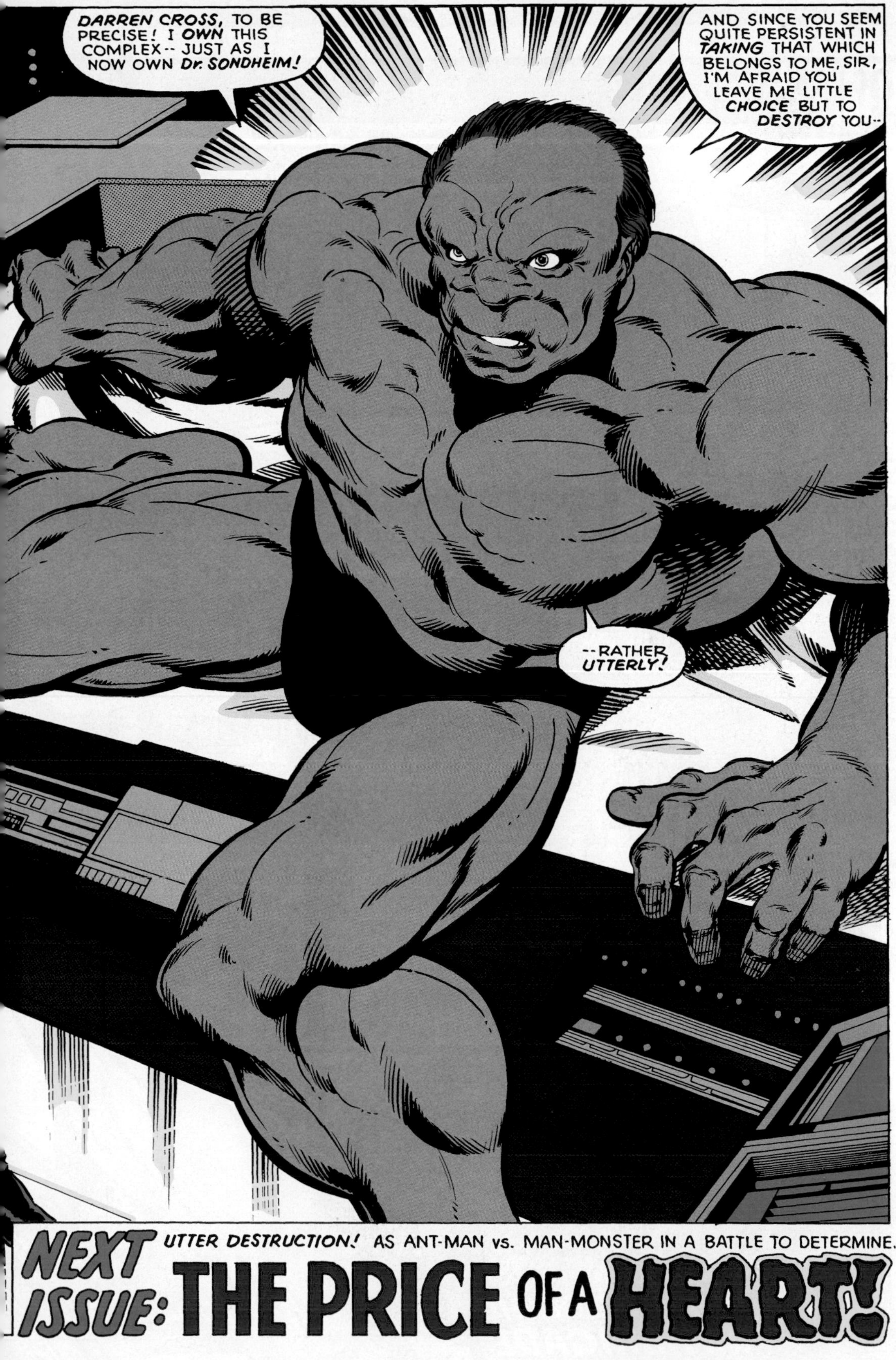
DARREN CROSS, TO BE PRECISE! I OWN THIS COMPLEX-- JUST AS I NOW OWN Dr. SONDHEIM!
AND SINCE YOU SEEM QUITE PERSISTENT IN TAKING THAT WHICH BELONGS TO ME, SIR, I'M AFRAID YOU LEAVE ME LITTLE CHOICE BUT TO DESTROY YOU--
--RATHER UTTERLY!

NEXT ISSUE: UTTER DESTRUCTION! AS ANT-MAN vs. MAN-MONSTER IN A BATTLE TO DETERMINE...

THE PRICE OF A HEART!

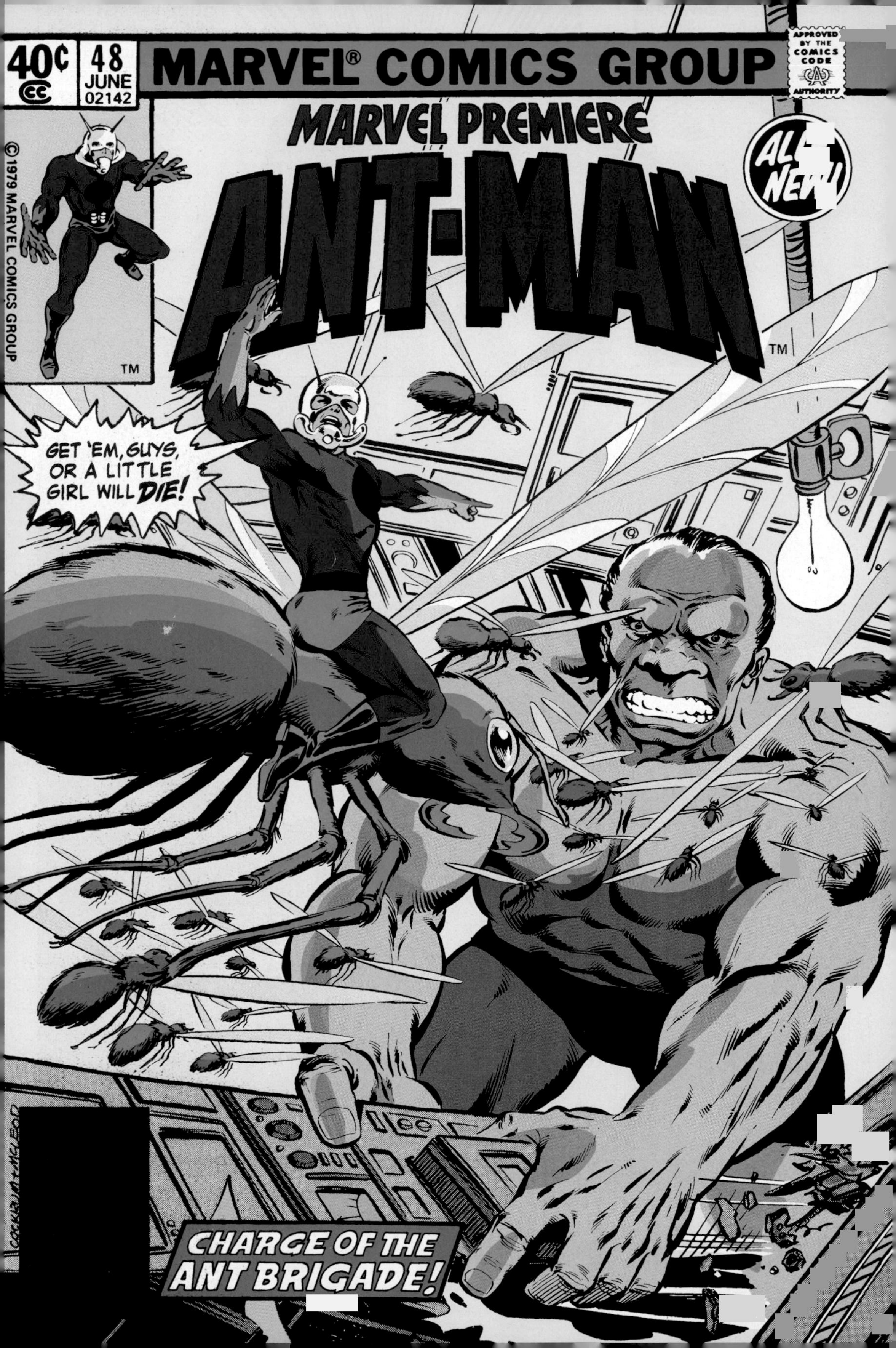

40¢
48
JUNE
02142
MARVEL® COMICS GROUP
APPROVED BY THE COMICS CODE AUTHORITY
MARVEL PREMIERE
ANT-MAN™
© 1979 MARVEL COMICS GROUP
GET 'EM, GUYS, OR A LITTLE GIRL WILL DIE!
CHARGE OF THE ANT BRIGADE!

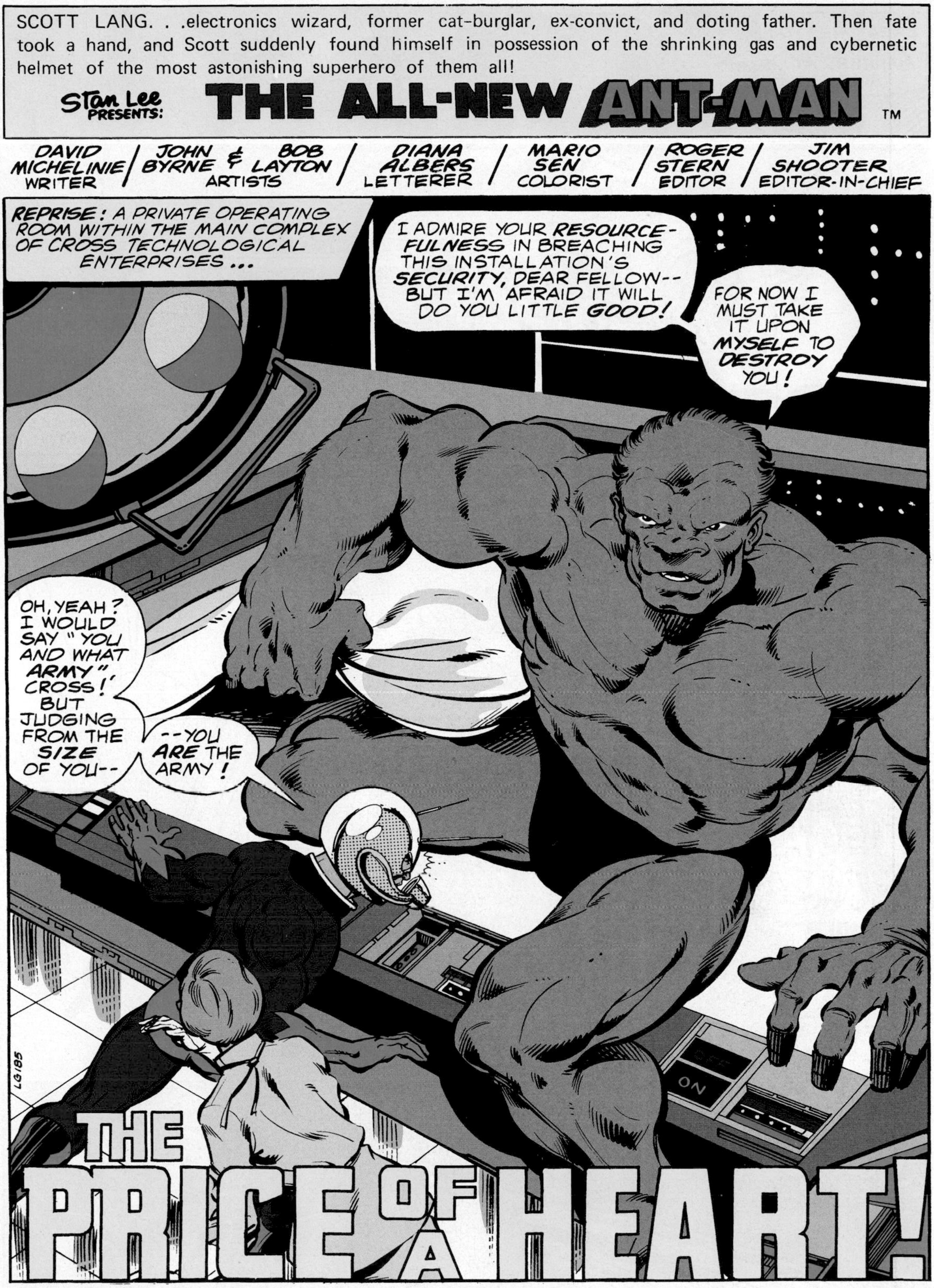
SCOTT LANG. . .electronics wizard, former cat-burglar, ex-convict, and doting father. Then fate took a hand, and Scott suddenly found himself in possession of the shrinking gas and cybernetic helmet of the most astonishing superhero of them all!
Stan Lee PRESENTS: THE ALL-NEW ANT-MAN ™
DAVID MICHELINIE WRITER / JOHN BYRNE & BOB LAYTON ARTISTS / DIANA ALBERS LETTERER / MARIO SEN COLORIST / ROGER STERN EDITOR / JIM SHOOTER EDITOR-IN-CHIEF
REPRISE: A PRIVATE OPERATING ROOM WITHIN THE MAIN COMPLEX OF CROSS TECHNOLOGICAL ENTERPRISES...
I ADMIRE YOUR RESOURCEFULNESS IN BREACHING THIS INSTALLATION'S SECURITY, DEAR FELLOW-- BUT I'M AFRAID IT WILL DO YOU LITTLE GOOD!
FOR NOW I MUST TAKE IT UPON MYSELF TO DESTROY YOU!
OH, YEAH? I WOULD SAY "YOU AND WHAT ARMY", CROSS! BUT JUDGING FROM THE SIZE OF YOU--
--YOU ARE THE ARMY!
OFF
ON
THE PRICE OF A HEART!

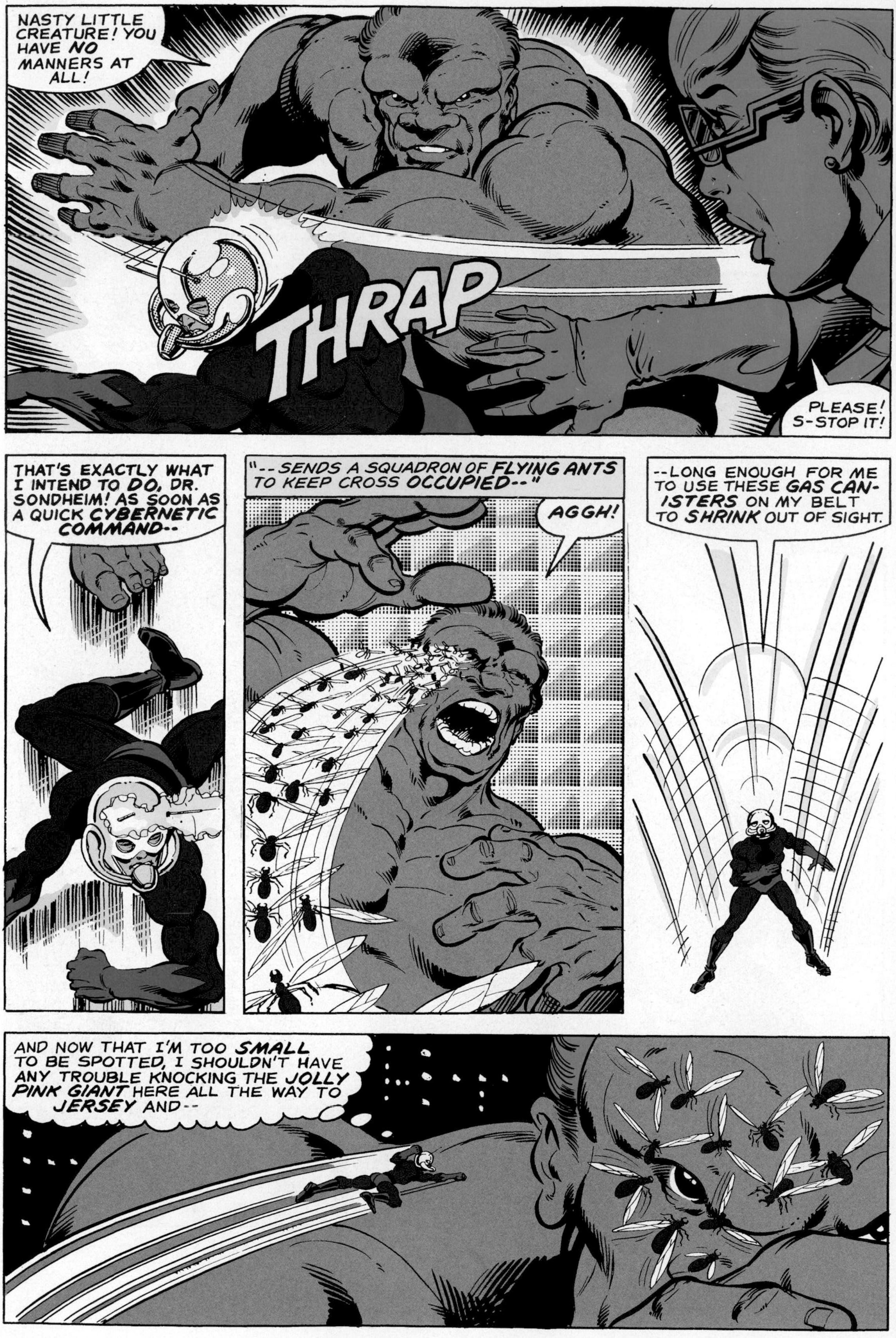
NASTY LITTLE CREATURE! YOU HAVE NO MANNERS AT ALL!
THRAP
PLEASE! S-STOP IT!
THAT'S EXACTLY WHAT I INTEND TO DO, DR. SONDHEIM! AS SOON AS A QUICK CYBERNETIC COMMAND--
"--SENDS A SQUADRON OF FLYING ANTS TO KEEP CROSS OCCUPIED--"
AGGH!
--LONG ENOUGH FOR ME TO USE THESE GAS CANISTERS ON MY BELT TO SHRINK OUT OF SIGHT.
AND NOW THAT I'M TOO SMALL TO BE SPOTTED, I SHOULDN'T HAVE ANY TROUBLE KNOCKING THE JOLLY PINK GIANT HERE ALL THE WAY TO JERSEY AND--

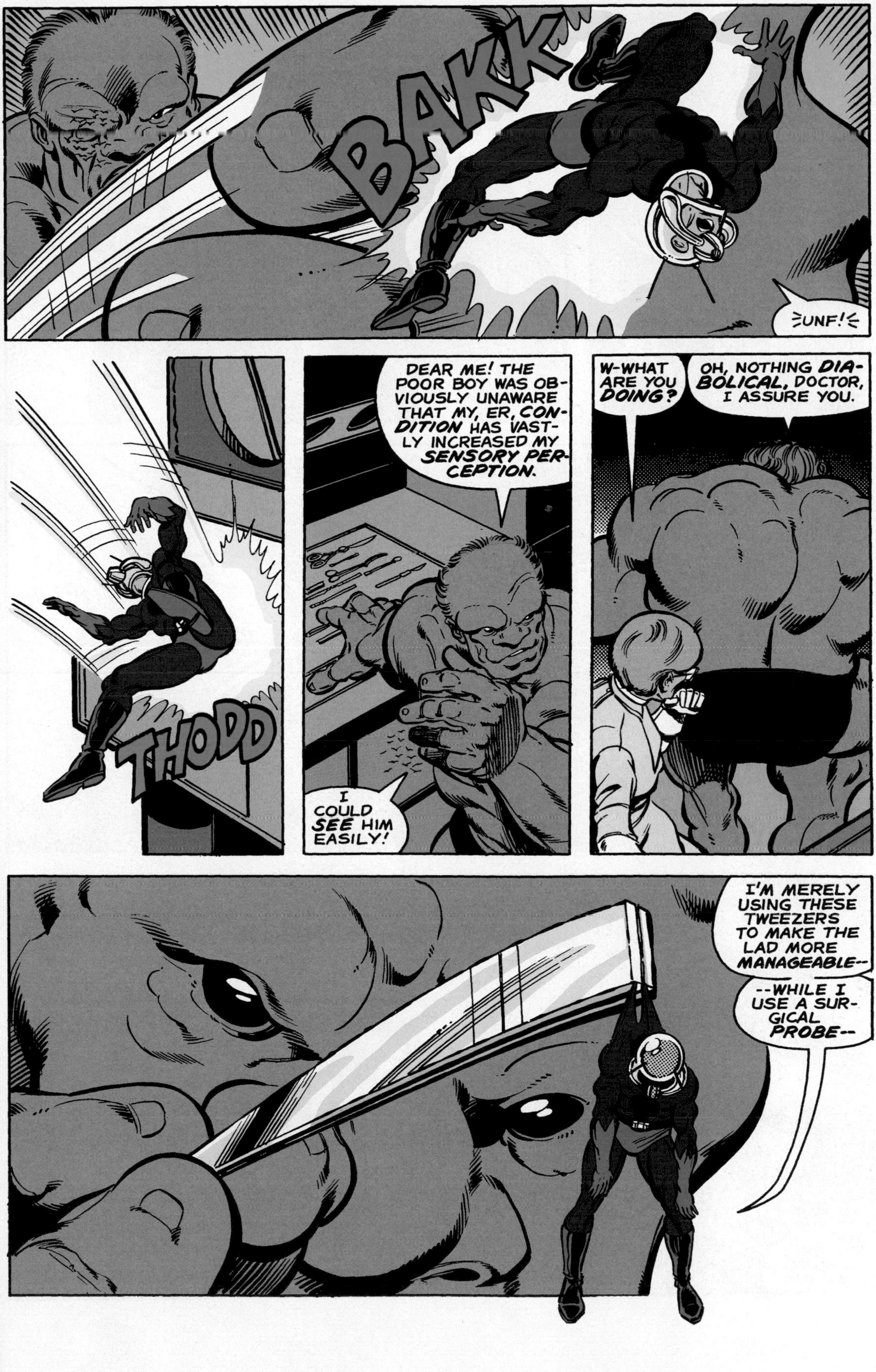
BAKK
UNF!
THODD
DEAR ME! THE POOR BOY WAS OBVIOUSLY UNAWARE THAT MY, ER, CONDITION HAS VASTLY INCREASED MY SENSORY PERCEPTION.
I COULD SEE HIM EASILY!
W-WHAT ARE YOU DOING?
OH, NOTHING DIABOLICAL, DOCTOR, I ASSURE YOU.
I'M MERELY USING THESE TWEEZERS TO MAKE THE LAD MORE MANAGEABLE--
--WHILE I USE A SURGICAL PROBE--

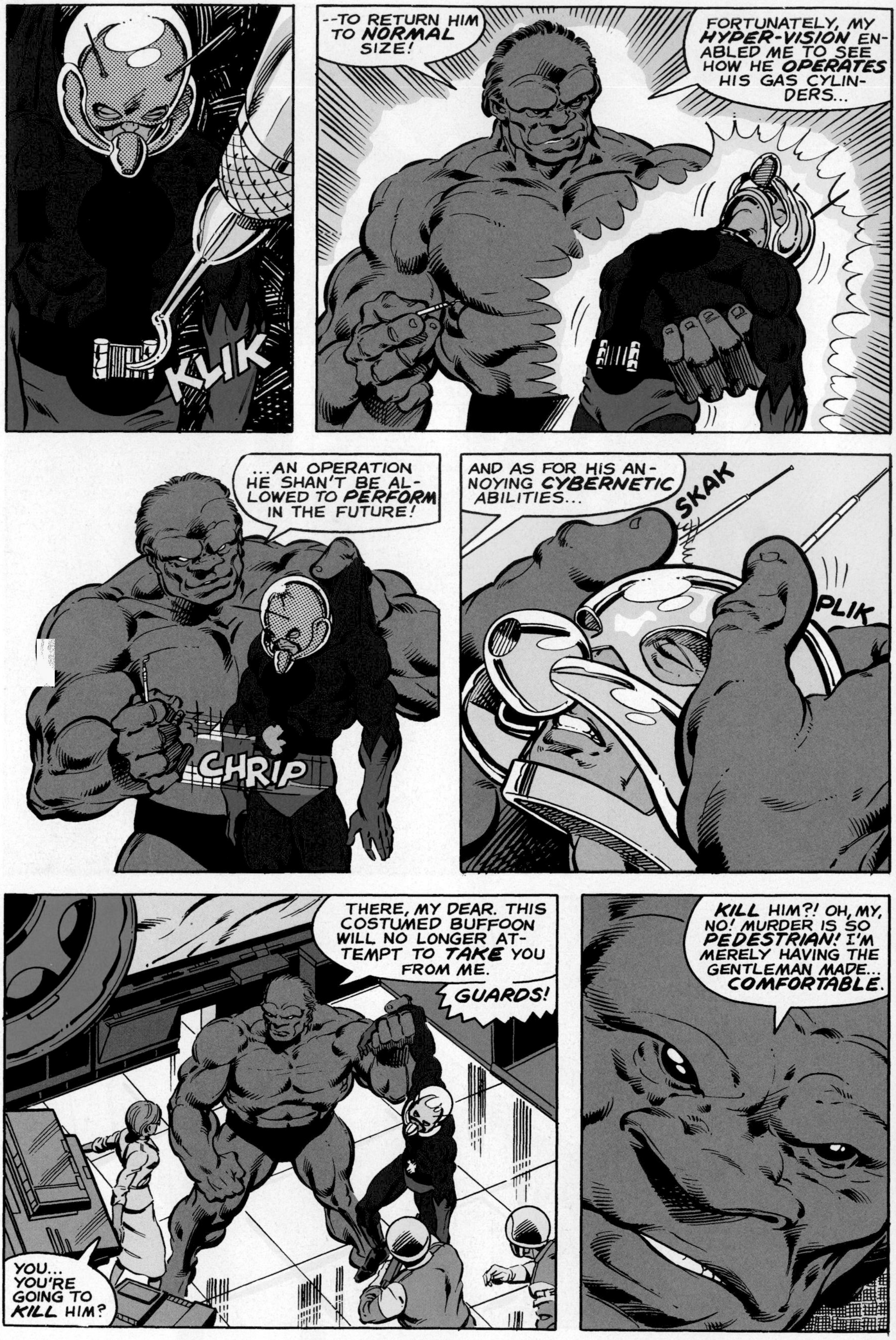
KLIK
--TO RETURN HIM TO NORMAL SIZE!
FORTUNATELY, MY HYPER-VISION ENABLED ME TO SEE HOW HE OPERATES HIS GAS CYLINDERS...
...AN OPERATION HE SHAN'T BE ALLOWED TO PERFORM IN THE FUTURE!
CHRIP
AND AS FOR HIS ANNOYING CYBERNETIC ABILITIES...
SKAK
PLIK
THERE, MY DEAR. THIS COSTUMED BUFFOON WILL NO LONGER ATTEMPT TO TAKE YOU FROM ME.
GUARDS!
YOU... YOU'RE GOING TO KILL HIM?
KILL HIM?! OH, MY, NO! MURDER IS SO PEDESTRIAN! I'M MERELY HAVING THE GENTLEMAN MADE... COMFORTABLE.

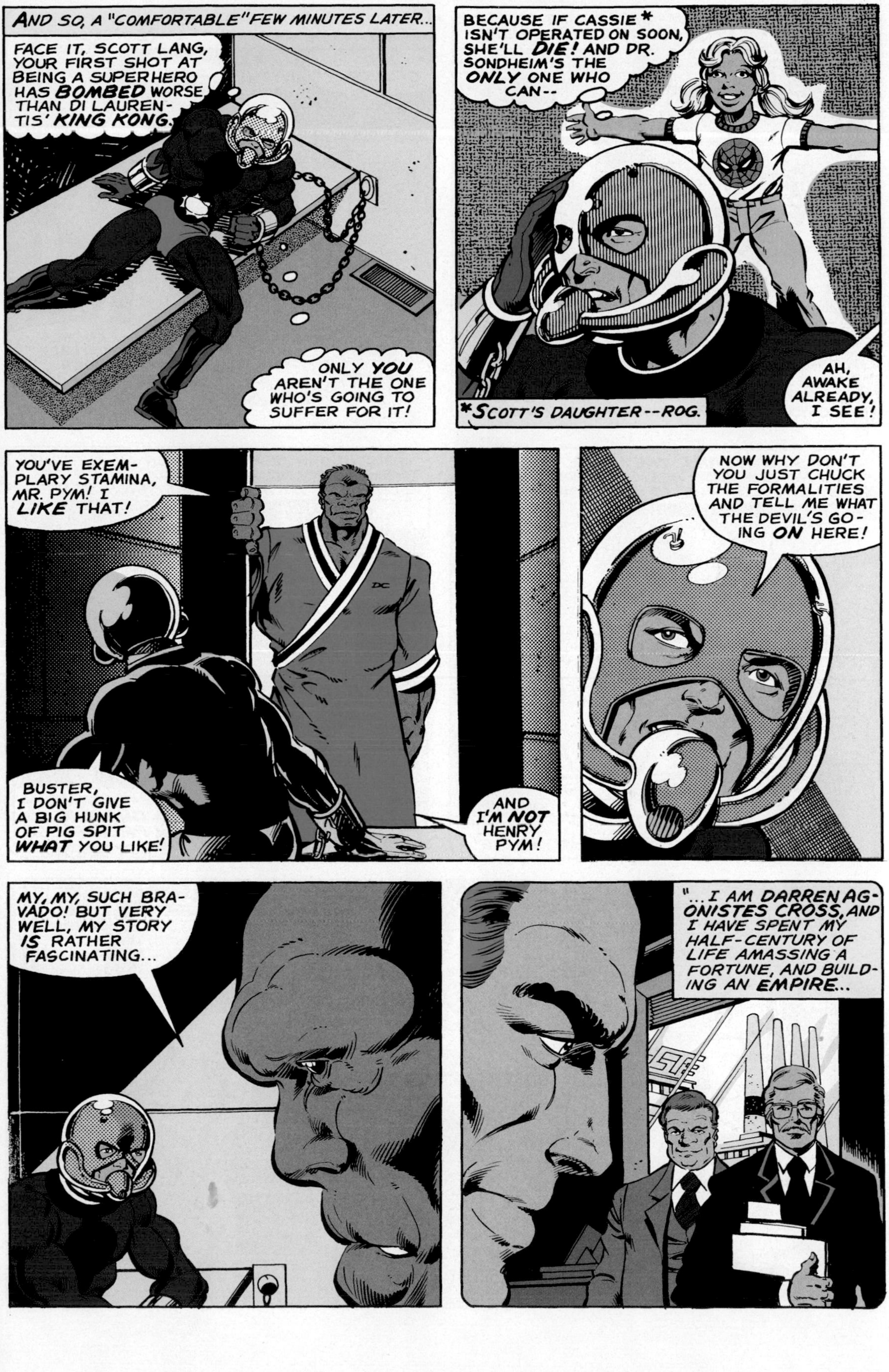
AND SO, A "COMFORTABLE" FEW MINUTES LATER...
FACE IT, SCOTT LANG, YOUR FIRST SHOT AT BEING A SUPERHERO HAS BOMBED WORSE THAN DI LAURENTIS' KING KONG.
ONLY YOU AREN'T THE ONE WHO'S GOING TO SUFFER FOR IT!
BECAUSE IF CASSIE* ISN'T OPERATED ON SOON, SHE'LL DIE! AND DR. SONDHEIM'S THE ONLY ONE WHO CAN--
*SCOTT'S DAUGHTER--ROG.
AH, AWAKE ALREADY, I SEE!
YOU'VE EXEMPLARY STAMINA, MR. PYM! I LIKE THAT!
BUSTER, I DON'T GIVE A BIG HUNK OF PIG SPIT WHAT YOU LIKE!
AND I'M NOT HENRY PYM!
NOW WHY DON'T YOU JUST CHUCK THE FORMALITIES AND TELL ME WHAT THE DEVIL'S GOING ON HERE!
MY, MY, SUCH BRAVADO! BUT VERY WELL, MY STORY IS RATHER FASCINATING...
"...I AM DARREN AGONISTES CROSS, AND I HAVE SPENT MY HALF-CENTURY OF LIFE AMASSING A FORTUNE, AND BUILDING AN EMPIRE...

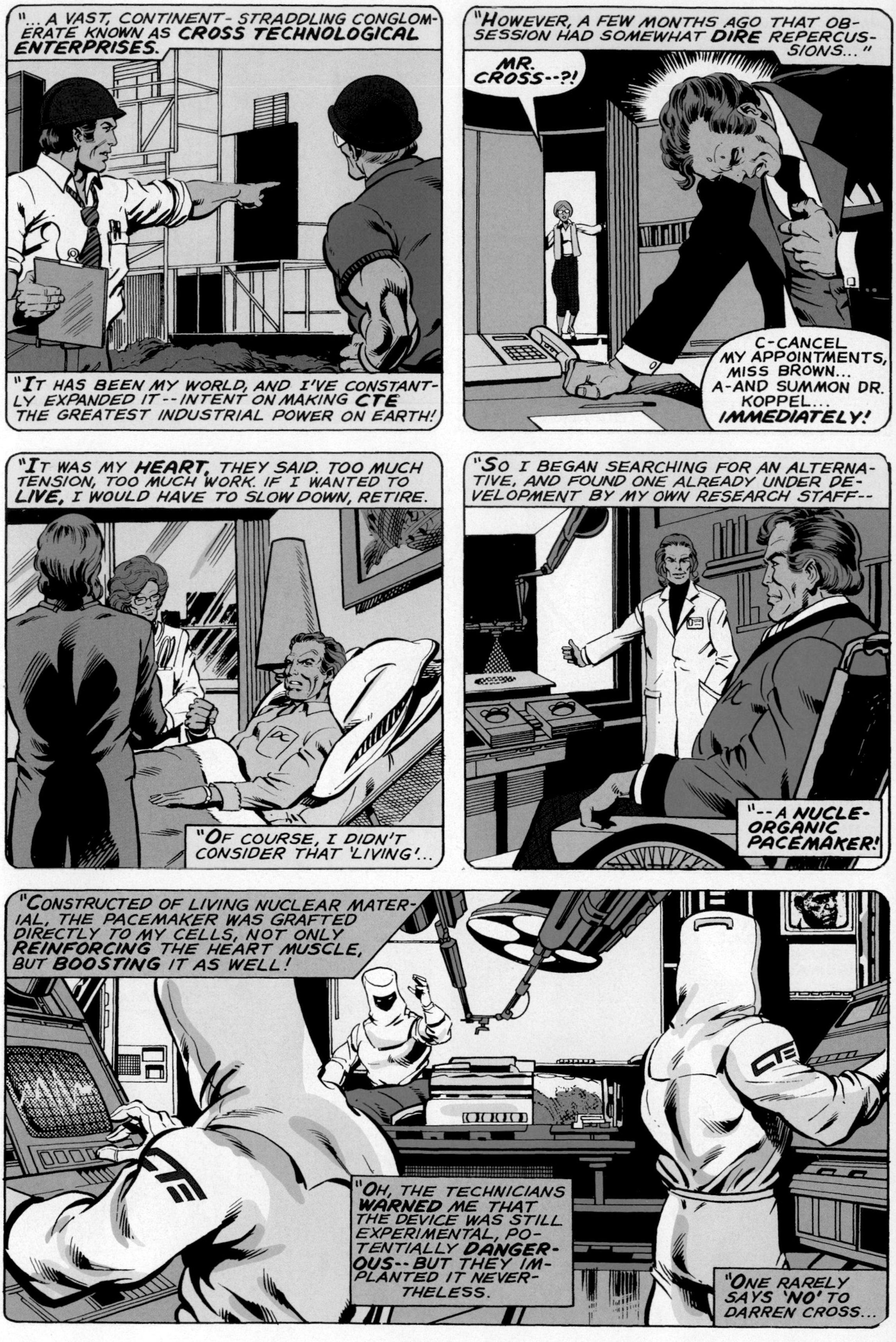
"... A VAST, CONTINENT-STRADDLING CONGLOMERATE KNOWN AS CROSS TECHNOLOGICAL ENTERPRISES.
"IT HAS BEEN MY WORLD, AND I'VE CONSTANTLY EXPANDED IT -- INTENT ON MAKING CTE THE GREATEST INDUSTRIAL POWER ON EARTH!
"HOWEVER, A FEW MONTHS AGO THAT OBSESSION HAD SOMEWHAT DIRE REPERCUSSIONS..."
MR. CROSS--?!
C-CANCEL MY APPOINTMENTS, MISS BROWN... A-AND SUMMON DR. KOPPEL... IMMEDIATELY!
"IT WAS MY HEART, THEY SAID. TOO MUCH TENSION, TOO MUCH WORK. IF I WANTED TO LIVE, I WOULD HAVE TO SLOW DOWN, RETIRE.
"OF COURSE, I DIDN'T CONSIDER THAT 'LIVING'...
"SO I BEGAN SEARCHING FOR AN ALTERNATIVE, AND FOUND ONE ALREADY UNDER DEVELOPMENT BY MY OWN RESEARCH STAFF--
"--A NUCLE-ORGANIC PACEMAKER!
"CONSTRUCTED OF LIVING NUCLEAR MATERIAL, THE PACEMAKER WAS GRAFTED DIRECTLY TO MY CELLS, NOT ONLY REINFORCING THE HEART MUSCLE, BUT BOOSTING IT AS WELL!
"OH, THE TECHNICIANS WARNED ME THAT THE DEVICE WAS STILL EXPERIMENTAL, POTENTIALLY DANGEROUS-- BUT THEY IMPLANTED IT NEVERTHELESS.
"ONE RARELY SAYS 'NO' TO DARREN CROSS...

"FOR A WHILE, THINGS WENT WELL, BUT THEN I BEGAN FEELING AN ODD... *PRESSURE* IN MY CHEST.

"IT WAS MOST UPSETTING--

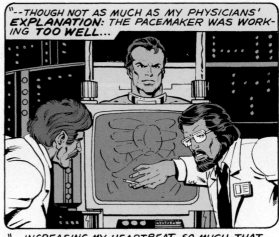

"--THOUGH NOT AS MUCH AS MY PHYSICIANS' *EXPLANATION:* THE PACEMAKER WAS WORKING *TOO WELL*...

"...INCREASING MY HEARTBEAT SO MUCH THAT MY ENTIRE CIRCULATORY SYSTEM WAS *ENLARGING!* AND THE NATURE OF THE BOOSTER MADE ITS REMOVAL CERTAIN DEATH!

"AT FIRST, I ALMOST *ENJOYED* THE INCREASED PERCEPTION AND STRENGTH MY ALTERED METABOLISM ENGENDERED. BUT THEN--

"--CAME THE RATHER UNFORTUNATE *COSMETIC* SIDE EFFECTS!

"SO IT WAS THAT I HAD GONE INTO *SECLUSION* BY THE TIME THE LEARNED MEN OF MEDICINE REVEALED THEIR *FINAL* DISCOVERY--

"--THAT THE ADDED STRAIN WAS *ERODING* MY HEART! NATURALLY, I HAD ANOTHER HEART *TRANSPLANTED*--ONLY THE PACEMAKER EXHAUSTED *THAT* ONE, TOO... AS WELL AS THE NEXT...

"...AND THE *NEXT*...

"THUS WAS IT DURING THE PERIOD OF DARK BROODING WHICH FOLLOWED THAT I LEARNED OF DR. SONDHEIM, AND HER ADVANCED TECHNIQUES IN CRITICAL FOCUS *LASER* SURGERY..."

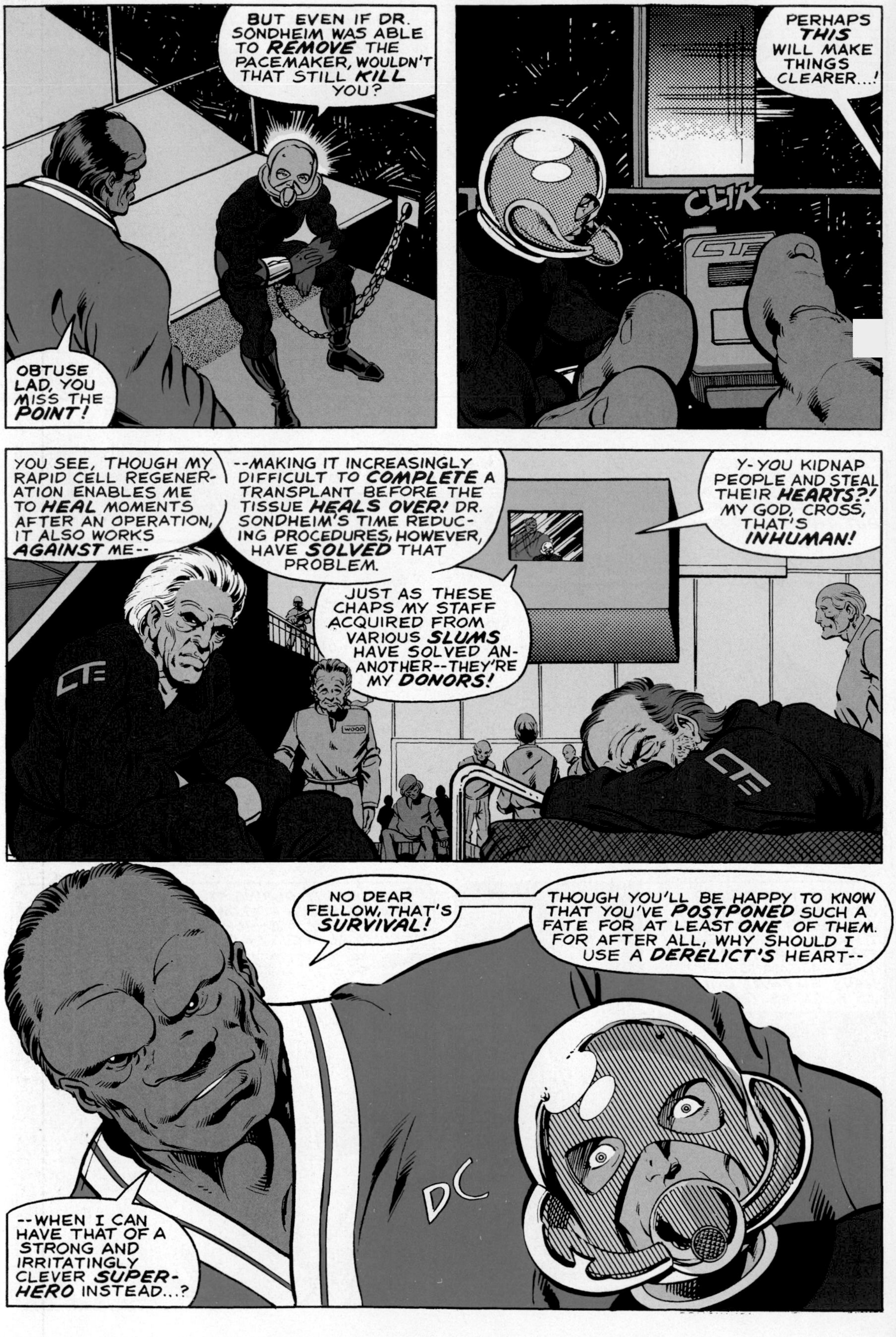
BUT EVEN IF DR. SONDHEIM WAS ABLE TO REMOVE THE PACEMAKER, WOULDN'T THAT STILL KILL YOU?
OBTUSE LAD, YOU MISS THE POINT!
PERHAPS THIS WILL MAKE THINGS CLEARER...!
CLIK
YOU SEE, THOUGH MY RAPID CELL REGENERATION ENABLES ME TO HEAL MOMENTS AFTER AN OPERATION, IT ALSO WORKS AGAINST ME--
--MAKING IT INCREASINGLY DIFFICULT TO COMPLETE A TRANSPLANT BEFORE THE TISSUE HEALS OVER! DR. SONDHEIM'S TIME REDUCING PROCEDURES, HOWEVER, HAVE SOLVED THAT PROBLEM.
JUST AS THESE CHAPS MY STAFF ACQUIRED FROM VARIOUS SLUMS HAVE SOLVED AN-ANOTHER--THEY'RE MY DONORS!
Y-YOU KIDNAP PEOPLE AND STEAL THEIR HEARTS?! MY GOD, CROSS, THAT'S INHUMAN!
NO DEAR FELLOW, THAT'S SURVIVAL!
THOUGH YOU'LL BE HAPPY TO KNOW THAT YOU'VE POSTPONED SUCH A FATE FOR AT LEAST ONE OF THEM. FOR AFTER ALL, WHY SHOULD I USE A DERELICT'S HEART--
--WHEN I CAN HAVE THAT OF A STRONG AND IRRITATINGLY CLEVER SUPER-HERO INSTEAD...?

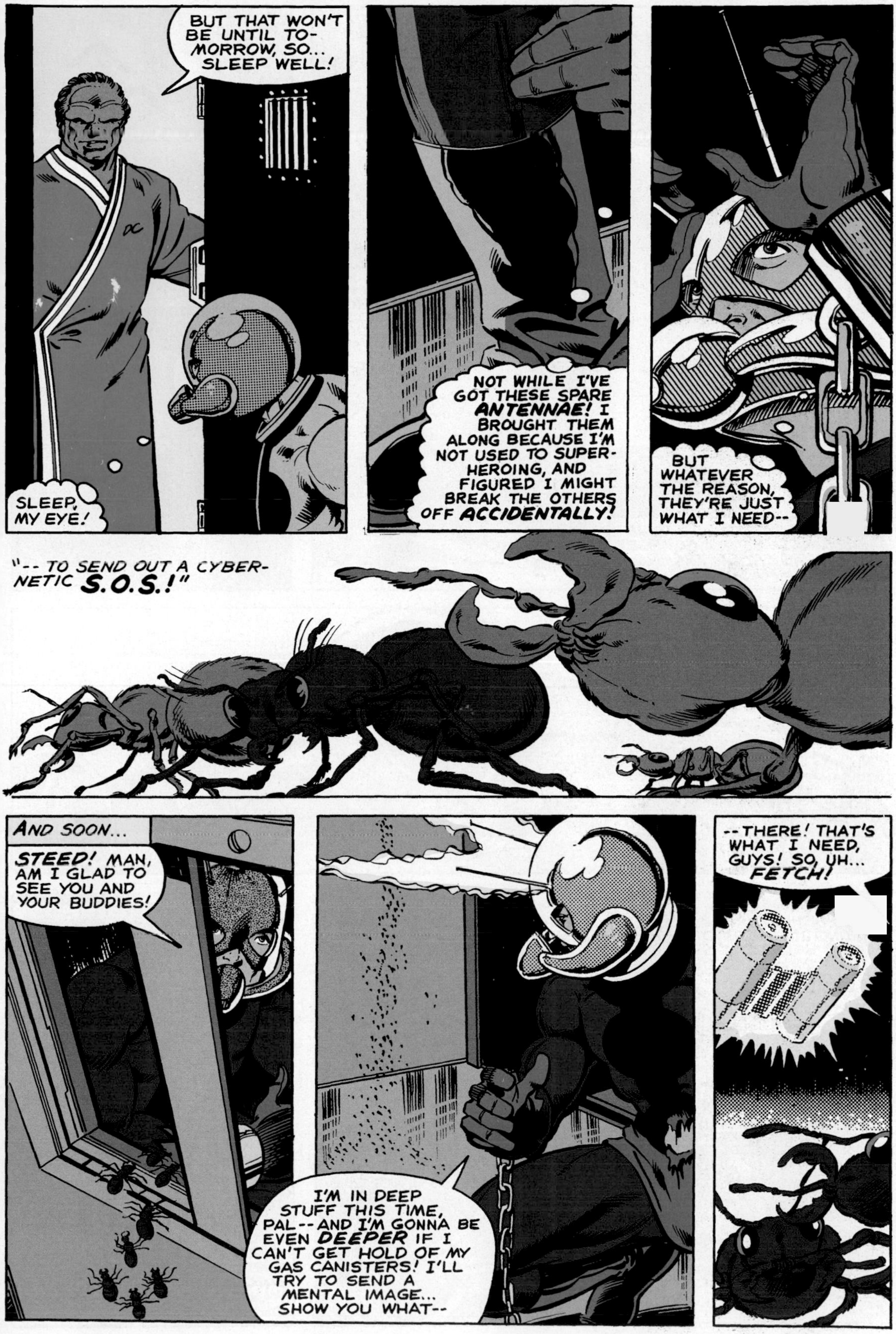

BUT THAT WON'T BE UNTIL TO-MORROW, SO... SLEEP WELL!
SLEEP, MY EYE!
NOT WHILE I'VE GOT THESE SPARE ANTENNAE! I BROUGHT THEM ALONG BECAUSE I'M NOT USED TO SUPER-HEROING, AND FIGURED I MIGHT BREAK THE OTHERS OFF ACCIDENTALLY!
BUT WHATEVER THE REASON, THEY'RE JUST WHAT I NEED--
"--TO SEND OUT A CYBER-NETIC S.O.S.!"
AND SOON...
STEED! MAN, AM I GLAD TO SEE YOU AND YOUR BUDDIES!
I'M IN DEEP STUFF THIS TIME, PAL--AND I'M GONNA BE EVEN DEEPER IF I CAN'T GET HOLD OF MY GAS CANISTERS! I'LL TRY TO SEND A MENTAL IMAGE... SHOW YOU WHAT--
--THERE! THAT'S WHAT I NEED, GUYS! SO, UH... FETCH!

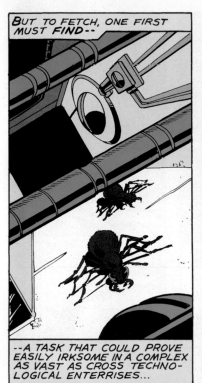

BUT TO FETCH, ONE FIRST MUST *FIND*--

THOUGH THE SIX-LEGGED SEARCHERS EVIDENCE NO SUCH FRUSTRATION--

--GOING ABOUT THEIR SCRU-TINY WITH A STOLID PRECISION THAT WOULD MAKE EX-CAT-BURGLAR SCOTT LANG PROUD--

--ESPECIALLY WHEN THEIR HOURS-CON-SUMING EXPLORATION PROVES *SUCCESSFUL!*

--A TASK THAT COULD PROVE EASILY IRKSOME IN A COMPLEX AS VAST AS CROSS TECHNO-LOGICAL ENTERRISES...

BUT BY THEN THE NIGHT IS NEARLY *OVER*. AND AS THE OBEDIENT ANTS STRUGGLE TO RETURN THE MASSIVE CANISTERS TO THEIR MASTER, THE QUESTION REMAINS: HAS THEIR SUCCESS COME IN--

--*TIME* SURE GOES FAST WHEN YOU'RE SHAKING IN YOUR BOOTS! I CAN'T BELIEVE IT'S ALMOST DAWN--AND I'VE GOT MY *LIFE* STAKED ON A BUNCH OF *BUGS!*

SOME-TIMES I--

--EH? WHAT'S THAT?

Y'KNOW, ERNIE, I'M REALLY GLAD MR. CROSS DECIDED TO PUT THE *SNUFFS* ON THAT ANT-MAN.

EVER SINCE THE LITTLE TWERP *DECKED* ME, I BEEN WANTIN' TO *STEP* ON 'IM MYSELF!

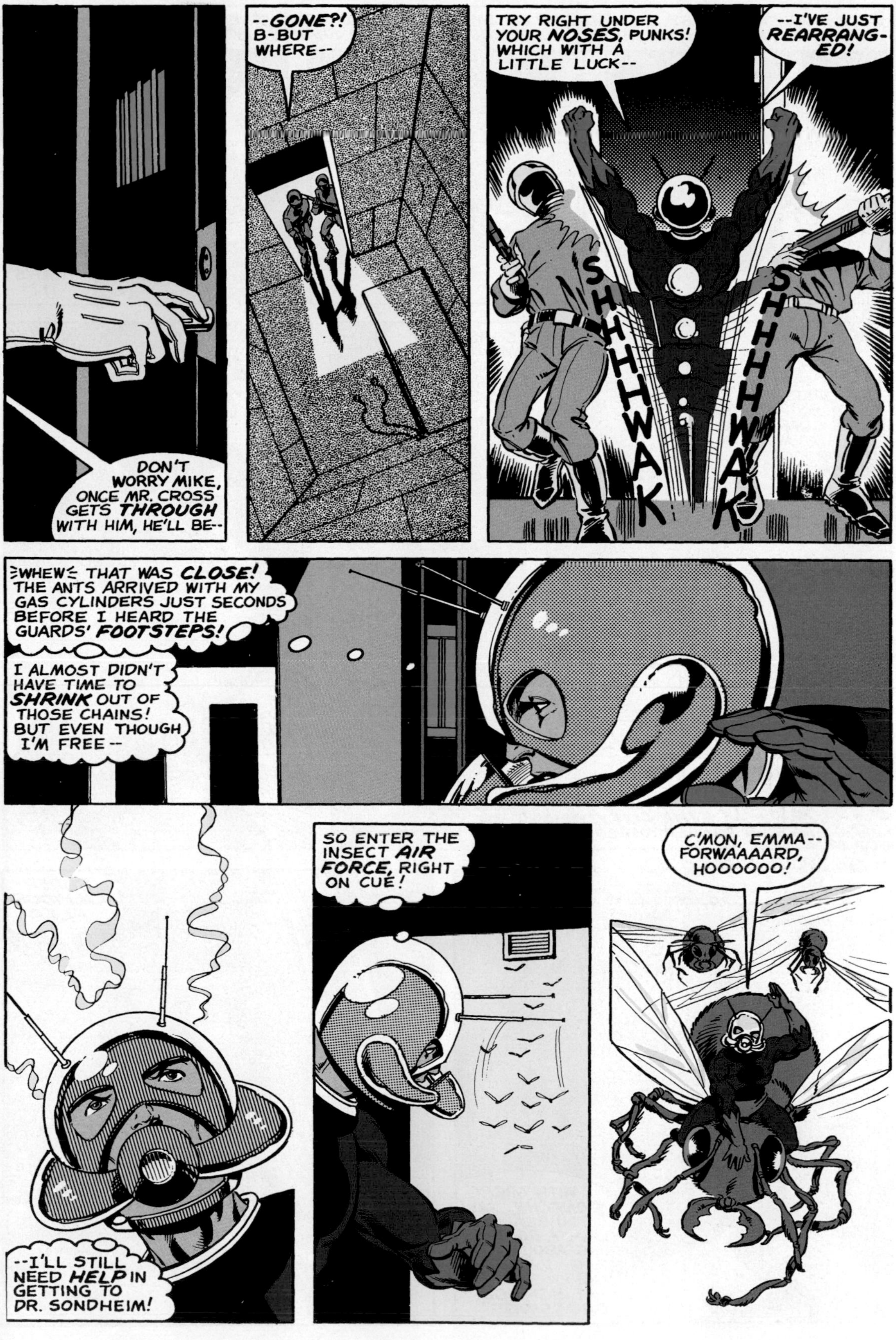
DON'T WORRY MIKE, ONCE MR. CROSS GETS THROUGH WITH HIM, HE'LL BE--
--GONE?! B-BUT WHERE--
TRY RIGHT UNDER YOUR NOSES, PUNKS! WHICH WITH A LITTLE LUCK--
--I'VE JUST REARRANG-ED!
SHHHHWAK
SHHHHWAK
WHEW THAT WAS CLOSE! THE ANTS ARRIVED WITH MY GAS CYLINDERS JUST SECONDS BEFORE I HEARD THE GUARDS' FOOTSTEPS!
I ALMOST DIDN'T HAVE TIME TO SHRINK OUT OF THOSE CHAINS! BUT EVEN THOUGH I'M FREE--
--I'LL STILL NEED HELP IN GETTING TO DR. SONDHEIM!
SO ENTER THE INSECT AIR FORCE, RIGHT ON CUE!
C'MON, EMMA-- FORWAAAARD, HOOOOOO!

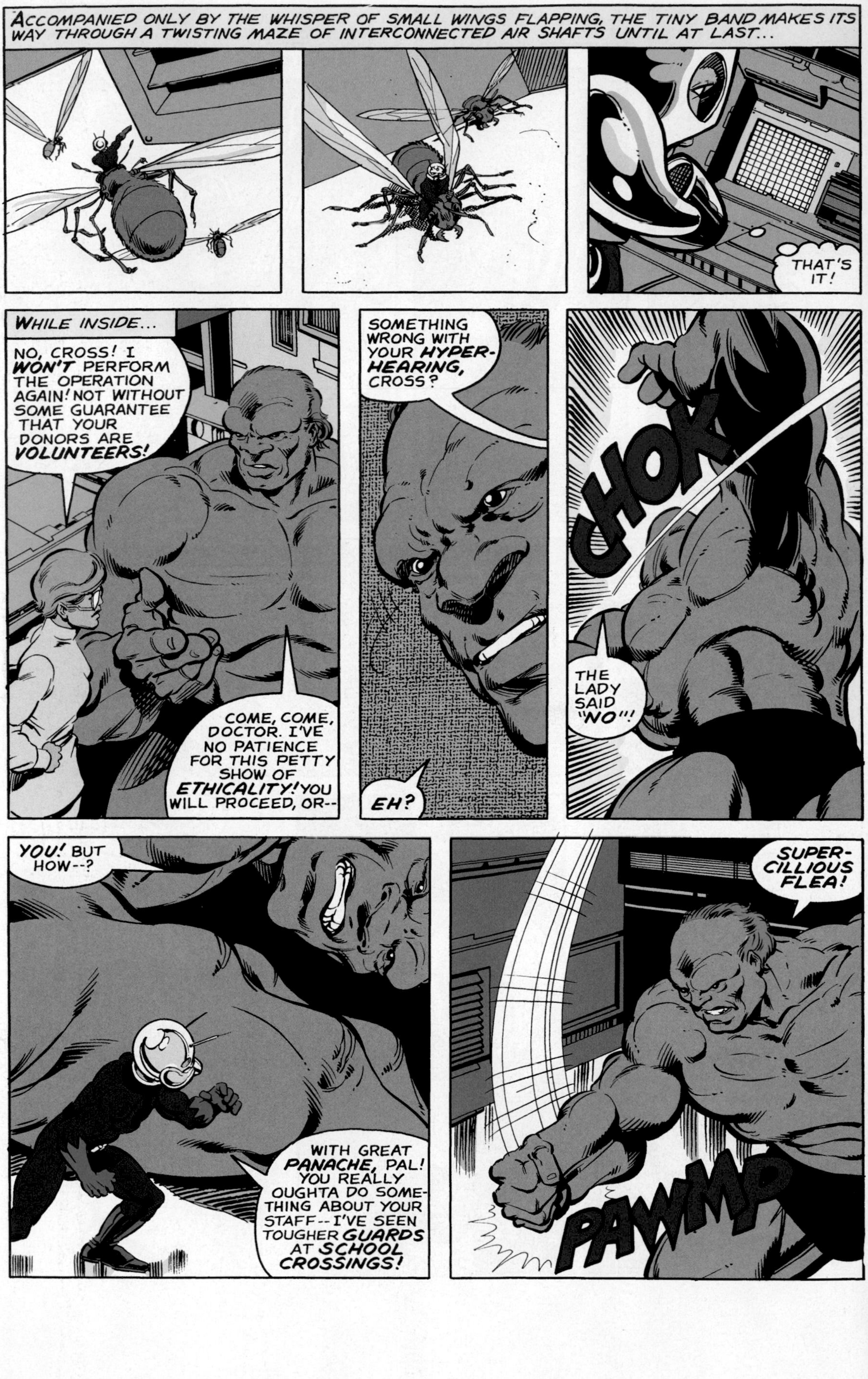

ACCOMPANIED ONLY BY THE WHISPER OF SMALL WINGS FLAPPING, THE TINY BAND MAKES ITS WAY THROUGH A TWISTING MAZE OF INTERCONNECTED AIR SHAFTS UNTIL AT LAST...
THAT'S IT!
WHILE INSIDE...
NO, CROSS! I WON'T PERFORM THE OPERATION AGAIN! NOT WITHOUT SOME GUARANTEE THAT YOUR DONORS ARE VOLUNTEERS!
COME, COME, DOCTOR. I'VE NO PATIENCE FOR THIS PETTY SHOW OF ETHICALITY! YOU WILL PROCEED, OR--
SOMETHING WRONG WITH YOUR HYPER-HEARING, CROSS?
EH?
CHOK
THE LADY SAID "NO"!
YOU! BUT HOW--?
WITH GREAT PANACHE, PAL! YOU REALLY OUGHTA DO SOME-THING ABOUT YOUR STAFF-- I'VE SEEN TOUGHER GUARDS AT SCHOOL CROSSINGS!
SUPER-CILLIOUS FLEA!
PAWMP

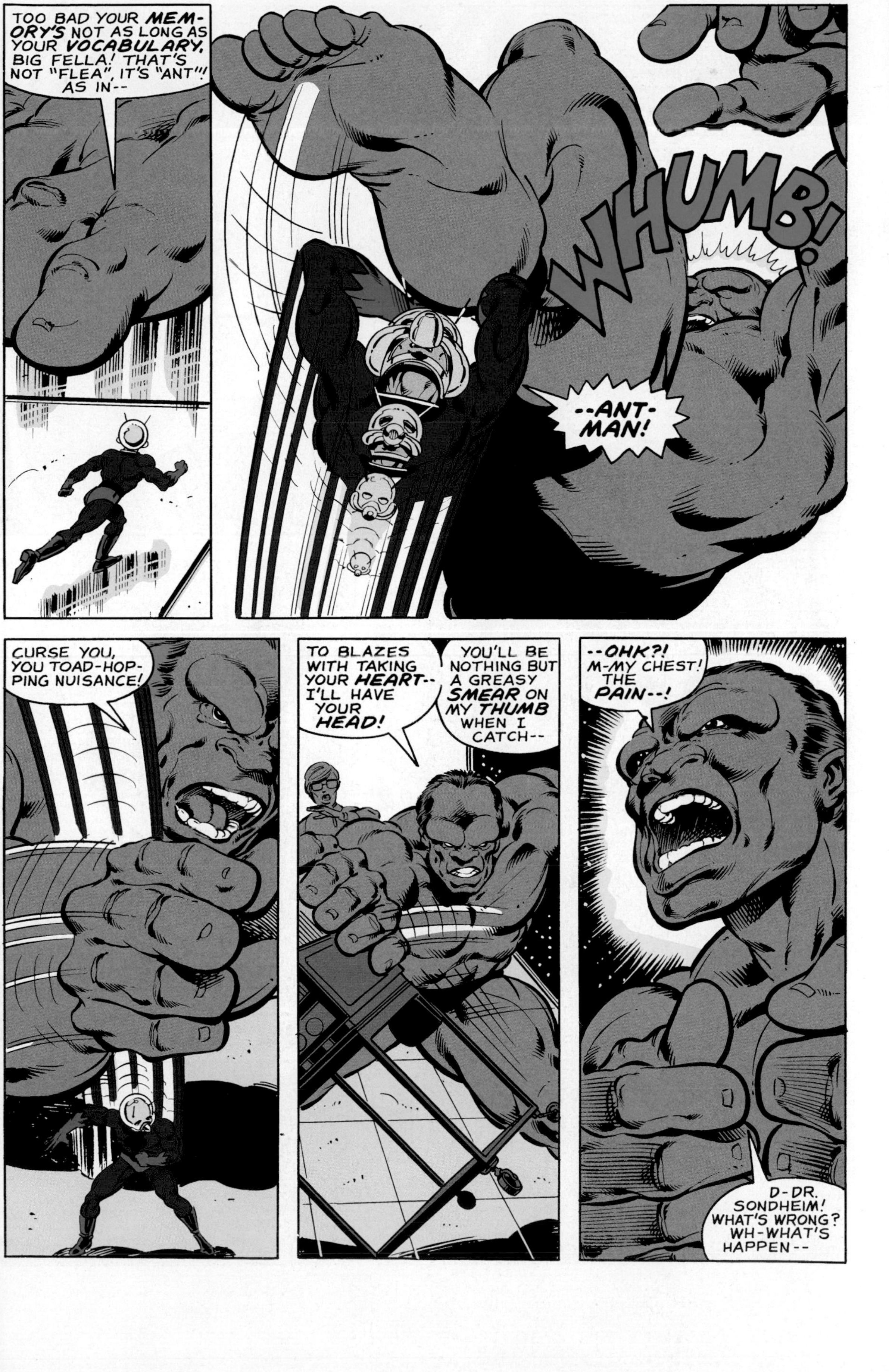
TOO BAD YOUR MEMORY'S NOT AS LONG AS YOUR VOCABULARY, BIG FELLA! THAT'S NOT "FLEA", IT'S "ANT"! AS IN--
WHUMB!
--ANT-MAN!
CURSE YOU, YOU TOAD-HOPPING NUISANCE!
TO BLAZES WITH TAKING YOUR HEART-- I'LL HAVE YOUR HEAD!
YOU'LL BE NOTHING BUT A GREASY SMEAR ON MY THUMB WHEN I CATCH--
--OHK?! M-MY CHEST! THE PAIN--!
D-DR. SONDHEIM! WHAT'S WRONG? WH-WHAT'S HAPPEN--

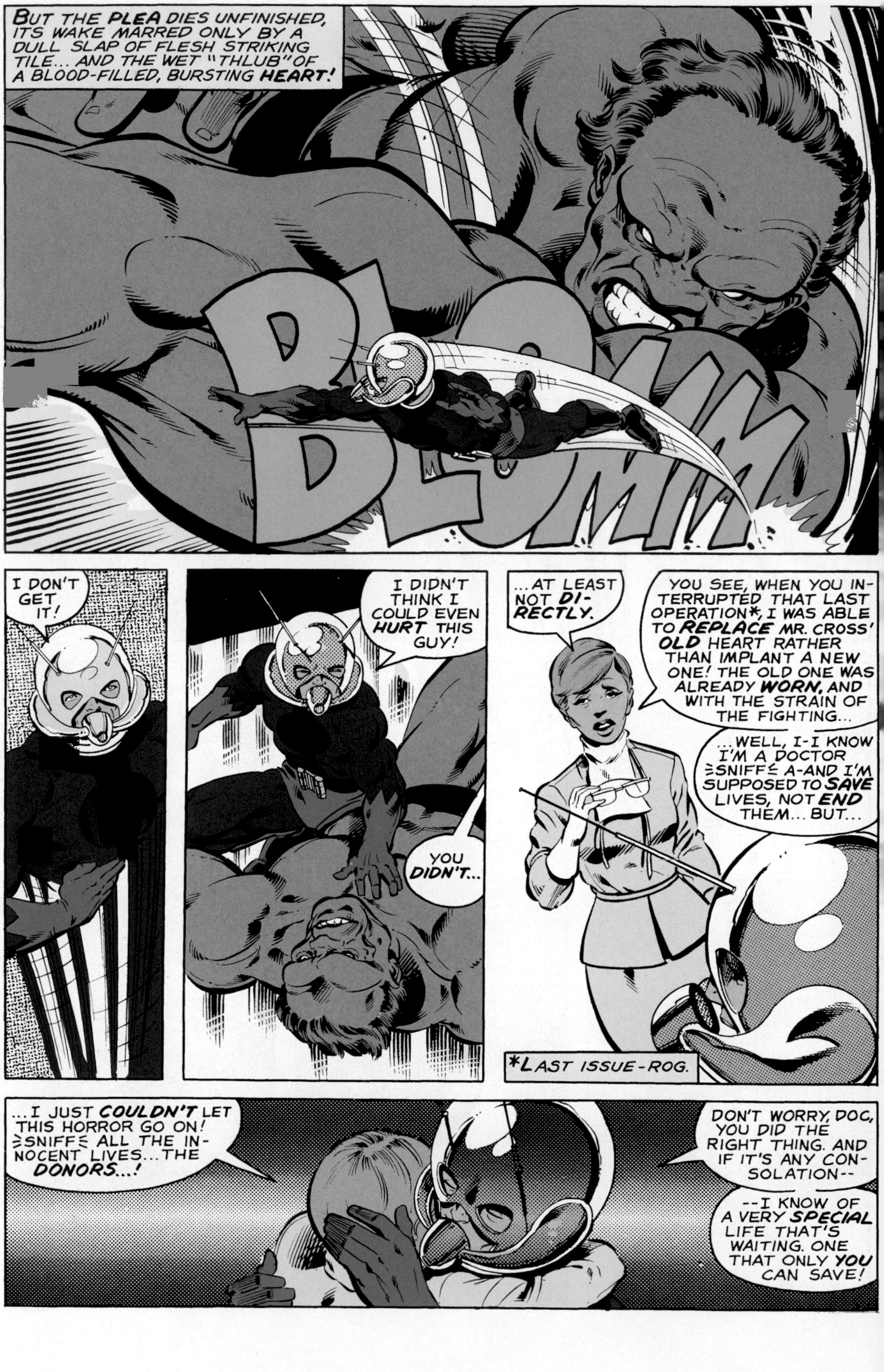

BUT THE PLEA DIES UNFINISHED, ITS WAKE MARRED ONLY BY A DULL SLAP OF FLESH STRIKING TILE... AND THE WET "THLUB" OF A BLOOD-FILLED, BURSTING HEART!
BLOOMM
I DON'T GET IT!
I DIDN'T THINK I COULD EVEN HURT THIS GUY!
YOU DIDN'T...
...AT LEAST NOT DI-RECTLY.
YOU SEE, WHEN YOU IN-TERRUPTED THAT LAST OPERATION*, I WAS ABLE TO REPLACE MR. CROSS' OLD HEART RATHER THAN IMPLANT A NEW ONE! THE OLD ONE WAS ALREADY WORN, AND WITH THE STRAIN OF THE FIGHTING...
...WELL, I-I KNOW I'M A DOCTOR ≷SNIFF≶ A-AND I'M SUPPOSED TO SAVE LIVES, NOT END THEM... BUT...
*LAST ISSUE-ROG.
...I JUST COULDN'T LET THIS HORROR GO ON! ≷SNIFF≶ ALL THE IN-NOCENT LIVES... THE DONORS...!
DON'T WORRY, DOC, YOU DID THE RIGHT THING. AND IF IT'S ANY CON-SOLATION--
--I KNOW OF A VERY SPECIAL LIFE THAT'S WAITING. ONE THAT ONLY YOU CAN SAVE!

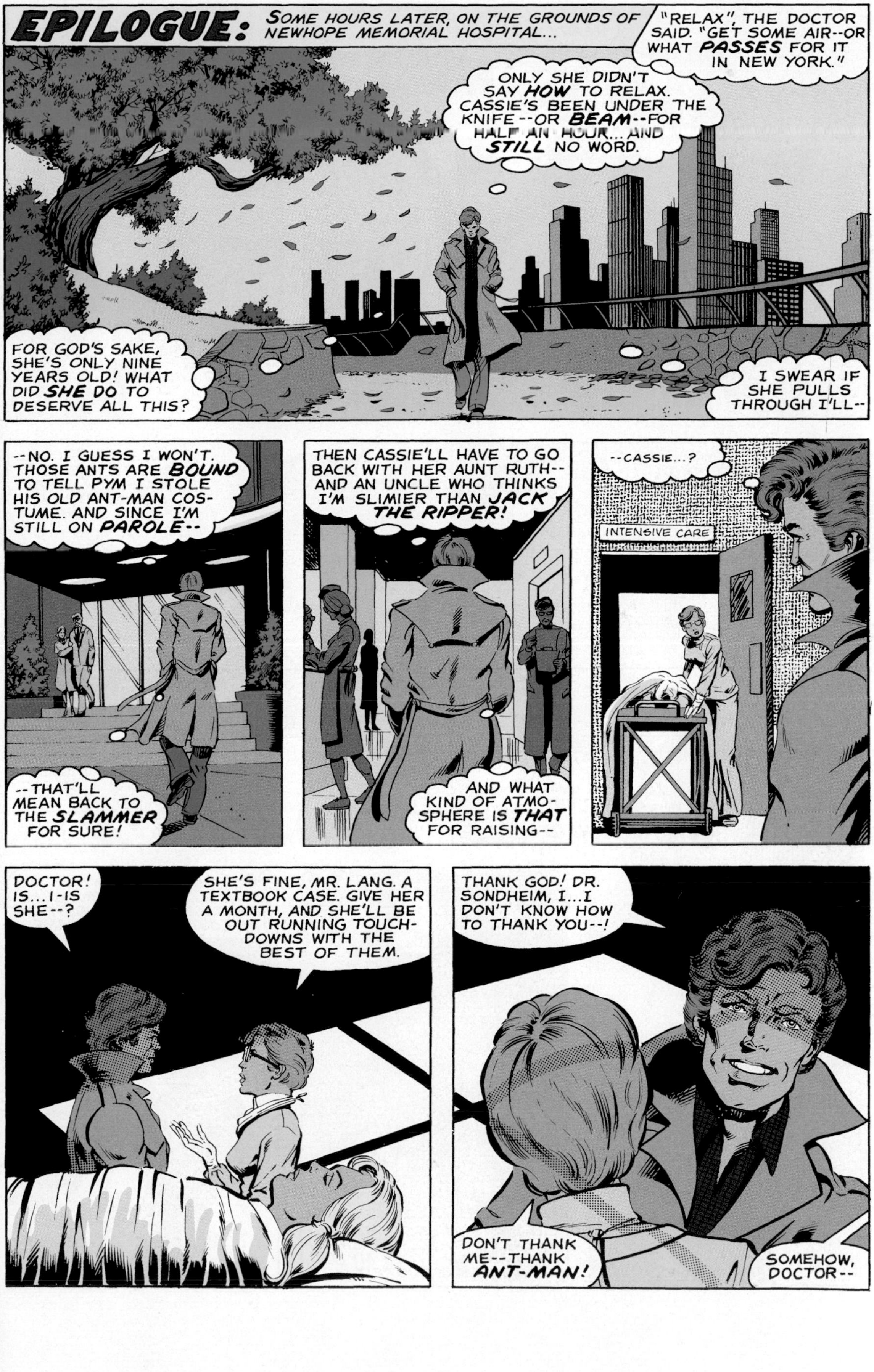
EPILOGUE:
SOME HOURS LATER, ON THE GROUNDS OF NEWHOPE MEMORIAL HOSPITAL...
"RELAX", THE DOCTOR SAID. "GET SOME AIR--OR WHAT PASSES FOR IT IN NEW YORK."
ONLY SHE DIDN'T SAY HOW TO RELAX. CASSIE'S BEEN UNDER THE KNIFE--OR BEAM--FOR HALF AN HOUR... AND STILL NO WORD.
FOR GOD'S SAKE, SHE'S ONLY NINE YEARS OLD! WHAT DID SHE DO TO DESERVE ALL THIS?
I SWEAR IF SHE PULLS THROUGH I'LL--
--NO. I GUESS I WON'T. THOSE ANTS ARE BOUND TO TELL PYM I STOLE HIS OLD ANT-MAN COSTUME. AND SINCE I'M STILL ON PAROLE--
--THAT'LL MEAN BACK TO THE SLAMMER FOR SURE!
THEN CASSIE'LL HAVE TO GO BACK WITH HER AUNT RUTH--AND AN UNCLE WHO THINKS I'M SLIMIER THAN JACK THE RIPPER!
AND WHAT KIND OF ATMOSPHERE IS THAT FOR RAISING--
--CASSIE...?
INTENSIVE CARE
DOCTOR! IS...I-IS SHE--?
SHE'S FINE, MR. LANG. A TEXTBOOK CASE. GIVE HER A MONTH, AND SHE'LL BE OUT RUNNING TOUCHDOWNS WITH THE BEST OF THEM.
THANK GOD! DR. SONDHEIM, I...I DON'T KNOW HOW TO THANK YOU--!
DON'T THANK ME--THANK ANT-MAN!
SOMEHOW, DOCTOR--

--I THINK HE'S ALREADY *GOTTEN* HIS REWARD!

WHA--YELLOW-JACKET! B-BUT, AREN'T YOU--?

NOT ANY MORE. I GAVE UP MY *ANT-MAN* IDENTITY SOME TIME AGO.

NOW, IF YOU'LL EXCUSE US, I'D LIKE TO HAVE A FEW WORDS WITH MR. LANG. IN PRIVATE.

UH, SURE. I'LL GO CHECK CASSIE INTO POST-OP. 'BYE.

OKAY, PYM, IF *YOU'RE* HERE, THEN YOU MUST KNOW THE WHOLE STORY. I'LL COME ALONG PEACEFULLY.

HEY, CALM DOWN. YOU'RE NOT GOING *ANYWHERE!*

I...I'M *NOT?*

NO. I DIDN'T COME HERE TO *ARREST* YOU-- I CAME TO *CONGRATULATE* YOU!

HUH? B-BUT WHY--?

SIMPLE: WHEN YOU BROKE INTO MY PLACE IN CRESSKILL, YOU NEUTRALIZED *MOST* OF THE DETECTION NETWORK--

--BUT NOT *ALL* OF IT!

"SO I WAS IN COSTUME AND READY WHEN YOU REACHED THE LAB AND STOLE MY OLD *ANT-MAN* OUTFIT.

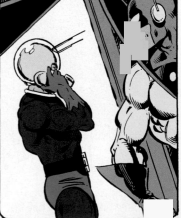

"CURIOUS AS TO WHY YOU'D *WANT* IT, I FOLLOWED YOU HOME...WATCHED YOU TEST OUT THE COSTUME'S HARDWARE...

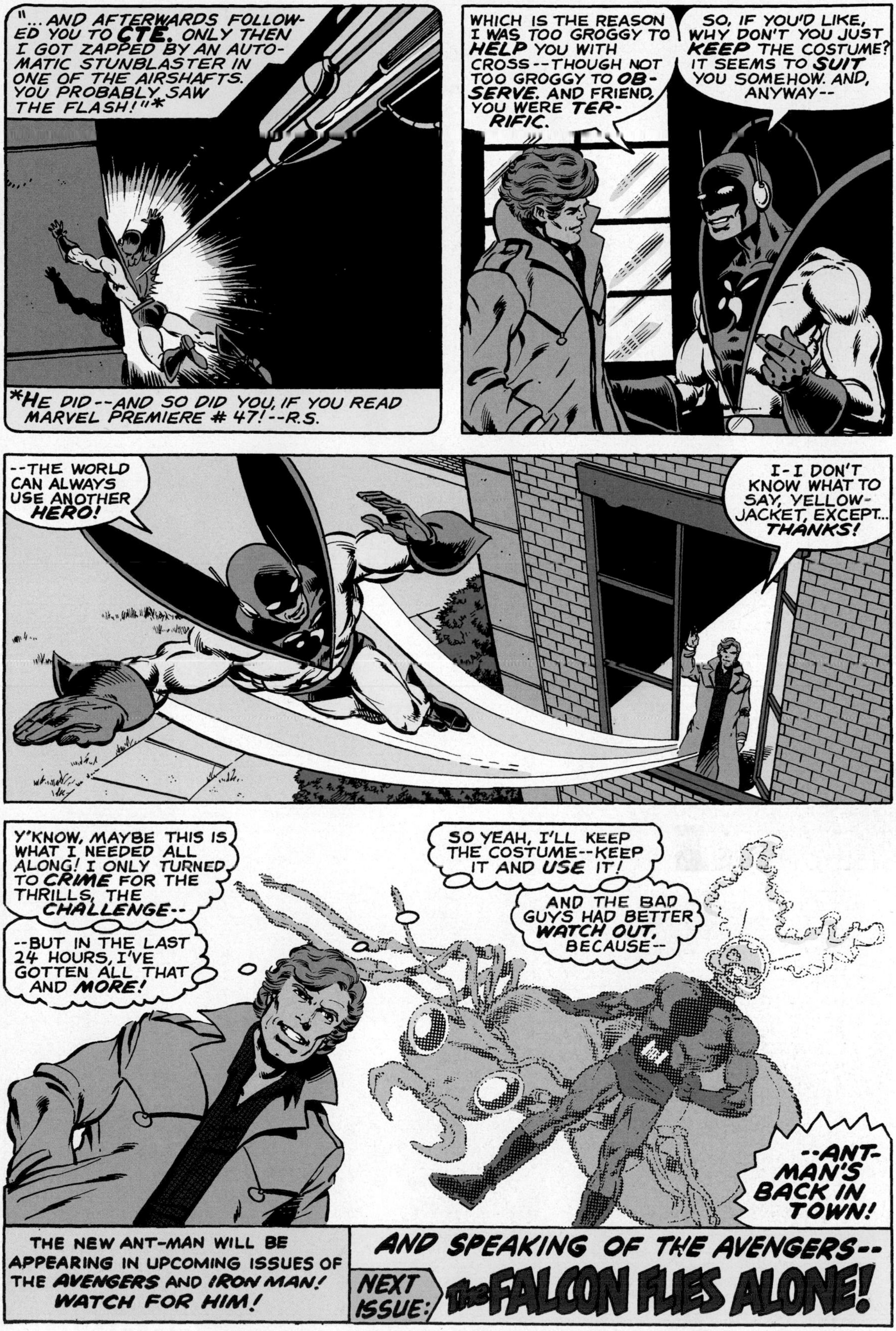
"...AND AFTERWARDS FOLLOWED YOU TO CTE. ONLY THEN I GOT ZAPPED BY AN AUTOMATIC STUNBLASTER IN ONE OF THE AIRSHAFTS. YOU PROBABLY SAW THE FLASH!"*
*HE DID--AND SO DID YOU, IF YOU READ MARVEL PREMIERE #47!--R.S.
WHICH IS THE REASON I WAS TOO GROGGY TO HELP YOU WITH CROSS--THOUGH NOT TOO GROGGY TO OBSERVE. AND FRIEND, YOU WERE TERRIFIC.
SO, IF YOU'D LIKE, WHY DON'T YOU JUST KEEP THE COSTUME? IT SEEMS TO SUIT YOU SOMEHOW. AND, ANYWAY--
--THE WORLD CAN ALWAYS USE ANOTHER HERO!
I-I DON'T KNOW WHAT TO SAY, YELLOWJACKET, EXCEPT... THANKS!
Y'KNOW, MAYBE THIS IS WHAT I NEEDED ALL ALONG! I ONLY TURNED TO CRIME FOR THE THRILLS, THE CHALLENGE--
--BUT IN THE LAST 24 HOURS, I'VE GOTTEN ALL THAT AND MORE!
SO YEAH, I'LL KEEP THE COSTUME--KEEP IT AND USE IT!
AND THE BAD GUYS HAD BETTER WATCH OUT, BECAUSE--
--ANT-MAN'S BACK IN TOWN!
THE NEW ANT-MAN WILL BE APPEARING IN UPCOMING ISSUES OF THE AVENGERS AND IRON MAN! WATCH FOR HIM!
AND SPEAKING OF THE AVENGERS--
NEXT ISSUE: The FALCON FLIES ALONE!

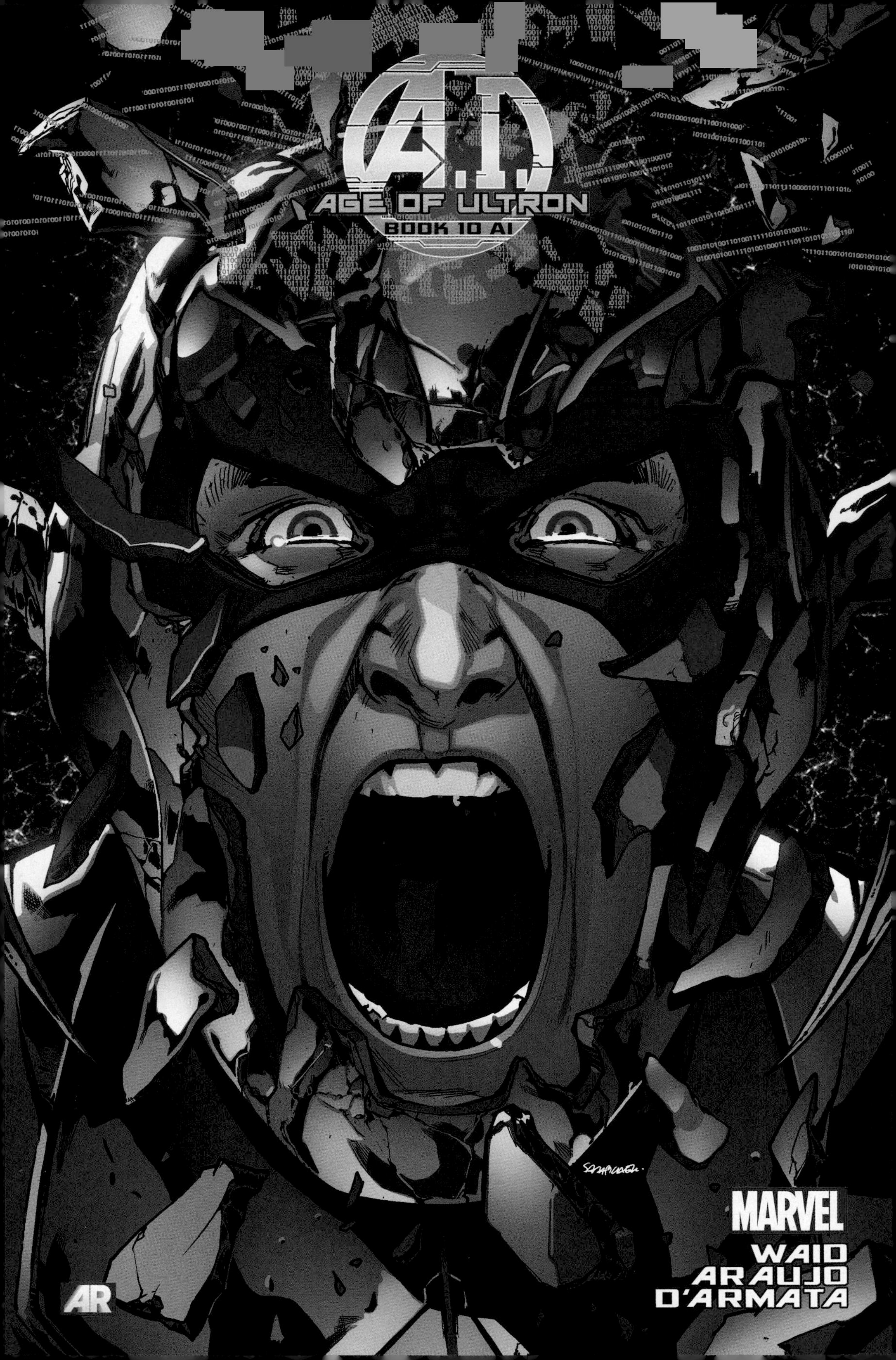
A.I.
AGE OF ULTRON
BOOK 10 AI
MARVEL
WAID
ARAUJO
D'ARMATA
AR

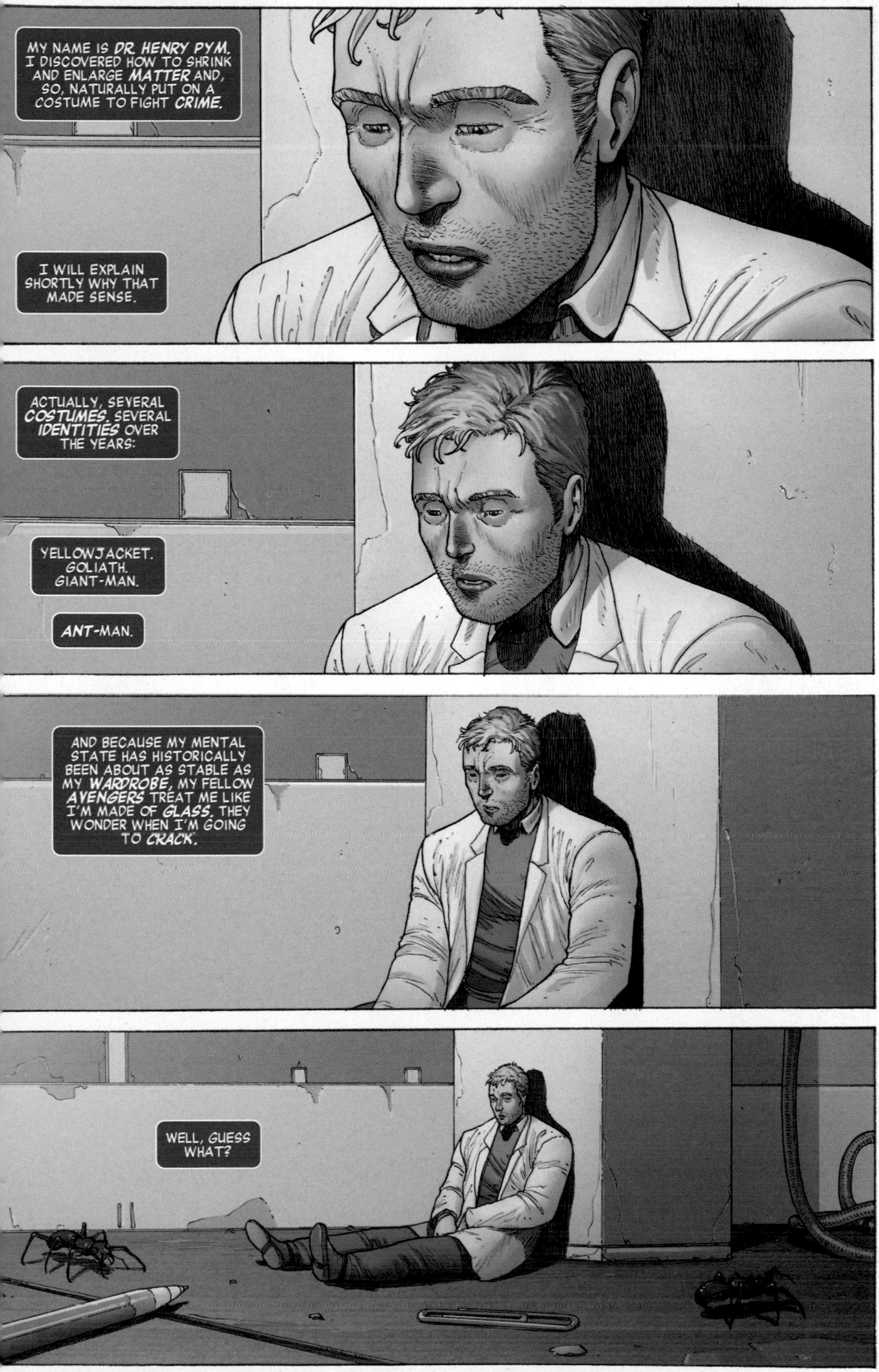

MY NAME IS DR. HENRY PYM. I DISCOVERED HOW TO SHRINK AND ENLARGE MATTER AND, SO, NATURALLY PUT ON A COSTUME TO FIGHT CRIME.
I WILL EXPLAIN SHORTLY WHY THAT MADE SENSE.
ACTUALLY, SEVERAL COSTUMES. SEVERAL IDENTITIES OVER THE YEARS:
YELLOWJACKET. GOLIATH. GIANT-MAN.
ANT-MAN.
AND BECAUSE MY MENTAL STATE HAS HISTORICALLY BEEN ABOUT AS STABLE AS MY WARDROBE, MY FELLOW AVENGERS TREAT ME LIKE I'M MADE OF GLASS. THEY WONDER WHEN I'M GOING TO CRACK.
WELL, GUESS WHAT?

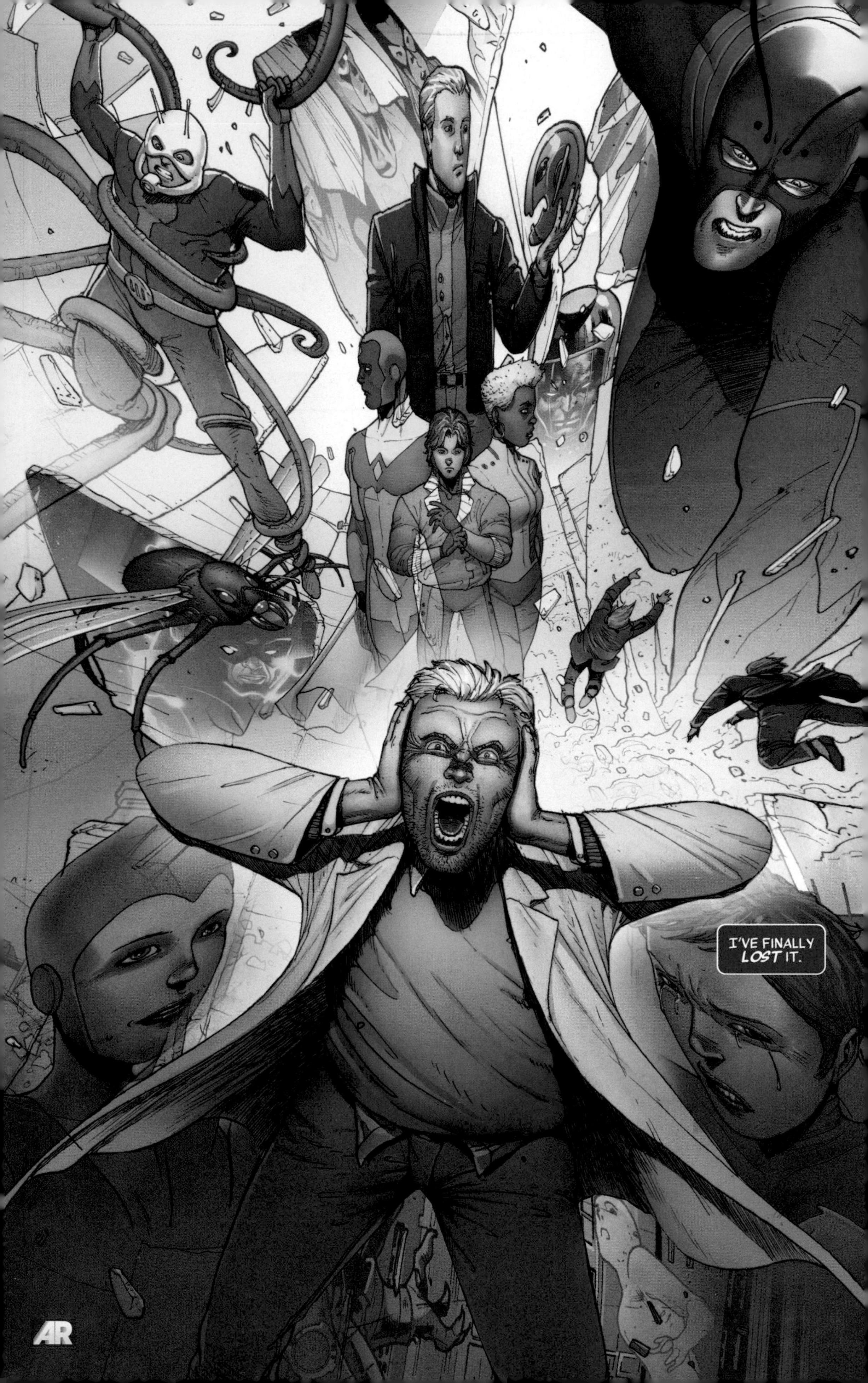
I'VE FINALLY LOST IT.

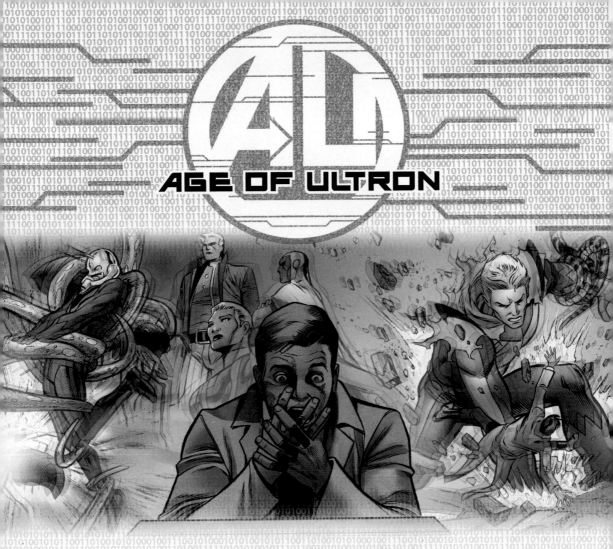

AGE OF ULTRON

PREVIOUSLY IN AGE OF ULTRON...

HANK PYM WAS A PIONEER WHEN IT CAME TO BEING A SUPER HERO. AS THE SIZE-CHANGING ANT-MAN, HE WAS A FOUNDING MEMBER OF THE AVENGERS. ON THEIR FIRST CASE, IT WAS HANK'S BRAINSTORM THAT WON THE DAY AGAINST LOKI--PERHAPS HIS FINEST MOMENT. SINCE THEN, HE HAS ADOPTED A VARIETY OF HEROIC IDENTITIES AND PERSONAS, BUT IN HIS HEART OF HEARTS, HE KNOWS IT NEVER GOT BETTER THAN BEATING LOKI.

HANK PYM WAS A PIONEER AS A SCIENTIST. AMONG HIS EARLY CREATIONS WAS AN ARTIFICIAL INTELLIGENCE CALLED ULTRON, WHICH WAS TOO SMART FOR ANYONE'S OWN GOOD. SENTIENT AND MALEVOLENT, THE ULTIMATE REBELLIOUS CHILD, THE ROBOTIC ULTRON WENT ROGUE AND BATTLED THE AVENGERS TIME AND AGAIN.

HANK PYM WAS A PIONEER AT GENOCIDE. ULTRON EVENTUALLY SUCCEEDED IN ERADICATING THE HUMAN RACE, AND ONLY A MAD TIME-TRAVEL GAMBLE BY THE AVENGERS--ALONG WITH AN ASSIST FROM A YOUNGER HANK PYM--MANAGED TO CHANGE HISTORY AND ELIMINATE ULTRON ONCE AND FOR ALL. ALONG THE WAY, HANK GOT A PEEK INTO AN ALTERNATE REALITY WHERE HE'D BEEN KILLED BEFORE HE WAS EVER ABLE TO INVENT ULTRON.

IT WAS NOT A WONDERFUL LIFE....

MARK WAID WRITER

ANDRE LIMA ARAUJO ARTIST

FRANK D'ARMATA COLOR ARTIST

VC'S CLAYTON COWLES LETTERER

SARA PICHELLI & MARTE GRACIA COVER ART

PAOLO RIVERA VARIANT COVER

JAKE THOMAS ASSISTANT EDITOR

LAUREN SANKOVITCH EDITOR

TOM BREVOORT EXECUTIVE EDITOR

AXEL ALONSO EDITOR IN CHIEF

JOE QUESADA CHIEF CREATIVE OFFICER

DAN BUCKLEY PUBLISHER

ALAN FINE EXECUTIVE PRODUCER

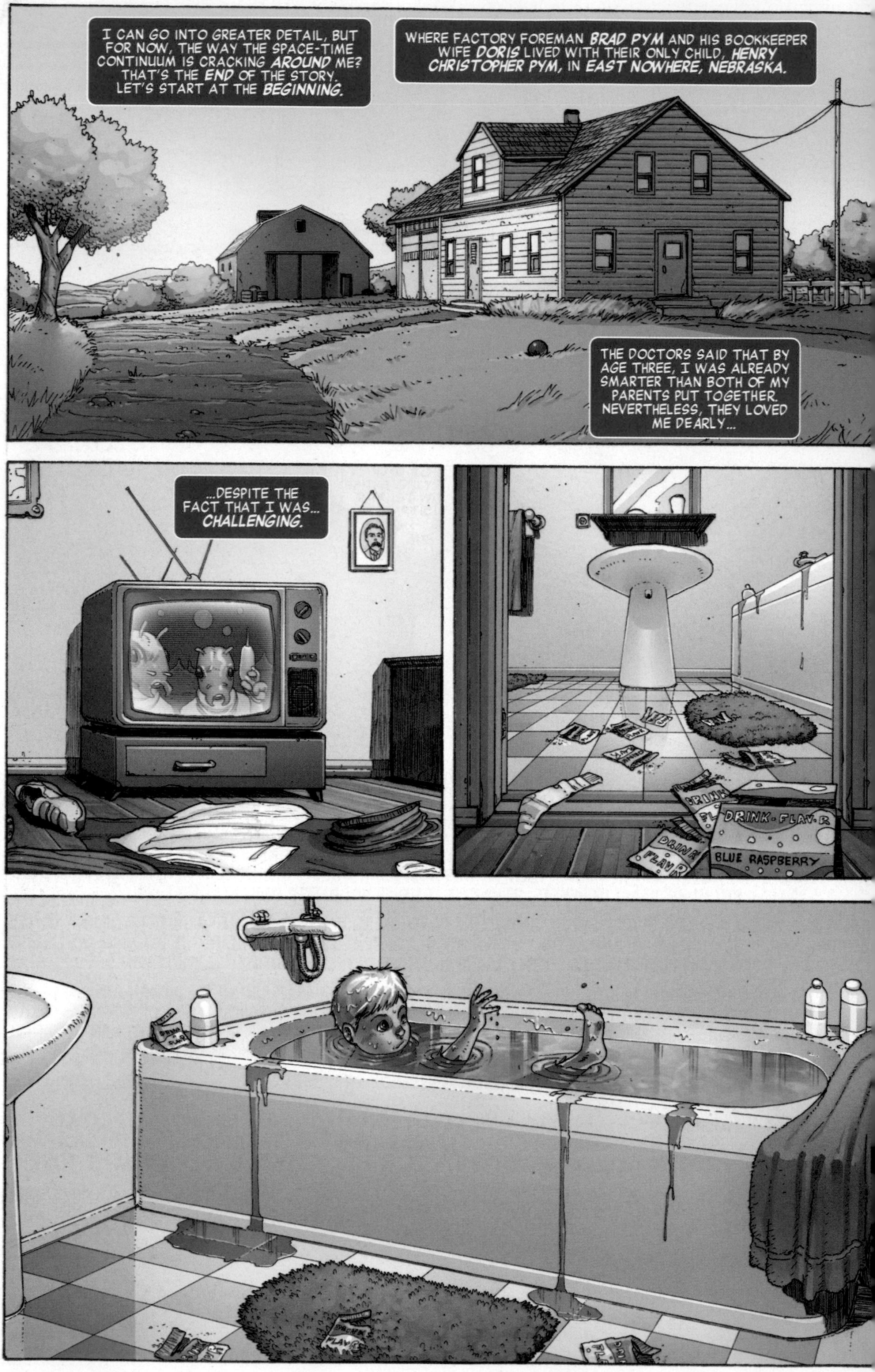
I CAN GO INTO GREATER DETAIL, BUT FOR NOW, THE WAY THE SPACE-TIME CONTINUUM IS CRACKING AROUND ME? THAT'S THE END OF THE STORY. LET'S START AT THE BEGINNING.
WHERE FACTORY FOREMAN BRAD PYM AND HIS BOOKKEEPER WIFE DORIS LIVED WITH THEIR ONLY CHILD, HENRY CHRISTOPHER PYM, IN EAST NOWHERE, NEBRASKA.
THE DOCTORS SAID THAT BY AGE THREE, I WAS ALREADY SMARTER THAN BOTH OF MY PARENTS PUT TOGETHER. NEVERTHELESS, THEY LOVED ME DEARLY...
...DESPITE THE FACT THAT I WAS... CHALLENGING.
DRINK-FLAV-R
BLUE RASPBERRY

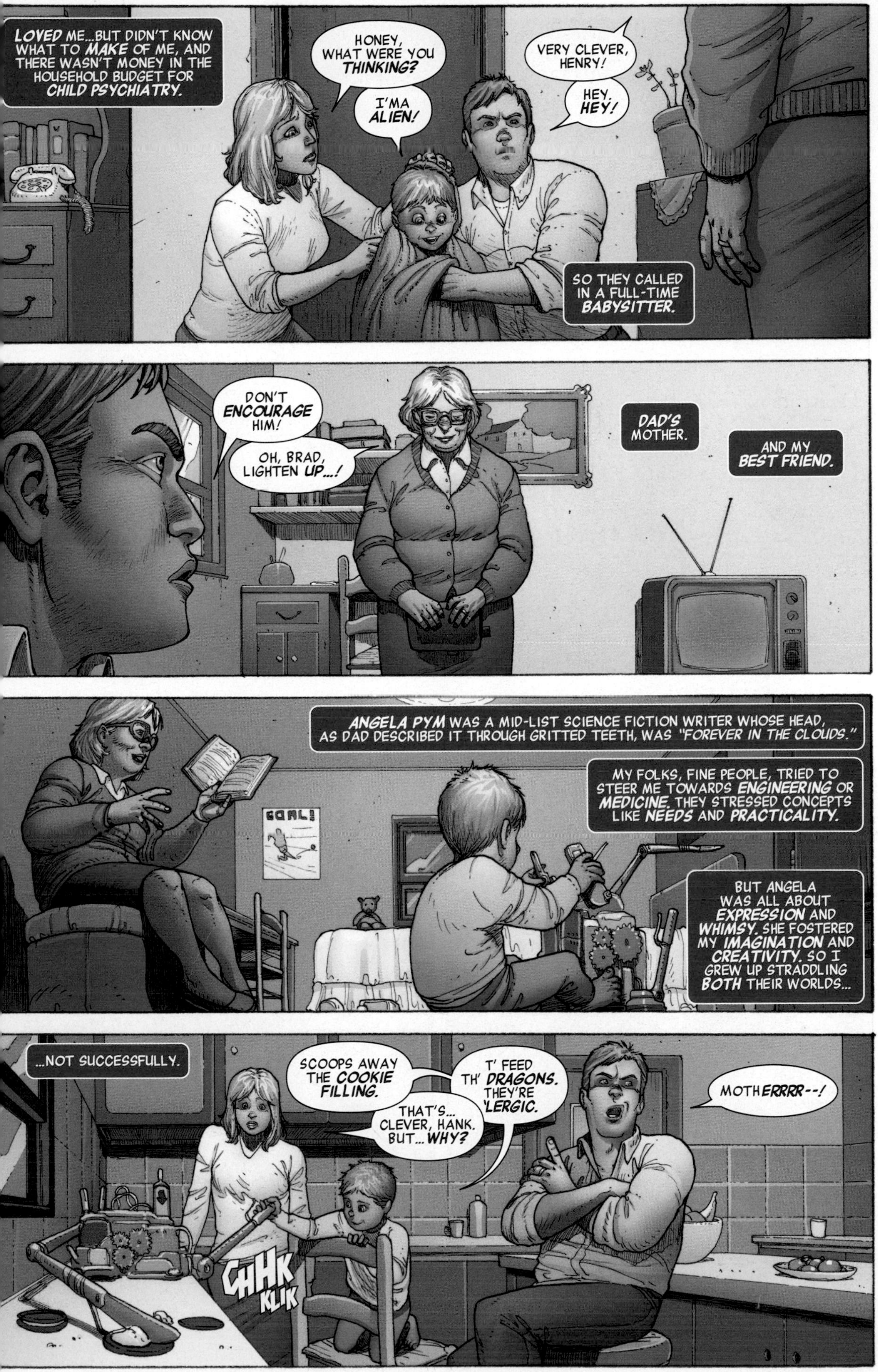
LOVED ME...BUT DIDN'T KNOW WHAT TO MAKE OF ME, AND THERE WASN'T MONEY IN THE HOUSEHOLD BUDGET FOR CHILD PSYCHIATRY.
HONEY, WHAT WERE YOU THINKING?
I'M A ALIEN!
VERY CLEVER, HENRY!
HEY. HEY!
SO THEY CALLED IN A FULL-TIME BABYSITTER.
DON'T ENCOURAGE HIM!
OH, BRAD, LIGHTEN UP...!
DAD'S MOTHER.
AND MY BEST FRIEND.
ANGELA PYM WAS A MID-LIST SCIENCE FICTION WRITER WHOSE HEAD, AS DAD DESCRIBED IT THROUGH GRITTED TEETH, WAS "FOREVER IN THE CLOUDS."
MY FOLKS, FINE PEOPLE, TRIED TO STEER ME TOWARDS ENGINEERING OR MEDICINE. THEY STRESSED CONCEPTS LIKE NEEDS AND PRACTICALITY.
GOAL!
BUT ANGELA WAS ALL ABOUT EXPRESSION AND WHIMSY. SHE FOSTERED MY IMAGINATION AND CREATIVITY. SO I GREW UP STRADDLING BOTH THEIR WORLDS...
...NOT SUCCESSFULLY.
SCOOPS AWAY THE COOKIE FILLING.
T' FEED TH' DRAGONS. THEY'RE 'LERGIC.
THAT'S... CLEVER, HANK. BUT... WHY?
MOTHERRRR--!
CHHK
KLIK

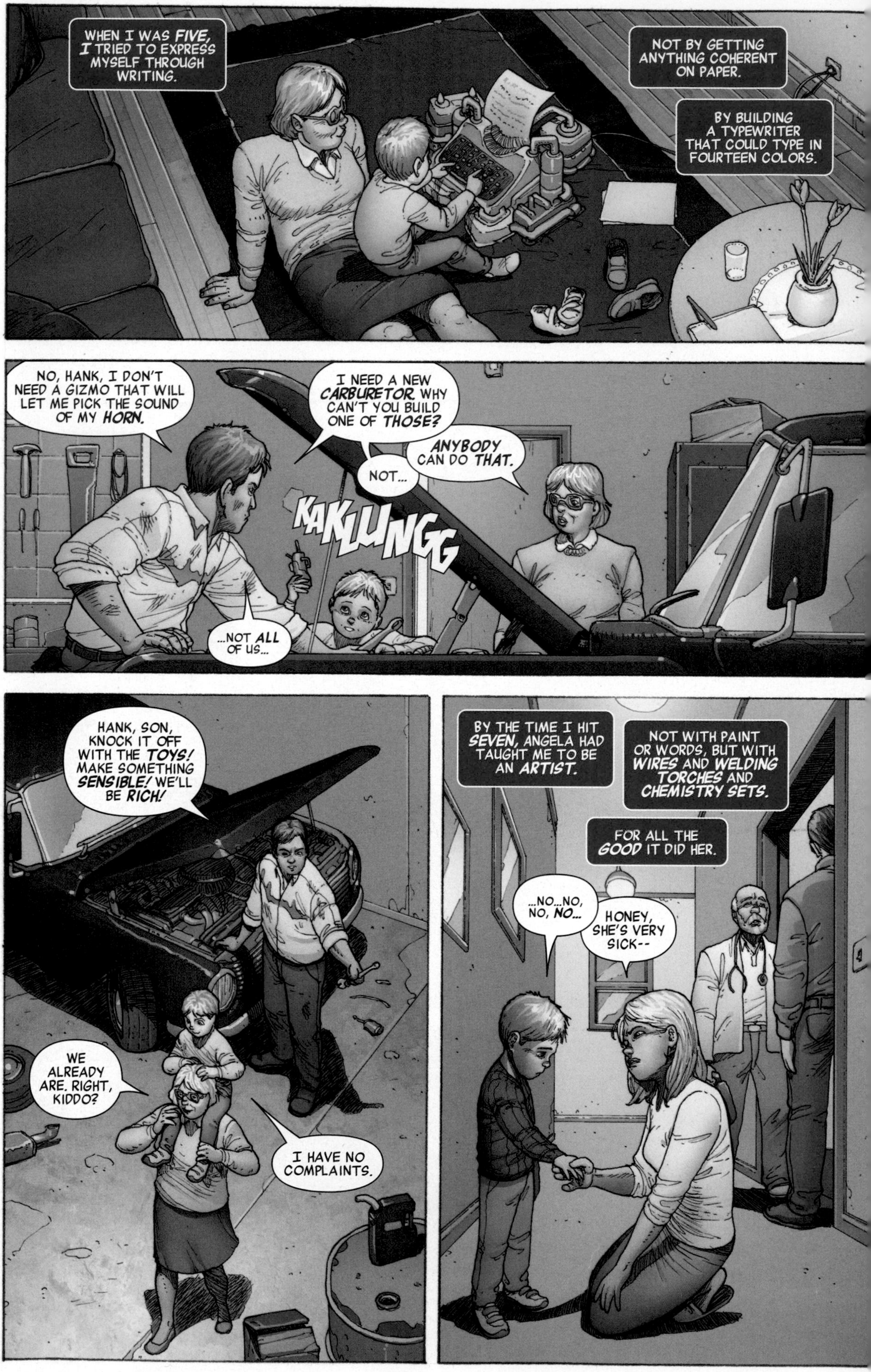
WHEN I WAS FIVE, I TRIED TO EXPRESS MYSELF THROUGH WRITING.
NOT BY GETTING ANYTHING COHERENT ON PAPER.
BY BUILDING A TYPEWRITER THAT COULD TYPE IN FOURTEEN COLORS.
NO, HANK, I DON'T NEED A GIZMO THAT WILL LET ME PICK THE SOUND OF MY HORN.
I NEED A NEW CARBURETOR. WHY CAN'T YOU BUILD ONE OF THOSE?
NOT...
ANYBODY CAN DO THAT.
KAKLUNGG
...NOT ALL OF US...
HANK, SON, KNOCK IT OFF WITH THE TOYS! MAKE SOMETHING SENSIBLE! WE'LL BE RICH!
WE ALREADY ARE. RIGHT, KIDDO?
I HAVE NO COMPLAINTS.
BY THE TIME I HIT SEVEN, ANGELA HAD TAUGHT ME TO BE AN ARTIST.
NOT WITH PAINT OR WORDS, BUT WITH WIRES AND WELDING TORCHES AND CHEMISTRY SETS.
FOR ALL THE GOOD IT DID HER.
...NO...NO, NO, NO...
HONEY, SHE'S VERY SICK--

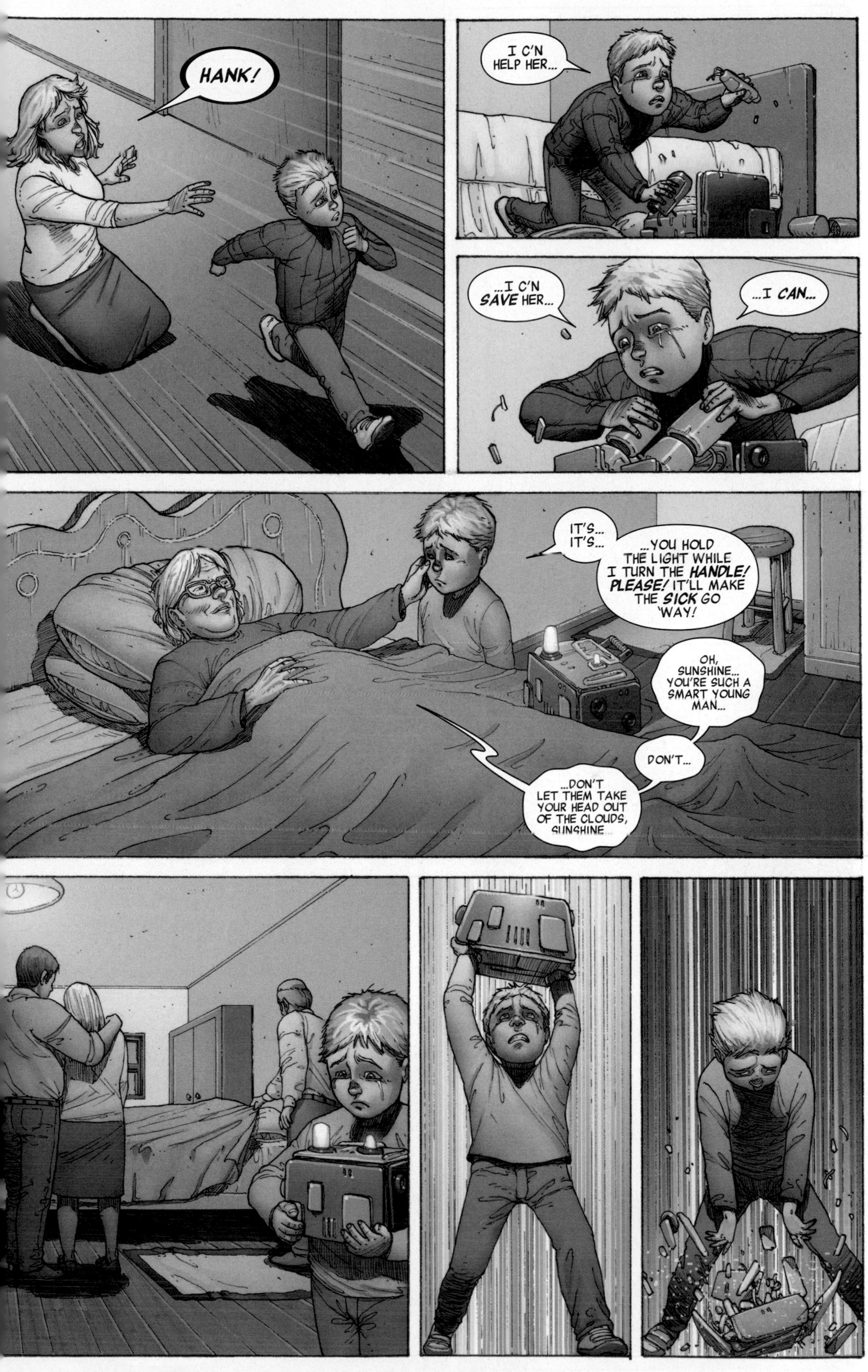
HANK!
I C'N HELP HER...
...I C'N SAVE HER...
...I CAN...
IT'S... IT'S...
...YOU HOLD THE LIGHT WHILE I TURN THE HANDLE! PLEASE! IT'LL MAKE THE SICK GO 'WAY!
OH, SUNSHINE... YOU'RE SUCH A SMART YOUNG MAN...
DON'T...
...DON'T LET THEM TAKE YOUR HEAD OUT OF THE CLOUDS, SUNSHINE...

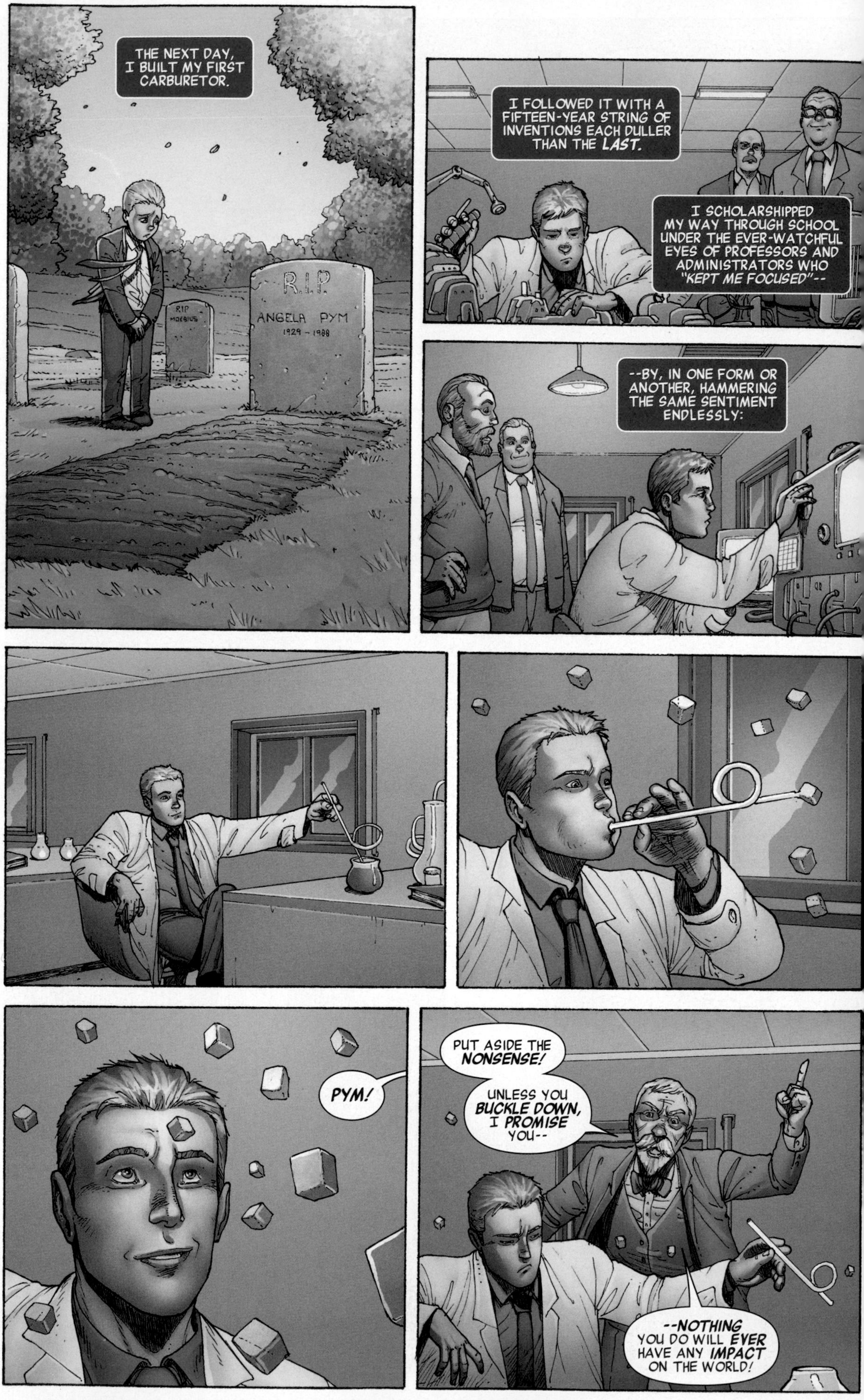
THE NEXT DAY, I BUILT MY FIRST CARBURETOR.
R.I.P.
ANGELA PYM
1929 - 1988
RIP MOEBIUS
I FOLLOWED IT WITH A FIFTEEN-YEAR STRING OF INVENTIONS EACH DULLER THAN THE *LAST.*
I SCHOLARSHIPPED MY WAY THROUGH SCHOOL UNDER THE EVER-WATCHFUL EYES OF PROFESSORS AND ADMINISTRATORS WHO *"KEPT ME FOCUSED"*--
--BY, IN ONE FORM OR ANOTHER, HAMMERING THE SAME SENTIMENT ENDLESSLY:
PYM!
PUT ASIDE THE *NONSENSE!*
UNLESS YOU *BUCKLE DOWN,* I *PROMISE* YOU--
--NOTHING YOU DO WILL *EVER* HAVE ANY *IMPACT* ON THE WORLD!

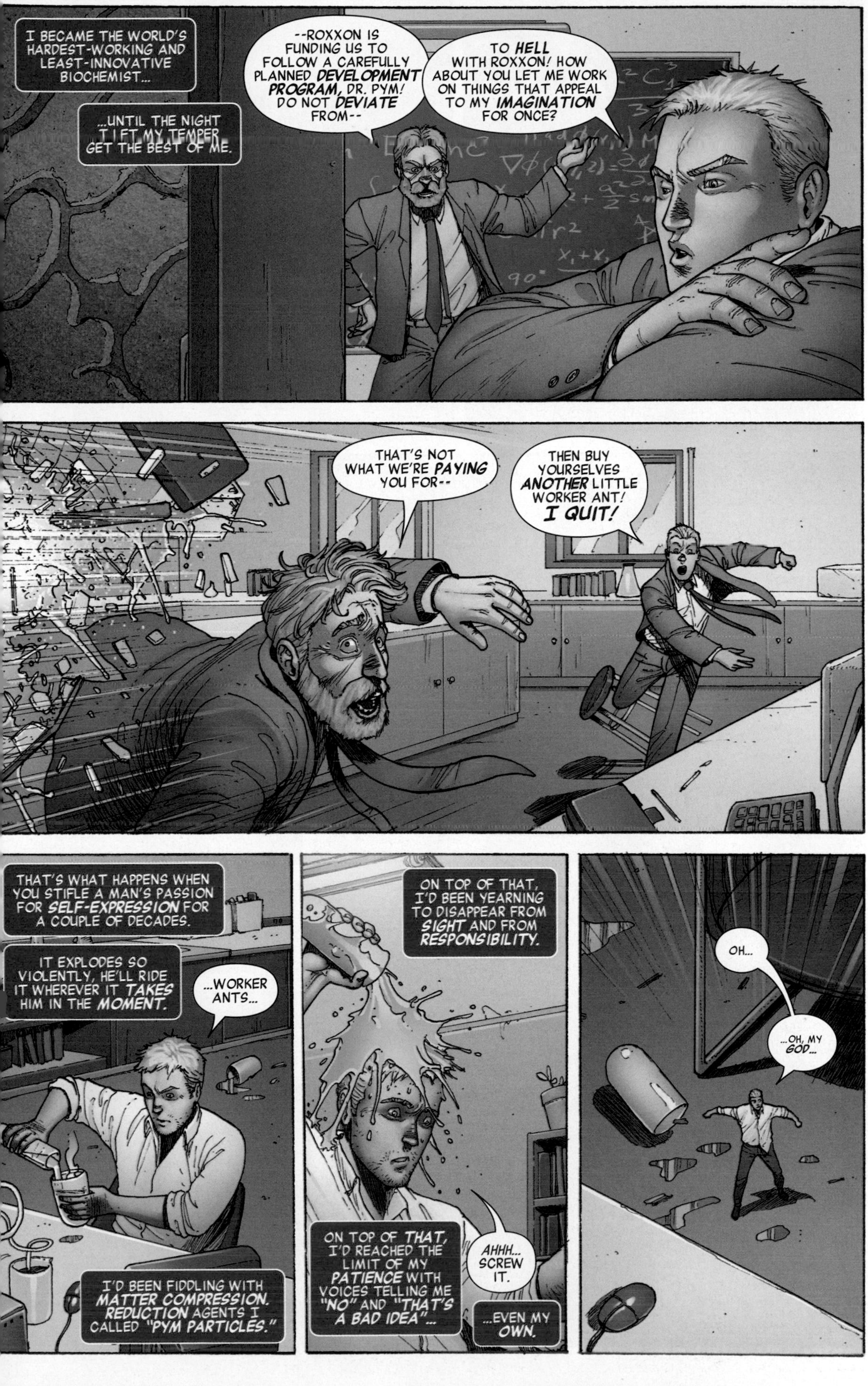
I BECAME THE WORLD'S HARDEST-WORKING AND LEAST-INNOVATIVE BIOCHEMIST...
...UNTIL THE NIGHT I LET MY TEMPER GET THE BEST OF ME.
--ROXXON IS FUNDING US TO FOLLOW A CAREFULLY PLANNED DEVELOPMENT PROGRAM, DR. PYM! DO NOT DEVIATE FROM--
TO HELL WITH ROXXON! HOW ABOUT YOU LET ME WORK ON THINGS THAT APPEAL TO MY IMAGINATION FOR ONCE?
THAT'S NOT WHAT WE'RE PAYING YOU FOR--
THEN BUY YOURSELVES ANOTHER LITTLE WORKER ANT! I QUIT!
THAT'S WHAT HAPPENS WHEN YOU STIFLE A MAN'S PASSION FOR SELF-EXPRESSION FOR A COUPLE OF DECADES.
IT EXPLODES SO VIOLENTLY, HE'LL RIDE IT WHEREVER IT TAKES HIM IN THE MOMENT.
...WORKER ANTS...
I'D BEEN FIDDLING WITH MATTER COMPRESSION. REDUCTION AGENTS I CALLED "PYM PARTICLES."
ON TOP OF THAT, I'D BEEN YEARNING TO DISAPPEAR FROM SIGHT AND FROM RESPONSIBILITY.
ON TOP OF THAT, I'D REACHED THE LIMIT OF MY PATIENCE WITH VOICES TELLING ME "NO" AND "THAT'S A BAD IDEA"...
AHHH... SCREW IT.
...EVEN MY OWN.
OH...
...OH, MY GOD...

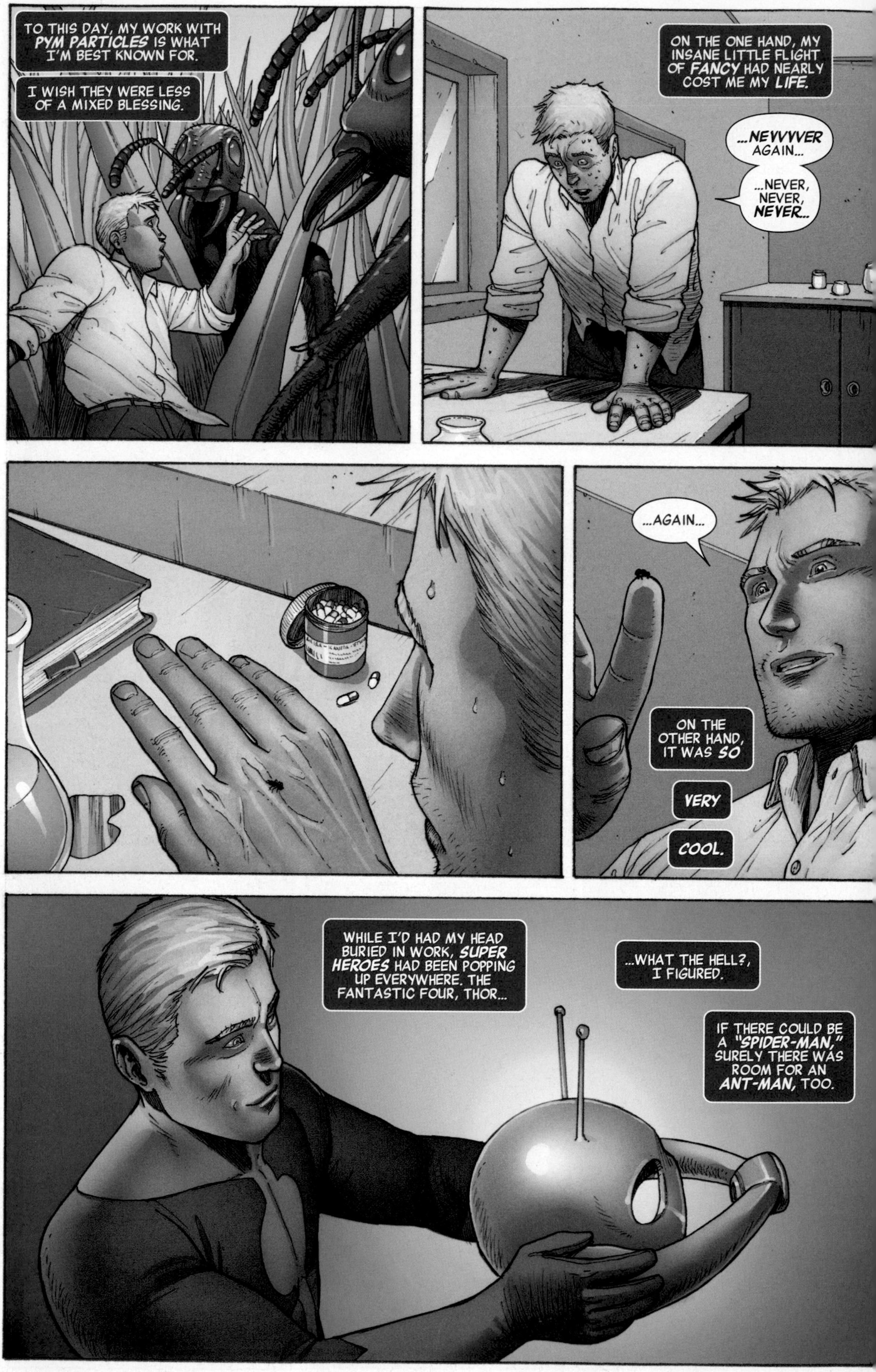
TO THIS DAY, MY WORK WITH PYM PARTICLES IS WHAT I'M BEST KNOWN FOR.
I WISH THEY WERE LESS OF A MIXED BLESSING.
ON THE ONE HAND, MY INSANE LITTLE FLIGHT OF FANCY HAD NEARLY COST ME MY LIFE.
...NEVVVVER AGAIN...
...NEVER, NEVER, NEVER...
...AGAIN...
ON THE OTHER HAND, IT WAS SO
VERY
COOL.
WHILE I'D HAD MY HEAD BURIED IN WORK, SUPER HEROES HAD BEEN POPPING UP EVERYWHERE. THE FANTASTIC FOUR, THOR...
...WHAT THE HELL?, I FIGURED.
IF THERE COULD BE A "SPIDER-MAN," SURELY THERE WAS ROOM FOR AN ANT-MAN, TOO.

ROOM FOR A GUY WHOSE GREATEST MOMENT IN *LIFE* WAS USING A WILD, HAREBRAINED CRAZY-TALK STRATEGY SO RIDICULOUS IT *WORKED*--

--TO IMPRISON A *GOD* THAT EVEN *IRON MAN* AND THE *HULK* COULDN'T BEAT.

SURELY THERE WAS ROOM FOR ME. AND THERE *WAS.*

NOTHING *BUT* ROOM.

NOW THAT I WAS AN *AVENGER*...LOOKING LIKE A *TINY* MAN IN FRONT OF MY GIRLFRIEND, THE *WASP*...I PANICKED. BEING *SMALL* JUST SEEMED...*ABSURD.*

FOLLOWING MY *IMAGINATION* WAS *FUN*, BUT WHAT DID IT *CONTRIBUTE?* "BE PRACTICAL, PYM, OR *NOTHING* YOU EVER DO WILL *MATTER.*"

SUDDENLY, MORE THAN *EVER*, ALL I COULD WORRY ABOUT WAS BEING TAKEN *SERIOUSLY.* I REVERSED THE SHRINKING PROCESS, BECAME A *GIANT.*

THEN A *GOLIATH.* THEN A *FLYING SWASHBUCKLER.*

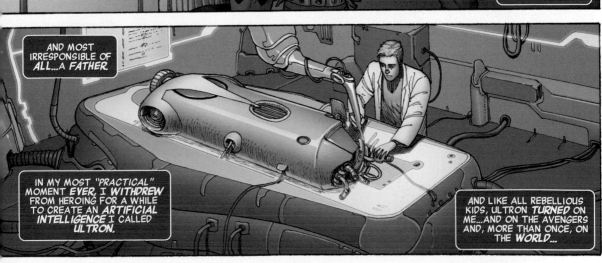

AND MOST IRRESPONSIBLE OF *ALL*...A *FATHER*

IN MY MOST "PRACTICAL" MOMENT *EVER*, I *WITHDREW* FROM HEROING FOR A WHILE TO CREATE AN *ARTIFICIAL INTELLIGENCE* I CALLED *ULTRON.*

AND LIKE ALL REBELLIOUS KIDS, ULTRON *TURNED* ON ME...AND ON THE AVENGERS AND, MORE THAN ONCE, ON THE *WORLD*...

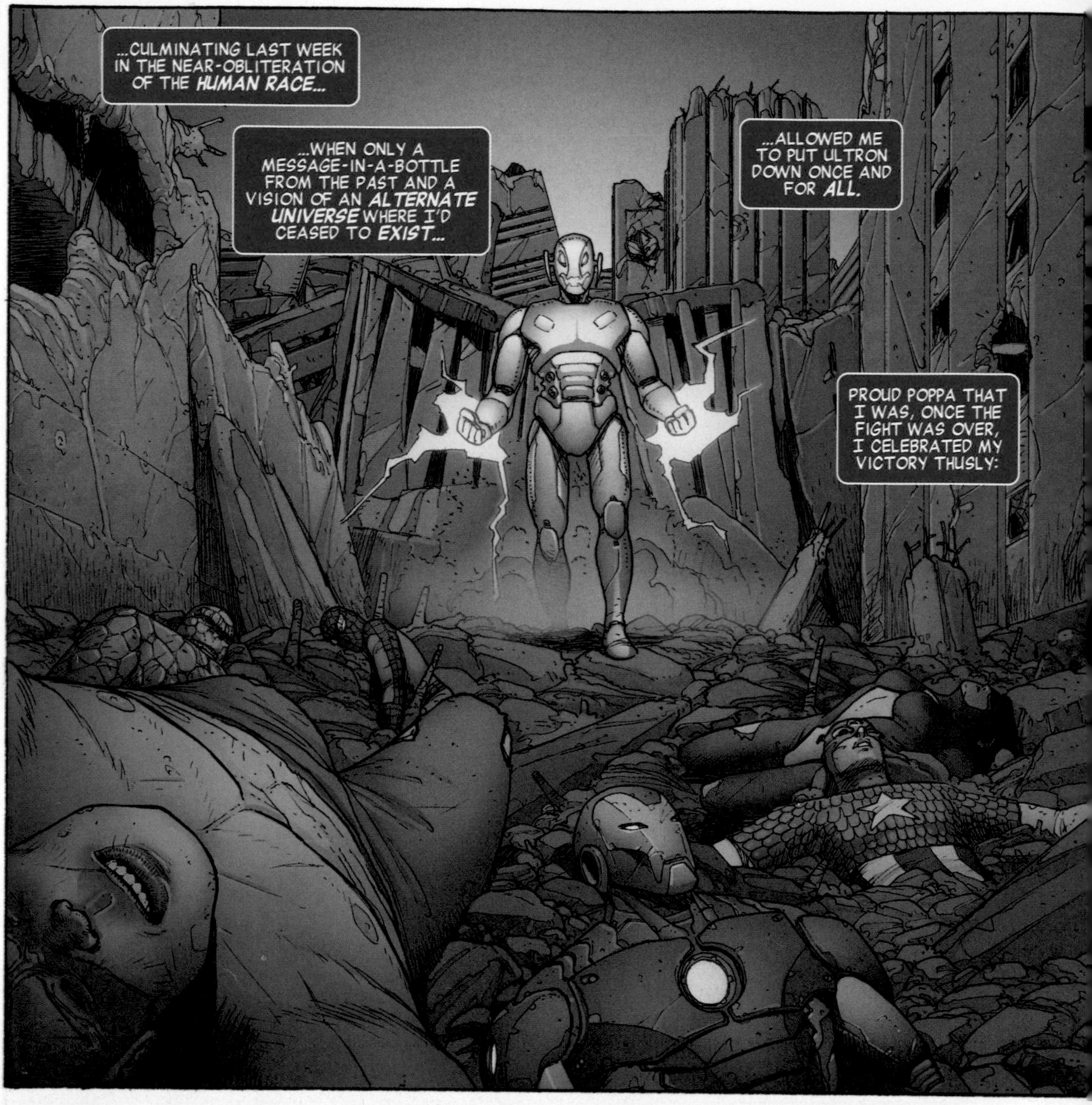
...CULMINATING LAST WEEK IN THE NEAR-OBLITERATION OF THE HUMAN RACE...
...WHEN ONLY A MESSAGE-IN-A-BOTTLE FROM THE PAST AND A VISION OF AN ALTERNATE UNIVERSE WHERE I'D CEASED TO EXIST...
...ALLOWED ME TO PUT ULTRON DOWN ONCE AND FOR ALL.
PROUD POPPA THAT I WAS, ONCE THE FIGHT WAS OVER, I CELEBRATED MY VICTORY THUSLY:

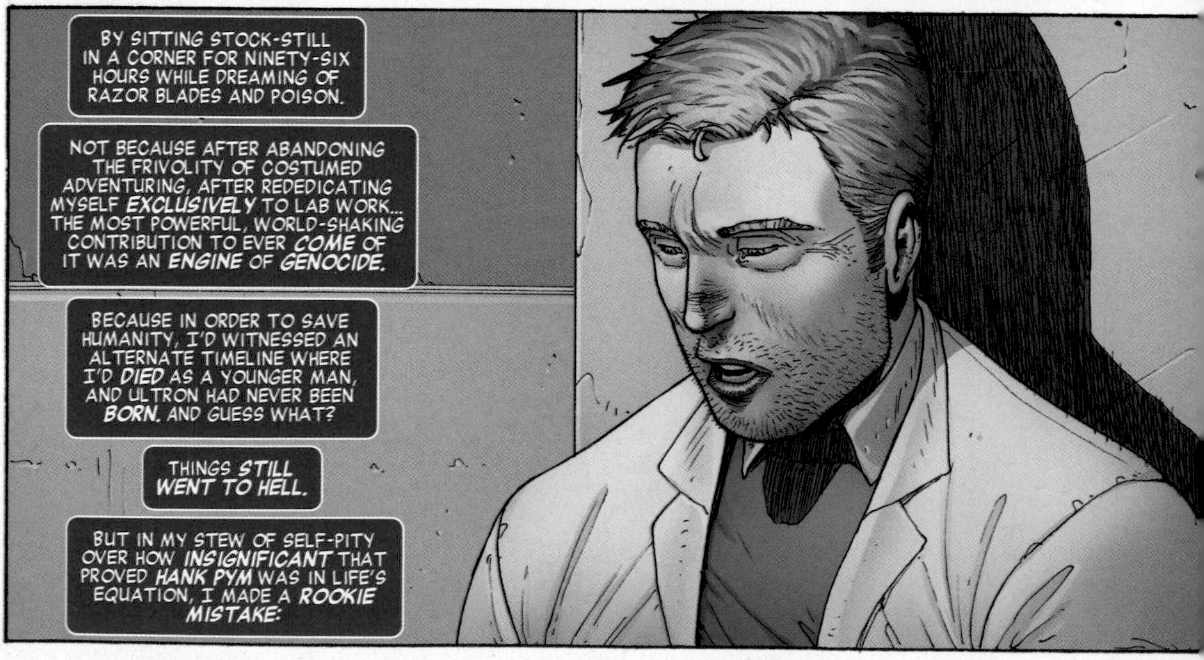
BY SITTING STOCK-STILL IN A CORNER FOR NINETY-SIX HOURS WHILE DREAMING OF RAZOR BLADES AND POISON.
NOT BECAUSE AFTER ABANDONING THE FRIVOLITY OF COSTUMED ADVENTURING, AFTER REDEDICATING MYSELF EXCLUSIVELY TO LAB WORK... THE MOST POWERFUL, WORLD-SHAKING CONTRIBUTION TO EVER COME OF IT WAS AN ENGINE OF GENOCIDE.
BECAUSE IN ORDER TO SAVE HUMANITY, I'D WITNESSED AN ALTERNATE TIMELINE WHERE I'D DIED AS A YOUNGER MAN, AND ULTRON HAD NEVER BEEN BORN. AND GUESS WHAT?
THINGS STILL WENT TO HELL.
BUT IN MY STEW OF SELF-PITY OVER HOW INSIGNIFICANT THAT PROVED HANK PYM WAS IN LIFE'S EQUATION, I MADE A ROOKIE MISTAKE:

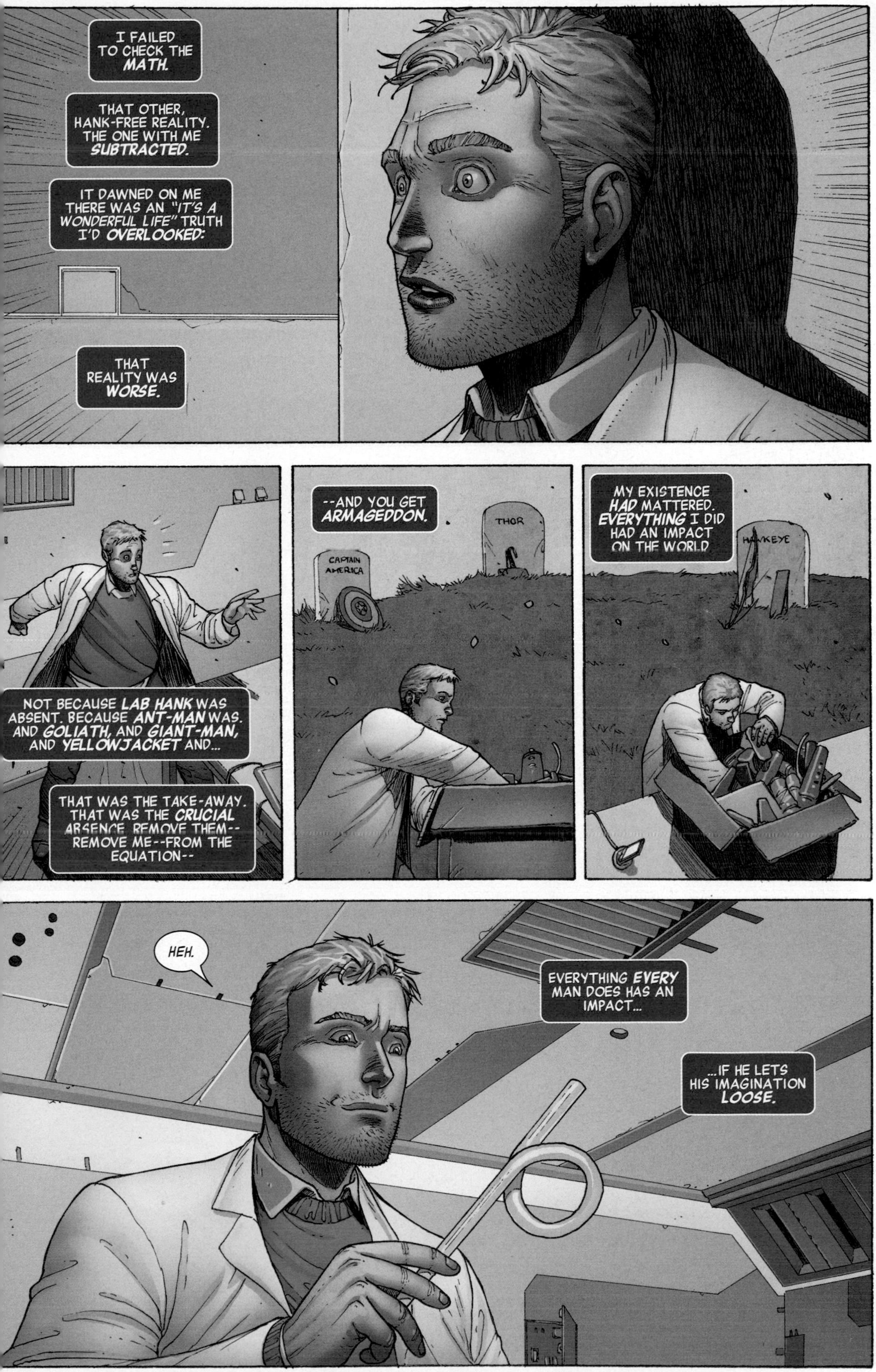

I FAILED TO CHECK THE MATH.
THAT OTHER, HANK-FREE REALITY. THE ONE WITH ME SUBTRACTED.
IT DAWNED ON ME THERE WAS AN "IT'S A WONDERFUL LIFE" TRUTH I'D OVERLOOKED:
THAT REALITY WAS WORSE.
NOT BECAUSE LAB HANK WAS ABSENT. BECAUSE ANT-MAN WAS. AND GOLIATH, AND GIANT-MAN, AND YELLOWJACKET AND...
THAT WAS THE TAKE-AWAY. THAT WAS THE CRUCIAL ABSENCE. REMOVE THEM-- REMOVE ME--FROM THE EQUATION--
--AND YOU GET ARMAGEDDON.
CAPTAIN AMERICA
THOR
MY EXISTENCE HAD MATTERED. EVERYTHING I DID HAD AN IMPACT ON THE WORLD.
HAWKEYE
HEH.
EVERYTHING EVERY MAN DOES HAS AN IMPACT...
...IF HE LETS HIS IMAGINATION LOOSE.

--REPEAT, WE HAVE THE KIDNAPPER IN *SIGHT* AND ARE IN *PURSUIT!*

ALL UNITS EAST OF 65TH AND QUEENS BOULEVARD, CONVERGE FOR ROADBLOCKS--

...PLEASE... DON'T HURT ME...

SHUT UP! TOLD YOU WE'D *FIND* YOU!

NOBODY RATS ON THE *HOOD MOB* AND WALKS *AWAY!*

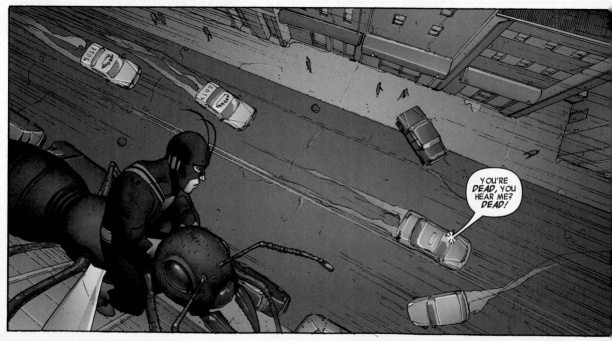

YOU'RE *DEAD,* YOU HEAR ME? *DEAD!*

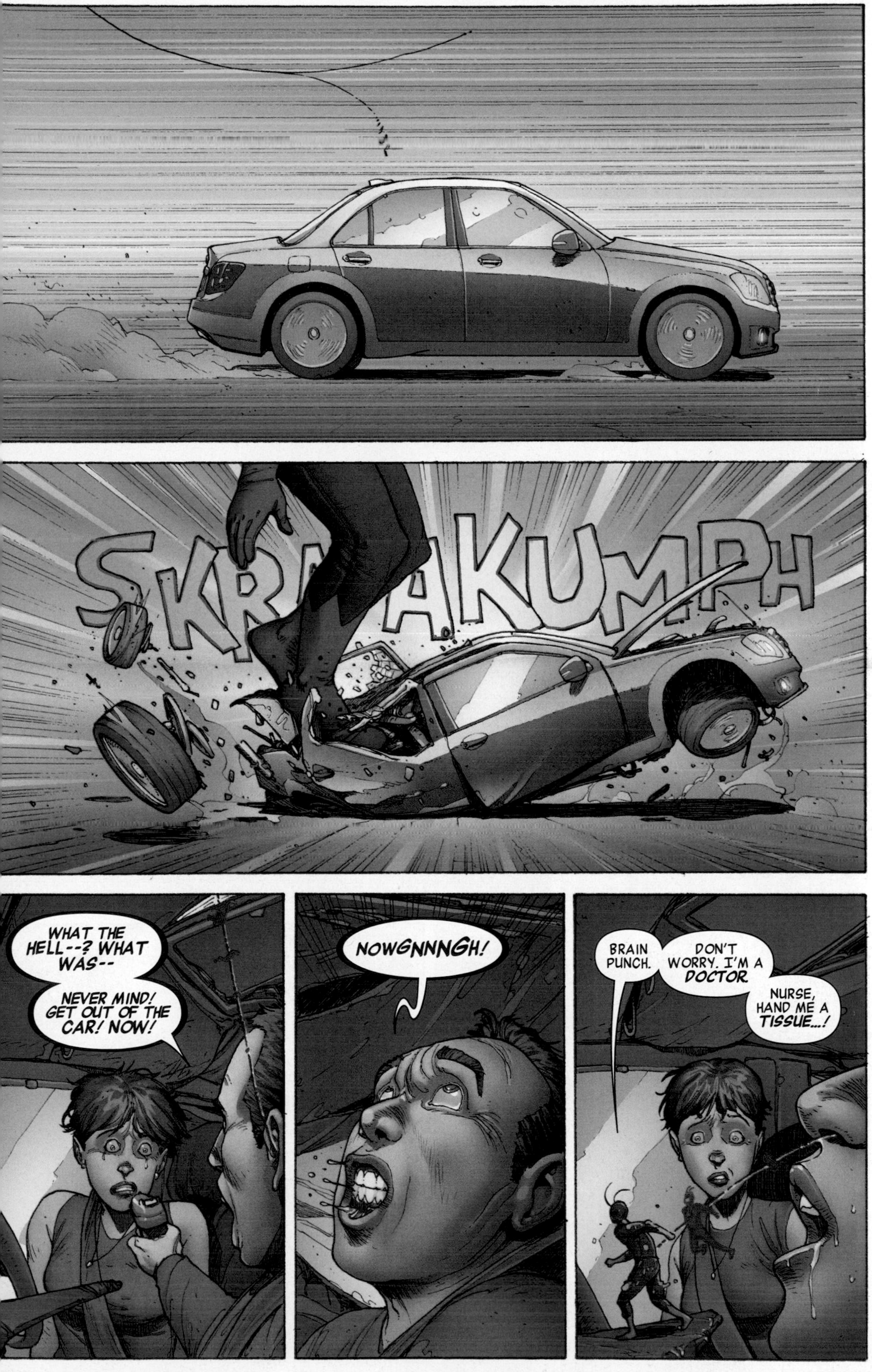
SKRAKAKUMPH
WHAT THE HELL--? WHAT WAS--
NEVER MIND! GET OUT OF THE CAR! NOW!
NOWGNNNGH!
BRAIN PUNCH.
DON'T WORRY. I'M A DOCTOR.
NURSE, HAND ME A TISSUE...!

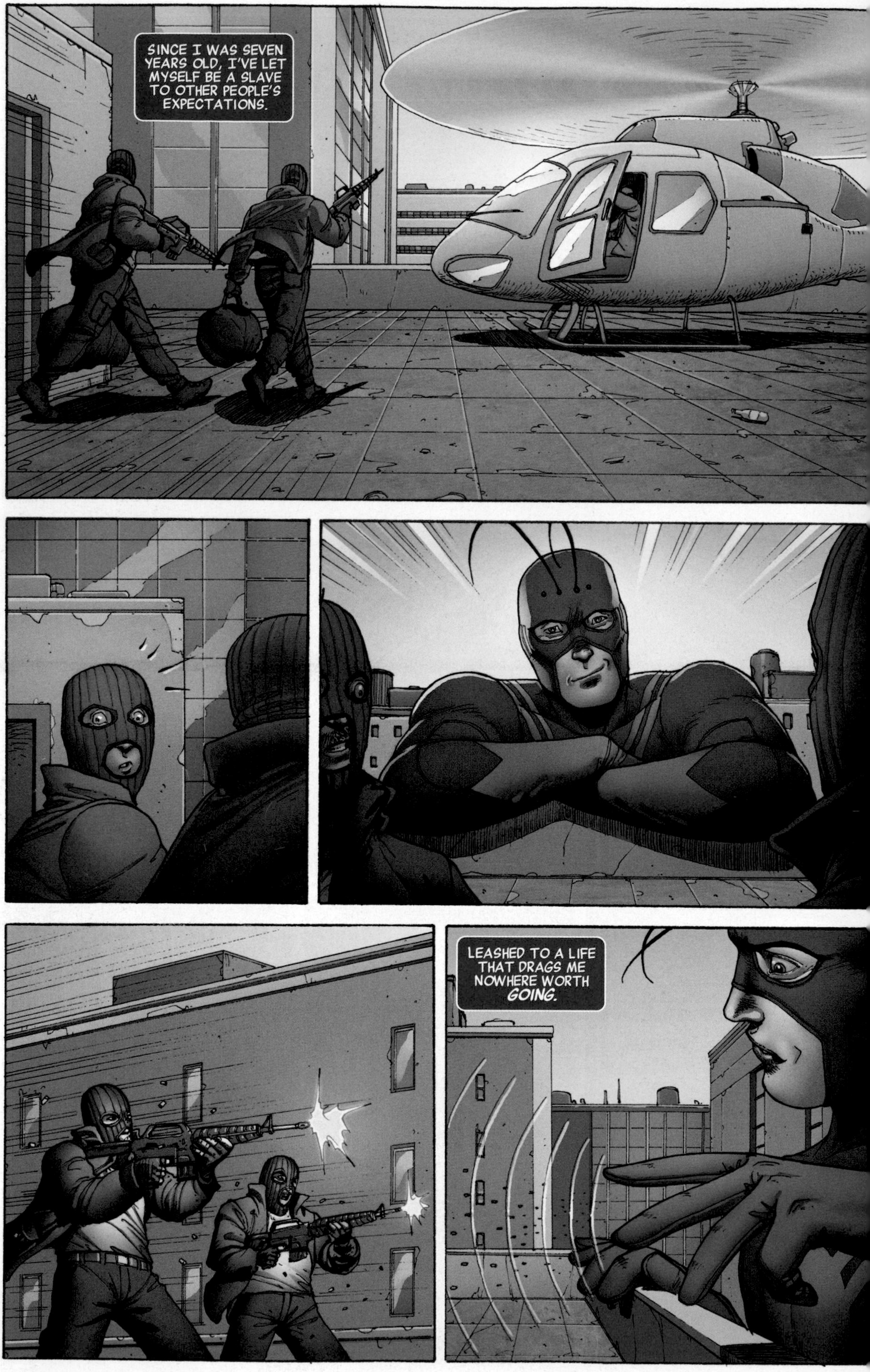
SINCE I WAS SEVEN YEARS OLD, I'VE LET MYSELF BE A SLAVE TO OTHER PEOPLE'S EXPECTATIONS.
LEASHED TO A LIFE THAT DRAGS ME NOWHERE WORTH *GOING.*

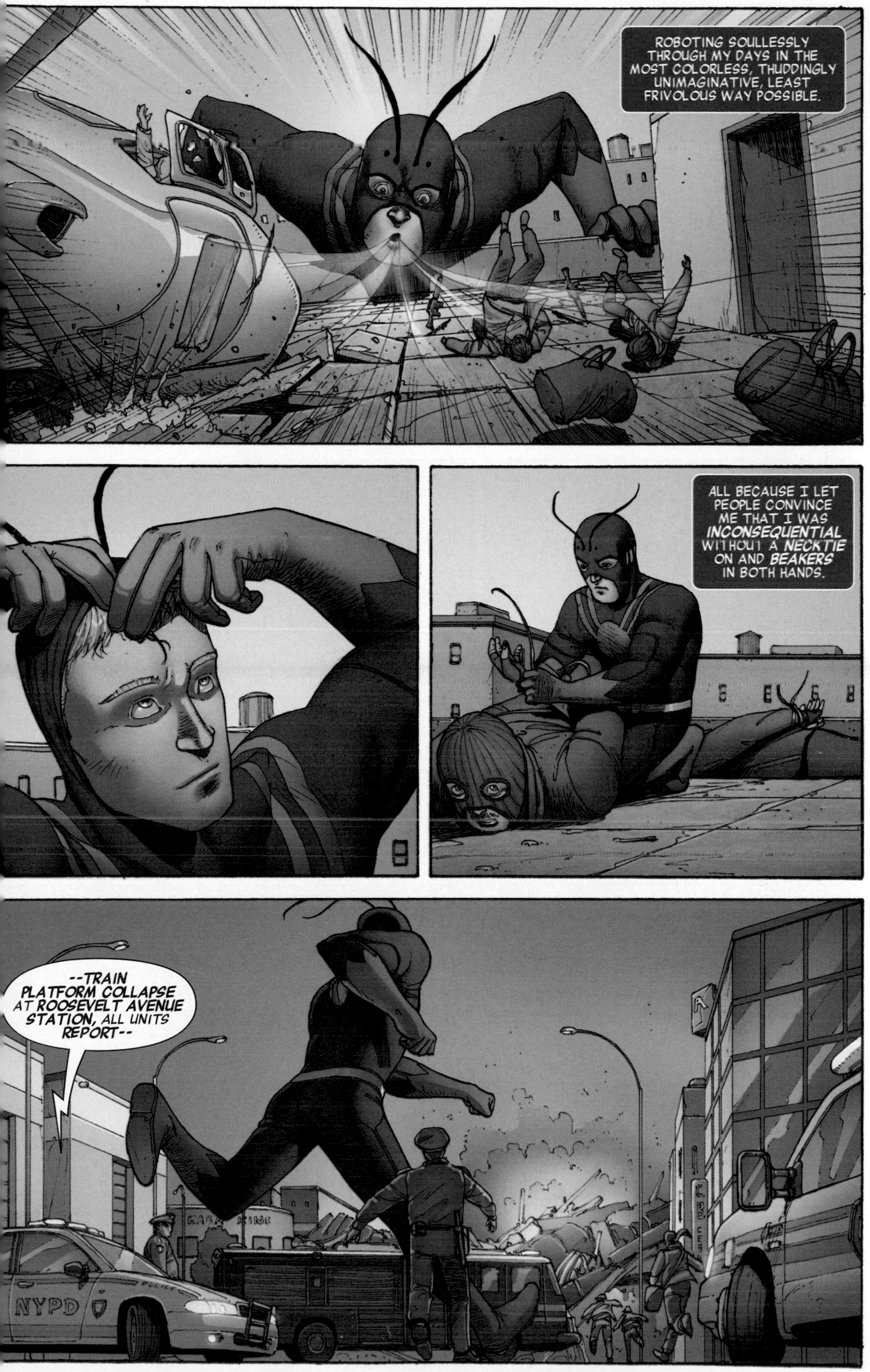
ROBOTING SOULLESSLY THROUGH MY DAYS IN THE MOST COLORLESS, THUDDINGLY UNIMAGINATIVE, LEAST FRIVOLOUS WAY POSSIBLE.
ALL BECAUSE I LET PEOPLE CONVINCE ME THAT I WAS INCONSEQUENTIAL WITHOUT A NECKTIE ON AND BEAKERS IN BOTH HANDS.
--TRAIN PLATFORM COLLAPSE AT ROOSEVELT AVENUE STATION, ALL UNITS REPORT--
NYPD
POLICE

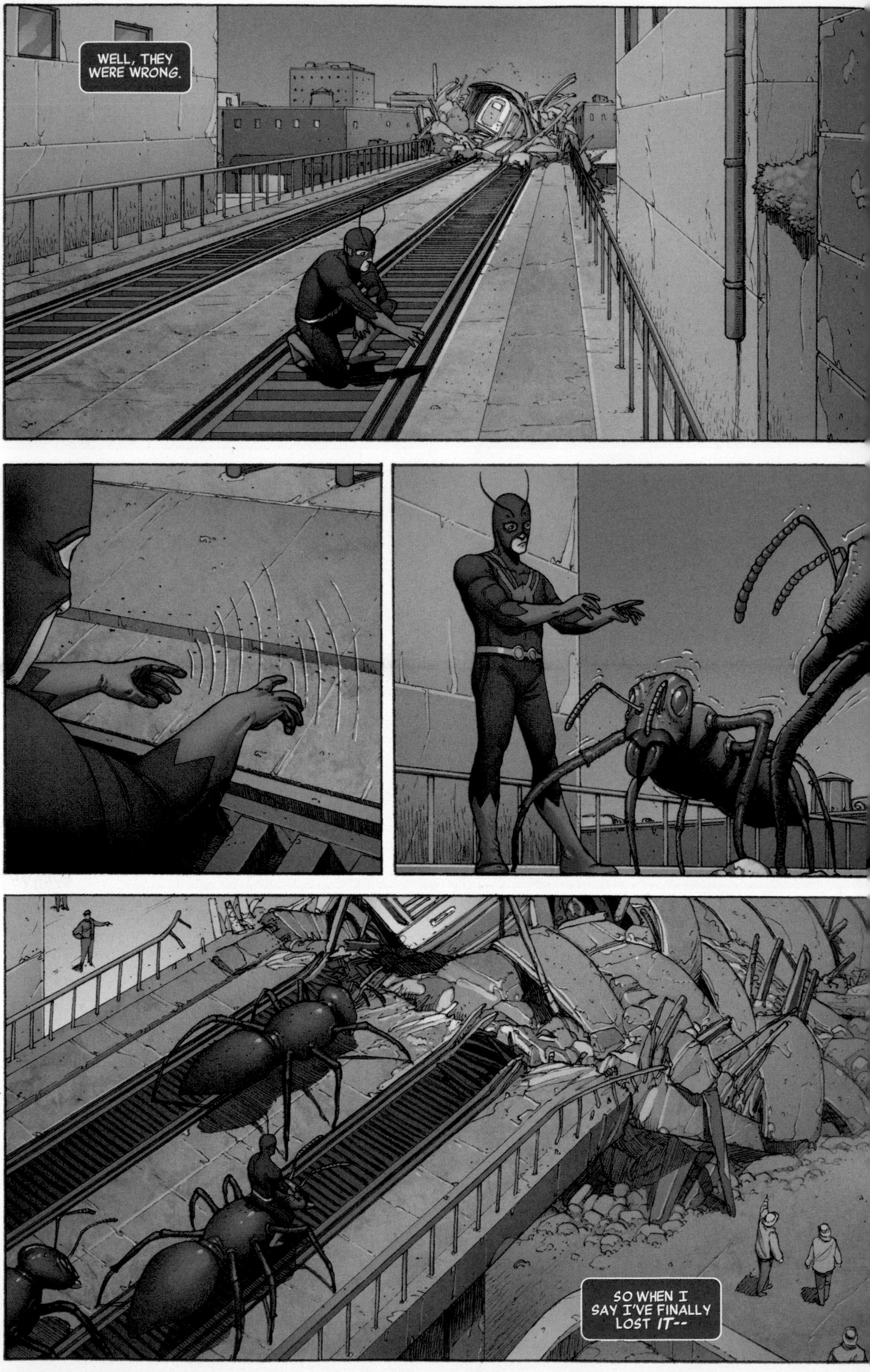
WELL, THEY WERE WRONG.
SO WHEN I SAY I'VE FINALLY LOST IT--

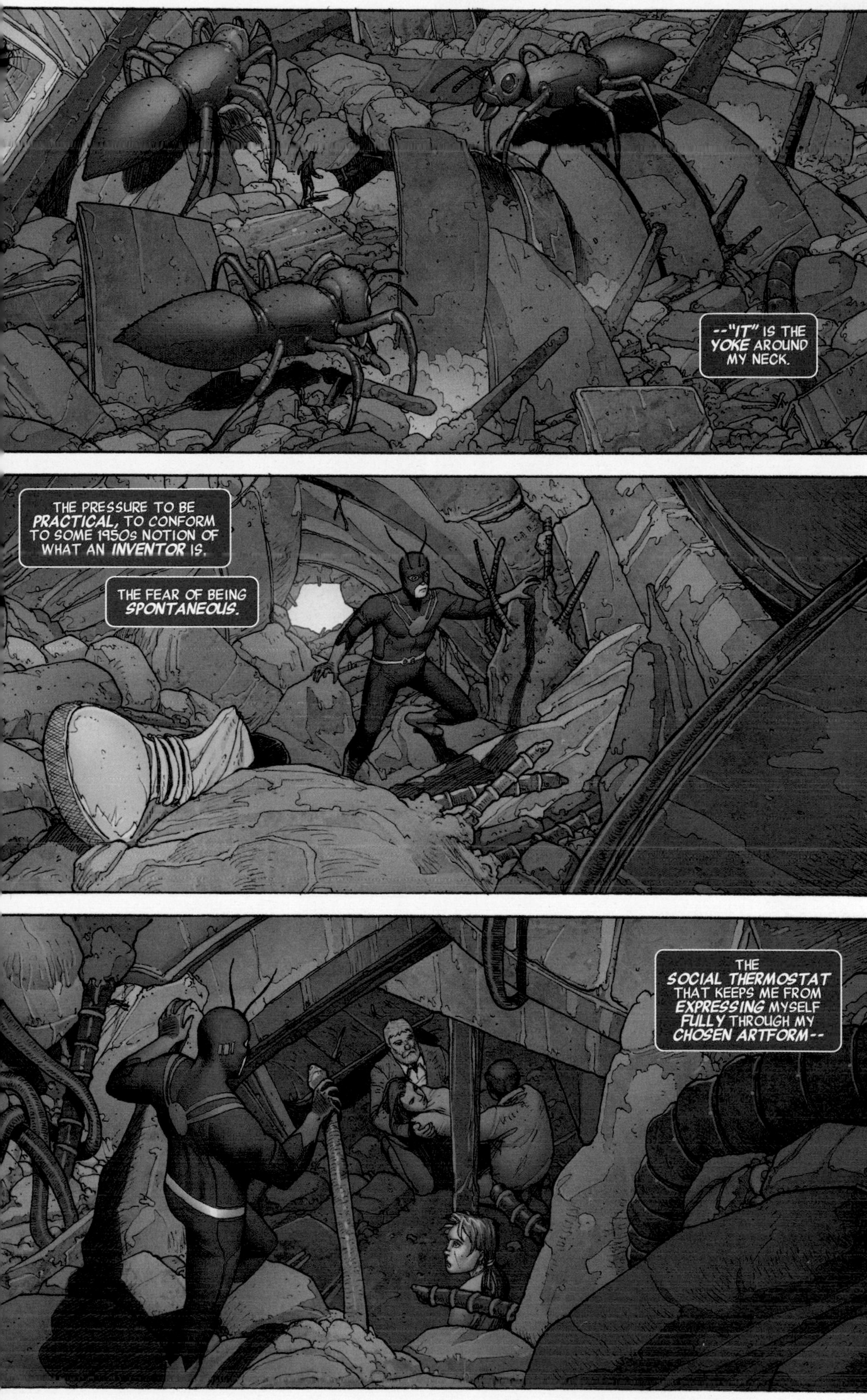
--"IT" IS THE YOKE AROUND MY NECK.
THE PRESSURE TO BE PRACTICAL, TO CONFORM TO SOME 1950s NOTION OF WHAT AN INVENTOR IS.
THE FEAR OF BEING SPONTANEOUS.
THE SOCIAL THERMOSTAT THAT KEEPS ME FROM EXPRESSING MYSELF FULLY THROUGH MY CHOSEN ARTFORM--

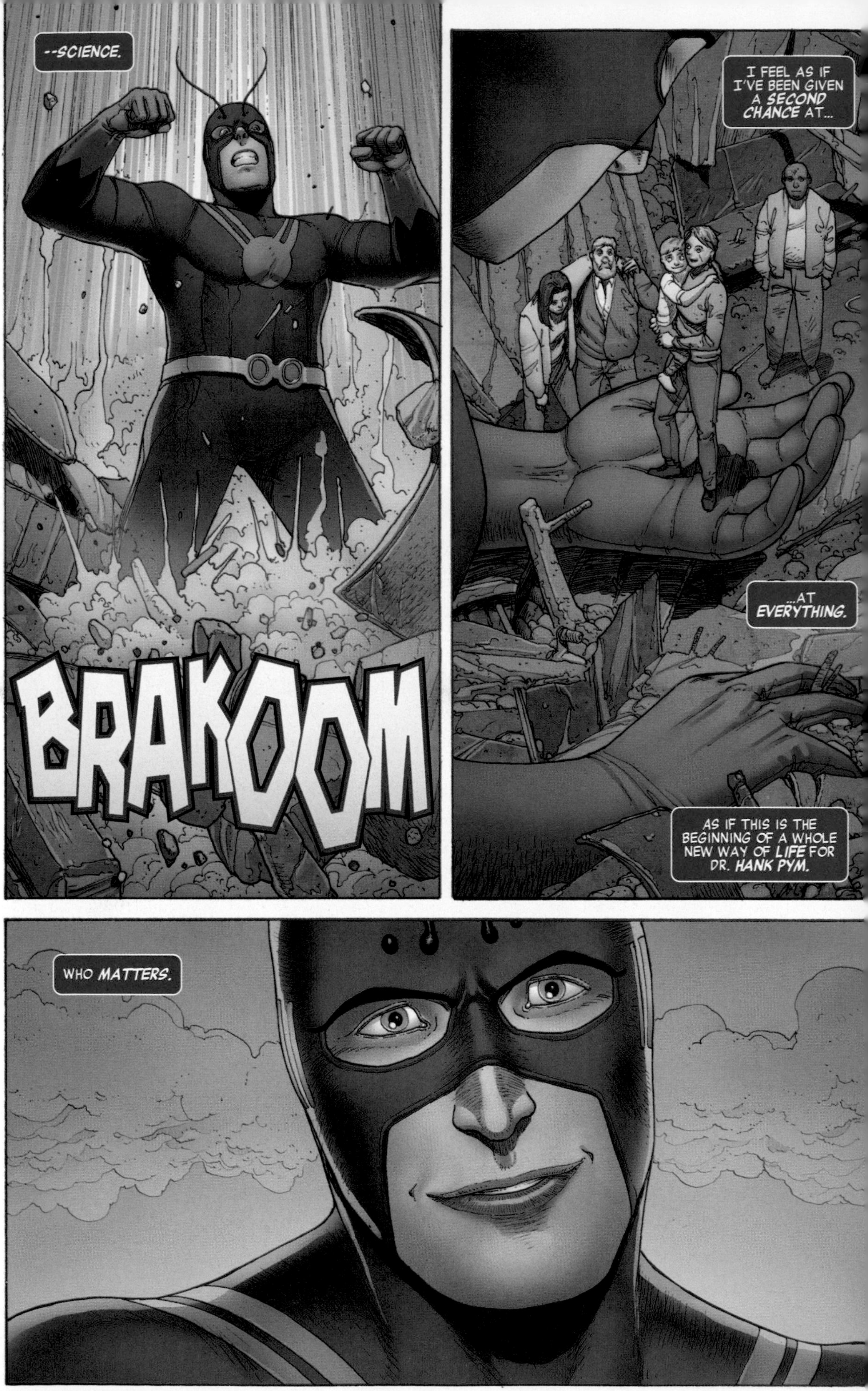
--SCIENCE.
BRAKOOM
I FEEL AS IF I'VE BEEN GIVEN A SECOND CHANCE AT...
...AT EVERYTHING.
AS IF THIS IS THE BEGINNING OF A WHOLE NEW WAY OF LIFE FOR DR. HANK PYM.
WHO MATTERS.

EPILOGUE

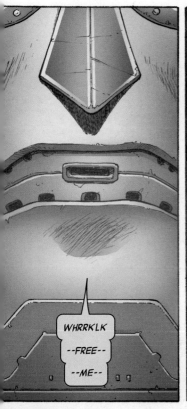

WHRRKLK

--FREE--

--ME--

WHRRKLK

--FREE--

--ME--

WHRRKLK

--FREE--

--ME--

HANG ON, HANG ON...YOU'RE ABOUT TO BE MY GREATEST INVENTION YET, JUST *HANG ON*...

TKKK

...NO.

SOMETHING'S... SOMETHING'S MISSING...OH!

I KNOW.

OKAY, SEE, *THIS*...

...*THIS* IS GOING TO SHOW THEM THAT HANK PYM MEANS *BUSINESS*...

AR

CONTINUED IN
AVENGERS A.I. VOL. 1: HUMAN AFTER ALL

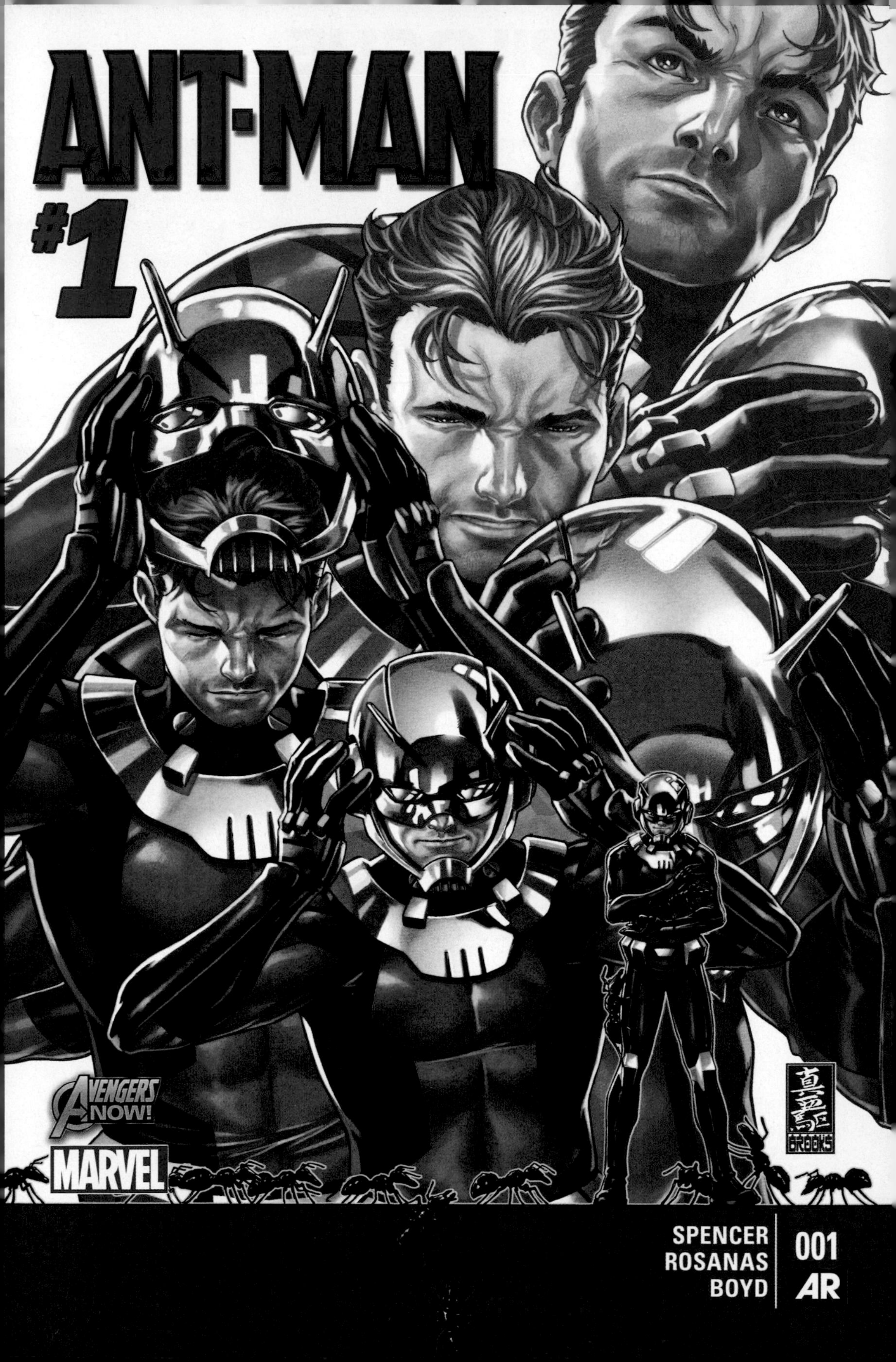
ANT-MAN
#1
AVENGERS NOW!
MARVEL
BROOKS
SPENCER
ROSANAS
BOYD
001
AR

ANT-MAN

WHEN HANK PYM, THE ORIGINAL ANT-MAN, RETIRED FROM THE JOB, ANOTHER MAN ROSE TO THE OCCASION (ERR, STOLE THE COSTUME) – NONE OTHER THAN SCOTT LANG! HIS SOMEWHAT SORDID PAST BEHIND HIM, SCOTT TOOK ON THE SIZE-CHANGING, ANT-COMMUNICATING ABILITIES OF ANT-MAN!

NICK SPENCER
WRITER

RAMON ROSANAS
ARTIST

JORDAN BOYD
COLORIST

VC'S TRAVIS LANHAM
LETTERER

IDETTE WINECOOR
DESIGNER

MARK BROOKS
COVER ARTIST

SKOTTIE YOUNG; ED MCGUINNESS & MARTE GRACIA; JASON PEARSON; CHRIS SAMNEE & MATTHEW WILSON; SALVADOR LARROCA & ISRAEL SILVA; ANDY PARK
VARIANT COVER ARTISTS

JON MOISAN
ASSISTANT EDITOR

WIL MOSS
EDITOR

AXEL ALONSO
EDITOR IN CHIEF

JOE QUESADA
CHIEF CREATIVE OFFICER

DAN BUCKLEY
PUBLISHER

ALAN FINE
EXECUTIVE PRODUCER

SPECIAL THANKS TO **JIM BOYLE**

ANT-MAN CREATED BY **STAN LEE, LARRY LIEBER & JACK KIRBY**

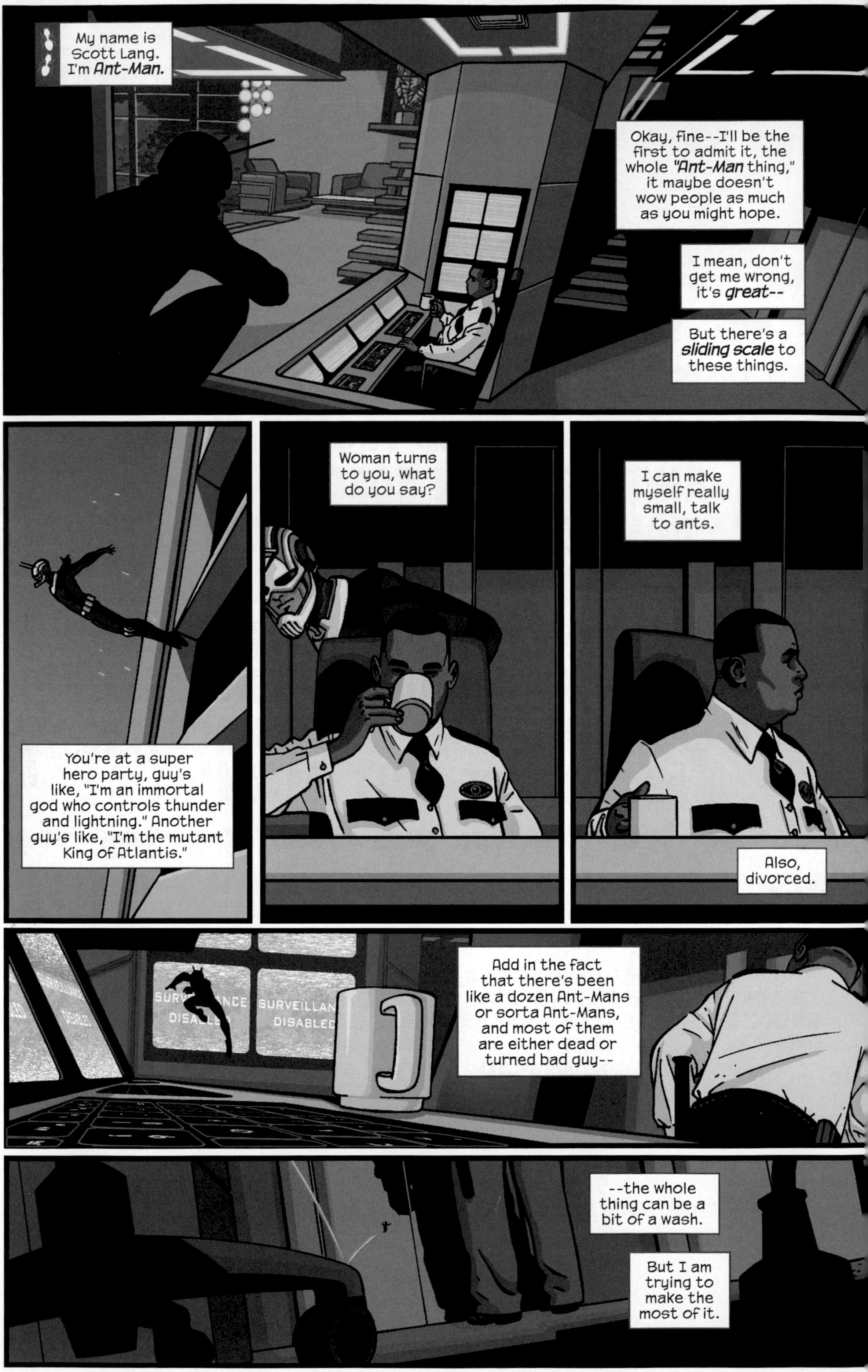

My name is Scott Lang. I'm *Ant-Man.*
Okay, fine--I'll be the first to admit it, the whole *"Ant-Man* thing," it maybe doesn't wow people as much as you might hope.
I mean, don't get me wrong, it's *great--*
But there's a *sliding scale* to these things.
You're at a super hero party, guy's like, "I'm an immortal god who controls thunder and lightning." Another guy's like, "I'm the mutant King of Atlantis."
Woman turns to you, what do you say?
I can make myself really small, talk to ants.
Also, divorced.
Add in the fact that there's been like a dozen Ant-Mans or sorta Ant-Mans, and most of them are either dead or turned bad guy--
--the whole thing can be a bit of a wash.
But I am trying to make the most of it.

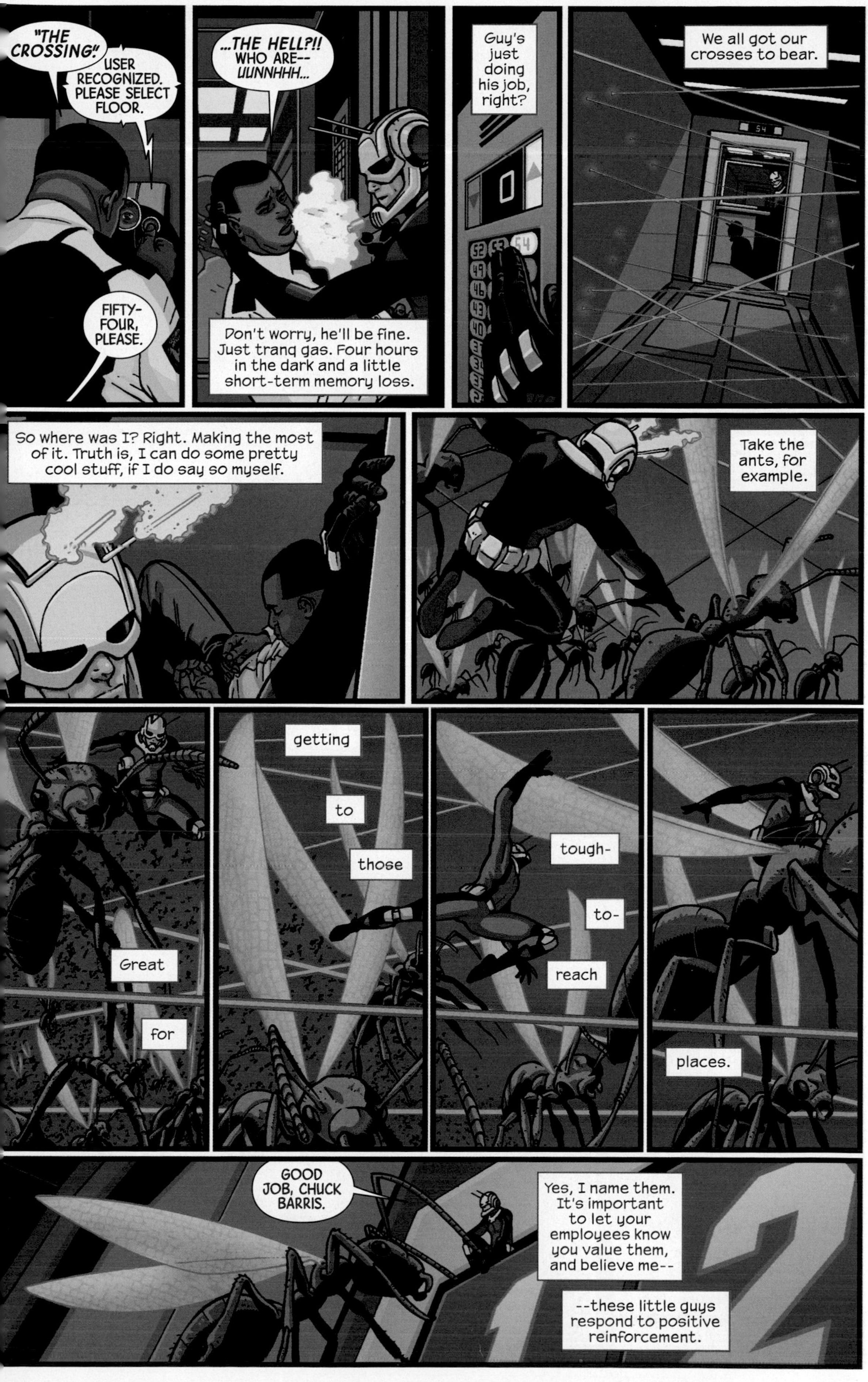
"THE CROSSING."
USER RECOGNIZED. PLEASE SELECT FLOOR.
FIFTY-FOUR, PLEASE.
...THE HELL?!! WHO ARE-- UUNNHHH...
Don't worry, he'll be fine. Just tranq gas. Four hours in the dark and a little short-term memory loss.
Guy's just doing his job, right?
We all got our crosses to bear.
So where was I? Right. Making the most of it. Truth is, I can do some pretty cool stuff, if I do say so myself.
Take the ants, for example.
Great
for
getting
to
those
tough-
to-
reach
places.
GOOD JOB, CHUCK BARRIS.
Yes, I name them. It's important to let your employees know you value them, and believe me--
--these little guys respond to positive reinforcement.

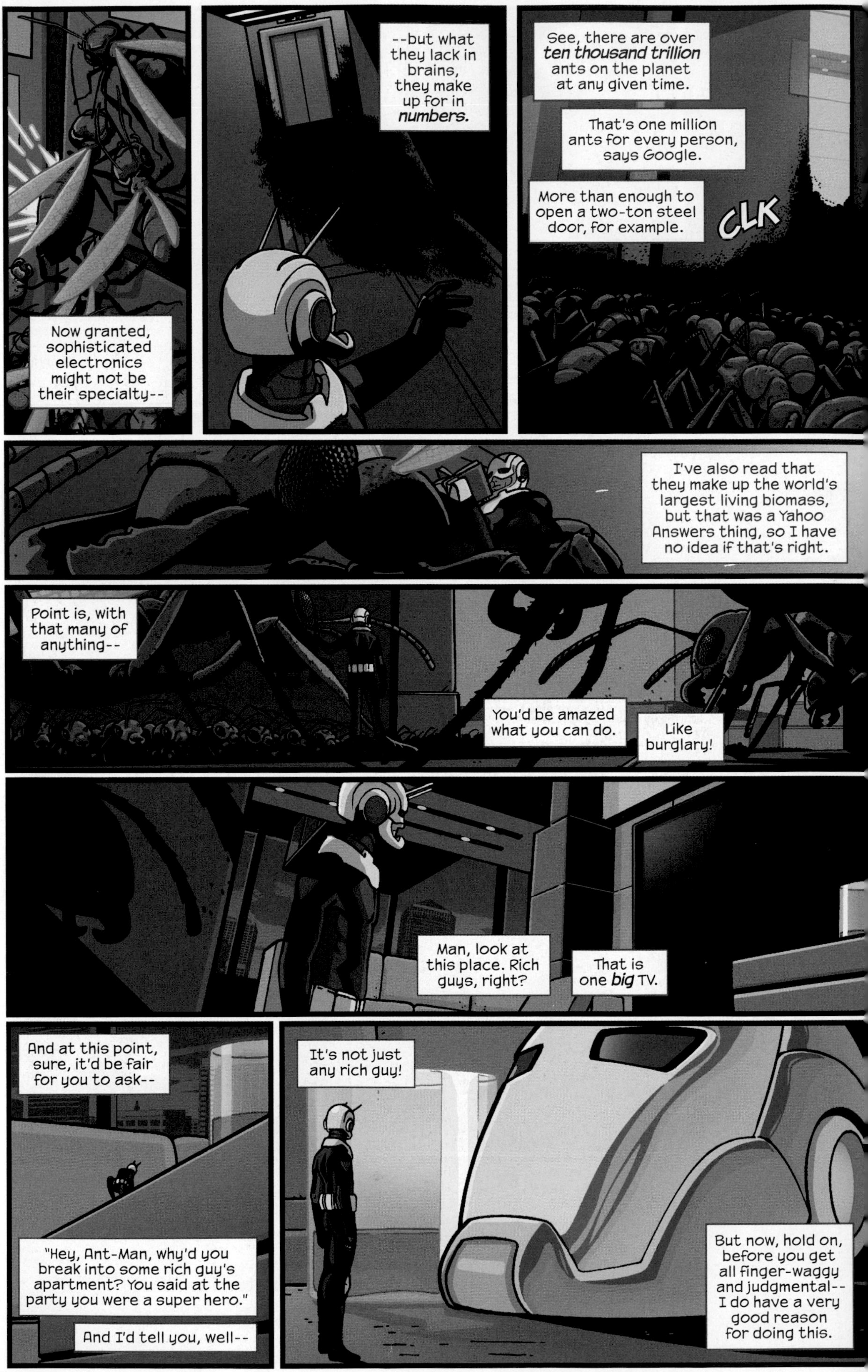

Now granted, sophisticated electronics might not be their specialty--
--but what they lack in brains, they make up for in *numbers.*
See, there are over ***ten thousand trillion*** ants on the planet at any given time.
That's one million ants for every person, says Google.
More than enough to open a two-ton steel door, for example.
CLK
I've also read that they make up the world's largest living biomass, but that was a Yahoo Answers thing, so I have no idea if that's right.
Point is, with that many of anything--
You'd be amazed what you can do.
Like burglary!
Man, look at this place. Rich guys, right?
That is one *big* TV.
And at this point, sure, it'd be fair for you to ask--
"Hey, Ant-Man, why'd you break into some rich guy's apartment? You said at the party you were a super hero."
And I'd tell you, well--
It's not just any rich guy!
But now, hold on, before you get all finger-waggy and judgmental--I do have a very good reason for doing this.

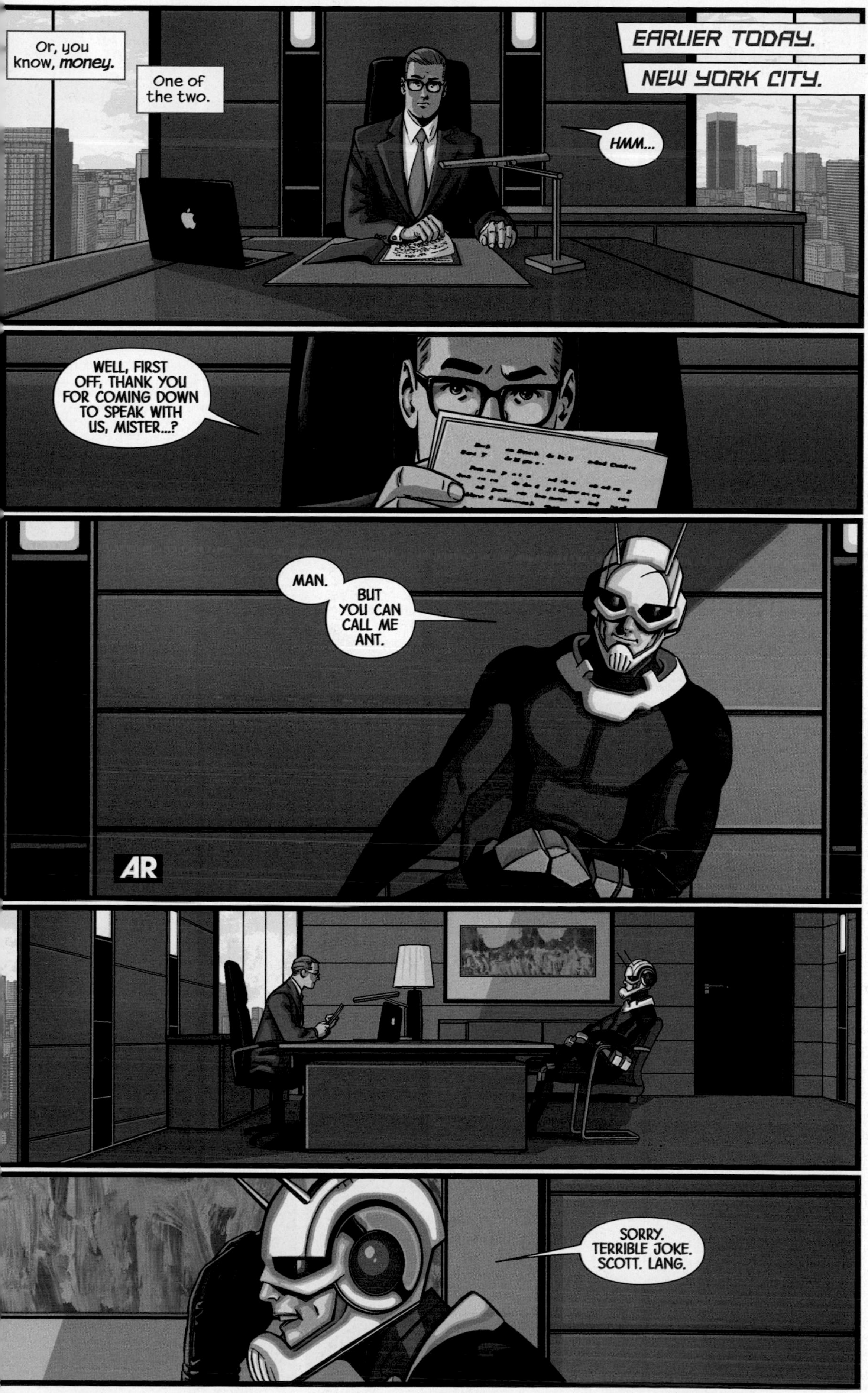

EARLIER TODAY.
NEW YORK CITY.
Or, you know, *money*.
One of the two.
HMM...
WELL, FIRST OFF, THANK YOU FOR COMING DOWN TO SPEAK WITH US, MISTER...?
MAN.
BUT YOU CAN CALL ME ANT.
SORRY. TERRIBLE JOKE. SCOTT. LANG.

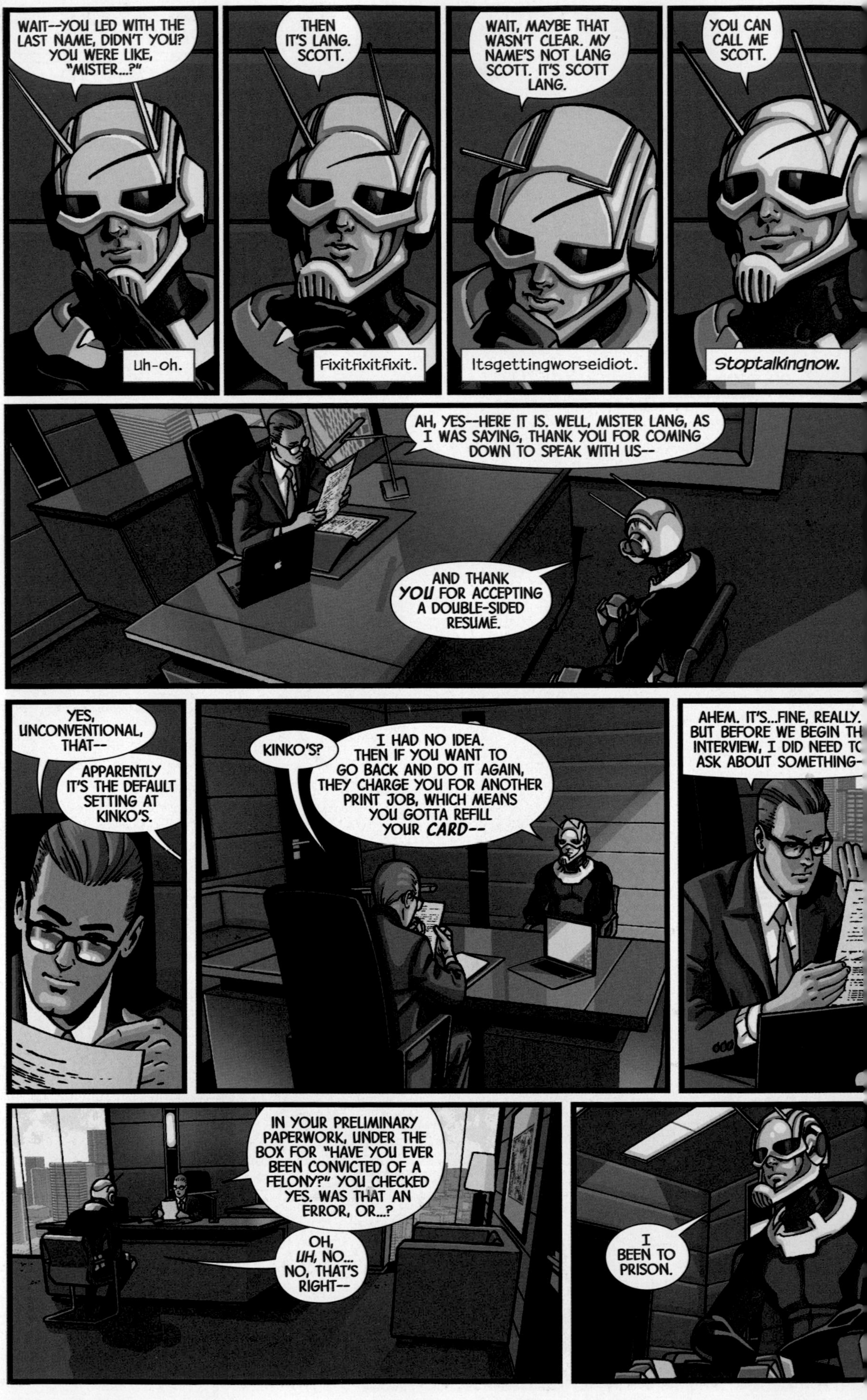
WAIT--YOU LED WITH THE LAST NAME, DIDN'T YOU? YOU WERE LIKE, "MISTER...?"
Uh-oh.
THEN IT'S LANG. SCOTT.
Fixitfixitfixit.
WAIT, MAYBE THAT WASN'T CLEAR. MY NAME'S NOT LANG SCOTT. IT'S SCOTT LANG.
Itsgettingworseidiot.
YOU CAN CALL ME SCOTT.
Stoptalkingnow.
AH, YES--HERE IT IS. WELL, MISTER LANG, AS I WAS SAYING, THANK YOU FOR COMING DOWN TO SPEAK WITH US--
AND THANK YOU FOR ACCEPTING A DOUBLE-SIDED RESUMÉ.
YES, UNCONVENTIONAL, THAT--
APPARENTLY IT'S THE DEFAULT SETTING AT KINKO'S.
KINKO'S?
I HAD NO IDEA. THEN IF YOU WANT TO GO BACK AND DO IT AGAIN, THEY CHARGE YOU FOR ANOTHER PRINT JOB, WHICH MEANS YOU GOTTA REFILL YOUR CARD--
AHEM. IT'S...FINE, REALLY. BUT BEFORE WE BEGIN TH INTERVIEW, I DID NEED TO ASK ABOUT SOMETHING-
IN YOUR PRELIMINARY PAPERWORK, UNDER THE BOX FOR "HAVE YOU EVER BEEN CONVICTED OF A FELONY?" YOU CHECKED YES. WAS THAT AN ERROR, OR...?
OH, UH, NO... NO, THAT'S RIGHT--
I BEEN TO PRISON.

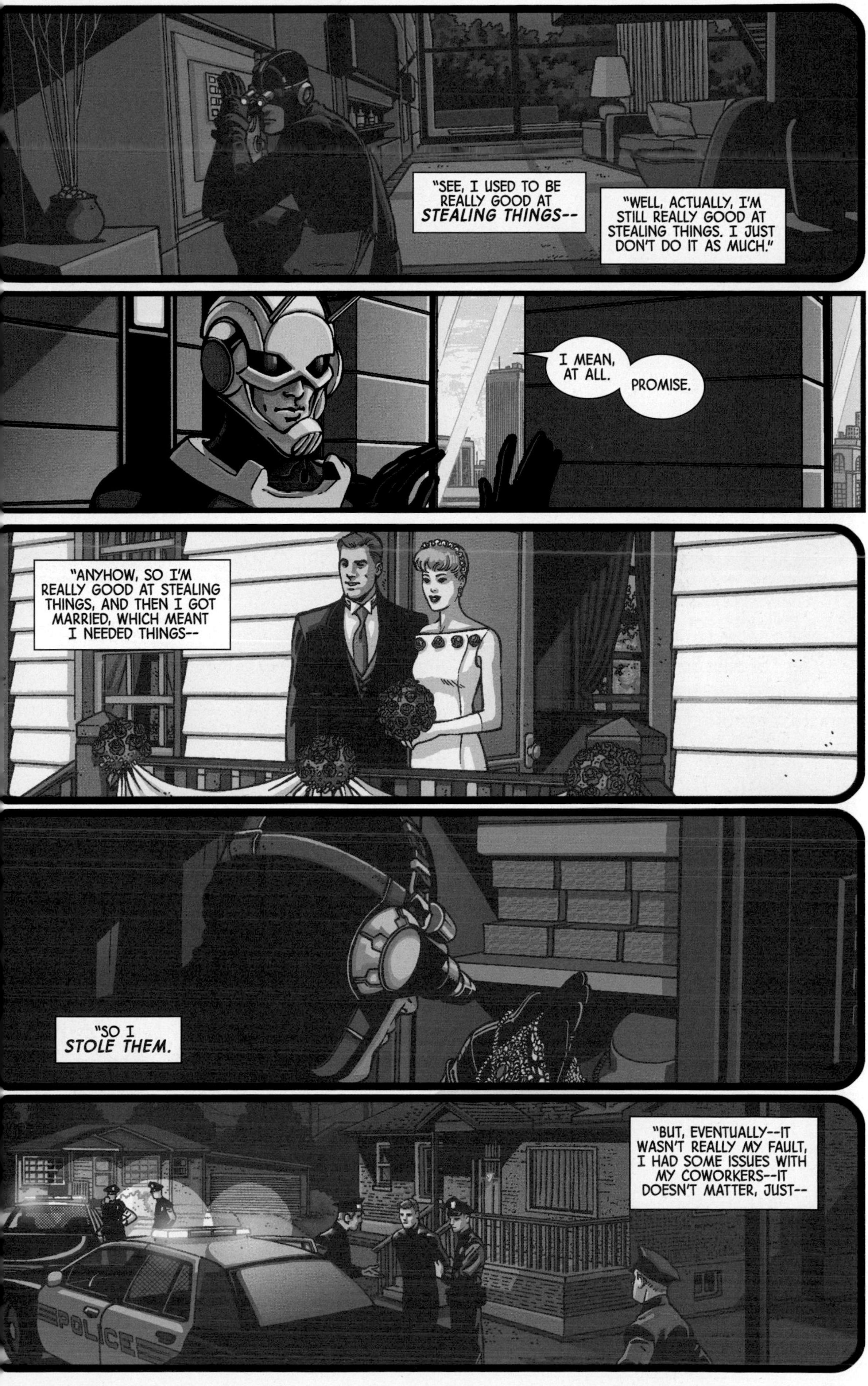
"SEE, I USED TO BE REALLY GOOD AT *STEALING THINGS*--
"WELL, ACTUALLY, I'M STILL REALLY GOOD AT STEALING THINGS. I JUST DON'T DO IT AS MUCH."
I MEAN, AT ALL.
PROMISE.
"ANYHOW, SO I'M REALLY GOOD AT STEALING THINGS, AND THEN I GOT MARRIED, WHICH MEANT I NEEDED THINGS--
"SO I *STOLE THEM.*
"BUT, EVENTUALLY--IT WASN'T REALLY MY FAULT, I HAD SOME ISSUES WITH MY COWORKERS--IT DOESN'T MATTER, JUST--
POLICE

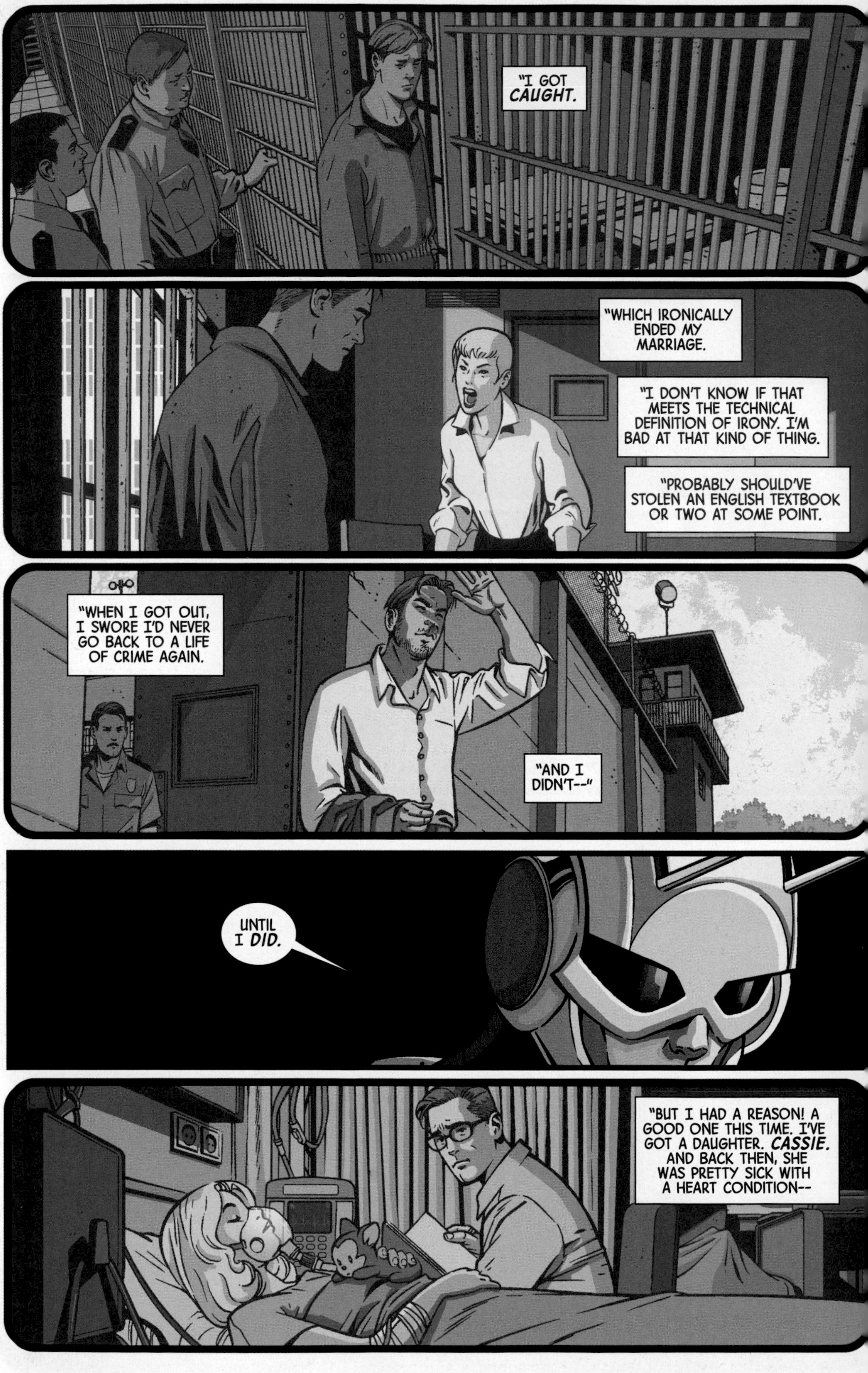
"I GOT CAUGHT.
"WHICH IRONICALLY ENDED MY MARRIAGE.
"I DON'T KNOW IF THAT MEETS THE TECHNICAL DEFINITION OF IRONY. I'M BAD AT THAT KIND OF THING.
"PROBABLY SHOULD'VE STOLEN AN ENGLISH TEXTBOOK OR TWO AT SOME POINT.
"WHEN I GOT OUT, I SWORE I'D NEVER GO BACK TO A LIFE OF CRIME AGAIN.
"AND I DIDN'T--"
UNTIL I DID.
"BUT I HAD A REASON! A GOOD ONE THIS TIME. I'VE GOT A DAUGHTER. CASSIE. AND BACK THEN, SHE WAS PRETTY SICK WITH A HEART CONDITION--

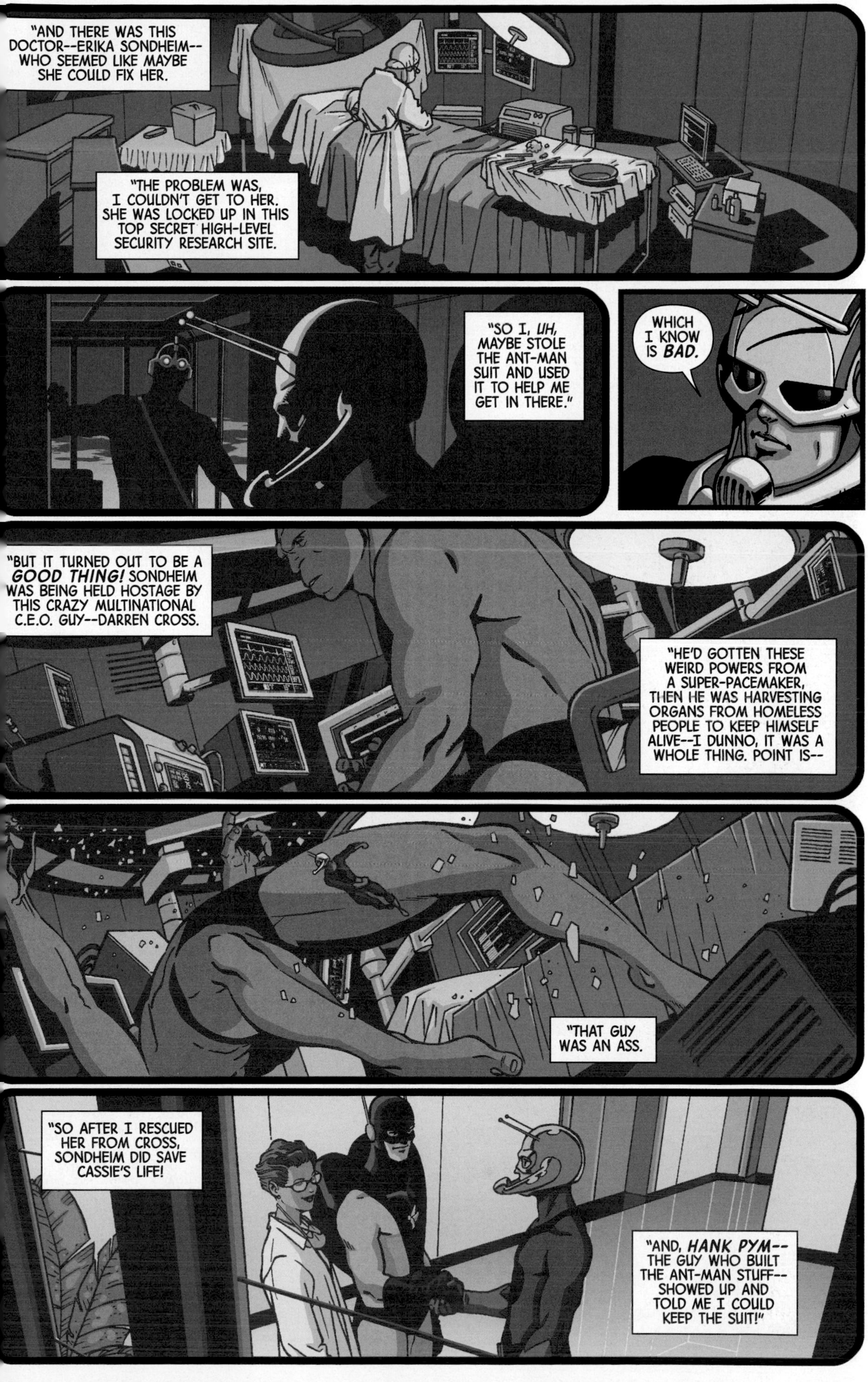
"AND THERE WAS THIS DOCTOR--ERIKA SONDHEIM--WHO SEEMED LIKE MAYBE SHE COULD FIX HER.
"THE PROBLEM WAS, I COULDN'T GET TO HER. SHE WAS LOCKED UP IN THIS TOP SECRET HIGH-LEVEL SECURITY RESEARCH SITE.
"SO I, *UH,* MAYBE STOLE THE ANT-MAN SUIT AND USED IT TO HELP ME GET IN THERE."
WHICH I KNOW IS ***BAD.***
"BUT IT TURNED OUT TO BE A ***GOOD THING!*** SONDHEIM WAS BEING HELD HOSTAGE BY THIS CRAZY MULTINATIONAL C.E.O. GUY--DARREN CROSS.
"HE'D GOTTEN THESE WEIRD POWERS FROM A SUPER-PACEMAKER, THEN HE WAS HARVESTING ORGANS FROM HOMELESS PEOPLE TO KEEP HIMSELF ALIVE--I DUNNO, IT WAS A WHOLE THING. POINT IS--
"THAT GUY WAS AN ASS.
"SO AFTER I RESCUED HER FROM CROSS, SONDHEIM DID SAVE CASSIE'S LIFE!
"AND, ***HANK PYM***--THE GUY WHO BUILT THE ANT-MAN STUFF--SHOWED UP AND TOLD ME I COULD KEEP THE SUIT!"

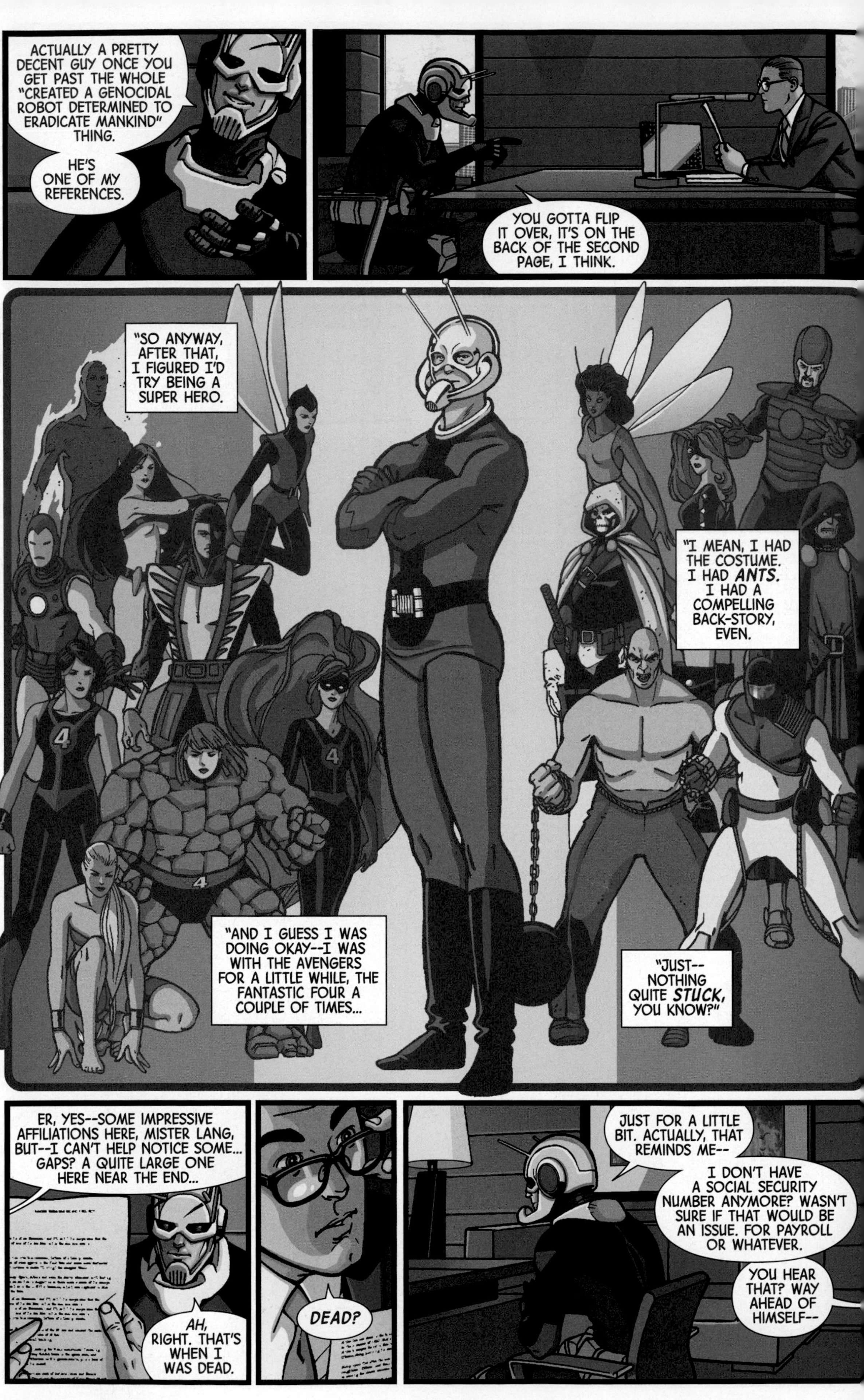
ACTUALLY A PRETTY DECENT GUY ONCE YOU GET PAST THE WHOLE "CREATED A GENOCIDAL ROBOT DETERMINED TO ERADICATE MANKIND" THING.
HE'S ONE OF MY REFERENCES.
YOU GOTTA FLIP IT OVER, IT'S ON THE BACK OF THE SECOND PAGE, I THINK.
"SO ANYWAY, AFTER THAT, I FIGURED I'D TRY BEING A SUPER HERO.
"I MEAN, I HAD THE COSTUME. I HAD ANTS. I HAD A COMPELLING BACK-STORY, EVEN.
"AND I GUESS I WAS DOING OKAY--I WAS WITH THE AVENGERS FOR A LITTLE WHILE, THE FANTASTIC FOUR A COUPLE OF TIMES...
"JUST--NOTHING QUITE STUCK, YOU KNOW?"
ER, YES--SOME IMPRESSIVE AFFILIATIONS HERE, MISTER LANG, BUT--I CAN'T HELP NOTICE SOME... GAPS? A QUITE LARGE ONE HERE NEAR THE END...
AH, RIGHT. THAT'S WHEN I WAS DEAD.
DEAD?
JUST FOR A LITTLE BIT. ACTUALLY, THAT REMINDS ME--
I DON'T HAVE A SOCIAL SECURITY NUMBER ANYMORE? WASN'T SURE IF THAT WOULD BE AN ISSUE. FOR PAYROLL OR WHATEVER.
YOU HEAR THAT? WAY AHEAD OF HIMSELF--

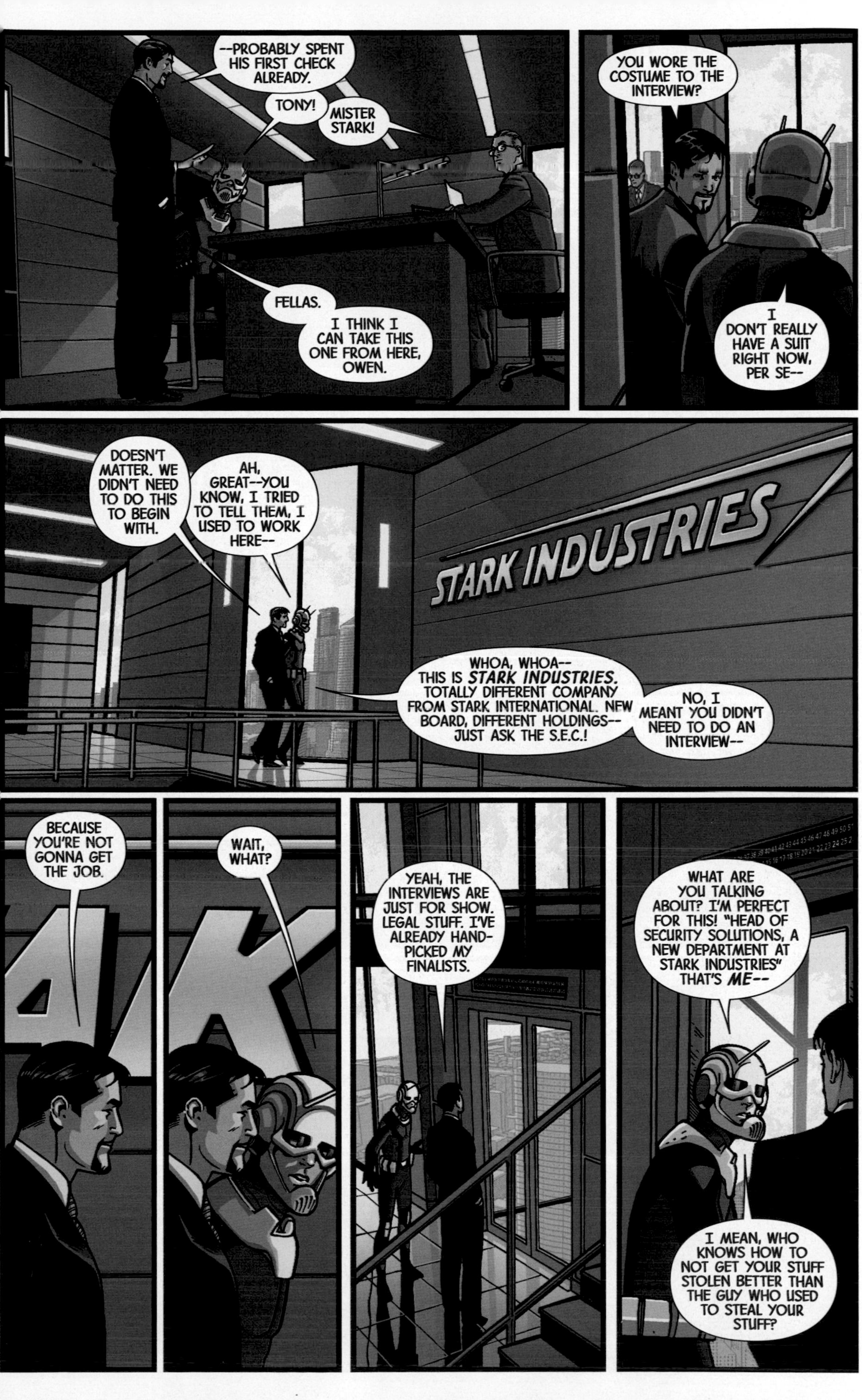
--PROBABLY SPENT HIS FIRST CHECK ALREADY.
TONY!
MISTER STARK!
FELLAS.
I THINK I CAN TAKE THIS ONE FROM HERE, OWEN.
YOU WORE THE COSTUME TO THE INTERVIEW?
I DON'T REALLY HAVE A SUIT RIGHT NOW, PER SE--
DOESN'T MATTER. WE DIDN'T NEED TO DO THIS TO BEGIN WITH.
AH, GREAT--YOU KNOW, I TRIED TO TELL THEM, I USED TO WORK HERE--
STARK INDUSTRIES
WHOA, WHOA-- THIS IS *STARK INDUSTRIES.* TOTALLY DIFFERENT COMPANY FROM STARK INTERNATIONAL. NEW BOARD, DIFFERENT HOLDINGS-- JUST ASK THE S.E.C.!
NO, I MEANT YOU DIDN'T NEED TO DO AN INTERVIEW--
BECAUSE YOU'RE NOT GONNA GET THE JOB.
WAIT, WHAT?
YEAH, THE INTERVIEWS ARE JUST FOR SHOW. LEGAL STUFF. I'VE ALREADY HAND-PICKED MY FINALISTS.
WHAT ARE YOU TALKING ABOUT? I'M PERFECT FOR THIS! "HEAD OF SECURITY SOLUTIONS, A NEW DEPARTMENT AT STARK INDUSTRIES" THAT'S *ME--*
I MEAN, WHO KNOWS HOW TO NOT GET YOUR STUFF STOLEN BETTER THAN THE GUY WHO USED TO STEAL YOUR STUFF?

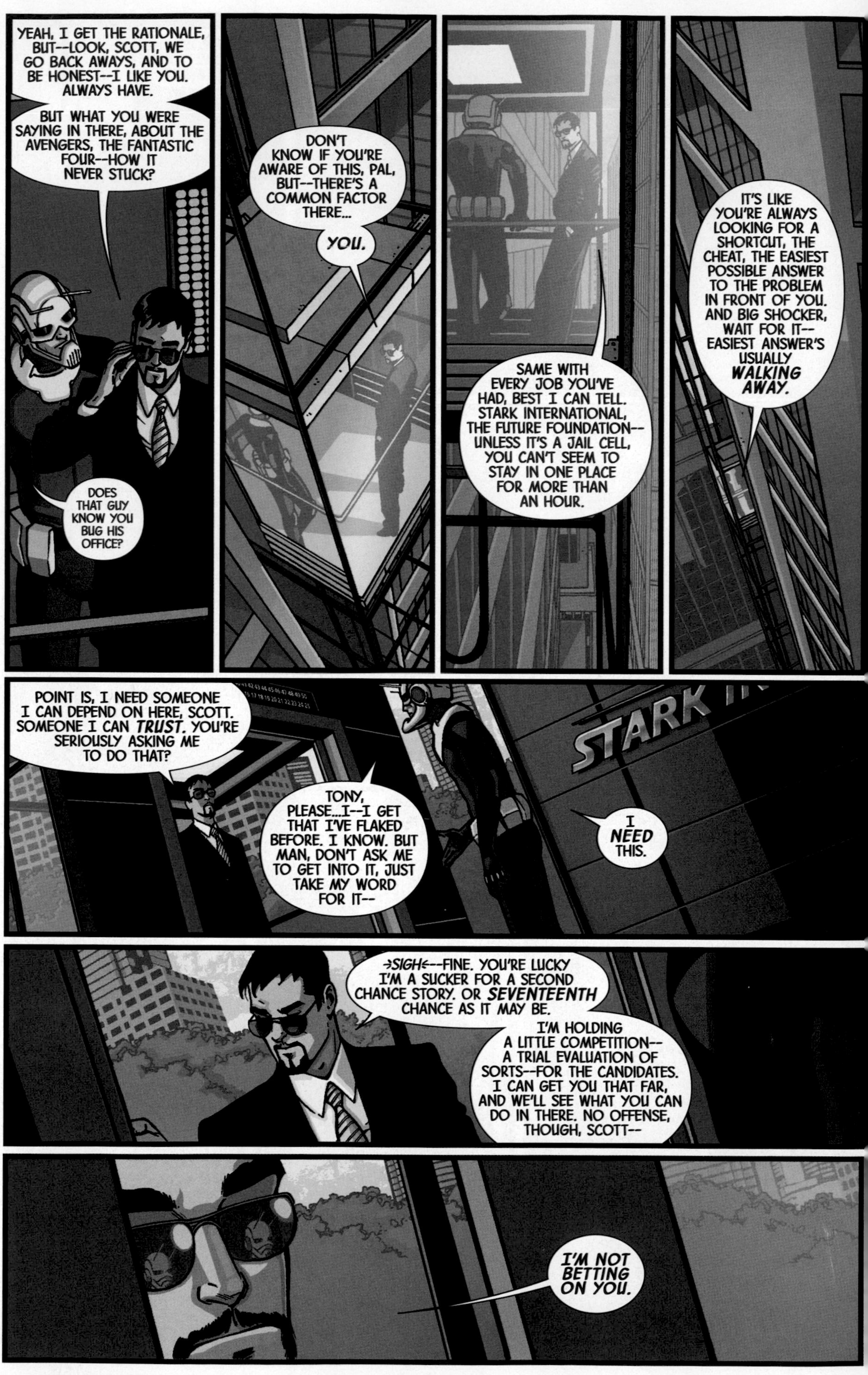
YEAH, I GET THE RATIONALE, BUT--LOOK, SCOTT, WE GO BACK AWAYS, AND TO BE HONEST--I LIKE YOU. ALWAYS HAVE.
BUT WHAT YOU WERE SAYING IN THERE, ABOUT THE AVENGERS, THE FANTASTIC FOUR--HOW IT NEVER STUCK?
DOES THAT GUY KNOW YOU BUG HIS OFFICE?
DON'T KNOW IF YOU'RE AWARE OF THIS, PAL, BUT--THERE'S A COMMON FACTOR THERE...
YOU.
SAME WITH EVERY JOB YOU'VE HAD, BEST I CAN TELL. STARK INTERNATIONAL, THE FUTURE FOUNDATION--UNLESS IT'S A JAIL CELL, YOU CAN'T SEEM TO STAY IN ONE PLACE FOR MORE THAN AN HOUR.
IT'S LIKE YOU'RE ALWAYS LOOKING FOR A SHORTCUT, THE CHEAT, THE EASIEST POSSIBLE ANSWER TO THE PROBLEM IN FRONT OF YOU. AND BIG SHOCKER, WAIT FOR IT--EASIEST ANSWER'S USUALLY WALKING AWAY.
POINT IS, I NEED SOMEONE I CAN DEPEND ON HERE, SCOTT. SOMEONE I CAN TRUST. YOU'RE SERIOUSLY ASKING ME TO DO THAT?
TONY, PLEASE...I--I GET THAT I'VE FLAKED BEFORE. I KNOW. BUT MAN, DON'T ASK ME TO GET INTO IT, JUST TAKE MY WORD FOR IT--
STARK
I NEED THIS.
→SIGH←--FINE. YOU'RE LUCKY I'M A SUCKER FOR A SECOND CHANCE STORY. OR SEVENTEENTH CHANCE AS IT MAY BE.
I'M HOLDING A LITTLE COMPETITION--A TRIAL EVALUATION OF SORTS--FOR THE CANDIDATES. I CAN GET YOU THAT FAR, AND WE'LL SEE WHAT YOU CAN DO IN THERE. NO OFFENSE, THOUGH, SCOTT--
I'M NOT BETTING ON YOU.

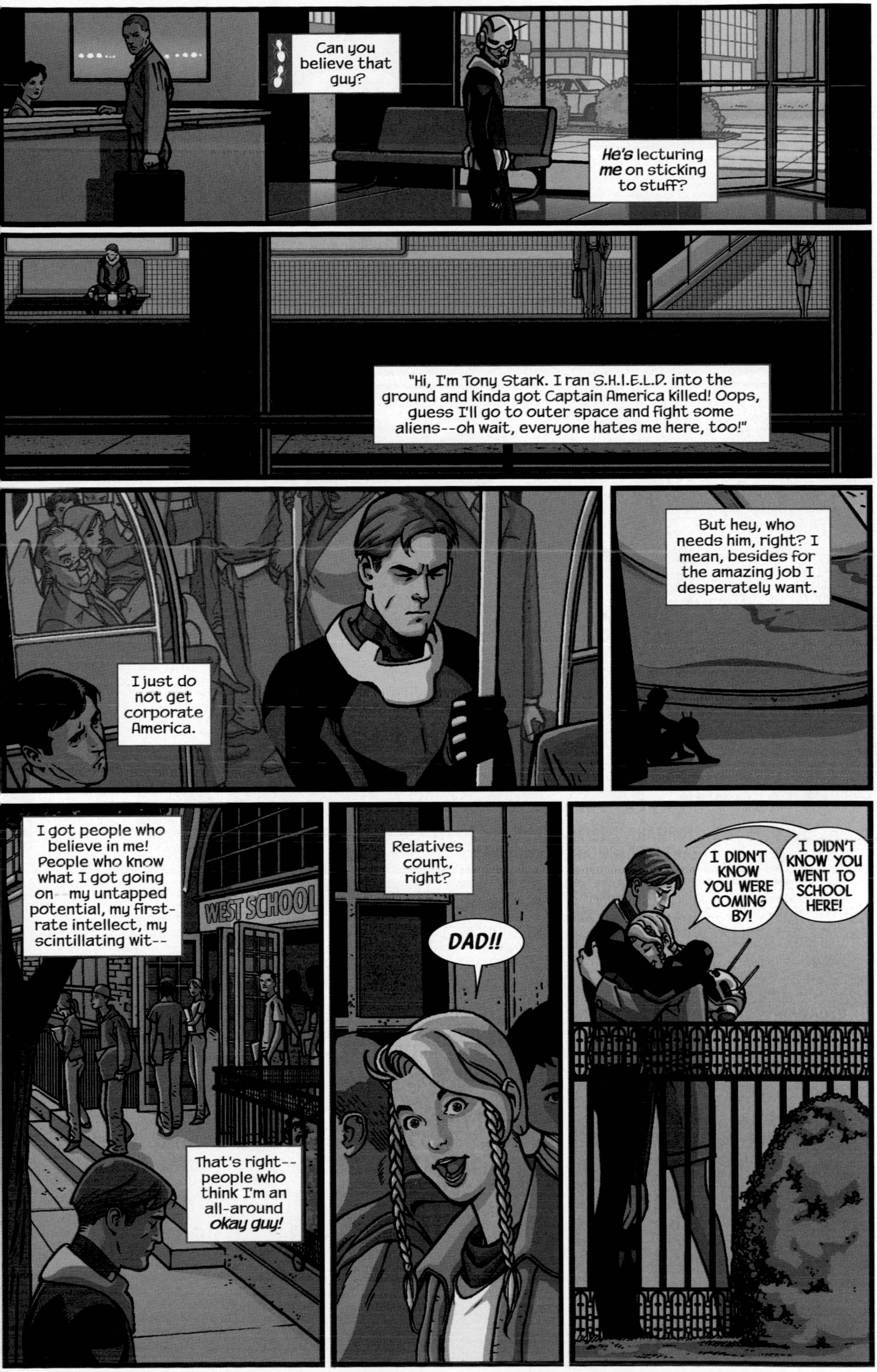
Can you believe that guy?
He's lecturing me on sticking to stuff?
"Hi, I'm Tony Stark. I ran S.H.I.E.L.D. into the ground and kinda got Captain America killed! Oops, guess I'll go to outer space and fight some aliens--oh wait, everyone hates me here, too!"
I just do not get corporate America.
But hey, who needs him, right? I mean, besides for the amazing job I desperately want.
I got people who believe in me! People who know what I got going on--my untapped potential, my first-rate intellect, my scintillating wit--
WEST SCHOOL
That's right--people who think I'm an all-around okay guy!
Relatives count, right?
DAD!!
I DIDN'T KNOW YOU WERE COMING BY!
I DIDN'T KNOW YOU WENT TO SCHOOL HERE!

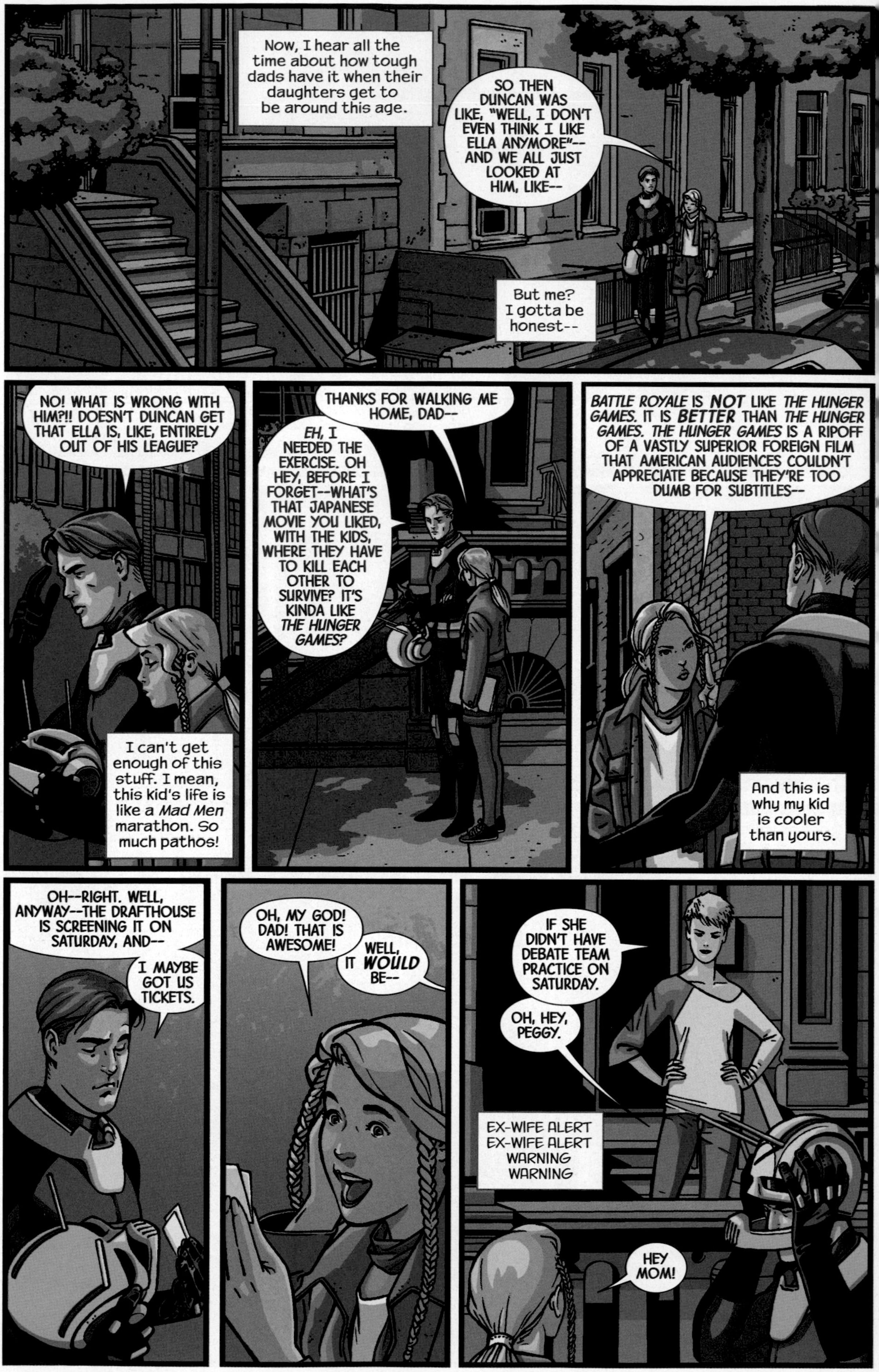

Now, I hear all the time about how tough dads have it when their daughters get to be around this age.
SO THEN DUNCAN WAS LIKE, "WELL, I DON'T EVEN THINK I LIKE ELLA ANYMORE"--AND WE ALL JUST LOOKED AT HIM, LIKE--
But me? I gotta be honest--
NO! WHAT IS WRONG WITH HIM?!! DOESN'T DUNCAN GET THAT ELLA IS, LIKE, ENTIRELY OUT OF HIS LEAGUE?
I can't get enough of this stuff. I mean, this kid's life is like a *Mad Men* marathon. So much pathos!
THANKS FOR WALKING ME HOME, DAD--
EH, I NEEDED THE EXERCISE. OH HEY, BEFORE I FORGET--WHAT'S THAT JAPANESE MOVIE YOU LIKED, WITH THE KIDS, WHERE THEY HAVE TO KILL EACH OTHER TO SURVIVE? IT'S KINDA LIKE *THE HUNGER GAMES?*
BATTLE ROYALE IS **NOT** LIKE *THE HUNGER GAMES*. IT IS **BETTER** THAN *THE HUNGER GAMES*. *THE HUNGER GAMES* IS A RIPOFF OF A VASTLY SUPERIOR FOREIGN FILM THAT AMERICAN AUDIENCES COULDN'T APPRECIATE BECAUSE THEY'RE TOO DUMB FOR SUBTITLES--
And this is why my kid is cooler than yours.
OH--RIGHT. WELL, ANYWAY--THE DRAFTHOUSE IS SCREENING IT ON SATURDAY, AND--
I MAYBE GOT US TICKETS.
OH, MY GOD! DAD! THAT IS AWESOME!
WELL, IT ***WOULD*** BE--
IF SHE DIDN'T HAVE DEBATE TEAM PRACTICE ON SATURDAY.
OH, HEY, PEGGY.
EX-WIFE ALERT EX-WIFE ALERT WARNING WARNING
HEY MOM!

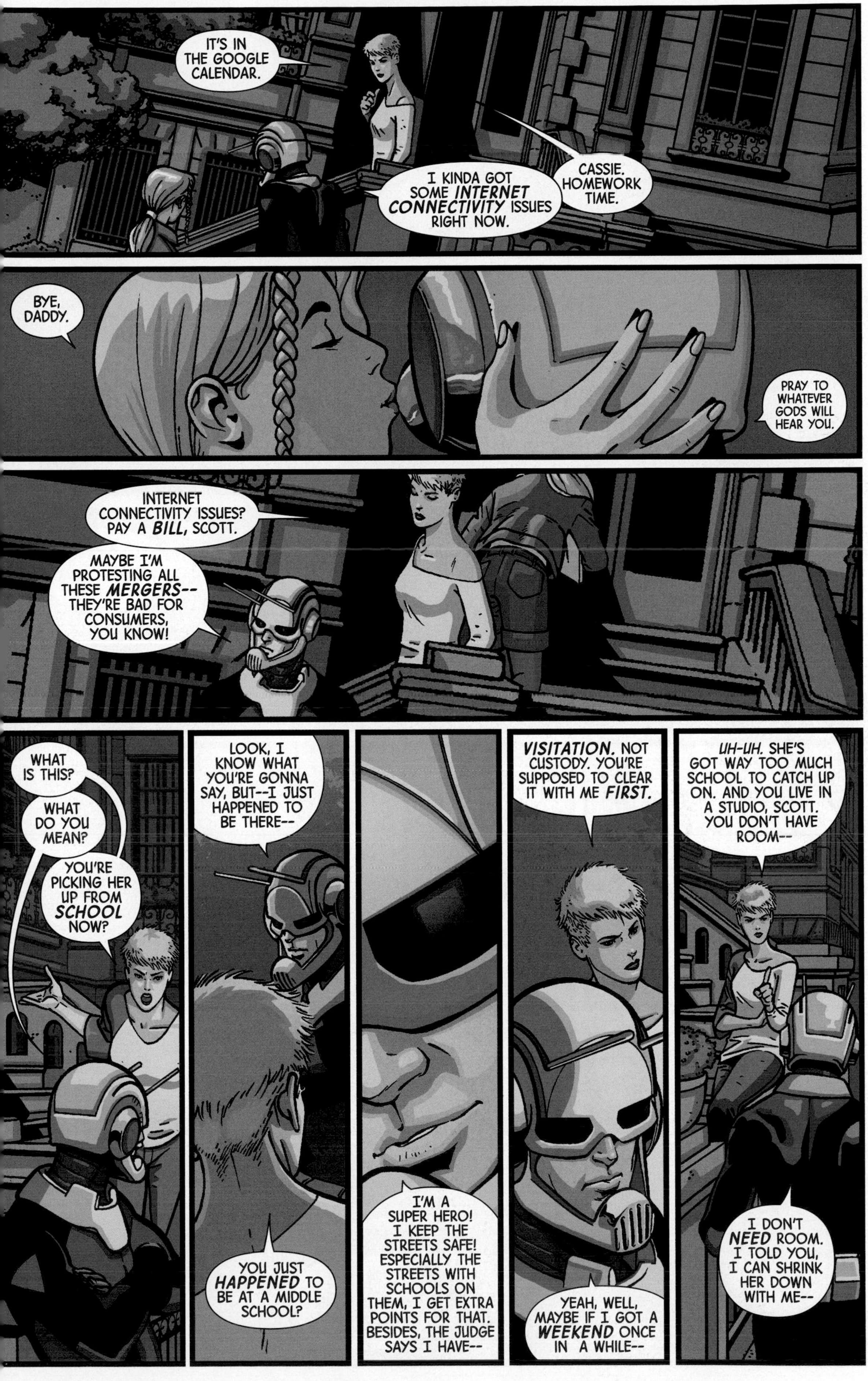
IT'S IN THE GOOGLE CALENDAR.
CASSIE. HOMEWORK TIME.
I KINDA GOT SOME INTERNET CONNECTIVITY ISSUES RIGHT NOW.
BYE, DADDY.
PRAY TO WHATEVER GODS WILL HEAR YOU.
INTERNET CONNECTIVITY ISSUES? PAY A BILL, SCOTT.
MAYBE I'M PROTESTING ALL THESE MERGERS-- THEY'RE BAD FOR CONSUMERS, YOU KNOW!
WHAT IS THIS?
WHAT DO YOU MEAN?
YOU'RE PICKING HER UP FROM SCHOOL NOW?
LOOK, I KNOW WHAT YOU'RE GONNA SAY, BUT--I JUST HAPPENED TO BE THERE--
YOU JUST HAPPENED TO BE AT A MIDDLE SCHOOL?
I'M A SUPER HERO! I KEEP THE STREETS SAFE! ESPECIALLY THE STREETS WITH SCHOOLS ON THEM, I GET EXTRA POINTS FOR THAT. BESIDES, THE JUDGE SAYS I HAVE--
VISITATION. NOT CUSTODY. YOU'RE SUPPOSED TO CLEAR IT WITH ME FIRST.
YEAH, WELL, MAYBE IF I GOT A WEEKEND ONCE IN A WHILE--
UH-UH. SHE'S GOT WAY TOO MUCH SCHOOL TO CATCH UP ON. AND YOU LIVE IN A STUDIO, SCOTT. YOU DON'T HAVE ROOM--
I DON'T NEED ROOM. I TOLD YOU, I CAN SHRINK HER DOWN WITH ME--

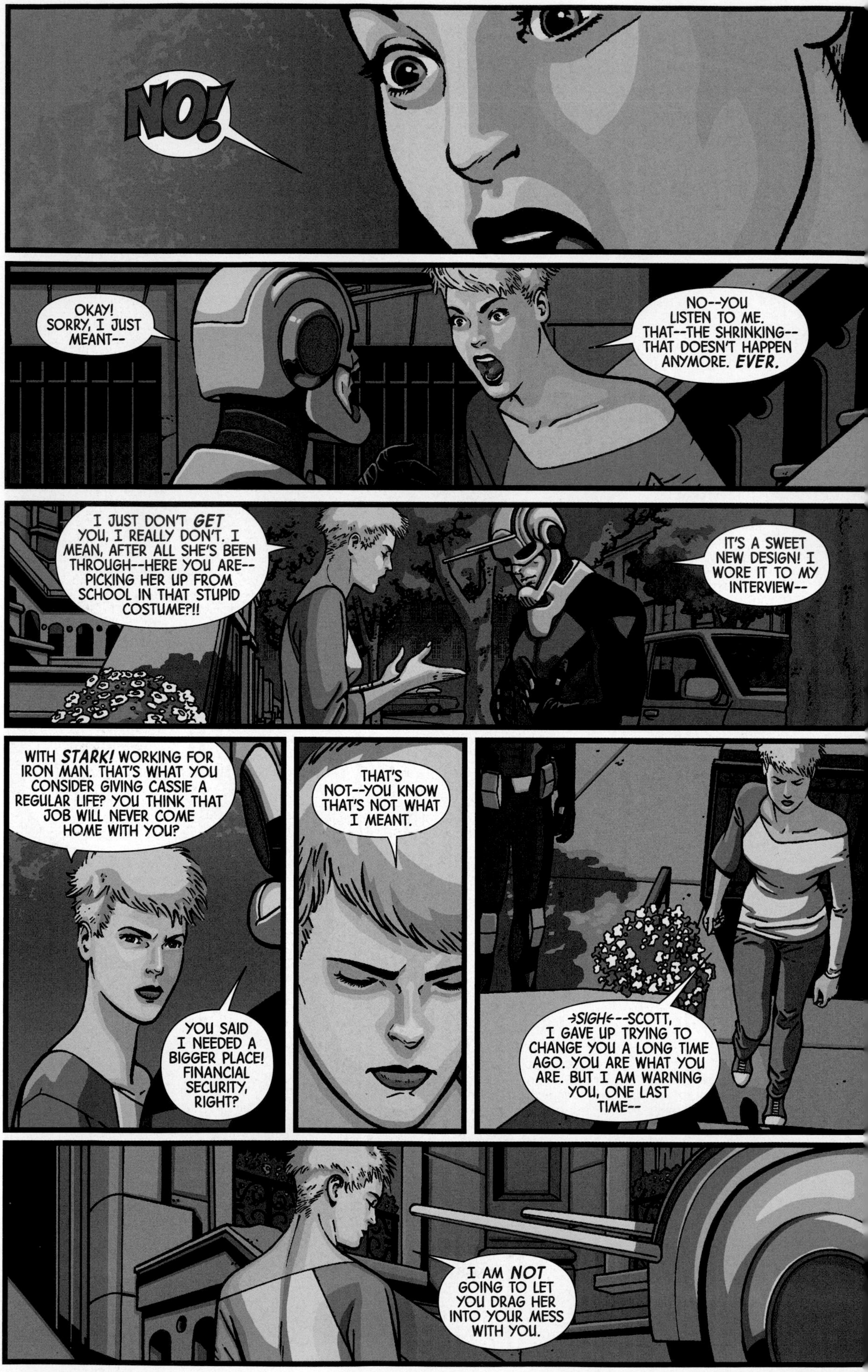
NO!
OKAY! SORRY, I JUST MEANT--
NO--YOU LISTEN TO ME. THAT--THE SHRINKING--THAT DOESN'T HAPPEN ANYMORE. EVER.
I JUST DON'T GET YOU, I REALLY DON'T. I MEAN, AFTER ALL SHE'S BEEN THROUGH--HERE YOU ARE--PICKING HER UP FROM SCHOOL IN THAT STUPID COSTUME?!!
IT'S A SWEET NEW DESIGN! I WORE IT TO MY INTERVIEW--
WITH STARK! WORKING FOR IRON MAN. THAT'S WHAT YOU CONSIDER GIVING CASSIE A REGULAR LIFE? YOU THINK THAT JOB WILL NEVER COME HOME WITH YOU?
YOU SAID I NEEDED A BIGGER PLACE! FINANCIAL SECURITY, RIGHT?
THAT'S NOT--YOU KNOW THAT'S NOT WHAT I MEANT.
→SIGH←--SCOTT, I GAVE UP TRYING TO CHANGE YOU A LONG TIME AGO. YOU ARE WHAT YOU ARE. BUT I AM WARNING YOU, ONE LAST TIME--
I AM NOT GOING TO LET YOU DRAG HER INTO YOUR MESS WITH YOU.

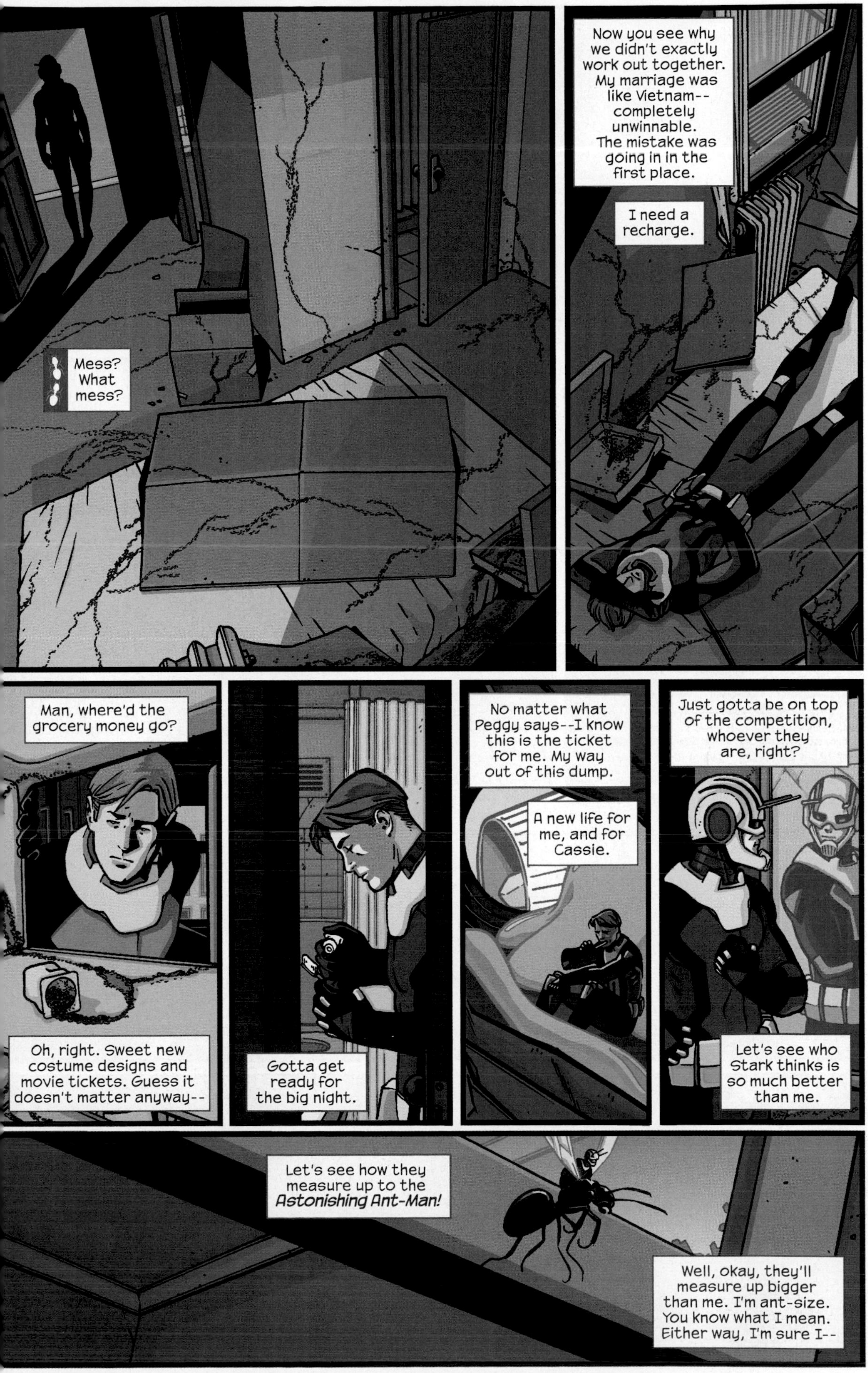
Mess? What mess?
Now you see why we didn't exactly work out together. My marriage was like Vietnam--completely unwinnable. The mistake was going in in the first place.
I need a recharge.
Man, where'd the grocery money go?
Oh, right. Sweet new costume designs and movie tickets. Guess it doesn't matter anyway--
Gotta get ready for the big night.
No matter what Peggy says--I know this is the ticket for me. My way out of this dump.
A new life for me, and for Cassie.
Just gotta be on top of the competition, whoever they are, right?
Let's see who Stark thinks is so much better than me.
Let's see how they measure up to the *Astonishing Ant-Man!*
Well, okay, they'll measure up bigger than me. I'm ant-size. You know what I mean. Either way, I'm sure I--

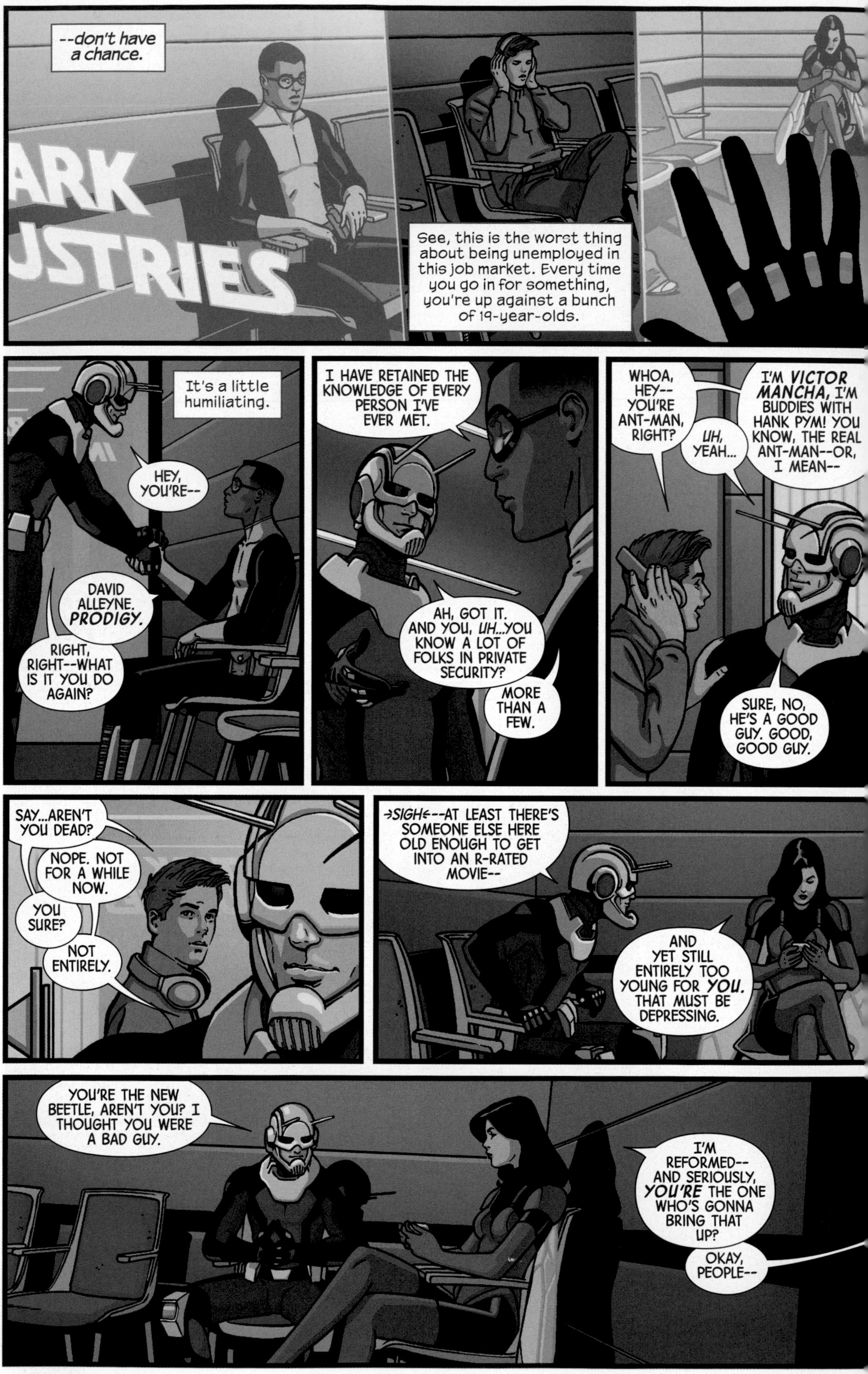
--don't have a chance.
ARK USTRIES
See, this is the worst thing about being unemployed in this job market. Every time you go in for something, you're up against a bunch of 19-year-olds.
It's a little humiliating.
HEY, YOU'RE--
DAVID ALLEYNE. PRODIGY.
RIGHT, RIGHT--WHAT IS IT YOU DO AGAIN?
I HAVE RETAINED THE KNOWLEDGE OF EVERY PERSON I'VE EVER MET.
AH, GOT IT. AND YOU, UH...YOU KNOW A LOT OF FOLKS IN PRIVATE SECURITY?
MORE THAN A FEW.
WHOA, HEY-- YOU'RE ANT-MAN, RIGHT?
UH, YEAH...
I'M VICTOR MANCHA, I'M BUDDIES WITH HANK PYM! YOU KNOW, THE REAL ANT-MAN--OR, I MEAN--
SURE, NO, HE'S A GOOD GUY. GOOD, GOOD GUY.
SAY...AREN'T YOU DEAD?
NOPE. NOT FOR A WHILE NOW.
YOU SURE?
NOT ENTIRELY.
→SIGH←--AT LEAST THERE'S SOMEONE ELSE HERE OLD ENOUGH TO GET INTO AN R-RATED MOVIE--
AND YET STILL ENTIRELY TOO YOUNG FOR YOU. THAT MUST BE DEPRESSING.
YOU'RE THE NEW BEETLE, AREN'T YOU? I THOUGHT YOU WERE A BAD GUY.
I'M REFORMED-- AND SERIOUSLY, YOU'RE THE ONE WHO'S GONNA BRING THAT UP?
OKAY, PEOPLE--

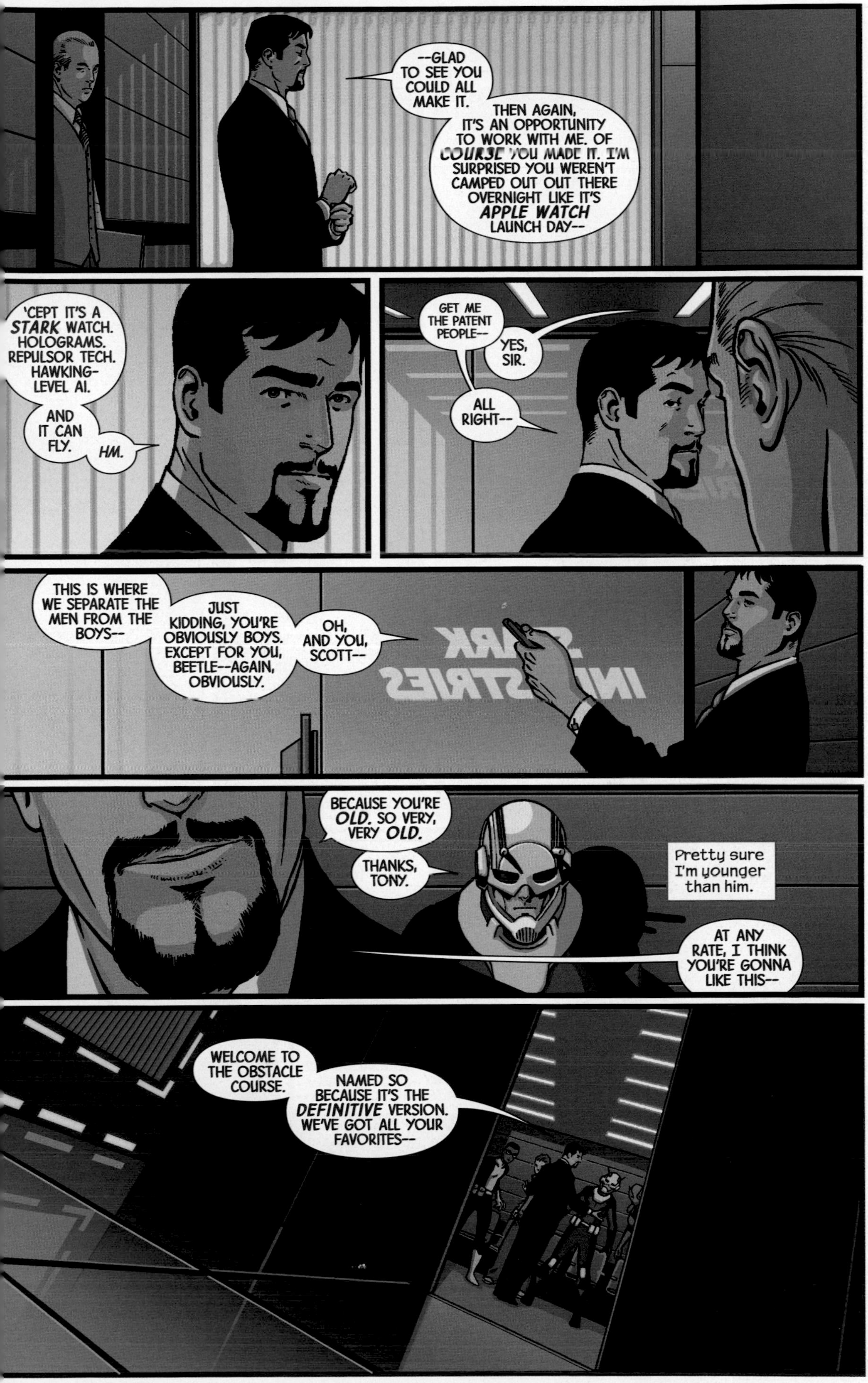
--GLAD TO SEE YOU COULD ALL MAKE IT.
THEN AGAIN, IT'S AN OPPORTUNITY TO WORK WITH ME. OF COURSE YOU MADE IT. I'M SURPRISED YOU WEREN'T CAMPED OUT OUT THERE OVERNIGHT LIKE IT'S APPLE WATCH LAUNCH DAY--
'CEPT IT'S A STARK WATCH. HOLOGRAMS. REPULSOR TECH. HAWKING-LEVEL AI.
AND IT CAN FLY.
HM.
GET ME THE PATENT PEOPLE--
YES, SIR.
ALL RIGHT--
THIS IS WHERE WE SEPARATE THE MEN FROM THE BOYS--
JUST KIDDING, YOU'RE OBVIOUSLY BOYS. EXCEPT FOR YOU, BEETLE--AGAIN, OBVIOUSLY.
OH, AND YOU, SCOTT--
BECAUSE YOU'RE OLD. SO VERY, VERY OLD.
THANKS, TONY.
Pretty sure I'm younger than him.
AT ANY RATE, I THINK YOU'RE GONNA LIKE THIS--
WELCOME TO THE OBSTACLE COURSE.
NAMED SO BECAUSE IT'S THE DEFINITIVE VERSION. WE'VE GOT ALL YOUR FAVORITES--

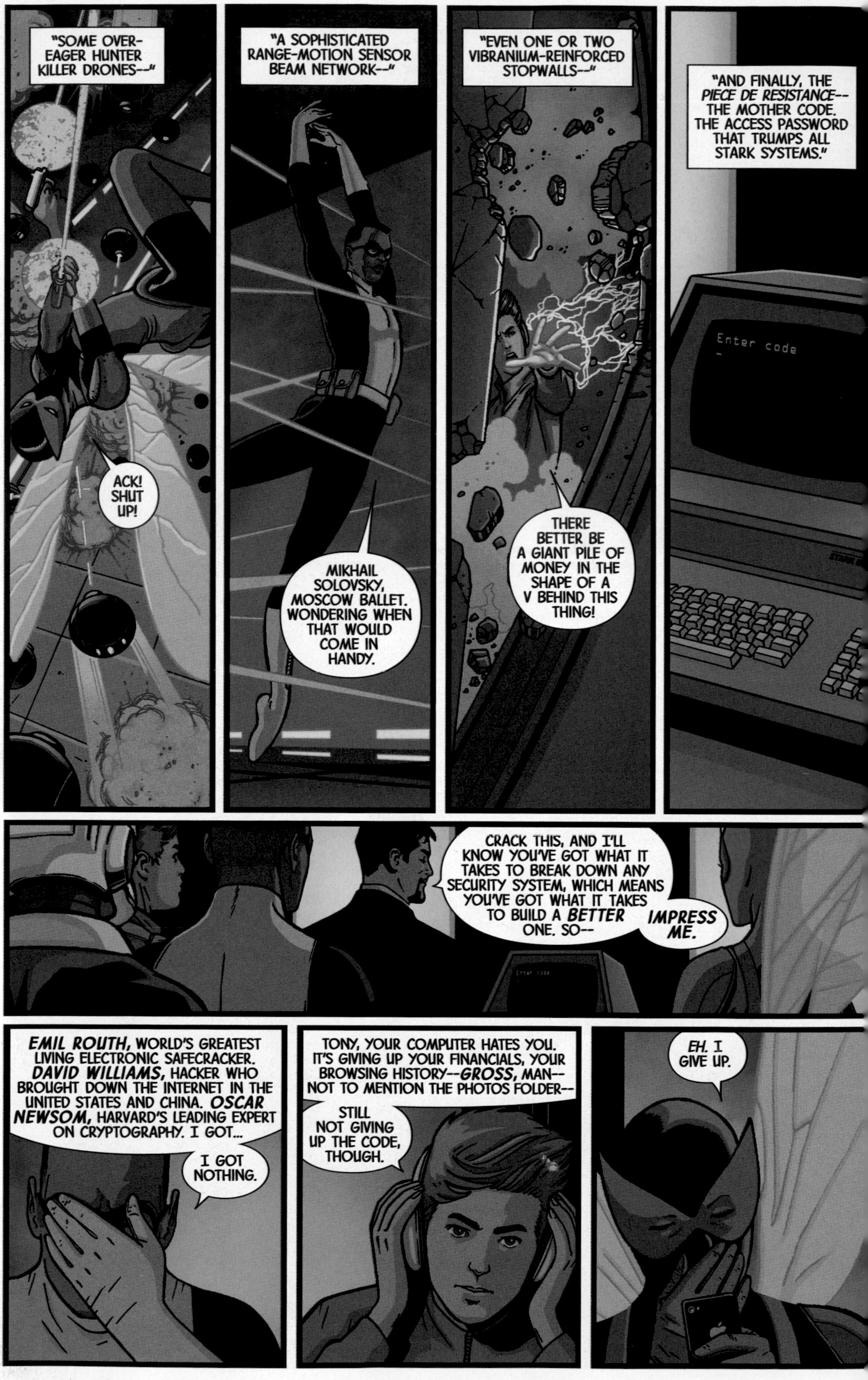
"SOME OVER-EAGER HUNTER KILLER DRONES--"
ACK! SHUT UP!
"A SOPHISTICATED RANGE-MOTION SENSOR BEAM NETWORK--"
MIKHAIL SOLOVSKY, MOSCOW BALLET. WONDERING WHEN THAT WOULD COME IN HANDY.
"EVEN ONE OR TWO VIBRANIUM-REINFORCED STOPWALLS--"
THERE BETTER BE A GIANT PILE OF MONEY IN THE SHAPE OF A V BEHIND THIS THING!
"AND FINALLY, THE *PIECE DE RESISTANCE*-- THE MOTHER CODE. THE ACCESS PASSWORD THAT TRUMPS ALL STARK SYSTEMS."
Enter code
CRACK THIS, AND I'LL KNOW YOU'VE GOT WHAT IT TAKES TO BREAK DOWN ANY SECURITY SYSTEM, WHICH MEANS YOU'VE GOT WHAT IT TAKES TO BUILD A ***BETTER*** ONE. SO--
IMPRESS ME.
EMIL ROUTH, WORLD'S GREATEST LIVING ELECTRONIC SAFECRACKER. ***DAVID WILLIAMS,*** HACKER WHO BROUGHT DOWN THE INTERNET IN THE UNITED STATES AND CHINA. ***OSCAR NEWSOM,*** HARVARD'S LEADING EXPERT ON CRYPTOGRAPHY. I GOT...
I GOT NOTHING.
TONY, YOUR COMPUTER HATES YOU. IT'S GIVING UP YOUR FINANCIALS, YOUR BROWSING HISTORY--***GROSS,*** MAN--NOT TO MENTION THE PHOTOS FOLDER--
STILL NOT GIVING UP THE CODE, THOUGH.
EH. I GIVE UP.

WELL, SCOTT-- YOU GONNA SHOW THESE KIDS HOW IT'S DONE?

WITH *PLEASURE,* TONY.

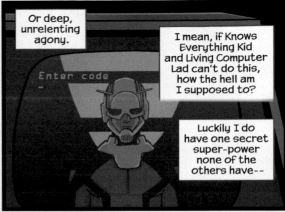

Or deep, unrelenting agony.

I mean, if Knows Everything Kid and Living Computer Lad can't do this, how the hell am I supposed to?

Luckily I do have one secret super-power none of the others have--

The power to fake *sick.*

See, with the Pym Particles, I can actually shrink individual parts of my body. Now this is not something most guys are usually in a rush to do, but in the case of the *digestive* system--

Can come in handy.

BLERGH!!

EWW!

OH MAN--

INSIDE THE HELMET!

OKAY, THAT'S ENOUGH--

TONY, I'M SORRY, I--I SHOULD'VE SAID SOMETHING. BEEN DEALING WITH A STOMACH FLU-- THOUGHT I COULD TOUGH IT OUT--

→SIGH←-- IT'S FINE--

LOOK, ALL OF YOU, HERE'S WHAT WE'RE GONNA DO. WE'LL RECONVENE TOMORROW MORNING AND GO THROUGH ALL OF THIS AGAIN, SEE IF WE GET SOME DIFFERENT RESULTS.

AND GOD KNOWS WE BETTER. I HAVE TO HIRE ONE OF YOU PEOPLE. RHODEY WON'T EVEN RETURN MY CALLS.

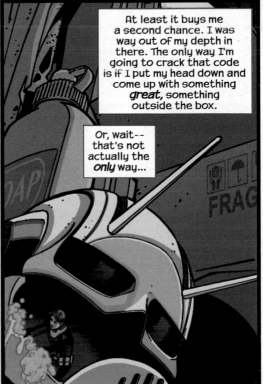

At least it buys me a second chance. I was way out of my depth in there. The only way I'm going to crack that code is if I put my head down and come up with something *great,* something outside the box.

Or, wait-- that's not actually the *only* way...

SOAP

FRAG

So yeah, this is how I ended up breaking into Tony Stark's apartment.

Y'know, on second thought--

Judge away.

Because if this is what I gotta do to give Cassie a better life, so be it. I know exactly where he'll have stored the mother code-- localized on his helmet. With the right gear, it's easy pickings.

I am in it to--

OH, TONY!!

Oh, come on!!

Beetle's hooking up with Stark now?!!

I can't believe this. That's totally cheating!

I mean, yeah, sure, this is cheating too, but-- this is different! In ways that are difficult to express!

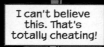

OPYING FILES 90 PERCENT

I HOPE YOU DON'T THINK THIS WILL GET YOU FAVORABLE TREATMENT TOMORROW AT THE COMPETITION.

IF I THOUGHT THAT WAS SOMETHING YOU COULD CONTROL, I WOULDN'T BE HERE.

Whatever. Tomorrow we'll see how her unmerited advantage does against my...unmerited advantage. For now, I just need to get out of here--

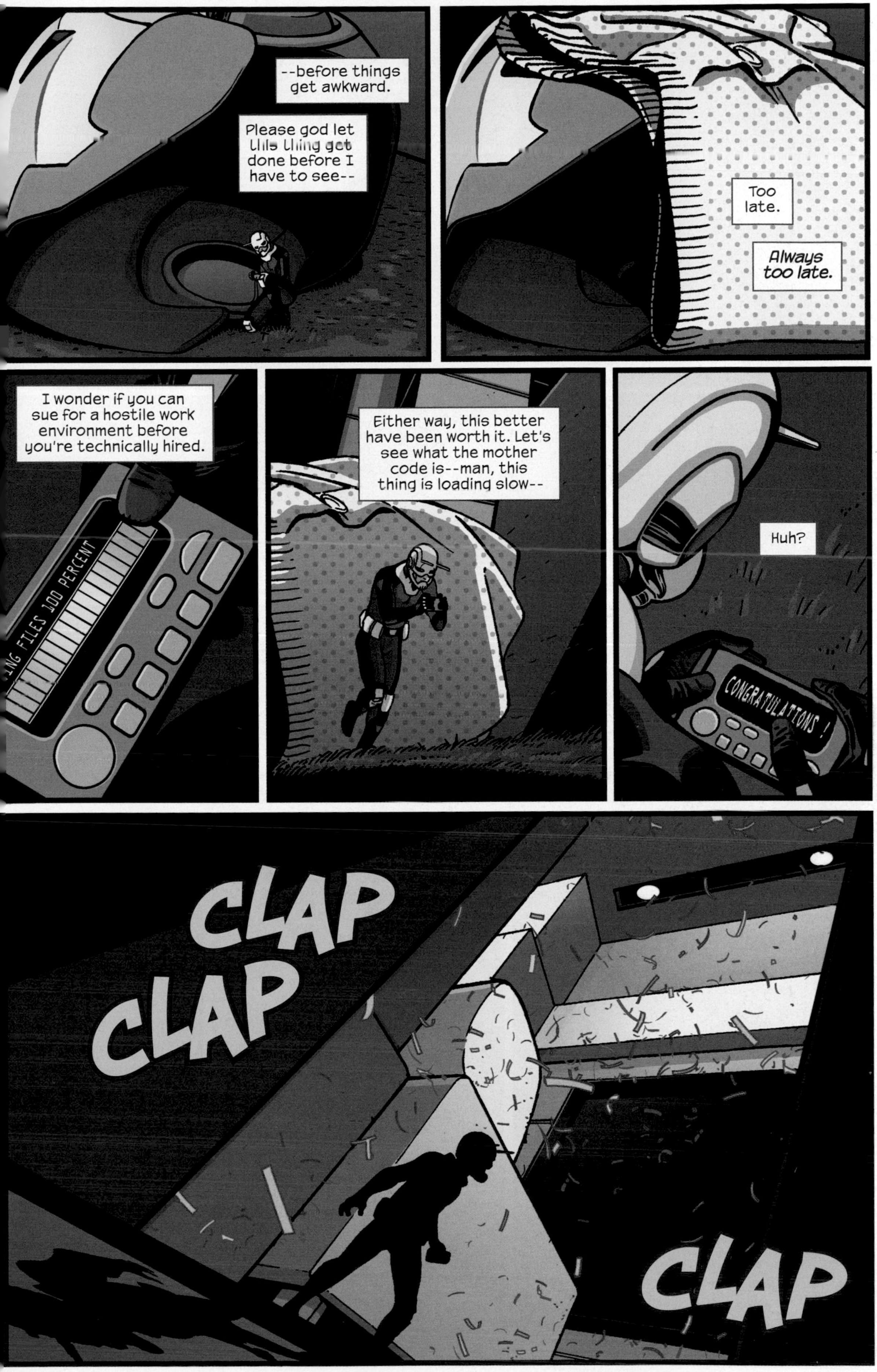

Please god let this thing get done before I have to see--
--before things get awkward.
Too late.
Always too late.
I wonder if you can sue for a hostile work environment before you're technically hired.
FILES 100 PERCENT
Either way, this better have been worth it. Let's see what the mother code is--man, this thing is loading slow--
Huh?
CONGRATULATIONS!
CLAP
CLAP
CLAP

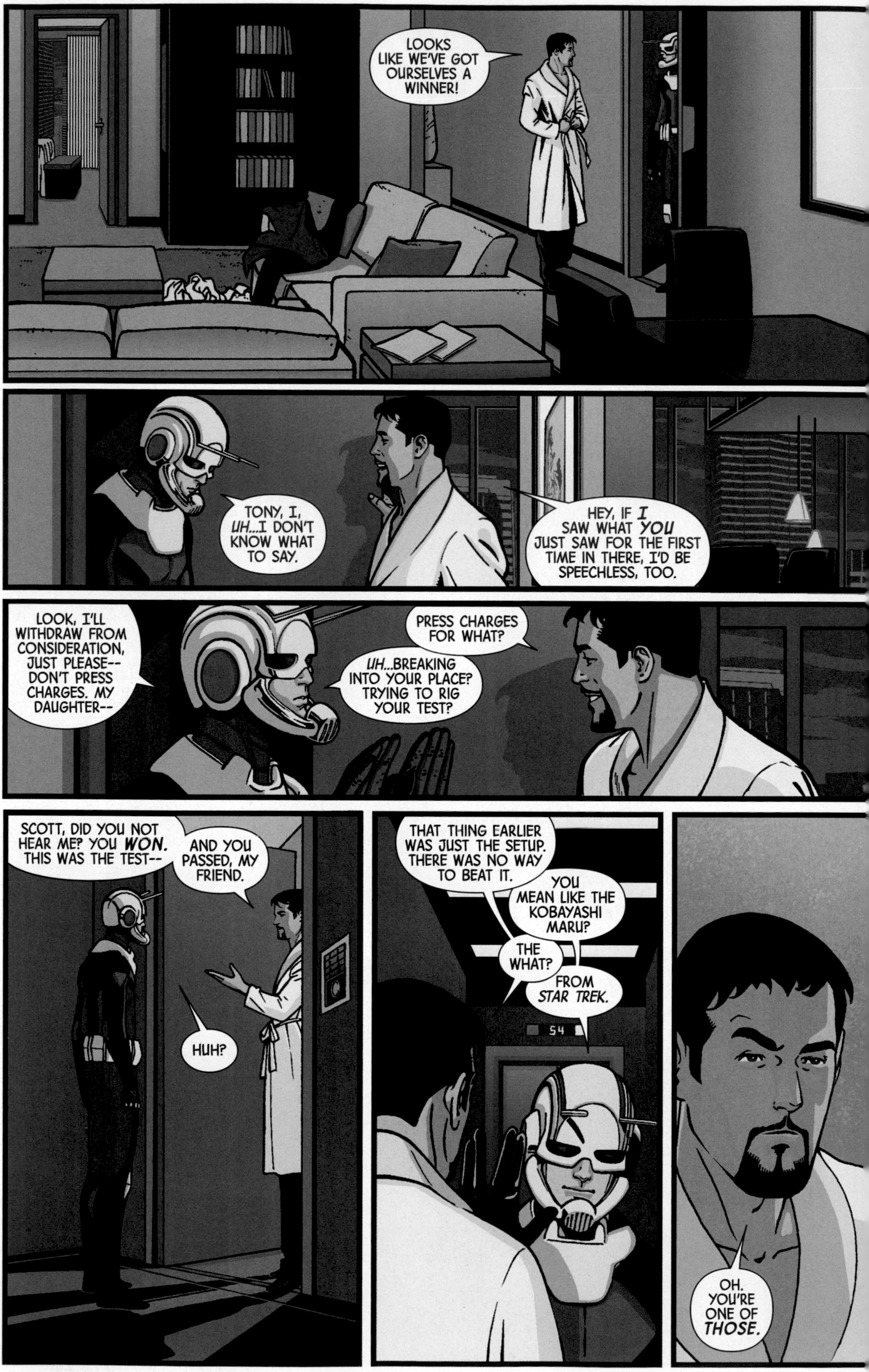

LOOKS LIKE WE'VE GOT OURSELVES A WINNER!
TONY, I, *UH*...I DON'T KNOW WHAT TO SAY.
HEY, IF *I* SAW WHAT *YOU* JUST SAW FOR THE FIRST TIME IN THERE, I'D BE SPEECHLESS, TOO.
LOOK, I'LL WITHDRAW FROM CONSIDERATION, JUST PLEASE-- DON'T PRESS CHARGES. MY DAUGHTER--
PRESS CHARGES FOR WHAT?
UH...BREAKING INTO YOUR PLACE? TRYING TO RIG YOUR TEST?
SCOTT, DID YOU NOT HEAR ME? YOU ***WON.*** THIS WAS THE TEST--
AND YOU PASSED, MY FRIEND.
HUH?
THAT THING EARLIER WAS JUST THE SETUP. THERE WAS NO WAY TO BEAT IT.
YOU MEAN LIKE THE KOBAYASHI MARU?
THE WHAT?
FROM *STAR TREK.*
54
OH. YOU'RE ONE OF ***THOSE.***

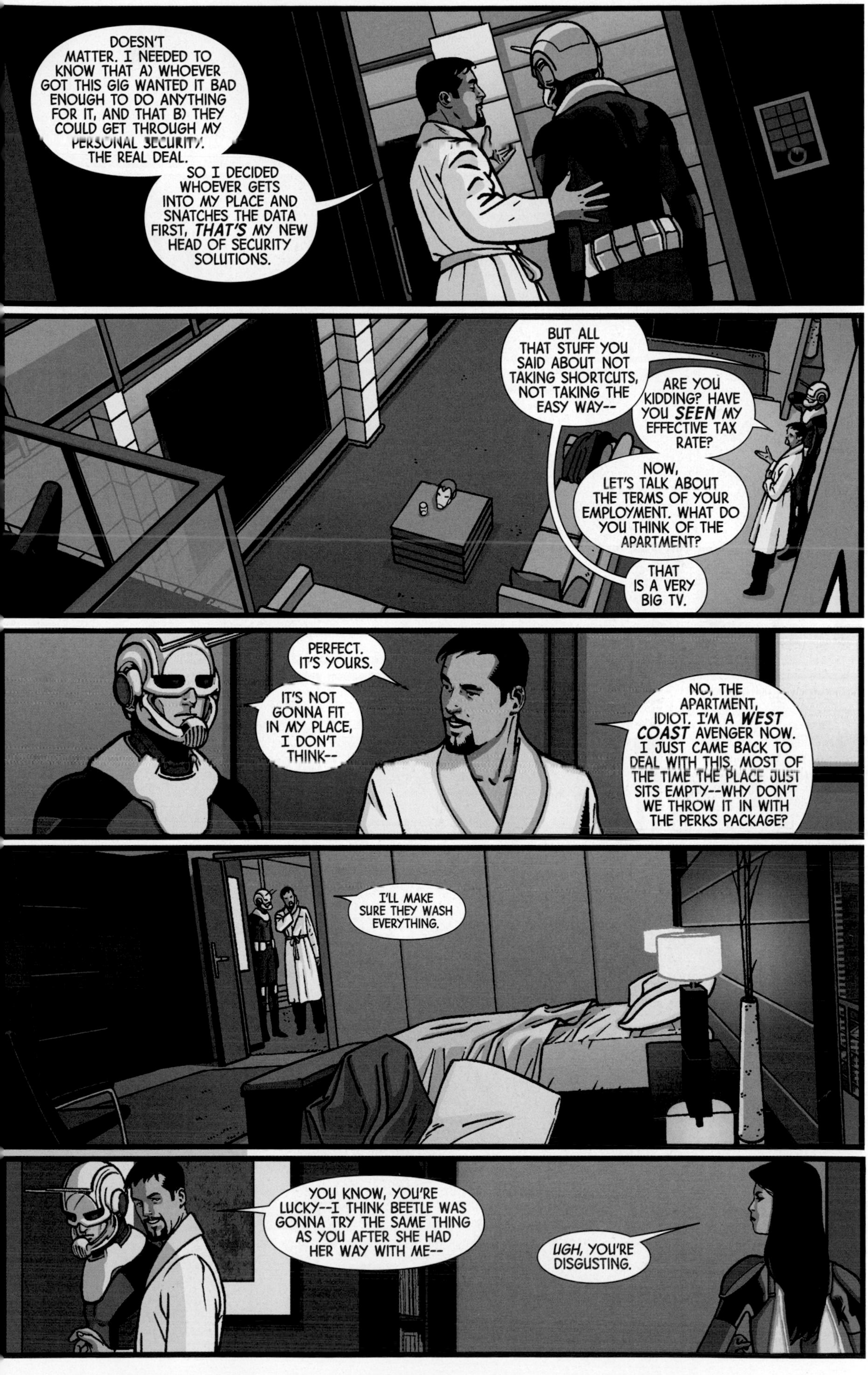
DOESN'T MATTER. I NEEDED TO KNOW THAT A) WHOEVER GOT THIS GIG WANTED IT BAD ENOUGH TO DO ANYTHING FOR IT, AND THAT B) THEY COULD GET THROUGH MY PERSONAL SECURITY. THE REAL DEAL.
SO I DECIDED WHOEVER GETS INTO MY PLACE AND SNATCHES THE DATA FIRST, *THAT'S* MY NEW HEAD OF SECURITY SOLUTIONS.
BUT ALL THAT STUFF YOU SAID ABOUT NOT TAKING SHORTCUTS, NOT TAKING THE EASY WAY--
ARE YOU KIDDING? HAVE YOU *SEEN* MY EFFECTIVE TAX RATE?
NOW, LET'S TALK ABOUT THE TERMS OF YOUR EMPLOYMENT. WHAT DO YOU THINK OF THE APARTMENT?
THAT IS A VERY BIG TV.
PERFECT. IT'S YOURS.
IT'S NOT GONNA FIT IN MY PLACE, I DON'T THINK--
NO, THE APARTMENT, IDIOT. I'M A *WEST COAST* AVENGER NOW. I JUST CAME BACK TO DEAL WITH THIS, MOST OF THE TIME THE PLACE JUST SITS EMPTY--WHY DON'T WE THROW IT IN WITH THE PERKS PACKAGE?
I'LL MAKE SURE THEY WASH EVERYTHING.
YOU KNOW, YOU'RE LUCKY--I THINK BEETLE WAS GONNA TRY THE SAME THING AS YOU AFTER SHE HAD HER WAY WITH ME--
UGH, YOU'RE DISGUSTING.

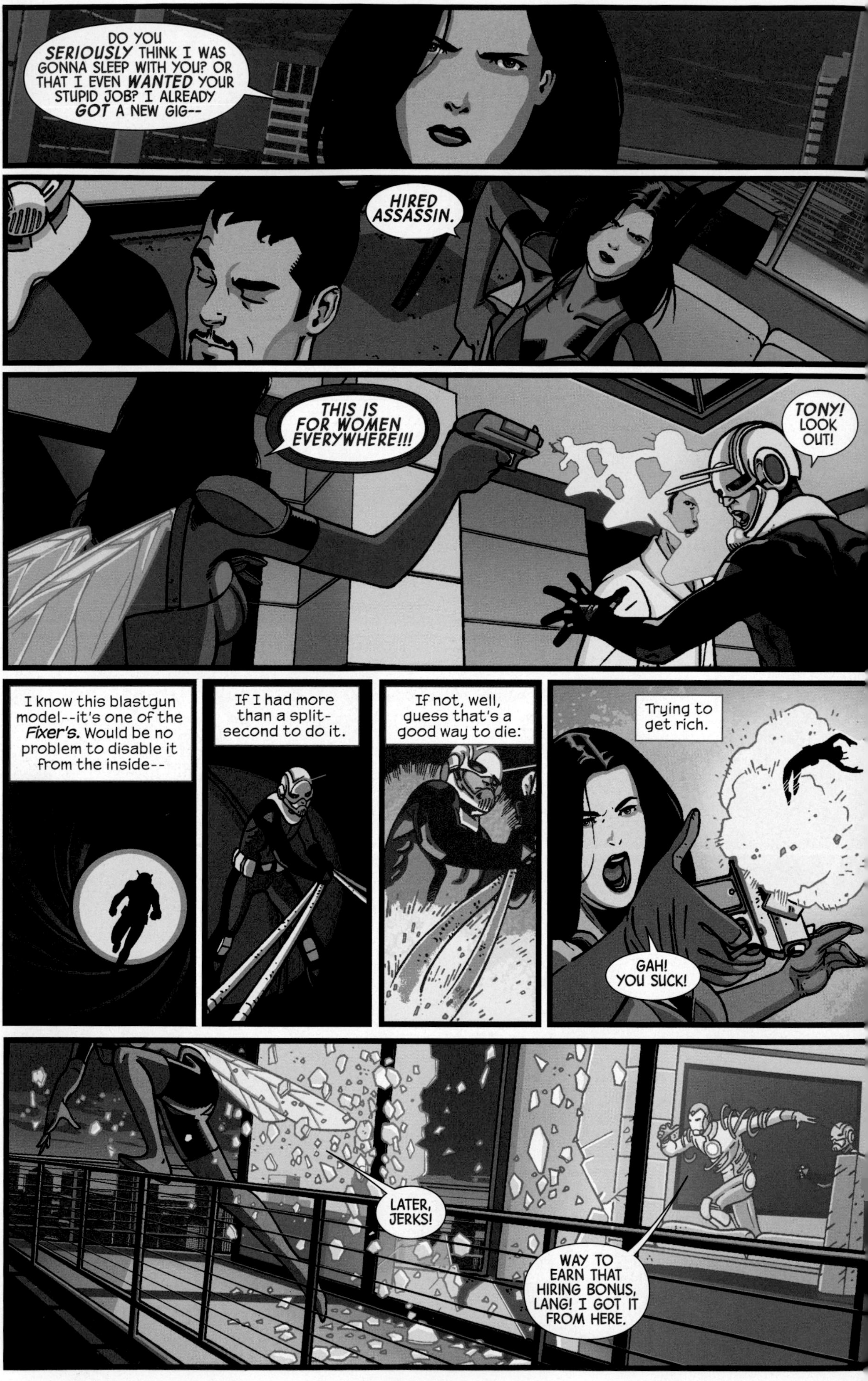
DO YOU SERIOUSLY THINK I WAS GONNA SLEEP WITH YOU? OR THAT I EVEN WANTED YOUR STUPID JOB? I ALREADY GOT A NEW GIG--
HIRED ASSASSIN.
THIS IS FOR WOMEN EVERYWHERE!!!
TONY! LOOK OUT!
I know this blastgun model--it's one of the Fixer's. Would be no problem to disable it from the inside--
If I had more than a split-second to do it.
If not, well, guess that's a good way to die:
Trying to get rich.
GAH! YOU SUCK!
LATER, JERKS!
WAY TO EARN THAT HIRING BONUS, LANG! I GOT IT FROM HERE.

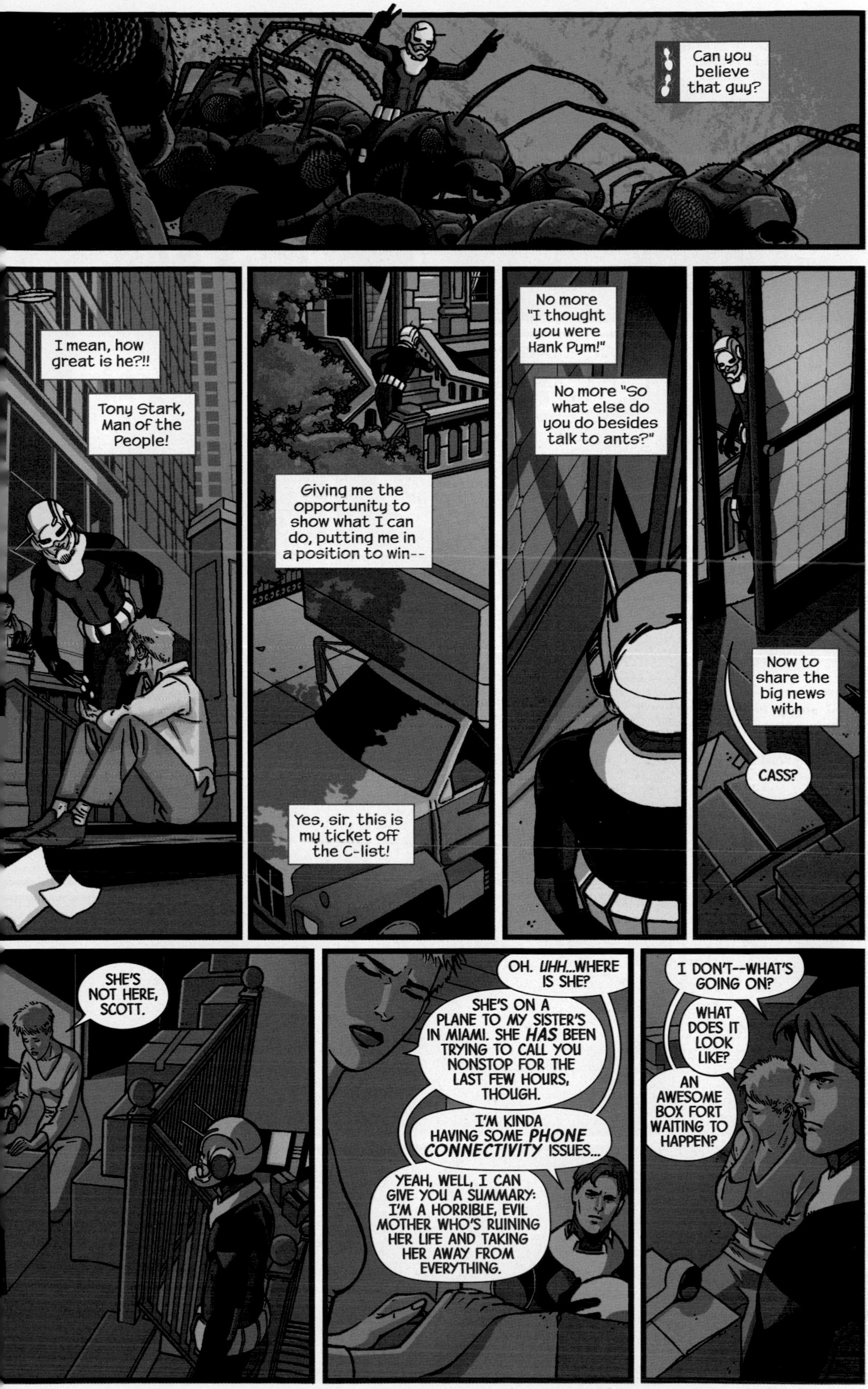

Can you believe that guy?
I mean, how great is he?!!
Tony Stark, Man of the People!
Giving me the opportunity to show what I can do, putting me in a position to win--
Yes, sir, this is my ticket off the C-list!
No more "I thought you were Hank Pym!"
No more "So what else do you do besides talk to ants?"
Now to share the big news with
CASS?
SHE'S NOT HERE, SCOTT.
OH. UHH...WHERE IS SHE?
SHE'S ON A PLANE TO MY SISTER'S IN MIAMI. SHE HAS BEEN TRYING TO CALL YOU NONSTOP FOR THE LAST FEW HOURS, THOUGH.
I'M KINDA HAVING SOME PHONE CONNECTIVITY ISSUES...
YEAH, WELL, I CAN GIVE YOU A SUMMARY: I'M A HORRIBLE, EVIL MOTHER WHO'S RUINING HER LIFE AND TAKING HER AWAY FROM EVERYTHING.
I DON'T--WHAT'S GOING ON?
WHAT DOES IT LOOK LIKE?
AN AWESOME BOX FORT WAITING TO HAPPEN?

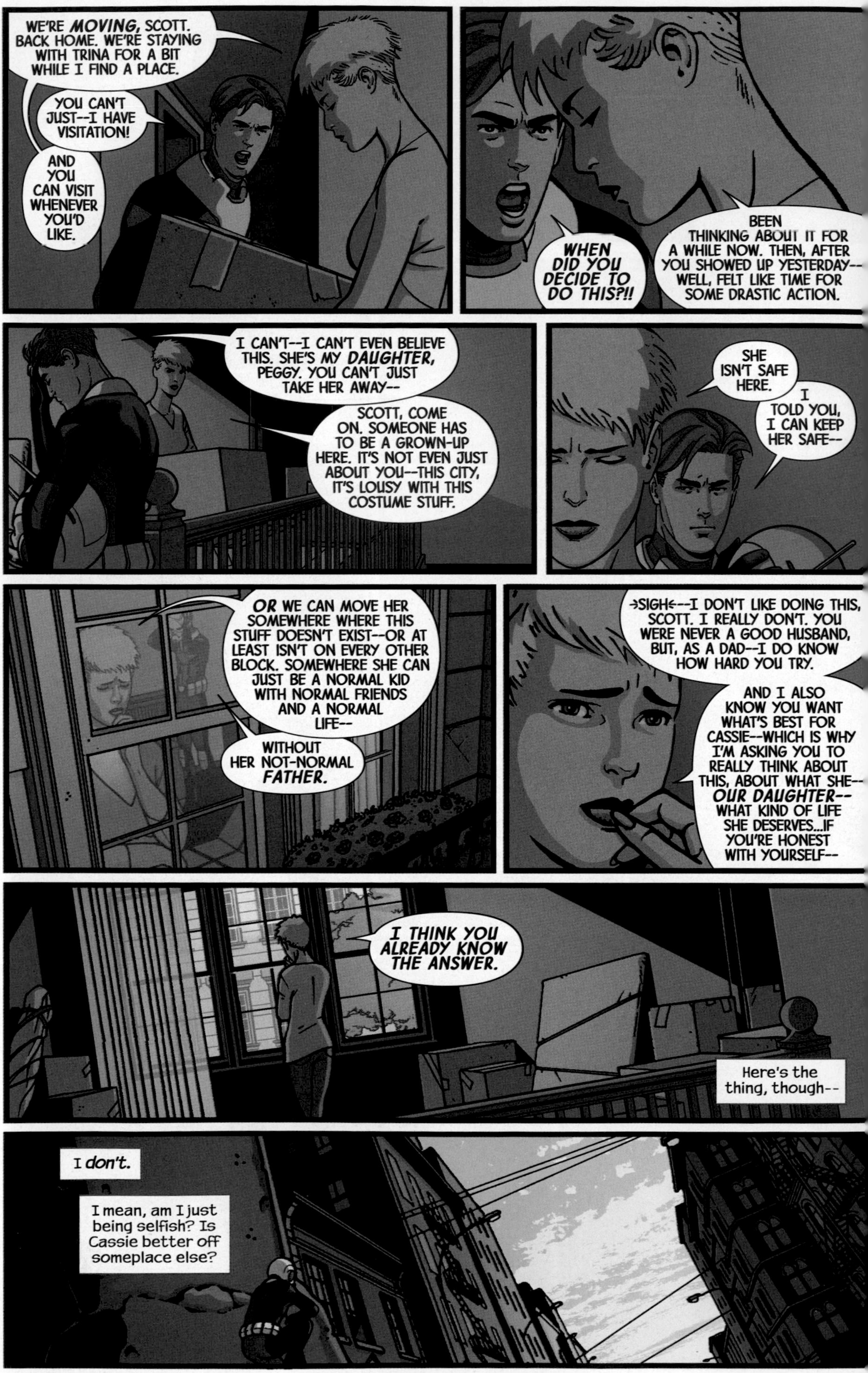
WE'RE *MOVING*, SCOTT. BACK HOME. WE'RE STAYING WITH TRINA FOR A BIT WHILE I FIND A PLACE.
YOU CAN'T JUST--I HAVE VISITATION!
AND YOU CAN VISIT WHENEVER YOU'D LIKE.
WHEN DID YOU DECIDE TO DO THIS?!!
BEEN THINKING ABOUT IT FOR A WHILE NOW. THEN, AFTER YOU SHOWED UP YESTERDAY--WELL, FELT LIKE TIME FOR SOME DRASTIC ACTION.
I CAN'T--I CAN'T EVEN BELIEVE THIS. SHE'S MY *DAUGHTER*, PEGGY. YOU CAN'T JUST TAKE HER AWAY--
SCOTT, COME ON. SOMEONE HAS TO BE A GROWN-UP HERE. IT'S NOT EVEN JUST ABOUT YOU--THIS CITY, IT'S LOUSY WITH THIS COSTUME STUFF.
SHE ISN'T SAFE HERE.
I TOLD YOU, I CAN KEEP HER SAFE--
OR WE CAN MOVE HER SOMEWHERE WHERE THIS STUFF DOESN'T EXIST--OR AT LEAST ISN'T ON EVERY OTHER BLOCK. SOMEWHERE SHE CAN JUST BE A NORMAL KID WITH NORMAL FRIENDS AND A NORMAL LIFE--
WITHOUT HER NOT-NORMAL *FATHER*.
→SIGH←--I DON'T LIKE DOING THIS, SCOTT. I REALLY DON'T. YOU WERE NEVER A GOOD HUSBAND, BUT, AS A DAD--I DO KNOW HOW HARD YOU TRY.
AND I ALSO KNOW YOU WANT WHAT'S BEST FOR CASSIE--WHICH IS WHY I'M ASKING YOU TO REALLY THINK ABOUT THIS, ABOUT WHAT SHE--*OUR DAUGHTER*--WHAT KIND OF LIFE SHE DESERVES...IF YOU'RE HONEST WITH YOURSELF--
I THINK YOU ALREADY KNOW THE ANSWER.
Here's the thing, though--
I *don't*.
I mean, am I just being selfish? Is Cassie better off someplace else?

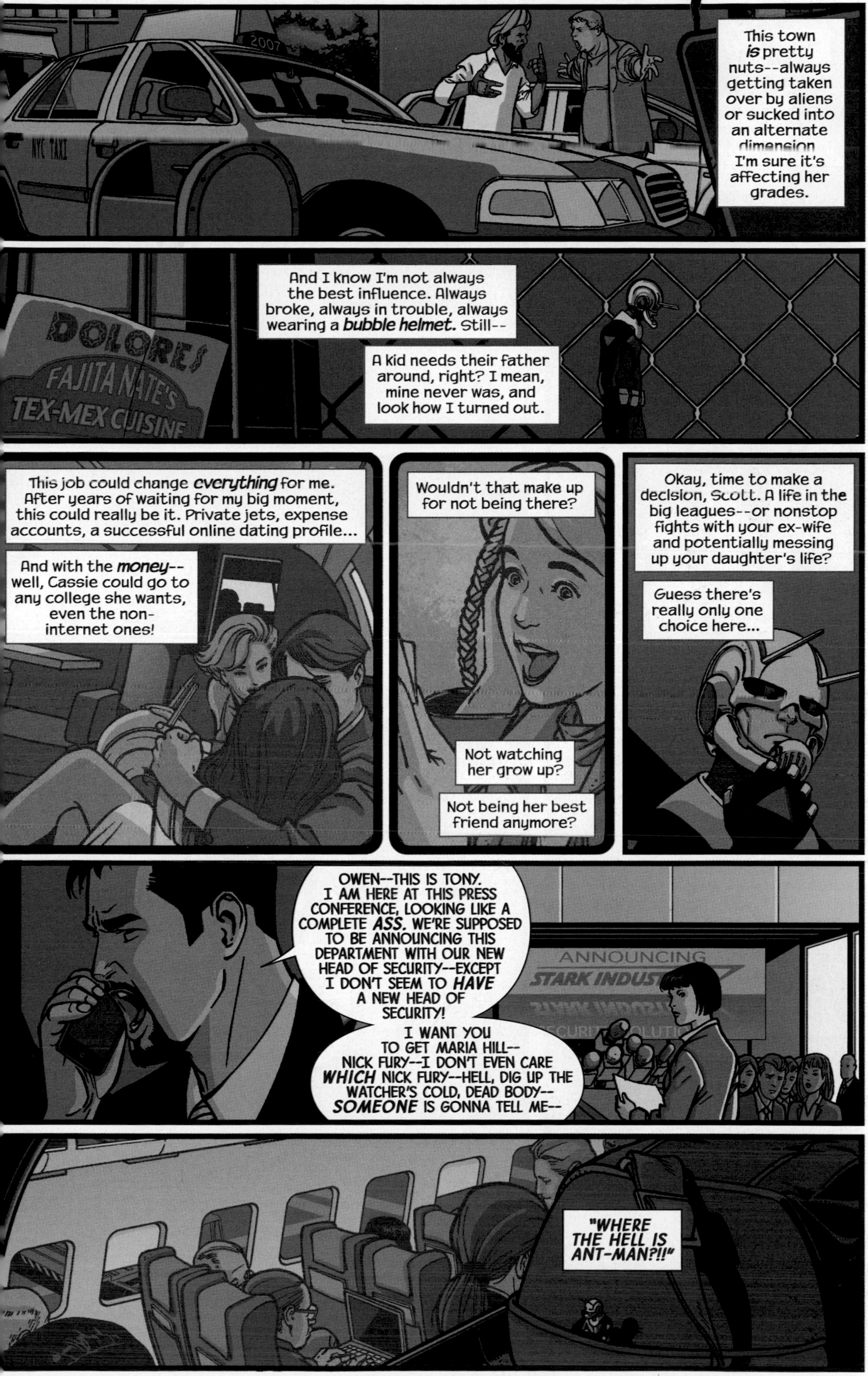
This town *is* pretty nuts--always getting taken over by aliens or sucked into an alternate dimension
I'm sure it's affecting her grades.
2007
NYC TAXI
And I know I'm not always the best influence. Always broke, always in trouble, always wearing a *bubble helmet.* Still--
A kid needs their father around, right? I mean, mine never was, and look how I turned out.
DOLORES
FAJITA NATE'S TEX-MEX CUISINE
This job could change *everything* for me. After years of waiting for my big moment, this could really be it. Private jets, expense accounts, a successful online dating profile...
And with the *money*--well, Cassie could go to any college she wants, even the non-internet ones!
Wouldn't that make up for not being there?
Not watching her grow up?
Not being her best friend anymore?
Okay, time to make a decision, Scott. A life in the big leagues--or nonstop fights with your ex-wife and potentially messing up your daughter's life?
Guess there's really only one choice here...
OWEN--THIS IS TONY. I AM HERE AT THIS PRESS CONFERENCE, LOOKING LIKE A COMPLETE *ASS.* WE'RE SUPPOSED TO BE ANNOUNCING THIS DEPARTMENT WITH OUR NEW HEAD OF SECURITY--EXCEPT I DON'T SEEM TO *HAVE* A NEW HEAD OF SECURITY!
I WANT YOU TO GET MARIA HILL--NICK FURY--I DON'T EVEN CARE *WHICH* NICK FURY--HELL, DIG UP THE WATCHER'S COLD, DEAD BODY--*SOMEONE* IS GONNA TELL ME--
ANNOUNCING
STARK INDUS
"WHERE THE HELL IS ANT-MAN?!!"

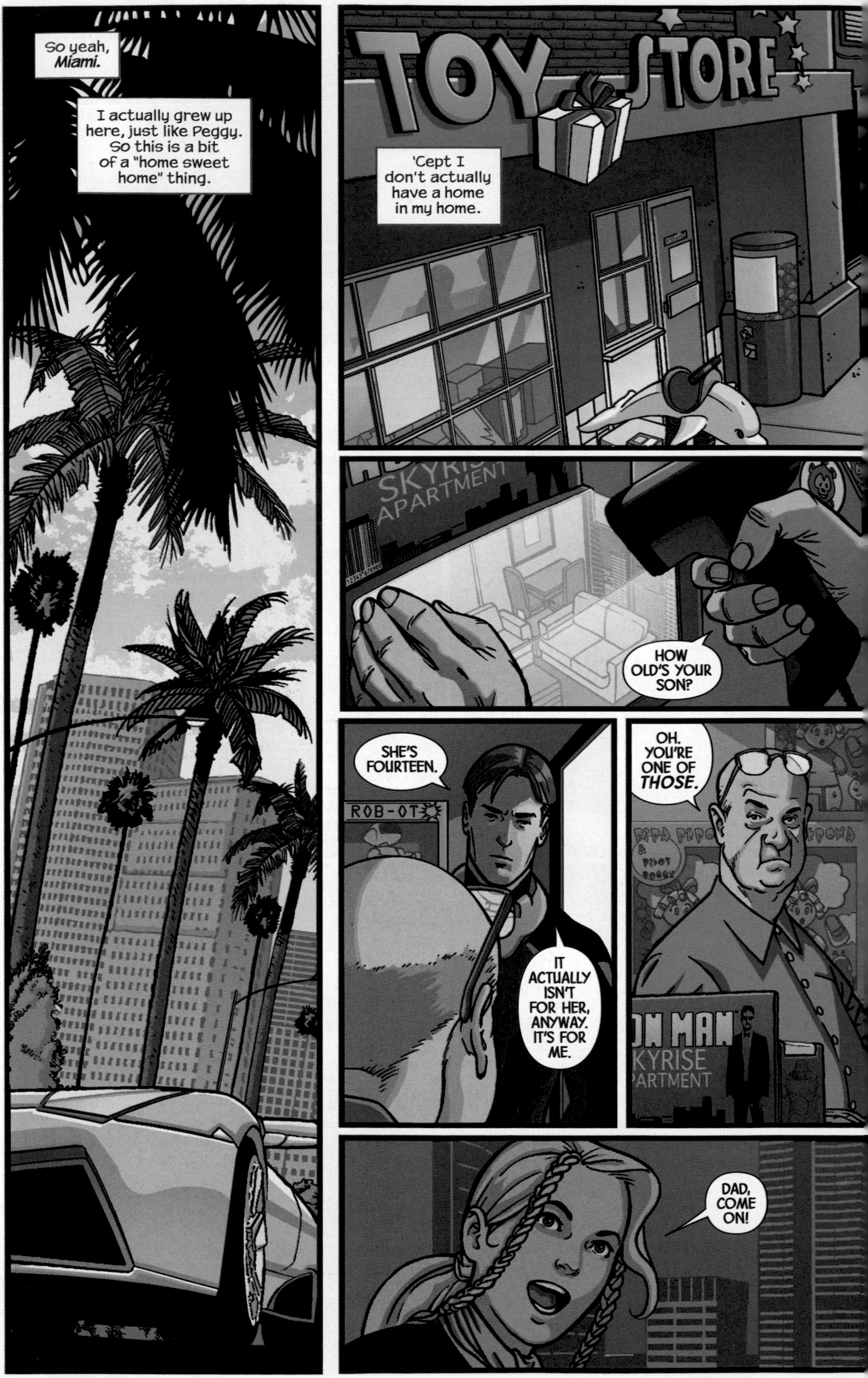
So yeah, *Miami.*
I actually grew up here, just like Peggy. So this is a bit of a "home sweet home" thing.
TOY STORE
'Cept I don't actually have a home in my home.
SKYRISE APARTMENT
HOW OLD'S YOUR SON?
SHE'S FOURTEEN.
ROB-OT
IT ACTUALLY ISN'T FOR HER, ANYWAY. IT'S FOR ME.
OH. YOU'RE ONE OF *THOSE.*
ON MAN
KYRISE
PARTMENT
DAD, COME ON!

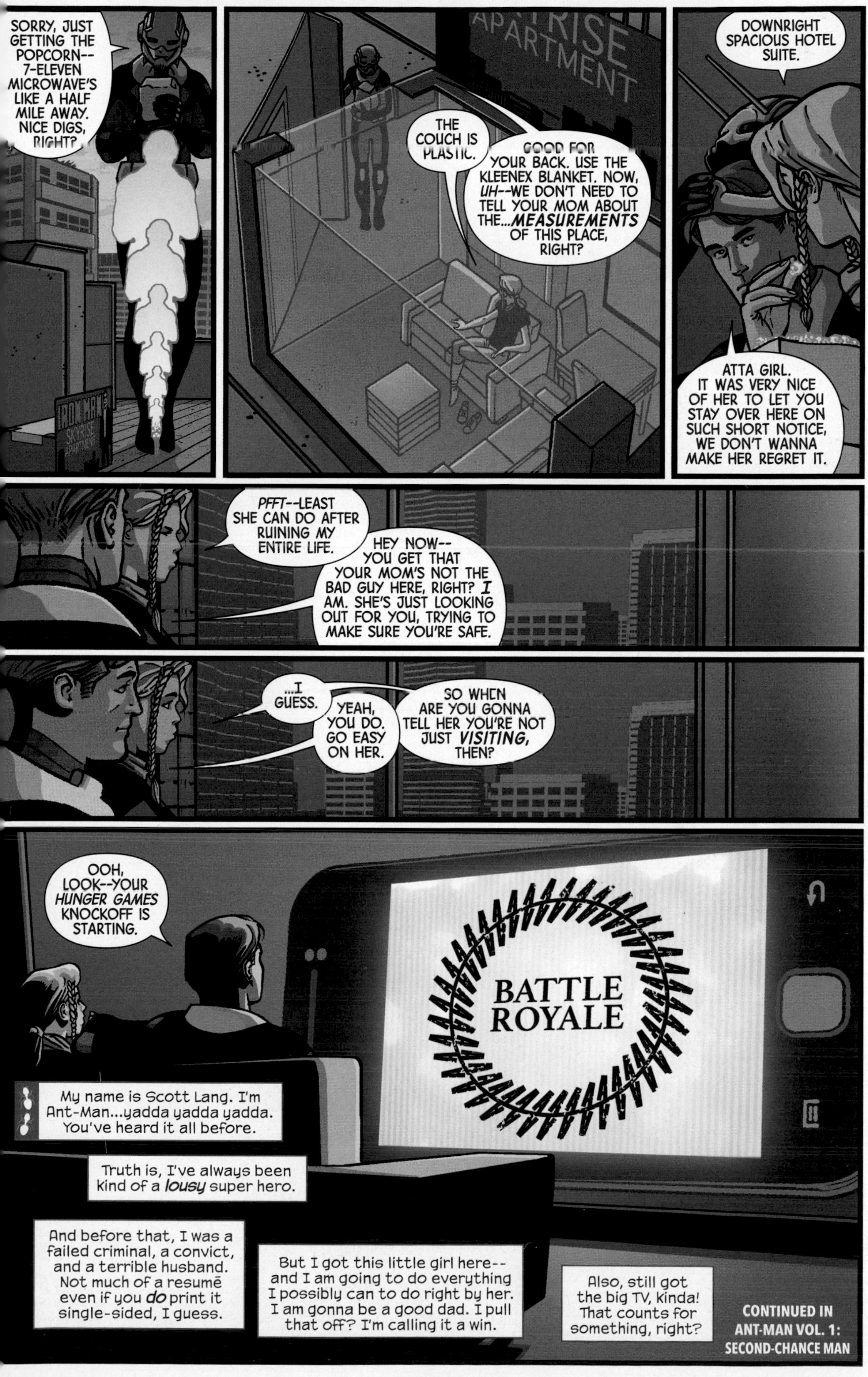
SORRY, JUST GETTING THE POPCORN-- 7-ELEVEN MICROWAVE'S LIKE A HALF MILE AWAY. NICE DIGS, RIGHT?
IRON MAN SKYRISE APARTMENT
SKYRISE APARTMENT
THE COUCH IS PLASTIC.
GOOD FOR YOUR BACK. USE THE KLEENEX BLANKET. NOW, UH--WE DON'T NEED TO TELL YOUR MOM ABOUT THE...MEASUREMENTS OF THIS PLACE, RIGHT?
DOWNRIGHT SPACIOUS HOTEL SUITE.
ATTA GIRL. IT WAS VERY NICE OF HER TO LET YOU STAY OVER HERE ON SUCH SHORT NOTICE, WE DON'T WANNA MAKE HER REGRET IT.
PFFT--LEAST SHE CAN DO AFTER RUINING MY ENTIRE LIFE.
HEY NOW-- YOU GET THAT YOUR MOM'S NOT THE BAD GUY HERE, RIGHT? I AM. SHE'S JUST LOOKING OUT FOR YOU, TRYING TO MAKE SURE YOU'RE SAFE.
...I GUESS.
YEAH, YOU DO. GO EASY ON HER.
SO WHEN ARE YOU GONNA TELL HER YOU'RE NOT JUST VISITING, THEN?
OOH, LOOK--YOUR HUNGER GAMES KNOCKOFF IS STARTING.
BATTLE ROYALE
My name is Scott Lang. I'm Ant-Man...yadda yadda yadda. You've heard it all before.
Truth is, I've always been kind of a lousy super hero.
And before that, I was a failed criminal, a convict, and a terrible husband. Not much of a resumé even if you do print it single-sided, I guess.
But I got this little girl here-- and I am going to do everything I possibly can to do right by her. I am gonna be a good dad. I pull that off? I'm calling it a win.
Also, still got the big TV, kinda! That counts for something, right?

CONTINUED IN ANT-MAN VOL. 1: SECOND-CHANCE MAN

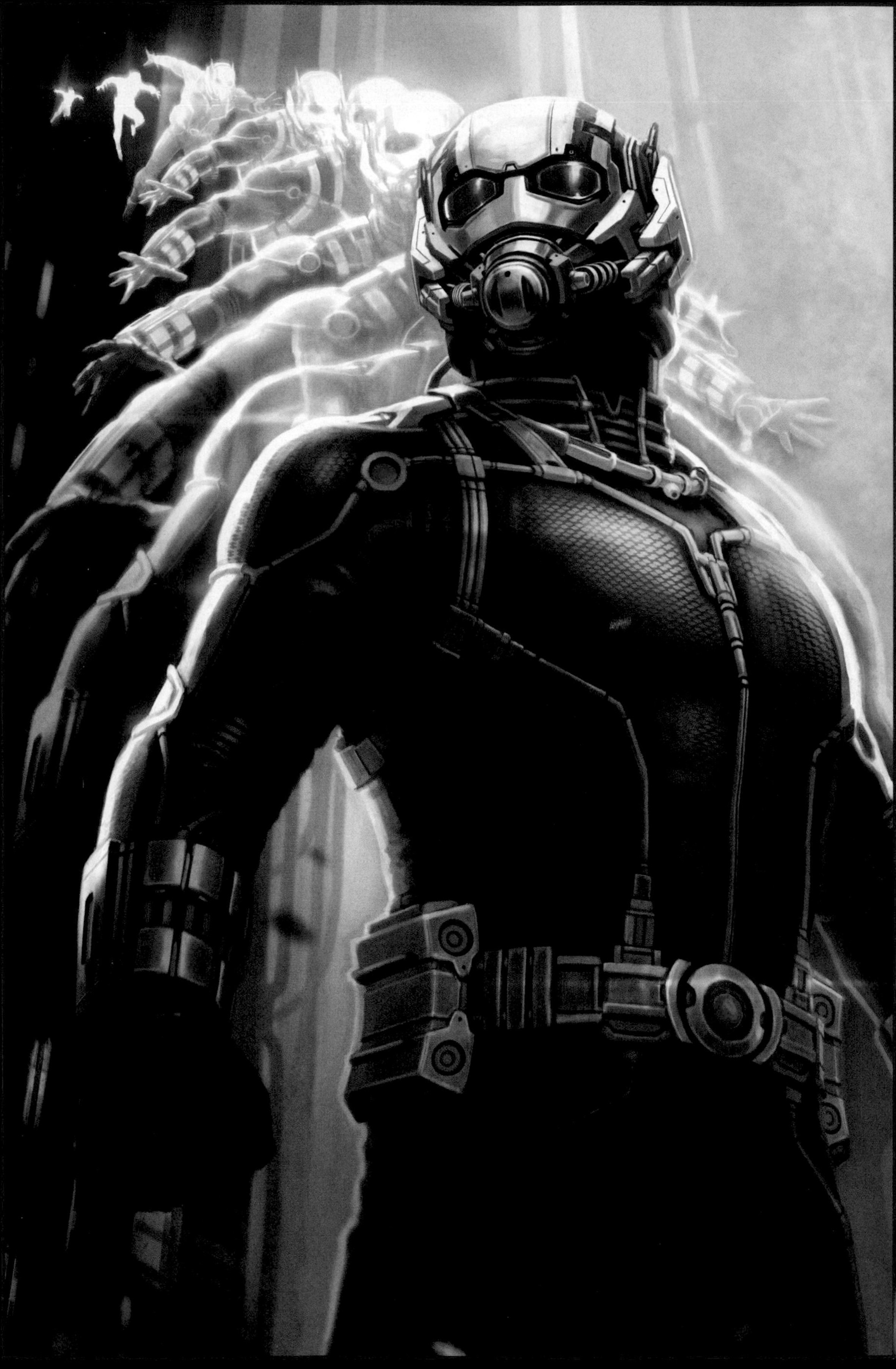

ANT-MAN #1 MOVIE VARIANT

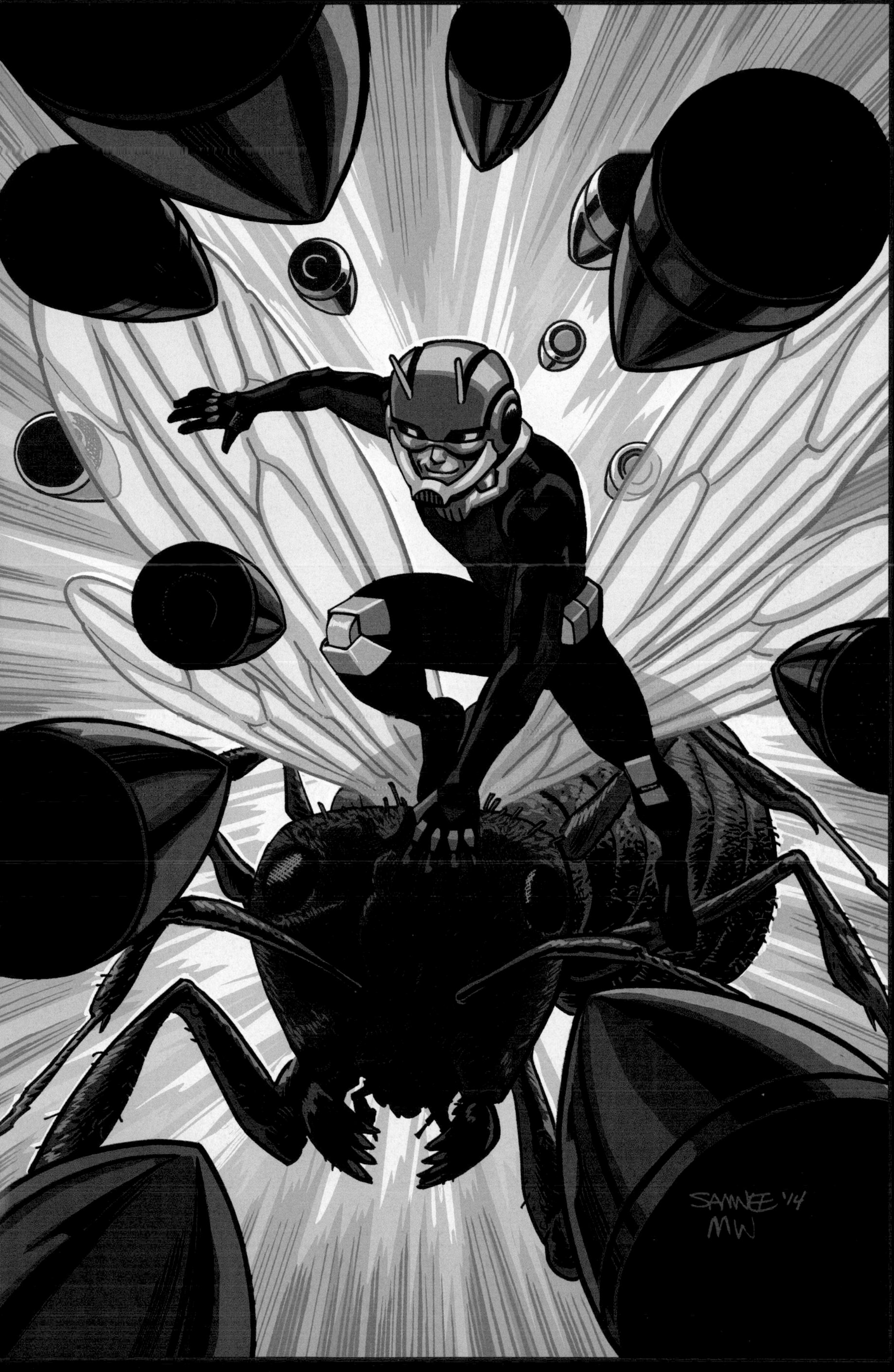
SAMNEE '14
MW

ANT-MAN #1 VARIANT BY **CHRIS SAMNEE & MATTHEW WILSON**

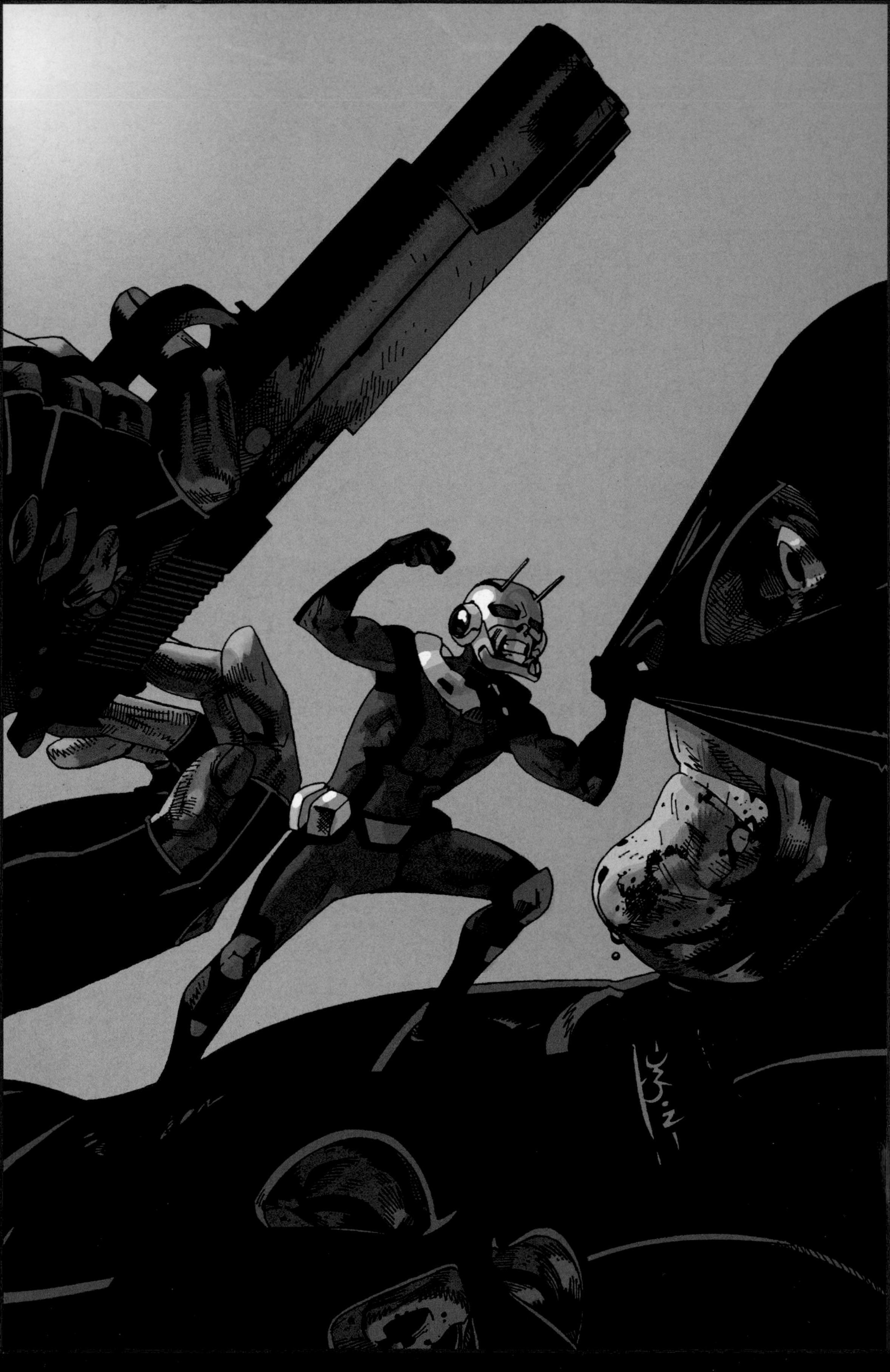

ANT-MAN #1 VARIANT BY JASON PEARSON

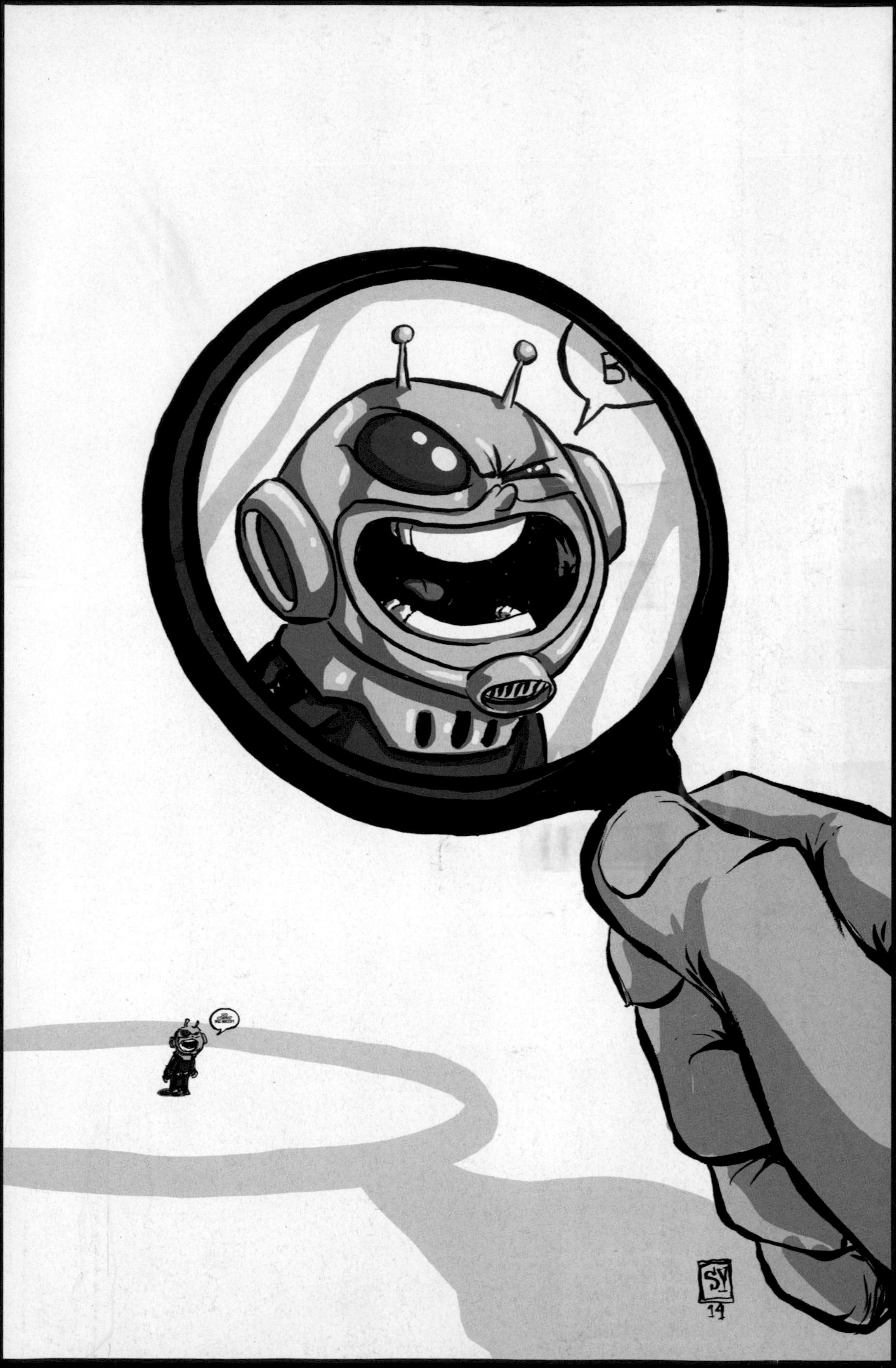

ANT-MAN #1 VARIANT BY **SKOTTIE YOUNG**

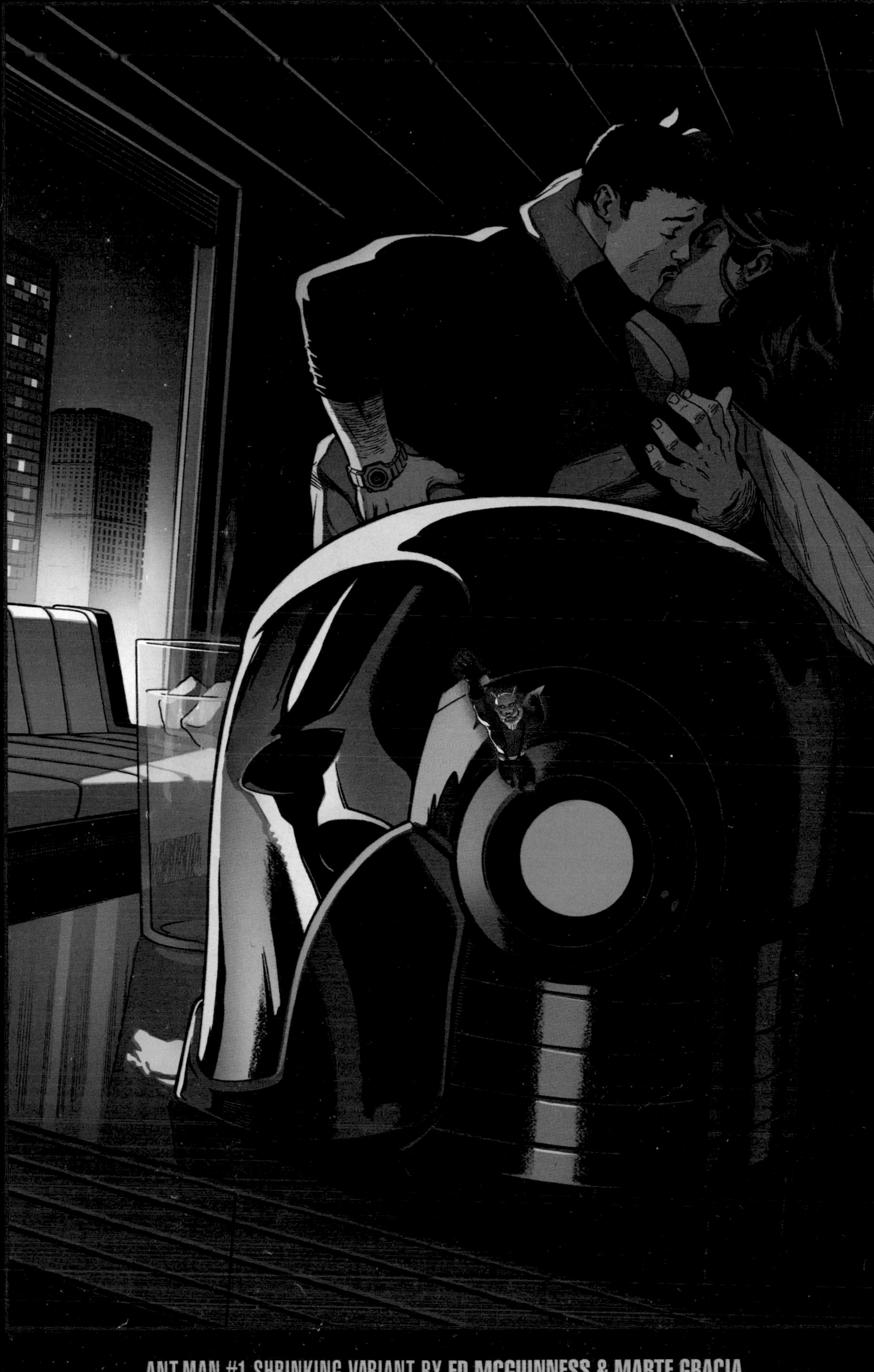

ANT-MAN #1 SHRINKING VARIANT BY ED MCGUINNESS & MARTE GRACIA